Lecture Notes in Computer Scien

Commenced Publication in 1973
Founding and Former Series Editors:
Gerhard Goos, Juris Hartmanis, and Jan van Leeuwen

Editorial Board

Nicolas Guelfi   Anthony Savidis (Eds.)

Rapid Integration of Software Engineering Techniques

Second International Workshop, RISE 2005
Heraklion, Crete, Greece, September 8-9, 2005
Revised Selected Papers

 Springer

Volume Editors

Nicolas Guelfi
University of Luxembourg
Faculty of Science, Technology and Communication
1359 Luxembourg, Luxembourg
E-mail: nicolas.guelfi@uni.lu

Anthony Savidis
Foundation for Research and Technology - Hellas (FORTH)
Institute of Computer Science
GR-70013 Heraklion, Crete, Greece
E-mail: as@ics.forth.gr

Library of Congress Control Number: 2006925116

CR Subject Classification (1998): D.2, F.3, K.6.1, K.6.3

LNCS Sublibrary: SL 2 – Programming and Software Engineering

ISSN   0302-9743
ISBN-10   3-540-34063-7 Springer Berlin Heidelberg New York
ISBN-13   978-3-540-34063-8 Springer Berlin Heidelberg New York

Springer is a part of Springer Science+Business Media

springer.com

© Springer-Verlag Berlin Heidelberg 2006
Printed in Germany

Typesetting: Camera-ready by author, data conversion by Scientific Publishing Services, Chennai, India
Printed on acid-free paper   SPIN: 11751113   06/3142   5 4 3 2 1 0

Preface

RISE 2005 (http://rise2005.ics.forth.gr/) was the second annual inter-national workshop of the ERCIM (European Research Consortium for Informatics and Mathematics - http://www.ercim.org/) Working Group on Rapid Integration of Software Engineering techniques (RISE - http://rise.uni.lu/). RISE is an international forum for researchers and practitioners interested in the advancement and rapid application of novel, integrated, or practical software engineering approaches being part of a methodological framework, which apply to the development of new or evolving applications and systems. RISE provides an opportunity to present and discuss the latest research results and ideas in the rapid and effective integration of software engineering techniques. Target application domains of interest to RISE include:

- Web-based software systems
- Mobile communication systems
- High-availability or mission-critical systems
- Resilient business and grid applications
- Ambient intelligence environments
- Embedded systems and applications
- User interface development
- Development environments
- Electronic entertainment
- Enterprise computing and applications

In particular, RISE 2005 focused on an open and inclusive set of key software engineering domains, which formed the focal point of the workshop, including, but not limited to:

- Software and system architectures
- Software reuse
- Software testing
- Software model checking
- Model-driven design and testing techniques
- Model transformation
- Requirements engineering
- Lightweight or practice-oriented formal methods
- Software processes and software metrics
- Automated software engineering
- Design patterns
- Design by contract
- Defensive programming
- Software entropy and software re-factoring

- Extreme programming
- Agile software development
- Programming languages
- Software dependability and trustworthiness

This second RISE workshop was, like RISE 2004, very successful and fruitful, almost doubling the number of submissions and of accepted papers, and leading to a high-quality two-day technical programme. Overall, RISE 2005 accomplished its objective to move a step forward in setting the ground towards a targeted, prestigious and open inter-national forum of high-quality research and development results in the arena of rapid integration of software engineering techniques.

All papers submitted to this workshop were peer reviewed by at least two members of the International Programme Committee. Acceptance was based primarily on originality and scientific contribution. Out of the 43 submissions received, 19 were selected for inclusion in the workshop technical programme. Six chaired thematic sessions were organized over a single workshop track, covering many aspects of the integration of complementary mature software engineering techniques. This year, the submissions addressed areas such as modelling safety case evolution, practical approaches in model mapping, context-aware service composition, techniques for representing product line core assets for automation, formal development of reactive fault-tolerant systems, stepwise feature introduction in practice, programming languages, aspects and contracts. The technical discussions that followed the paper presentations were tape recorded, and the transcripts can be found on the RISE 2005 website (http://rise2005.ics.forth.gr/).

The keynote speech was delivered by Bertrand Meyer, Chair of Software Engineering at ETH Zurich, Founder and Chief Architect of Eiffel Software in California, and inventor of the Design by Contract™ method. His inspiring talk as well as active participation during the discussion sessions contributed to the overall success of the workshop.

The editors wish to thank the keynote speaker and the authors for their valuable contribution in making RISE 2005 a truly outstanding event of high-quality contributions, as well as all the Programme Committee members who actively participated in the review process in a timely and quality fashion. Finally, we are thankful to Springer LNCS for publishing the RISE 2005 proceedings under this volume (the RISE 2004 post-proceedings are published as Springer LNCS Vol. 3475).

September 2005   Nicolas Guelfi
                                                             Anthony Savidis

Organization

RISE 2005 was organized by the Institute of Computer Science (ICS), Foundation for Research and Technology Hellas (FORTH).

Programme Chairs

Anthony Savidis   ICS-FORTH - *Programme and Organization Chair*
Nicolas Guelfi   FNR, Univ. Luxembourg - *General Workshop Chair*

International Programme Committee

Arve Aagesen Finn   NTNU, Norway
Avgeriou Paris   Fraunhofer IPSI Concert, Germany
Bertolino Antonia   CNR-ISTI, Italy
Bicarregui Juan   CCLRC, UK
Bolognesi Tommaso   CNR-ISTI, Italy
Born Marc   Fraunhofer FOKUS, Germany
                           University of Geneva, Switzerland
Carrez Cyril   NTNU, Norway
Dony Christophe   LIRMM, France
Fitzgerald John   DCS, Newcastle, UK
Greenough Chris   CCLRC-CSE CG, UK
Guelfi Nicolas   FNR, Luxembourg
Haajanen Jyrki   VTT, Finland
Issarny Valérie   INRIA, France
Klint Paul   CWI, The Netherlands
Mistrik Ivan   Fraunhofer IPSI IM, Germany
Mens Tom   FWO-Mons-Hainaut University TM, Belgium
Moeller Eckhard   Fraunhofer FOKUS, Germany
Monostori Laszlo   SZTAKI, Hungary
Pimentel Ernesto   SpaRCIM, Spain
Reggio Gianna   DISI, Genoa, Italy
Romanovsky Alexander   DCS, Newcastle, UK
Rosener Vincent   FNR, Luxembourg
Savidis Anthony   CS-FORTH, Greece
Schieferdecker Ina   Fraunhofer FOKUS, Germany

Local Organization

Maria Papadopoulou   ICS-FORTH
George Paparoulis   ICS-FORTH
Maria Bouhli   ICS-FORTH
Yannis Georgalis   ICS-FORTH

Sponsoring Institutions

This workshop was supported by ERCIM and by the ERCIM Working Group (WG) on Rapid Integration of Software Engineering Techniques (RISE).

Table of Contents

Invited Keynote Speech (Abstract)

Doing More with Contracts: Towards Automatic Tests and Proofs

Bertrand Meyer

ETH Zurich (Swiss Federal Institute of Technology),
Department of Computer Science,
CH-8092 Zürich, Switzerland
Bertrand.Meyer@inf.ethz.ch

Abstract. Equipping software with contracts, especially in the case of library components, opens up a whole range of applications. I will describe two of them, part of current work in the chair of software engineering at ETH. The first is automatic, "push-button" testing of contract-equipped components. The second is mathematical proof that such components satisfy their contracts. In both cases the effort is made more interesting by the existence of library versions that are fully contracted" thanks to the use of model classes based on set-theoretical concepts. Both the tests and the proofs apply to actual libraries as used in practical software development.

N. Guelfi and A. Savidis (Eds.): RISE 2005, LNCS 3943, p. 1, 2006.

Using Stepwise Feature Introduction in Practice: An Experience Report

Ralph-Johan Back, Johannes Eriksson, and Luka Milovanov

Turku Centre for Computer Science,
Åbo Akademi University, Department of Computer Science,
Lemminkäisenkatu 14, FIN-20520 Turku, Finland
{backrj, joheriks, lmilovan}@abo.fi

Abstract. Stepwise Feature Introduction is an incremental method and software architecture for building object-oriented system in thin layers of functionality, and is based on the Refinement Calculus logical framework. We have evaluated this method in a series of real software projects. The method works quite well on small to medium sized software projects, and provides a nice fit with agile software processes like Extreme Programming. The evaluations also allowed us to identify a number of places where the method could be improved, most of these related to the way inheritance is used in Stepwise Feature Introduction. Three of these issues are analyzed in more detail here: diamond inheritance, complexity of layering and unit testing of layered software.

1 Introduction

Stepwise Feature Introduction (SFI) [1] is a bottom-up software development methodology based on incremental extension of the object-oriented system with a single new feature at a time. It proposes a layered software architecture and uses Refinement Calculus [2, 3] as the logical framework.

Software is constructed in SFI in thin layers, where each layer implements a specific feature or a set of closely related features. The bottom layer provides the most basic functionality, with each subsequent layer adding more and more functionality to the system. The layers are implemented as class hierarchies, where a new layer inherits all functionality of previous layers by sub-classing existing classes, and adds new features by overriding methods and implementing new methods. Each layer, together with its ancestors, constitutes a fully executable software system.

Layers are added as new features are needed. However, in practice we cannot build the system in this purely *incremental* way, by just adding layer after layer. Features may interact in unforeseen ways, and a new feature may not fit into the current design of the software. In such cases, one must *refactor* the software so that the new feature fits better into the overall design. Large refactorings may also modify the layer structure, e.g. by changing the order of layers, splitting layers or removing layers altogether.

An important design principle of SFI is that each extension should preserve the functionality of all previous layers. This is known as *superposition refinement* [4]. A superposition refinement can add new operations and attributes to a class, and may override

N. Guelfi and A. Savidis (Eds.): RISE 2005, LNCS 3943, pp. 2–17, 2006.

old operations. However, when overriding an old operation, the effect of the old operation on the old attributes has to be preserved (but new attributes can be updated freely). No operations or attributes can be removed or renamed.

Consider as an example a class that provides a simple text widget in a graphical user interface. The widget works only with simple ASCII text. A new feature that could be added as an extension to this widget could be, e.g., formatted text (boldface, italics, underlined, etc). Another possible extension could be a clipboard to support cut and paste. We could carry out both these extensions in parallel and then construct a new class that inherits from both the clipboard text widget and the styles text widget using multiple inheritance (this is called a *feature combination*), possibly overriding some of the operations to avoid undesirable feature interaction. Or, we could first implement the clipboard functionality as an extension of the simple text widget, being careful to preserve all the old features, and then introduce styles as a new layer on top of this. Alternatively, we could first add styles and then implement a clipboard on top of the styles layer. The three approaches are illustrated in Figure 1.

A component is divided into layers in SFI. Layers will often cut across components, so that the same layering structure is imposed on a number of related components. As an example, consider building an editor that displays the text widget. In the first layer we have a simple editor that only displays the simple ASCII text widget. Because of the superposition property of extension this simple editor can in fact also use the CutAndPaste, Styles or BetterText widgets, but it cannot make use of the new features. We need to add some features to the simple editor so that the functionality of the

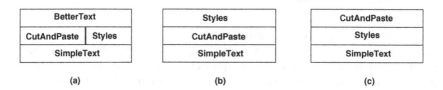

Fig. 1. Alternative extension orders

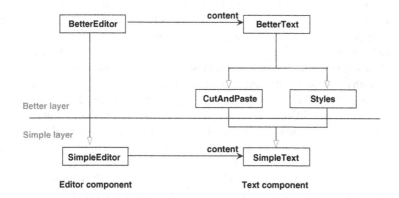

Fig. 2. Interacting components

extended widget can be accessed (menu items for cut and paste, or for formatting, or toolbar buttons for the same purpose). We do this by constructing a new an extension of the simple editor (a better editor), which uses the `BetterText` widget and gives the user access to the new functionality. The situation is illustrated in Figure 2.

The new editor is, however, restricted to only work on the better text widget, because the features it assumes are only available on this level. Hence, there are two layers in the design, the Simple layer and the Better layer.

Stepwise Feature Introduction has been tried out in a number of real software projects. This allows us now to evaluate the merits of this approach and to spot possible drawbacks as well as opportunities for improvement. Our purpose in this paper is to report on these case studies, and to provide a first evaluation of the approach, together with some suggestions on how to improve the method.

The paper is structured as following: Section 2 present the software projects where SFI was applied. We summarize our experience with the methodology in Section 3. In Sections 4–6 we then consider in more detail three interesting issues that arose from our experiments with Stepwise Feature Introduction. The problems with implementing feature combinations using multiple inheritance is discussed in Section 4. The problem of class proliferation is discussed in Section 5, where metaprogramming is considered as one possible way of avoiding unneccessary classes. In Section 6, we show how to adapt unit testing to also test for correct superposition refinement. We end with a short summary and some discussion on on-going and future work.

2   SFI Projects in Gaudi

The software projects where SFI was evauated were all carried out in the Gaudi Software Factory at Åbo Akademi University. The Gaudi Software Factory is an academic environment for building software for the research needs and for carrying out practical experiments in Software Engineering [5]. Our research group defines the setting, goals and methods to be used in the Factory, but actual construction of the software is done in the factory, following a well-defined software process. The work is closely monitored, and provides a lot of data and measures by wich the software process and its results can be evaluated. The software process used in Gaudi is based on agile methods, primarily *Extreme Programming* [6], together with our own extensions.

We will here describe four software projects where Stepwise Feature Introduction was used throughout. The settings for all these projects were similar: the software had to be built with a tight schedule, and the Gaudi software process had to be followed. The programmers employed for these projects (4–6 persons) were third-fifth year students majoring in Computer Science or related areas. Each project had a customer who had final saying on the functionality to be implemented. The projects were also supervised by a coach (a Ph.D. student specializing in Software Engineering), whose main task was to guide the use of the software process and to control that the process was being followed. There has also been one industrial software project [7] with SFI, but this is outside the scope of this paper, as it was not carried out in the Gaudi Factory, and the software process used was not monitored in a sufficiently systematic manner.

All of the projects used SFI, but the ways in which the method was applied differed from project to project. We describe the projects in chronological order below. For each project, we present the goals: both for the software product that was to be built, and for the way in which SFI was to be evaluated in this project. We give a general overview of the software architecture, show how SFI was implemented, what went right and what went wrong, and discuss the lessons learned from the project.

2.1 Extreme Editor

The Extreme Editor project [8] was the first application of SFI in practice. It ran for three months during the summer 2001 and involved six programmers. The programming language of the project was Python [9]. The software product to be built was an outlining editor which became a predecessor for the Derivation Editor described in Section 2.2. The goal for the project was to obtain the first experience from practical application of SFI with a dynamically typed programming language. There were no technical guidelines for the application of SFI except that the extension mechanism for classes (the feature introduction—Section 1) should be inheritance.

Figure 3 shows the layered architecture of the Extreme Editor. There were eight layers in the system. Each layer introduced new functionality into the system, without breaking the old features. The software was structured into these layers in an ad hoc way. A new layer extended its predecessor by inheriting its corresponding classes and possibly introducing one or more new classes. There were no physical division of the

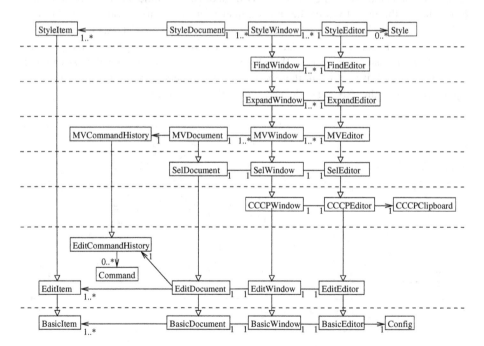

Fig. 3. The layers of the editor

software into the layers on the level of the file system: each class name had a prefix—the name of the layer where the class belongs to. More on the architecture of the software and detailed description of the layers can be found in the technical report [8].

The feedback on SFI from this project was rather positive. The method supported building software with a layered architecture quite well. The developers found it rather easy to add new features as new layers. The fact that functionality of the system was divided into layers made the overall structure of the system clearer to all the programmers. Another advantage was "bug identification": the layered structure made it easy to find the layer in which the bug occured and its location in the source code.

On the other hand, even in the three-month project, as more features were implementer and the more classes were introduced into the system, it was getting harder to navigate among them without any tool support, any automatic documentation describing the layer structure and without a systematic naming convention for classes, layers and methods. We also found that SFI requires a special way of unit testing (the testing classes should be extended in the same way as the ordinary classes of the system). More on unit testing will be discussed in Section 6.

2.2 Editor for Mathematical Derivations

MathEdit [10] was an effort to implement tool support for structured derivations and is currently the largest project developed using the SFI methodology. MathEdit was developed in the Gaudi Software Factory as two successive summer projects, in 2002 and 2003. One of the objectives of the first summer project was to try out feature combination by multiple inheritance. The second objective of the project was to assess how well a new team could embrace an existing SFI codebase and continue its development. The continuation project in 2003 shared only one out of four developers with the 2002 project. Still, it turned out that the new programmers were able to start working productively with the existing code base within the first three weeks.

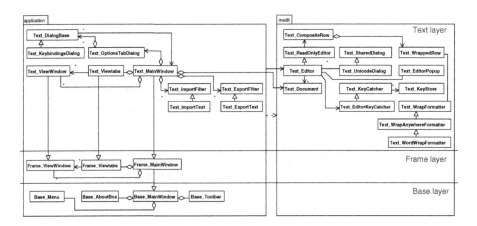

Fig. 4. The first three layers of MathEdit, unit tests excluded

MathEdit consists of totally 16 layers. A description of each layer and its major features can be found in [10]. Classes are associated with layers based on naming conventions. A diagram showing the classes of the first three layers (unit test classes excluded) can be seen in Figure 4. Due to space considerations, we do not display a complete class diagram for MathEdit.

On the highest level, MathEdit is separated into three major components: a document-view component (medit), the application-level user interface (application) and a mathematical profile plug-in. The medit and application components are layered as described above. The layering cross-cuts these top-level components, so the layering is *global*. The profile component was designed as a plug-in, so it was not layered—users should be able to write custom profiles without having to care about the internal layer structure of MathEdit.

Combining two layers using multiple inheritance was attempted but ultimately abandoned in the MathEdit project. The main reason were practical problems arising from the use of multiple inheritance; e.g., classes in the graphical toolkit used (Qt) did not support multiple inheritance well. Also, the development team was quite small, so it did not seem fruitful to work on two features in parallel as if they were independent, when it was already known that the features would be combined later on. Instead, a feature was implemented with extensibility in mind, so that it was easy to add the next feature in a new layer. The gains of parallel development would probably be much higher in a larger project, but this still remains to be evaluated.

The MathEdit application is executable with any layer as the top layer, providing the functionality of this layer and all layers below. The gives us the possibilities to fall back to an earlier working version in case of malfunction, and to locate bugs that were introduced in a some unknown layer. We simply implement a test that exposes the bug and run it with different top layers. The lowest layer that exhibits the erroneous behavior is either harboring the bug, or triggering a bug in a previous layer.

2.3   Software Construction Workbench

The Software Construction Workbench (SCW) project (summer – fall 2002) was an effort to build a prototype for IDE supporting Stepwise Feature Introduction and Python. This application was built in Python, as an extension of the System Modeling Workbench [11]. The main feature are modeling software systems in a SFI fashion with UML, automatic Python code generation and execution of the constructed system and support for unit tests in the environment. SCW also included basic support for Design by Contract [12] and reverse engineering.

As far as SFI is concerned, the goals in this project were to get further feedback on the practical application of the methods, to try out the layered approach to unit testing (discussed in Section 6) and to try out new naming conventions (described below in this section). A special feature of this project was that it used its own medicine: the software needed to support software development with SFI was built itself using this method. Since the architecture of the SCW is rather complex, we do not present it here, for the reader's convenience. Instead, we illustrate how the SFI method was applied in this project on a small and simplified fragment of the software.

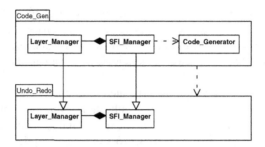

Fig. 5. Layer structure, Python implementation

Figure 5 shows an example of the layer structure implementation. SFI layers were implemented using Python's packaging mechanism: each SFI layer corresponds to a Python package. To show that a layer is a successor of another layer we draw a dependency from the successor to its ancestor; in practice this dependency was the Python import statement. The mechanism for extension of classes was inheritance, as shown in Figure 5. Every class, once introduced, keeps its original name through all of its extensions. This was simple to implement: Python packages provide a namespace so we had no conflicts with the names of the classes.

A class can be extended with new methods and/or some inherited methods can be overwritten. When an old method is overwritten in the next class extension, it is a good practice to have a call to the original method inside the body of the extended method. According to the developers, the implemented layered structure of the software together with the name conventions really clarified the software. The Software Construction Workbench project was carried out as two subprojects, such that half of the developers were new in the second subproject, and in the beginning had no understanding of the software at all. Nevertheless, the new programmers were able to take over the code easily because of the division of features into layers. The new programmers also commented that the layering made it much easier to navigate in the code, modify code and search for bugs.

The SCW project showed that in order to use the SFI methods properly and efficiently, tool support is really needed. Because of the way Python packaging was used to implement the SFI layers, it took a lot of time to divide the code into directories corresponding to the layers. Building software according to SFI also promotes refactoring (a practice enforced in our Software Factory). For example, when changing something in the lower layer, it can often affect the successive layers, so they should be slightly changed. According to the developers a simple tool helping with the navigation among the layer structure, i.e. from ancestor to successor and the other way around, would here save a lot of time.

2.4 Personal Financial Planner

The Personal Financial Planner project [13] (FiPla) was the first application of SFI with a statically typed language—Eiffel [14]. The software goal for the project was to build a personal financial planner. The features required of this product type include

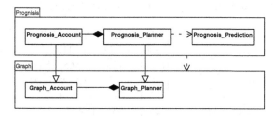

Fig. 6. Layer structure, Eiffel implementation

tracking of actual events (manually or automatically), planning (such as budgeting and creating scenarios), and showing future scenarios.

SFI was evaluated in this project to see how the method would work with a statically typed language. Another goal was to see how well the SFI layers layers correspond to the short release cycles used in the Gaudi Software Factory [5], so that each short iteration starts a new layer. Finally we also wanted to see how well SFI and Design by Contract [12] fit together.

SFI layers in Eiffel are implemented using Eiffel clusters. However, unlike Python packages, a cluster in Eiffel does not provide a namespace for the classes. It means that all names of the classes in the Eiffel software system should have unique name, so it was impossible to have the same naming convention as in the SCW project. For this purpose we used another naming convention, where each class name should have the name of the layer that the class belongs to as a prefix. Figure 6 shows a simplified fragment of the software architecture.

SFI worked well with Eiffel when we applied the methods in the same way as in our Python projects. Structuring the software system into layers according to the small releases defined by the customer turned out to be a good idea. However, a few important technical issues that needed improvement were found. These issues only came up when using SFI with a statically typed language.

The extension of classes using pure inheritance did not work well with Eiffel. The types of the parameters and return value of redefined routines should be at least of conforming types. Eiffel does not support parametrized polymorphism, hence, the number of parameters should be constant in all extensions of a routine. It is possible to overcome these limitations using routine renaming or rewriting a routine completely previously undefining it with Eiffel's *undefine* statement. The last case is, however, not recommended since it will not be a real extension of the routine.

To avoid these problems one must pay more attention to the overall system architecture and plan a bit further ahead then just for the next iteration. Extensive refactoring was needed in some cases, when the planning had not been done carefully enough. To refactor a SFI system efficiently, tool support was again deemed necessary.

3   Experience of Using SFI

In this section we summarize our experience from using SFI in the software projects mentioned above, based on the quantitative and qualitative data that was collected

Table 1. Basic product metrics for SFI projects

	EE	MathEdit	SCW	FiPla
LOC	3300	44372	16334	8572
Test LOC	1360	4198	14565	2548
Total LOC	4660	48570	30899	11120
Classes	52	427	66	59
Test classes	23	53	42	25
Methods	344	3790	610	331
Test methods	85	279	355	177
LOC/class	63	104	247	145
LOC/test class	59	79	347	102
Methods/class	6.6	8.9	9.2	6.0
Test methods/class	3.7	5.3	8.5	7.0

during these projects. Table 1 shows some basic code metrics for the presented SFI projects. It is easy to see that even in small projects like Extreme Editor and FiPla, the number of classes is growing fast. On the one hand this helps with debugging: as the developers were often commenting, it is easy to find the source of a bug in the code because of the separation of functionality into the layers. On the other hand, managing a large number of classes manually eventually becomes quite complicated, suggesting that tool support for navigation among successive layers, classes and methods is needed.

SFI is a bottom-up approach for constructing software systems and is therefore not that well suited for developing graphical user interfaces. Constructing good GUIs is a complicated task in itself and needs to combine different approaches such as bottom-up, top-down, use of state charts and designer tools. Our experience showed that when using SFI, it is better to separate GUI development from the construction of the core of the system.

Stepwise Feature Introduction fits well in our software process and in general in the Extreme Programming philosophy of introducing small changes one at a time in a software project [5, 15]. The division of the system into layers can be driven by the XP iteration planning process. When the development team negotiates with the customer about what new features should be implemented for the next small release, it is then easy to see what should be included in the next layer. Every layer in SFI system together with its ancestor layers represent a functional, working system. Hence, each layer corresponds to a small release, making it easy to package a specific release so that the customer can do the acceptance testing.

We obtained good results regarding the practical usability of SFI from our projects. SFI has a formal basis and provides a sound way of structuring software, and SFI designs often capture the core concerns of the software (the features) more explicitly than many traditional OO designs. We have also identified some shortcomings in the method that we need to work on. The use of inheritance as an extension mechanism can be cumbersome and does introduce some complexity of its own into the system. SFI occasionally makes it difficult to add a feature that does not fit well into the layer hierarchy. In order to make SFI practically usable, it will be necessary to devise another extension mechanism or introduce SFI-aware development tools (such a tool is currently being worked on, as explained in Section 7).

In the remaining sections, we will discuss in more depth three specific issues that came up during our experiments, and which we think merit a much closer analyzis.

4   Feature Combination and Diamond Inheritance

SFI suggests combining two or more independently developed layers into a feature combination layer (see Section 1). As each layer may contain an extension of the same class, the feature combination layer combines the extensions of a class from each layer into a new subclass using multiple inheritance. It is then the responsibility of the new layer to synchronize the two independent features in a meaningful way.

Multiple inheritance is significantly more complex than single inheritance for both language implementors and programmers. What constitutes correct use of multiple inheritance in object-oriented software is a subject of some controversy. Bir Singh [16] lists the four main uses of multiple inheritance, none of which correspond to the way it is used in SFI (combination of two implementations with a potentially large number of common methods):

– combination of multiple independent protocols;
– mix and match, where two or more classes are designed specially for combination;
– submodularity, to factor out similar subparts for improved system design;
– separation of interface and implementation.

This may suggest that multiple inheritance as implemented in most programming languages might not be ideal for feature combination as originally proposed in SFI. We will here focus on one serious design problem encountered numerous times in our experiments, namely *diamond inheritance*.

Diamond inheritance occurs when two or more ancestors of a class share the same base class. This situation arises fairly often in large systems, especially if the class hierarchy has a common root. In SFI diamond inheritance is likely to occur because of the way inheritance is used as a layer extension mechanism, especially if one uses the suggested feature combination.

An example of a situation in which the diamond pattern typically occurs in an SFI design can be seen in Figure 7. The Basic layer contains two classes, `BasicAccount` and a derived class `BasicCheckingAccount`, the latter supposedly having some extended behavior such as allowing withdrawals greater than the balance. In this case the programmer used inheritance to be able to handle objects of the two account types uniformly, i.e. to achieve polymorphism. Let us now assume that in the next layer (the Better layer), support for multiple currencies is added, and that this feature requires both `BasicAccount` and `BasicCheckingAccount` to be extended into `BetterAccount` and `BetterCheckingAccount` respectively. However, to preserve polymorphism, `BetterAccount` must also be extended to `BetterCheckingAccount`. We notice that mixing the two usage patterns of inheritance results in a diamond structure in the design.

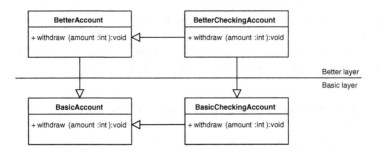

Fig. 7. Diamond inheritance

Diamond inheritance causes difficulty when the same method is implemented in more than one base class. In this example the `withdraw` method
of `BetterCheckingAccount` depends on functionality implemented in both
`BasicCheckingAccount` and `BetterAccount`, and calls both (in some order). However, each of these calls trigger a call to `BasicAccount.withdraw`, resulting in two
calls to this method. The code in `BasicAccount.withdraw` is thus executed twice,
which is not the intended behavior (the sum is withdrawn twice from the account). The
same situation occurs commonly with constructors—the constructor of the common
base class in the diamond is called twice. This results in data structures and resources
being initialized twice, potentially leading to resource leaks.

In the example case, when implementing `BetterCheckingAccount.withdraw` we
want to call the `withdraw` method of both base classes, but `BasicAccount.withdraw`
must be called only once. In Python 2.3, which was actually designed with inheritance
diamonds in mind [17], this is possible using the built-in `super` function which creates
a linearization of the class hierarchy and returns for a given class the previous class
in the linearization. By replacing direct calls to `__init__` with `super` the desired call
order can be achieved. The drawback is that since we are no longer explicitly calling
the base class method, we might not be sure which method actually gets called without
considering the linearization of the whole class hierarchy. Because this would make the
class design more complex we have not used `super` in any of our Python projects.

Most SFI projects developed in the Gaudi Software Factory have avoided diamond
inheritance by not using multiple inheritance for feature combination or for mixing polymorphic extension with stepwise extension. Consequently we have not been able to add
features to a base class in a polymorphic inheritance hierarchy using SFI layers. However,
many times features are better implemented using *delegation*, where an object uses another object (the delegatee) to perform an operation. In this case we can simply replace
the delegatee with a more advanced version in a higher layer. E.g., MathEdit heavily
uses the *Bridge* and *Decorator* design patterns [18] to avoid inheritance diamonds.

5   Avoiding Trivial Classes with Metaprogramming

One problem discovered early on was that some SFI-supporting metaprogramming
framework had to be implemented to reduce complexity that was primarily caused by

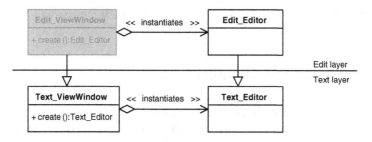

Fig. 8. Subclassing to override factory method

proliferating factory methods. This problem occurs whenever one class (the factory) is responsible for creating instances of another class (the product), and subclassing the product to add a new feature results in having to subclass the factory only to override the factory method so that it creates an instance of the new product class. An example from MathEdit is illustrated in Figure 8.

The class `Text_ViewWindow` creates an object of type `Text_Editor` in the Text layer. In the Edit layer the `Editor` class is extended with a feature that does not affect the behavior of `ViewWindow` in any other way than that it now has to instantiate objects of type `Edit_Editor` instead of `Text_Editor`. A class `Edit_ViewWindow` (grayed out) has to be introduced only to override the factory method that creates the `Editor` object.

Since frequent subclassing and deep inheritance hierarchies are commonplace in SFI designs, this situation will occur whenever a product class is subclassed and results in a large number of trivial factory subclasses, cluttering the design and increasing the code size. To avoid introducing these subclasses the metaprogramming framework of MathEdit implements a routine that given a class name returns the correct Python class for the running layer (Python classes are first-class objects which can easily be passed around; in more static languages one might need to do this in compile time using e.g. macro substitutions). If a certain class is not extended in the current layer, the routine searches backwards in the layer stack until it finds the most recent class definition. For example, calling the routine to get the `ViewWindow` class when running layer Edit would return `Text_ViewWindow`.

A substantial problem we encountered with deep inheritance hierarchies is that the control flow through the call chains of overridden methods becomes difficult to overview. The programmers generally thought it was hard to grasp the order of method calls and how the object state changes in response to the calls, especially with many nested method calls. Also, finding a method declaration in the code could require searching through several classes in the inheritance chain, unless the programmer knew exactly in which layer the method was implemented. One programmer commented that "a drawback with having so many hierarchical levels is that you start to forget methods and variables that you defined on the lowest levels."

Our experience indicates that the refactoring stage of SFI is of very high importance for keeping the design clean. Especially when working with unstable requirements, features can not easily be added on top of each other. The programmers found some of the refactorings to be difficult and error-prone, partly because inheritance creates a rather tight coupling between classes. However, a good test harness will substantially aid in the detection of such errors.

6   Unit Testing of Superposition

Unit testing is testing of individual hardware or software units or groups of related units [19]. Extensive, automated unit testing has been proposed as an efficient way of detecting errors introduced by changes in the software [6, 20]. A *unit test* exercises some subset of the software's behavior and validates it against its specification. Unit testing frameworks frequently group *test methods* into *test case classes*, which can further be aggregated into *test suites*. The complete *test harness*, consisting of all test suites, can then be executed with a single command.

SFI architectures should maintain the superposition refinement relationship between extensions and their bases—class invariants established in previous layers should not be violated in subsequent layers. A layered unit testing architecture allows us to easily create and maintain a test suite that aids in the detection of such violations, typically caused by programmer error or design mistakes. By writing tests for only new functionality and inheriting existing testing functionality, we introduce the requirement that a test introduced in one layer should also pass in all subsequent layers.

Most of our projects have utilized a unit testing architecture based on inheriting test cases. Our experience has shown it to be useful in practice; especially with many layers programmers easily forget assumptions and requirements introduced in a lower layer— if these are reflected in unit tests for the lower layer, possible violations are detected also when running tests for higher layers.

We assume that for testing we use a unit testing framework that provides us at least with a test case class. When constructing test cases in bottom layers, all test cases inherit the class from the testing framework. Test cases of the extended classes in successive layers should be extensions of the test cases from previous layers using the same extension mechanism as the application classes—inheritance. If an inherited method of an application class is overridden and extended with new functionality, the corresponding test method should be extended accordingly. If the body of the extended method contains a call to its ancestor method, the same technique should be applied in the body of the corresponding test method. This allows us to test both new and old functionality by writing tests just for the new functionality.

An example of a basic testing scenario with two layers can be seen in Figure 9. The Simple layer contains one application class (`SimpleText`) and its associated test class (`SimpleTextTest`), which tests the `insert` method of `SimpleText`. The Better layer extends `SimpleText` into `BetterText` by overriding `insert` and adding the `paste` method; correspondingly the `BetterTextTest` test case extends `SimpleTextTest` to override `testInsert` and adds a new test method for the paste method (`testPaste`). The new `testInsert` method should test directly only the new functionality introduced in `BetterText`, it should call the `testInsert` method from the Simple layer to test that the old functionality of insertion is preserved in `BetterText`. In this way, we test that `BetterText` is in fact a superposition refinement of `SimpleText`.

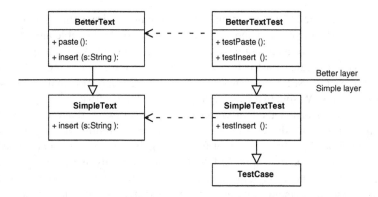

Fig. 9. Layered test cases

We have used the PyUnit [21] unit testing framework, which is essentially a Python version of the JUnit testing framework for Java [20]. The programmers found it easy to write tests in Python using PyUnit. No special compilation cycle for tests is required, and grouping all tests into a single suite makes it easy to run the tests often; programmers were encouraged to run the tests before committing any new code to the main source.

A number of open source testing frameworks for Eiffel are available. The Gobo [22] tool was used in our project for unit testing. Gobo test cases work similarly to PyUnit; the programmer subclasses a predefined test class and adds test methods. However, because the Gobo test framework is not integrated into the EiffelStudio environment, it was necessary to set up two different projects, one for compiling the system and one for compiling the tests and the system. The programmers found this arrangement inconvenient.

7   Conclusion and Future Work

We have above described our results from using Stepwise Feature Introduction, a formally defined method, in practical software engineering projects. The central idea in SFI is that layers are built stepwise as superposition refinements on top of each other; using class inheritance as the extension mechanism. Also, each layer together with lower layers should constitute a fully executable application.

We have carried out several case studies in Stepwise Feature Introduction. Our experience from these studies has shown us that SFI works well for structuring, debugging and testing the software under development. Combining SFI with an agile process like Extreme Programming provides architectural structure and guidance to an otherwise quite ad hoc software process, and has allowed us to deliver good working software in a timely manner. It is easy for developers to learn how to apply SFI, and the layer structure helps developers to understand the software architecture.

The main difficulties in applying the method have been caused by lack of automation and, to some extent, conflicting use of class inheritance. These observations point to a need for a generic SFI-supporting programming environment. Many of the programming tasks involved in applying SFI can require considerable amount of time. However, most of them can be automated, which would provide a great help for the programmers. The Software Construction Workbench (Section 2.3) was the first attempt to build tool support for SFI, but it was Python-specific. A number of smaller case studies also showed that SCW somewhat too rigidly restricted the software architecture.

SFI-style extensions adds a new dimension to software diagrams, which can become quite large and difficult to overview. We are currently building and experimenting with SOCOS, a prototype tool for constructing and reasoning about software systems, that is intended to support SFI. SOCOS is essentially an editor for *refinement diagrams* [3]. Refinement diagrams have exact semantics and a mathematical base in lattice theory and refinement calculus. A software system is presented to the user as a three-dimensional diagram containing *software parts* and *dependencies* between parts.

The SOCOS system is currently in early stages and the framework is still being worked on. Our current focus is on developing an environment for constructing layered software systems and reasoning about their correctness on both architectural and behavioral levels. Stepwise Feature Introduction, using either inheritance or another layer extension mechanism, is intended to be the main method by which features are added to the system. The goal is to create a tool for correctness-preserving, incremental construction of SFI-layered software systems.

References

1. Back, R.J.: Software construction by stepwise feature introduction. In: ZB '02: Proceedings of the 2nd International Conference of B and Z Users on Formal Specification and Development in Z and B, Springer-Verlag (2002) 162–183
2. Back, R.J.J., Akademi, A., Wright, J.V.: Refinement Calculus: A Systematic Introduction. Springer-Verlag New York, Inc., Secaucus, NJ, USA (1998)
3. Back, R.J.: Incremental software construction with refinement diagrams. Technical Report 660, TUCS – Turku Centre for Computer Science, Turku, Finland (2005)
4. Back, R.J., Sere, K.: Superposition refinement of reactive systems. Formal Aspects of Computing **8** (1996) 324–346
5. Back, R.J., Milovanov, L., Porres, I.: Software development and experimentation in an academic environment: The Gaudi experience. In: Proceedings of the 6th International Conference on Product Focused Software Process Improvement – PROFES 2005, Oulu, Finland. (2005)
6. Beck, K.: Extreme Programming Explained: Embrace Change. The XP Series. Addison-Wesley (1999)
7. Anttila, H., Back, R.J., Ketola, P., Konkka, K., Leskela, J., Rysä, E.: Coping with increasing SW complexity - combining stepwise feature introduction with user-centric design. In: Human Computer Interaction, International Conference (HCII2003), Crete, Greece (2003)
8. Back, R.J., Milovanov, L., Porres, I., Preoteasa, V.: An experiment on extreme programming and stepwise feature introduction. Technical Report 451, TUCS – Turku Centre for Computer Science, Turku, Finland (2002)
9. Lutz, M.: Programming Python. O'Reily (1996)
10. Eriksson, J.: Development of a mathematical derivation editor. Master's thesis, Åbo Akademi University, Department of Computer Science (2004)

11. Back, R.J., Björklund, D., Lilius, J., Milovanov, L., Porres, I.: A workbench to experiment on new model engineering applications. In Stevens, P., Whittle, J., Booch, G., eds.: UML 2003 – The Unified Modeling Language. Model Languages and Applications. 6th International Conference, San Francisco, CA, USA, October 2003, Proceedings Volume 2863 of LNCS, Springer (2003) 96–100
12. Meyer, B.: Object-Oriented Software Construction. second edn. Prentice Hall (1997)
13. Back, R.J., Hirkman, P., Milovanov, L.: Evaluating the XP customer model and design by contract. In: Proceedings of the 30th EUROMICRO Conference, IEEE Computer Society (2004)
14. Meyer, B.: Eiffel: The Language. second edn. Prentice Hall (1992)
15. Back, R.J., Milovanov, L., Porres, I., Preoteasa, V.: XP as a framework for practical software engineering experiments. In: Proceedings of the Third International Conference on eXtreme Programming and Agile Processes in Software Engineering - XP2002. (2002)
16. Singh, G.B.: Single versus multiple inheritance in object oriented programming. SIGPLAN OOPS Mess. 6 (1995) 30–39
17. Simionato, M.: The Python 2.3 method resolution order. http://www.python.org/2.3/mro.html (2003)
18. Gamma, E., Helm, R., Johnson, R., Vlissides, J.: Design Patterns: Elements of Reusable Object-Oriented Software. Addison-Wesley (1995)
19. Institute of Electrical and Electronics Engineers: IEEE Standard Computer Dictionary: A Compilation of IEEE Standard Computer Glossaries. New York (1990)
20. Beck, K., Gamma, E.: Test-Infected: Programmers Love Writing Tests. Java Report (1998) 37–50
21. Purcell, S.: PyUnit. http://pyunit.sourceforge.net/ (2004)
22. Bezault, E.: Gobo Eiffel Test. http://www.gobosoft.com/eiffel/gobo/getest/ (2001)

Rapid System Development Via Product Line Architecture Implementation

Mauro Caporuscio, Henry Muccini, Patrizio Pelliccione, and Ezio Di Nisio

Dipartimento di Informatica,
Università dell'Aquila,
I-67010 L'Aquila, Italy
{caporusc, muccini, pellicci, dinisio}@di.univaq.it

Abstract. Software Product Line (SPL) engineering allows designers to reason about an entire family of software applications, instead of a single product, with a strategic importance for the rapid development of new applications. While much effort has been spent so far in understanding and modeling SPLs and their architectures, very little attention has been given on how to systematically enforce SPL architectural decisions into the implementation step.

In this paper we propose a methodological approach and an implementation framework, based on a plugin component-based development, which allows us to move from an architectural specification of the SPL to its implementation in a systematic way. We show the suitability of this framework through its application to the TOOL●one case study SPL.

1 Introduction

The Software Product Line (SPL) technology has been introduced for the rapid development of new applications, by reusing as much as possible assets (i.e., components, known requirements or design elements, models, artifacts) identified in relation with specific application domains. The characteristic that distinguishes SPLs from previous efforts is *predictive* versus *opportunistic* software reuse [1]: instead of creating libraries of general purpose components, hoping they will be used in future development, SPLs make a predictive analysis of such artifacts which may be reused and integrated for the development of domain-specific products. Many approaches have been undertaken to deal with SPL during the entire life-cycle. At the requirement level, known notations have been extended to deal with SPL specific concepts (e.g., [2, 3]). At the software architecture level, formalisms have been introduced to model software architecture of product lines (e.g., [4, 5, 6]). At the design level, various approaches have been proposed so far (e.g, [2]). At the implementation level, some approaches and tools have been presented for SPL coding (e.g., [7, 8]).

While systematic tools and approaches have been proposed to specify SPL requirements, architectures and design artifacts, little attention has been paid on how to systematically integrate those steps. In particular, very few attention has been paid on *how to systematically implement the architecture of an SPL.*

N. Guelfi and A. Savidis (Eds.): RISE 2005, LNCS 3943, pp. 18–33, 2006.

Thus, constraints and decisions taken during architectural analysis cannot be easily propagated down to the product implementation.

Goal of this paper is to propose a *methodological support* and an *implementation framework* for establishing an effective and rapid integration and transition from SPL architectural specifications (usually referred as Product Line Architecture – PLA) to the implementation of the selected products in the SPL. The methodological support takes into consideration six different steps (shown in Figure 1), where (*a*) the PLA is specified in term of mandatory, optional and variant components, (*b*) a decision process is applied (*c*) to derive the specification of a certain product architecture (PA), (*d*) a constraint model is derived from the PLA and PA specifications, (*e*) the framework is configured taking into account architectural decisions and constraints, and (*f*) the product implementation is generated. The implementation framework (called N-PLA) fulfills the role of a plugin engine (managing plugins, lookup, communication) and provides capabilities for enforcing PLA level decisions and constraints. The product architecture is implemented using plug-in technology.

The novelty of our approach resides in the following aspects:

- the system development can automatically move from the specification stage to the implementation one;
- PLA-level decisions and choices are automatically enforced into the selected implementation. Structural, communication and dependency constraints identified at the PLA and PA level are identified and handled by the framework. Components are automatically assembled in order to conform to the architectural specification;
- SPL *evolution* is handled by the implementation framework itself. Whenever a component is added, removed or modified in the architectural specification, the framework catches the modification and handles it;
- *reusability*, well addressed at the architectural level by the PLA is reflected and stressed also at the implementation level.

The following of this paper is organized such as Section 2 introduces the concept of PLA, presents our methodology and the N-PLA implementation framework, Section 3 describes the TOOL•one SPL case study and how it is being implemented within the framework. Section 4 introduces related work while Section 5 concludes the paper.

2   From Product Line Architecture Modeling to Implementation

A Software Architecture provides high-level abstractions for representing the structure, behavior, and key properties of complex software systems [9]. Software Architecture models the system in terms of components and connectors, where components represent abstract computational subsystems, and connectors formalize the interactions among components.

When dealing with the software architecture of a product family, the concept of Product Line Architecture (PLA) [10, 11, 5] has been introduced as an emerging evolution to SA modeling for product family. Whereas an SA defines the structure and behavior of a single product, a PLA precisely captures, in a single specification, the overall architecture of a suite of closely-related products [10]. A PLA specification focuses on modeling *mandatory elements* (which are present in the architecture of each product), *optional elements* (which may or may not be present in a product), *variant elements* (which can be mandatory or optional, and can be chosen to be one of a number of different alternatives) [12] (see Figure 1, top-left portion), and explicitly models connection and communication constraints.

Once a number of variation points have been introduced in a PLA, it becomes necessary to be able to resolve variability in order to select one product architecture out of the overall PLA. This process is usually implemented using a *Decision Process* (e.g., [13, 7]) which allows the selection of optional and variant components (Figure 1, bottom-left portion) in order to choose a desired product architecture (PA). While notations and tools have been introduced in order to provide mechanisms to capture an entire family of architectures [13, 6], very few attention has been spent on investigating product line architecture implementation, that is, how architectural decisions and constraints may drive the implementation of a certain product.

In this section we describe our methodological approach and the associated implementation framework for PLA implementation.

2.1   Product Line Implementation: Our Methodology

Establishing an effective connection between SPL architectural models and their implementation is a relevant problem, as also remarked in [11], ch. 1, "one of the primary tasks of software architects is to establish and communicate to the rest of the team the important concepts necessary for effective software design and implementation".

In particular, what we believe is really challenging is:

- **enforcing the implementation adherence to PLA-level constraints:** When modeling an SPL and its PLA, many constraints are explicitly or implicitly identified: *structural constraints* are those related to the PLA model, in the form of mandatory, optional and variant elements; *communication constraints* dictate which components may communicate and how; *dependency constraints* establish how the selection of a component may require or exclude the selection of other components.
- **allowing software evolution, both at the PLA and product architecture level:** A relevant problem associated with an architecture is *managing evolution* [14, 5]: the *SPL may evolve*, requiring new versions of existing components or new components; the single *products* (members of the product line) may evolve. New features may be added, letting the product spinning off from the initial SPL; SPL evolution may *affect already deployed products*.

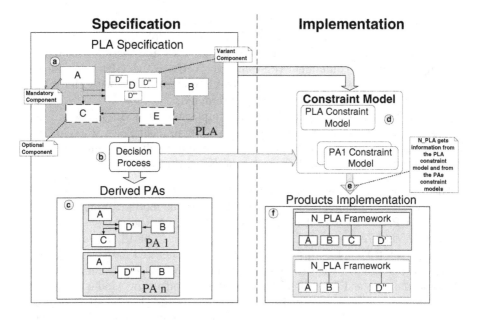

Fig. 1. Metodology Idea

The methodology we propose helps in creating a more deeply connection between the architectural specification and its implementation through six main steps (see Figure 1):

Step a): The PLA is specified in terms of mandatory, optional and variant components by using current modeling techniques and tools (PLA modeling tools are outlined in Section 4).

Steps b and c): A decision process is applied to the PLA specification for deriving a product architecture (PA) and the related constraint models. Clearly, it is impossible to fully automatize these steps: the product selection needs to be made by the software developer, however, PLA modeling tools allow for automatic PA derivation. The framework automatically generates the PA Constraint Model that is an XML file containing all the choices made by the user. For each selected PA a PA Constraint Model is generated.

Step d): Structural, communication and dependency constraints expressed in the architectural model are elicited from the PLA specification and automatically embedded in a PLA Constraint Model. This step is fully automated. The PLA Constraint Model is an XML file containing a representation of the PLA in terms of components (mandatory, optional and variant) and relations between them. In other words the PLA Constraint Model is a textual representation (XML format) of the PLA understandable by the N-PLA framework. While the PA Constraint Model is used to startup and instantiate the PA, the PLA Constraint Model is used to guide PA evolution. In fact, even if a PA can evolve, it must always comply to the PLA constraints.

Step e): For each PA, the N-PLA framework selects and loads the desired components from a component repository (i.e., the "plugin" directory). Components are Java bytecode packaged in .jar files and loaded through the `Plugin Manager` component (described in Section 2.2). N-PLA provides instructions on how components have to interact to match with the related Constraint Model. This step is fully automated.

Step f): N-PLA produces the product implementation. In particular, the selected product is implemented through a plugin technology, where mandatory and optional components are implemented as plugin components and, constraints are managed directly by the N-PLA framework.

The use of N-PLA as development environment, allows runtime selection and deselection of components, thus handling runtime modifications. Moreover, whenever a PA or PLA evolves, the framework adapts the implementation to conform to the PA or the PLA specification. In case of PLA evolution, the PLA Constraint Model is updated and each PA generated and instantiated is checked to be conform with the new PLA. In case of PA evolution, if the new PA conforms to the PLA, then the related PA Constraint Model is updated and the implementation modified. If a component is added or removed, a plugin needs to be added or removed. If the way components communicate changes, the communication information in N-PLA needs to be modified. This step is automatized.

In the next Section we show how the N-PLA framework works.

2.2   Product Line Implementation: The N-PLA Framework

The N-PLA framework [15] here proposed supports the designers with automatic transformations from the design to the implementation, automatically enforcing PLA-level decisions and choices into the selected implementation. Structural, communication and dependency constraints identified at the PLA level are mechanically caught and handled by the framework. Components are automatically assembled in order to conform to the architectural specification. N-PLA handles also SPL evolution: whenever a component is added or removed or changed in the architectural specification, the framework catches the modification and handles it.

Many different implementation frameworks have been developed so far for component based programming [16] such as JavaBeans [17] and COM [18]. Although these systems are widely accepted as standard reference models, they are not well suited for our purposes, since they do not allow for components addition and removal at runtime. More precisely, bindings between components are predefined and fixed, making architectural mutations impossible. On the contrary, what we need is a framework able to decouple components by achieving both modification of bindings, and components addition and removal.

The N-PLA framework overcomes this problem through a plugin-based infrastructure where components are N-PLA plugins, written in Java and loaded when needed by N-PLA. The framework itself is implemented in Java. Its

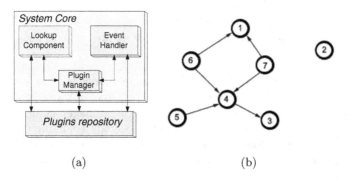

(a)   (b)

Fig. 2. a) N-PLA Software Architecture b) Plugin loading dependencies

plugin framework architecture is shown in Figure 2.a and is composed by two components:

- a *System Core*, which provides the core elements of the N-PLA plugin framework. While the `Plugin Manager` handles the loading and unloading of plugins, the `Event-based communication Handler` and the `Lookup-Component` manage the communication between components. From one side in the event-based system the components binding policy completely resides into the event handler which is responsible for switching events from a component to the others. Furthermore, architectural link modification will simply reflect in modifying the dispatching policy. Thus, while the event-dispatcher allows for a decoupled communication between components, it has the drawback in the added overhead and in the noise for results retrieving. In the case of synchronous call invocations, it is advised to avoid this communication handler. On the other side the Lookup-Component, that is able to retrieve the reference of a component through its ID, requires that the plugin that is interested to communicate with another plugin must necessarily know details on the interface of the target plugin. Moreover, the Lookup-Component, extracting information by the PLA XML[1], assures that the communication policies stated into the PLA design are respected.
- a *Plugin Repository*, which contains mandatory, optional and variant components.

While the plugin repository is just a site where the plugin are collected, the system core requires an extensive analysis in terms of its components *Plugin Manager*, *Event-Handler*, and *Lookup-Component*.

Plugin Manager: The plugin manager component is responsible for loading and unloading components. This component receives the PLA XML specification and extracts all the structural information that are used to define the policy regulating the plugins loading that each implemented PA must respect. In particular:

---

[1] We assume PLA and PA are both modeled in XML (as, for example, in [13]).

- each mandatory component must be contained into all implementations;
- optional components can be loaded or not;
- for a variant component the plugin manager assures that at least one of its alternatives is loaded.

For example, referring to Figure 1, the plugin manager, that contains the XML blueprint of the PLA, assures that an incorrect PA composed of only the plugins A and B is not loadable. The Plugin Manager assures also that dependencies between loaded components are respected. Assuming the existence of an acyclic dependency graph, where nodes are components in the PLA, and the direct arcs are the dependencies among components, the algorithm, at each step, loads the plugins (associated to the nodes) without dependencies (exiting arcs). After the deletion of each node representing plugins loaded, and its entering arcs, the process is iterated. In this manner all the plugins are loaded with respect to the stated dependencies. An example is reported in Figure 2.b, where the numbers inside the nodes represent one possible loading order. Whenever the PA or PLA specification have to change, the plugin manager dynamically revises the implementation in order to make it conform to the evolved architecture. If the component that must be removed, substituted or that is involved in the communication that is changing, is in a not stable state (i.e. it is computing or it is waiting for a result), the plugin manager temporary suspends the distribution of calls coming from stable components, waiting for a system stable state.

Event-Handler: The event handler component handles the event-based communications among plugins. Each plugin has an XML file specification that contains:

- plugin name,
- the plugin main class and others required information,
- binding information between received events and their internal methods.

The event is an object that contains the event ID and the list of parameters that should be passed to the bound method. The event handler is implemented as a queue able to maintain the publication order. For example, Figure 3.a shows the binding between an event $<E>$ and plugin methods for the component Sub_1.

The event handler analyzes the XML file for each plugin and builds a table (see the Figure 3.b) containing the event name, the event publisher and the list of components subscribed for the event. Therefore, referring to Figure 3.a and Figure 3.b, when Pub_i submits the event E, the event handler forwards the event to $Sub_1, \cdots, Sub_n$ in terms of methods invocation; in the case of Sub_1 the method **meth** of the class $Class$ is invoked with parameters "par_1",$\cdots$,"par_m". Whenever the PA or PLA specification change, the event handler updates the dispatching policy table, in order to make the implementation conform to the architectural specification.

Lookup-Component: This component allows for a direct communication between a pair of components. In fact, it is able to discover a component from

Event	Publisher	List of Subscribers
E		
"par$_1$"	Pub_i	$[Sub_1, \cdots, Sub_n]$
...		
"par$_m$"		
...	...	...

$< E > \implies Class.\mathbf{meth}(\text{"par}_1\text{"},\cdots,\text{"par}_m\text{"})$

(a)   (b)

Fig. 3. a) Mapping between events and plugin services b) Event-Handler dispatching policy

Client Component	Server Component
$Comp_1$	$Comp_2$
	$Comp_3$
	...
$Comp_3$	$Comp_1$
$Comp_i$	...

Fig. 4. Event Dispatching Policy

its ID and to return its interface containing all information needed to profit of the offered services. To do that each plugin specializes the abstract class *Plug-Data*, contained into the core component, adding the methods representing the exported services. The abstract class PlugData contains the method *lookup* that allows for plugins discovery. Thus, each plugin, using its class PlugData, that inherits the method lookup, can obtain the interface of each other plugin from the plugin ID. In this case the communication constraints can be assured. In fact the Lookup-Component can determine (see Figure 4) with which components a specified component can communicate and in case the communication is not allowed at the PLA level, the Lookup-Component returns *null*.

Currently, the N-PLA framework has been partially implemented and in the prototypal version available so far the *Plugin Manager* and the *Lookup-Component* do not allow for runtime changes (i.e., they work at compile time), and the *Event-Handler* does not handle binding between publisher and subscriber.

3   Product Line Architecture for Software Architecture Analysis: A Case Study

This section describes the application of the proposed methodology for implementing a PLA for Software Architecture (SA) analysis.

The analysis of functional and non-functional properties is a non-trivial task to perform along with the whole software life-cycle. Usually such activity requires the software engineer to have deep knowledge of formal languages and methods. However, since this is in contrast to the necessity to have short time-to-market, such activities are often skipped out. Hence, the use of support tools will easy and speed up the overall process. In [19], Cortellessa et al. faced such a problem

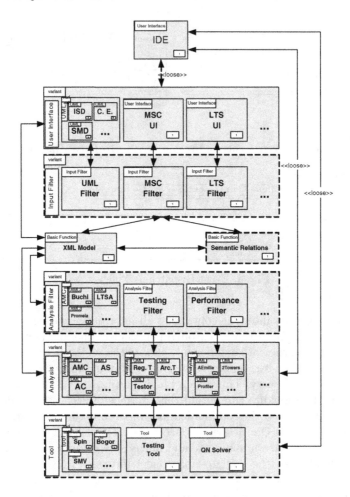

Fig. 5. The PLA for SA Analysis

by proposing TOOL•one, a framework for integration of functional and non-functional analysis.

Step a): Exploiting the Software Architecture of TOOL•one we derived a generic PLA for architectural analysis support tools (shown in Figure 5) that presents the following set of mandatory and optional components:

Mandatory Components:

- the *IDE* that implements the main window of the tool and is responsible to manage and coordinate the User Interface and the underlining analysis tools.
- *User Interface* which is a *variant* component for editing formal specification by means of diagrammatic notation. Referring to Figure 5 it is worth

noticing that the UML component is actually *variant*. In fact, since UML defines different kind of diagrams, it would be convenient to have the possibility of selecting one or more of them.

– the *XML Model* which manages the shared data structures. The use of XML representation of data allows for easily integration and management of a wide-range of different analysis.

– *Analysis* is a *variant* component responsible for performing the analysis of interest. It contains a set of *variant* components, representing the different kind of analysis, which in turn are composed of subset of *variant* components. In fact, for each kind of analysis there exist a number of various approaches implemented by different components.

Optional Components:

– the *Input Filter* is a *variant* component eventually needed to translate the visual editor output into the XML representation used by the *XML Model*

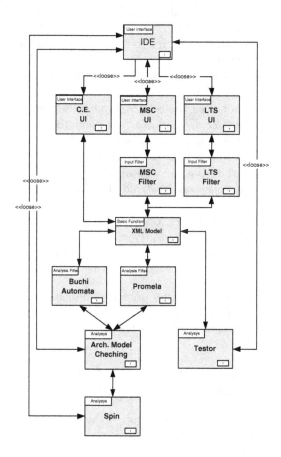

Fig. 6. The PA of CHARMY

component. In fact there may exist visual editors that already export their output as XML.

– *Analysis Filter:* is a *variant* component amenable to eventually translate or manipulate the XML model depending to the analysis to be carried on.

– *Tool* represents the set of additional components eventually needed to perform the desired analysis.

Step b) and c): From the PLA presented in *Step a*, we have instantiated the PA of CHARMY [20], a tool for supporting the design of Software Architectures and its validation against functional requirements (shown in Figure 6)[2].

In particular CHARMY is implemented by the following components:

Component Repository[3]:

– the *IDE* which implements the main window of the tool and is responsible to manage and coordinate the editors and the underlining analysis;

– the *CE UI* component which allows editing Software Architecture by means of components and connectors;

– the *LTS UI* editor which permits to specify the component behavior by means of state machines;

– the *MSC UI* editor which allows expressing interactions among components by means of message exchange;

– while *CE UI* does not need the related Input-Filter (it already exports its output in XML), the *LTS UI* and *MSC UI* come together with their input-filters components which are responsible to translate such diagrams into the XML representation that will be passed to the *XML Model* component;

– on the analysis side, the repository contains the *Architectural Model Checking* component for consistency analysis and the *TeStor* component for model-based testing;

– since the *Architectural Model Checking* requires Büchi automata and Promela code as input, the respective analysis-filters are needed in order to extract and translate data of interest from the XML Model representation.

Since *Architectural Model Checking* does not implement a model checker it self, the *Spin* [21] component is required for performing the overall analysis.

Finally, the XML file that represents the Constraint Model of CHARMY is constructed.

Step d): The PLA Constraint Model of TOOL•one is generated. A sketch of the XML file is here reported:

---

[2] Actually, while CHARMY v1.x does not comply to this SA, CHARMY v2.0 is still under construction and it is fully compliant with this work.

[3] Even though the Repository should contain all the components described by the PLA, the current prototype implements only those components needed to build the CHARMY PA.

XML of the TOOL•one PLA

```
<PLA_Constraint_Model name="Toolone">
<component type="mandatory" name="IDE" ID= "1">
    <connectionsList>
        <con type="loose">2</con>
        <con type="loose">7</con>
    </connectionsList>
</component>
<varcomponent type="mandatory" name="UserInterface" ID= "2">
    <connectionsList>
        <con type="async">1</con>
        <con type="async">4</con>
    </connectionsList>
    <componentAlternatives>
        <varcomponent type="mandatory" name="UML" ID= "2.1">
            <connectionsList>
                <con type="async">3.1</con>
            </connectionsList>
                <componentAlternatives>
                <component type="mandatory" name="ISD" ID= "2.1.1"/>
                <component type="mandatory" name="C.E." ID= "2.1.2"/>
                <component type="mandatory" name="SMD" ID= "2.1.3"/>
            </componentAlternatives>
                . . .
        </varcomponent>
    </componentAlternatives>
</varcomponent>
    . . .
</PLA_Constraint_Model>
```

Step e): Given such a component repository and the *Constraint Model* derived from the PLA and the PA XML description (Steps c) and d) of Figure 1) we proceed on running N-PLA.

Supposing that the *Decision Process* is correct, N-PLA parses the given PA deriving the set of plugins that composes the initial application configuration and extracting the constraints and relations between the components. In particular, when the *Plugin Manager* (refer to Figure 2) is launched, it processes the information presented above in order to load right plugins and properly initialize both the *Lookup-Component* and the *Event-Handler*.

In particular:

- The *Plugin Manager* retrieves from the PA the information about tight relations (links without stereotypes in Figure 5 and Figure 6) and build the an access policy table of the *Lookup-Component* (see Figure 7.a). When a plugin p asks for the reference of a plugin q to the *Lookup-Component*, the latter checks if p appears into the table. If there exists a row in which p and q are correlated, then the reference of q will be returned to p.
- The *Plugin Manager* also retrieves information about loosely relations (stereotyped links in Figure 5 and Figure 6) and build the table (shown in Figure 7.b) in which the *Event-Handler* keeps track of the architectural dispatching policy defined by the PA. When a publisher p sends an event e to the *Event-Handler*, the latter checks if such event appears into the table. If there exists a row in which e and p are correlated, then e will be dispatched to all plugins in subscriber list. In particular, Event-dispatching is implemented as method callback respecting the bindings defined into the XML plugin description (an example is given in Figure 8).

Client Comp.	Server Comp.
XML Model	CE UI
	...
	Büchi Automata
	...
	Testor
Testor	XML Model

(a) Lookup Access Policy

Event	Publisher	List of Subscribers
AMC_START "depth"	IDE	[Arc. MC]
RESULT	Arc. MC	[IDE]
DRAW "object"	IDE	[CE, MSC, LTS]

(b) Event Dispatching Policy

Fig. 7. Dispatching Policy

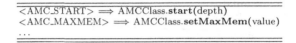

<AMC_START> $\implies$ AMCClass.**start**(depth)
<AMC_MAXMEM> $\implies$ AMCClass.**setMaxMem**(value)
...

Fig. 8. Mapping between events and plugin services

Step f): Finally, once all connections among components have been established, the CHARMY product is finished and can be used for performing analysis of interest.

4 Related Work

In this section we briefly report on Product Line Architecture Modeling tools and Product Line Implementation processes and tools.

4.1 Product Line Architecture Modeling

Ménage [13] and Koala [6] represent the state of the art in PLA specification. (ACME Studio and UML have been used for product line modeling too).

Ménage [13] is an environment for managing evolving architectures in SPL. It provides a definition of how to represent PLAs (addressing variabilities and also evolution) and a graphical environment which facilitates the specification, in the defined representation, of PLAs. Ménage uses xADL 2.0 [22] XML schemas as the representation format.

Koala, instead, is an ADL specially designed for modeling embedded software for consumer electronics. It inherits from the Darwin architecture description language the main concepts and ideals, even though it is more oriented to notations and concepts commonly used in consumer electronics products. Koala allows specifying hierarchical architectures, it makes a distinction between component types and instances, it permits to construct configurations by instantiating components and connectors and explicitly models optional interfaces.

4.2 Product Line Implementation

KobrA (Component-based Application Development) [7] is a software process- and product- centric engineering approach which uses a component-based approach in each phase of the development process. The KobrA implementation process provides guidelines on how UML artifacts used for specifying the SPL, may be used during the implementation phase. However, and differently from N-PLA, it does not provide implementation support.

Another interesting work has been proposed in [8] where the Pure::Variant approach and tool support for SPL is provided. The tool seems to cover all steps of SPL development, from requirements to product generation. The specification-to-implementation features will be further investigated when the product will be released.

Other tools proposed by the SPL community include Holmes [23], which supports SPL development and whose architecture is based on JavaSpaces, PuLSE-BEAT [24] which supports all steps of the scoping process, and [25] which supports top-down as well as bottom-up traceability in product families. None of such approaches and tools seem to support implementation of SPLs. For sake of completeness, somehow related to our topic are also Koala [6], xADL [22](with its C2 framework) and DiscoTect [26] (for architecture recovery).

5   Conclusions and Future Work

We presented a methodological approach and the N-PLA implementation framework for implementing product architectures, by enforcing constraints and allowing for reconfiguration. The TOOL•one PLA has been presented, together with one PA and some information on how it has been implemented in N-PLA.

With respect to a non-framework implementation, N-PLA imposes to use certain interfaces and packaging rules (as in any framework) but this cost allows for an automated loading of components, communication and constraints automatic handling. It is however necessary to impose a rigid structure in order to provide the N-PLA features.

With respect to other plugin-based frameworks (e.g., Eclipse and MagicBeans) we are currently evaluating N-PLA main advantages and limitations. The added value of N-PLA is on the ability to load the XML representations for the PLA and the PA and to manage consistently the loading of the plugins and the communication between them. Thus, if we think to use another plugin based tool (for example Eclipse), an extension is required in order to provide the potentiality of N-PLA.

Many enhancement are in mind for future work. A validation engine needs to be created for accomplishing two different tasks:

– validating the PLA specification conformance to feature and requirements. In fact, being assured the PA implementation conforms to the PA specification is not enough, if the PLA model itself has not been formally validated a-priori.
– Assuming a PA may have its own properties and constraints, a validation engine needs to be proposed to monitor the implementation execution conformance to the PA specification.

References

1. Krueger, C.W.: Introduction to Software Product Lines.
   http://www.softwareproductlines.com/introduction/introduction.html (2004)
2. Gomaa, H.: Designing Software Product Line with UML - from use cases to pattern-based software architectures. Object Technology Series. (2004)
3. Bertolino, A., Fantechi, A., Gnesi, S., Lami, G., Maccari, A.: Use Case Description of Requirements for Product Lines. In: International Workshop on Requirements Engineering for Product Lines - REPL02, Essen, Germany (2002)
4. Clements, P., Northrop, L.M.: Software Product Lines: Practices and Patterns. 1st edn. Addison-Wesley Pub Co (2001)
5. Garg, A., Critchlow, M., Chen, P., van der Westhuizen, C., van der Hoek, A.: An Environment for Managing Evolving Product Line Architectures. In: ICSM '03: Proceedings of the International Conference on Software Maintenance, IEEE Computer Society (2003) 358
6. van Ommering, R., van der Linden, F., Kramer, J., Magee, J.: The Koala Component Model for Consumer Electronics Software. Computer **33**(3) (2000) 78–85
7. Atkinson, C., Bayer, J., Bunse, C., Kamsties, E., Laitenberger, O., Laqua, R., Muthig, D., Paech, B., Wüst, J., Zettel, J.: Component-Based Product-Line Engineering with UML. Addison-Wesley (2001)
8. Pure::variants. http://www.pure-systems.com (2005)
9. Garlan, D.: Formal Modeling and Analysis of Software Architecture: Components, Connectors, and Events. In: Formal Methods for Software Architectures, Lecture Note in Computer Science, 2804 (2003) 1–24
10. Bosch, J.: Design and Use of Software Architectures: Adopting and Evolving a Product-Line Approach. ACM Press/Addison-Wesley Publishing Co. (2000)
11. Jazayeri, M., Ran, A., van der Linden, F.: Software architecture for product families: principles and practice. Addison-Wesley Publishing Co. (2000)
12. Jaring, M., Bosch, J.: Representing Variability in Software Product Lines: A Case Study. In: SPLC. (2002) 15–36
13. The Ménage Project: (University of California, Irvine) http://www. isr.uci.edu/projects/menage.
14. Bass, L., Clements, P., Kazman, R.: Software Architecture in Practice, second edition. SEI Series in Software Engineering. Addison-Wesley Professional (2003)
15. N-PLA Project. N-PLA Web Page.
    http://www.di.univaq.it/di/project.php?id=16 (2005)
16. Szyperski, C.: Component Software. Beyond Object Oriented Programming. Addison Wesley (1998)
17. Sun Microsystems, Inc.: JavaBeans. (http://java.sun.com/products/javabeans)
18. Platt, D.S.: Understanding COM+. Microsoft Press (1999)
19. Cortellessa, V., Di Marco, A., Inverardi, P., Mancinelli, F., Pelliccione, P.: A framework for the integration of functional and non-functional analysys of software architectures. Electr. Notes Theor. Comput. Sci., Proocedings of the International Workshop on Test and Analysis of Component Based Systems (TACoS), Barcelona (116: 31-44 (2005)) (2005)
20. CHARMY Project. Charmy Web Site. http://www.di.univaq.it/charmy (2004)
21. (SPIN Home page: http://cm.bell-labs.com/cm/cs/what/spin/index.html)
22. xADL 2.0 Architecture Description Language.
    http://www.isr.uci.edu/projects/xarchuci/ (2005)

23. Succi, G., Yip, J., Pedrycz, W.: Holmes: an intelligent system to support software product line development. In: ICSE '01: Proceedings of the 23rd International Conference on Software Engineering, IEEE Computer Society (2001) 829–830

24. Schmid, K., Schank, M.: PuLSE-BEAT – A Decision Support Tool for Scoping Product Lines. In: IW-SAPF-3: Proceedings of the International Workshop on Software Architectures for Product Families, Springer-Verlag (2000) 65–75

25. Lago, P., Niemelä, E., Vliet, H.V.: Tool support for traceable product evolution. In: CSMR. (2004) 261–269

26. Yan, H., Garlan, D., Schmerl, B., Aldrich, J., Kazman, R.: Discotect: A system for discovering architectures from running systems. In: IEEE Proc. of the 26th Int. Conf. on Software Engineering. (2004) 470–479

User Centred Rapid Application Development

Edward Lank[1,2], Ken Withee[2], Lisa Schile[3], and Tom Parker[3]

[1] David R. Cheriton School of Computer Science, University of Waterloo,
Waterloo, Ontario, Canada
lank@cs.uwaterloo.ca
[2] Computer Science Department, San Francisco State University,
San Francisco, California, USA
withee@withee.com
[3] Biology Department, San Francisco State University,
San Francisco, California, USA
lschile@sfsu.edu, parker@sfsu.edu

Abstract. This paper describes our experiences modifying the Rapid Application Development methodology for rapid system development to design a data gathering system for mobile fieldworkers using handheld computers in harsh environmental conditions. In our development process, we integrated User-Centred Design as an explicit stage in the Rapid Application Development (RAD) software engineering methodology. We describe our design process in detail and present a case study of its use in the development of a working system. Finally, we use the design of the working system to highlight some of the lessons learned, and provide guidelines for the design of software systems for mobile data collection.

In pursuing this project, we worked with field ecologists monitoring the evolution of coastal wetlands in the San Francisco Bay Area. The overall goal of the ecology project was to provide accurate information on the impact development has on these wetland areas. While the architecture of our system is tuned to the specific needs of the ecologists with whom we worked, the design process and the lessons we learned during design are of interest to other software engineers designing for similar work practices.

1 Introduction and Background

Recently, much interest has been paid to supporting the information needs of biologists, specifically with respect to the collection, analysis, and management of large data sets. While much of the work is geared toward genomic data, other fields of biology also suffer from inadequate data collection and management processes. In this paper, we describe our development process that resulted in the design of a data collection application for ecologists studying plant species in the sensitive coastal wetlands area near our institution.

The wetlands project measures species and frequency of vegetation at randomly generated data points in an area of ecological interest. Figure 1 depicts a region of interest with sampling points. Data points are loaded into a GPS

N. Guelfi and A. Savidis (Eds.): RISE 2005, LNCS 3943, pp. 34–49, 2006.

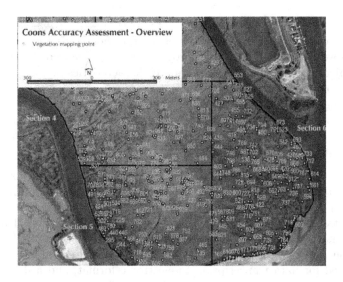

Fig. 1. Computer generated data collection points are displayed on a map, and the researchers collectively assign data points in the field

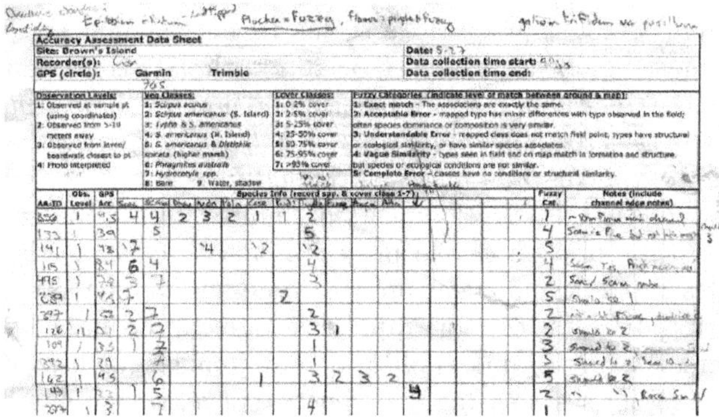

Fig. 2. Data sheet used to record field data. The data is captured using numerical scales.

system and ecologists travel to each of the data points, recording species and frequency data for the vegetation located there.

To record data, each team used a clipboard with a sheet of paper attached. Information is recorded using fixed numerical scales (See Figure 2). The use of numerical scales speeds the recording process and minimizes transcription errors. To analyze the numerical data collected, the data is transcribed into a spreadsheet application. The transcription of one day of paper-based field observations typically takes two or three days of data entry time in the laboratory. Our goal in this project was to enable electronic data collection, thus eliminating transcription.

While a complete description of the data collection practices of ecologists is beyond the scope of this paper, one important question is whether the fieldwork techniques we observed in our target project can be generalized. Certain aspects of any project are unique, while others are characteristics of the general work practice across many or all projects.

The ecologists we work with perform fieldwork constantly. In follow-up interviews with our user group and other biologists, several themes that are common across current biological fieldwork practice came to light. Typical practices include:

1. The use of numerical scales or other shorthand symbols or shorthand notations to simplify data capture and to minimize transcription errors is common.
2. The data collected are predictable. Biologists know the species of vegetation (or animals, soil moisture content, etc.) that they expect to find at a given location, and how much variability is likely in measured values.
3. The need for data transcription to electronic format, and a desire for this process to happen quickly, are generally true of many projects.
4. The use of pen and paper is typical in the field, due to paper's tactile characteristics and to the persistence of data recorded on paper despite mishaps, i.e. *"If it falls in the mud, I can still read it."*

One other important characteristic seems to be common across biological domains. The most significant hassle associated with data collection is the transcription process in the lab. As one participant noted: *"Transcribing is error prone ... knowing whether something is a 4 or a 9, lining up numbers with names ... It takes a lot of time and no one likes [doing] it."*

A constraint on system development for limited term biological fieldwork projects, where the duration of the project is measured in weeks or months, is the need for a rapid development process to design and deploy systems early in the fieldwork project. To support rapid development for mobile fieldwork, we present a modified form of rapid application development we used in the design and deployment of our system. Rapid application development (RAD) is an iterative software development methodology described, originally, by James Martin [11]. Since its inception, many authors have identified difficulties associated with software development using RAD methodology [1] [8].

To overcome problems with typical RAD methodologies, we introduce User Centred Rapid Application Development (UCRAD). UCRAD is a three-stage process. In the first stage, user interface design is combined with the elicitation of requirements. In the second stage, a high fidelity prototype is evolved into a functional system that is gradually deployed in the field. Finally, we maintain the deployed application through constant tailoring to the data collection process.

This paper is organized as follows. In Related Work, we outline some previous work in the design of data collection systems for ecologists, and some related work in the use of Pocket PC devices and PDAs for data collection in other fields. Next, we describe the User-Centred Rapid Application Development methodology we evolved during the course of the design of the system. We briefly describe the system architecture we designed and its success as a vehicle for data collection for field biologists. Finally, we conclude by outlining lessons learned during the evolution of our design process.

2   Related Systems

In this section, we focus on data capture or data recording systems designed for handheld computers. The use of handheld computers, such as Personal Digital Assistants (PDAs), as data collection devices has been studied in a number of fields as diverse as Emergency Response [16], Learning environments [6] [13], and even in Human-Computer Interaction during usability trials [7]. Of particular interest to us is the use of handhelds in the ecological sphere.

One significant use of PDAs in ecological fieldwork environments is the work by Pascoe et al. for use in observing giraffe behaviour in Kenya and in support of archaeologists [12]. In their project, many of the characteristics of field biologist users were identified, including:

- Dynamic user configuration, specifically the fact that data capture occurs in hostile environments while walking, crawling, or running.
- Limited attention capacity, due to the need to record data while making observations.
- High-speed interaction, due to the fact that giraffes move and an observer may need to record a lot of data rapidly to capture a complete picture of giraffe behaviour.
- Context dependency, specifically the need to know location and timing information.

While the work of Pascoe et al. does identify many characteristics of users in fieldwork environments, their focus on ecologists observing animals has an effect on user characteristics. As well, while an understanding of users is important, there is a need to understand how these characteristics play out in design, and to develop methodologies for successful design.

Other related work that merits mention includes the use of PDAs as location-aware guides in indoor environments [4], or as guide systems for use on university campuses [6]. Finally, we note that many researchers are working on a complete understanding of context, in various fields, including scientific inquiry [5].

In these research systems, the focus of research is on how best to use handheld computers such as PDAs to support data collection tasks. The design process is not the focus of this work.

Beyond the research domain, several companies design solutions for mobile data collection. One well-known company is Fieldworker[1], which builds integrated solutions involving GPS, data servers, and PDAs to collect field data. Fieldworker distributes a development environment to aid in the deployment of sophisticated applications. While reviewers have liked the advanced features

---

[1] http://www.fieldworker.com/

Fieldworker Pro supports [15], there is a clear delineation to be made between Integrated Development Environments like Fieldworker Pro and software development processes which is our focus here. Fieldworker is a tool to support software development methodologies. The focus of this paper is a software development methodology which we have developed to design applications for mobile fieldworkers.

3   User-Centred Rapid Application Development

The goal of our project is the design of data collection applications for use in limited term fieldwork projects that are common in ecology and other biological fields. The limited term nature of these projects, ranging in duration from weeks to months, requires an agile software development process.

Agile development methodologies, including Extreme Programming, are difficult to manage. For example, in Extreme Programming (XP), Bellotti et al. note that teams "must have a good grip on customer requirements ... by the time you engage in XP in order to prioritize engineering effectively" [2]. While XP does allow rapid development, the "Customer is King" aspect of design requires an ability, on the part of the customer or fieldworker, to prioritize features. This was absent in our development, as the ecologists had no experience with technology. Working with them to prioritize engineering required providing them with some experience with the technology prior to requirements specification.

Researchers also note that iterative development methodologies often result in poor quality software due to the need to specify system architecture and system logic early, in conjunction with evolving requirements [8]. This need to specify architecture first is also a characteristic of standard software development processes such as the Universal Software Development Process [10]. If the goal is to develop functional software in a short timeframe, eliciting requirements is often too time consuming a process to separate from development, but the need to specify a target for development still exists. When looking at RAD methodology, our goal was to combine software development with the elicitation of requirements and allow the prioritization of engineering to evolve with the project.

To compensate for a lack of requirements, we modified traditional RAD methodology to allow the early stages of development to focus on eliciting requirements. Figure 3 depicts our RAD process for developing software for mobile fieldworkers. The process has three stages. In the first stage, high-fidelity prototypes are developed to design and evaluate the user interface and to manage project risk. In the second stage, the prototype is evolved into a functioning system by creating the back-end architecture. Finally, we deploy the full-featured application and continually tune the application to the evolving requirements of the fieldworker. Each stage is iterative in nature, and follows a basic RAD style deployment, where a prototype is developed, tested in the field, and evaluated via a joint meeting between clients and developers.

We designed this process for the express purpose of deploying a highly usable application in two to three weeks. We try to accelerate the development process

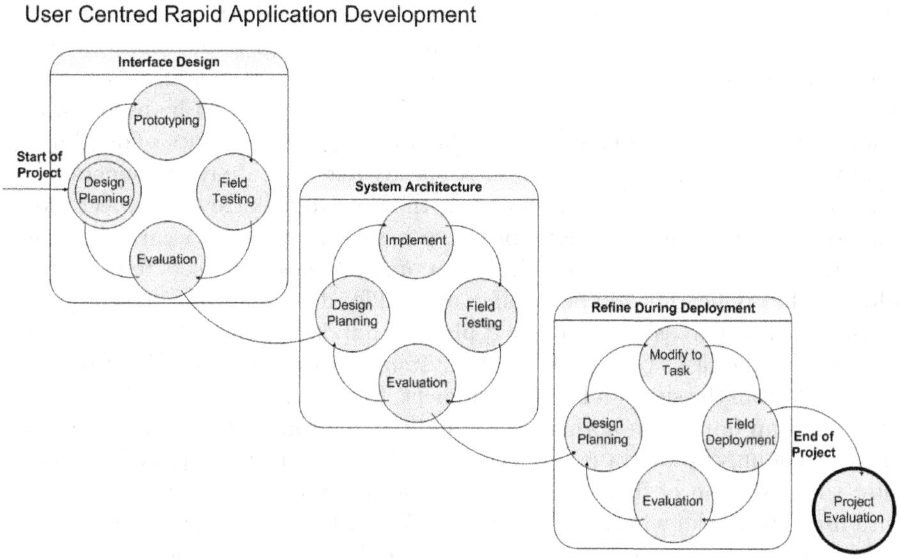

User Centred Rapid Application Development

Fig. 3. Our software development process for field biology

by giving biologists some experience using technology in the field early and to give developers, here a Master's student in Computer Science, some understanding of the requirements of the biological process early.

Early iterations occur in approximately four days. This works well in conjunction with many ecological projects. The typical data collection process we have observed in field ecology involves biologists spending one or two days collecting data in the field, followed by two or three days transcribing the data recorded on paper in the field into electronic format and doing some early analysis of the data. By matching our iteration to the biologists' data collection cycle, we prototyped a high quality user interface in approximately four iterations over a two week period and then added the back end application logic over a one to two week period. During the last week of the development cycle, the biologists used our application for data collection, but continued to maintain paper data collection as a back-up until the application development cycle entered the third stage.

There are two main goals to the first stage of development. First, functional and non-functional requirements must be developed for the overall project. Second, we wish to manage risk and determine whether the project will result in a worthwhile software artefact. To do this, we focus specifically on the design and implementation of a high-fidelity user interface.

Focusing on the user interface allows us to accomplish our goals in a number of ways. Eliciting requirements in any domain is a challenging task, particularly when the users have no frame of reference. In our case, working with field ecologists, the most significant hurdle we faced was the lack of experience on the part of the ecologists with technology in the field. While we had significant experience designing applications, we lacked experience with ecological fieldwork environments. A common language for expressing requirements was missing, as was any experience on the part of the user with what technology would be useful in the field. Focusing on the development of a high-fidelity user interface allowed us to work with the ecologists to concurrently specify and validate requirements. Second, and equal to eliciting requirements is the need to manage user expectations and user buy-in. With high fidelity prototypes, we can represent accurately to our users the functionality of the final application, and allow our users to determine whether the application will be an effective tool for data collection. Third, in any user-centred design task, work context plays an important role. There is a need to specify both the tasks performed by the system and the constraints on that task that result from the surrounding environment. However, the introduction of technology has an impact on both the task and the environment, and we wanted to measure not only how data was currently collected, but how an application could alter the paradigm of data collection, and what were the liabilities associated with use of technology in the environment. We worked to understand the impact of our technology due to two factors that together determine successful design for mobile fieldworkers. The first is rapid data input. Fieldwork is the most costly component in any data collection task in the ecological sphere, and we need to ensure that electronic data capture is not significantly slower than paper-based data collection. The second is data integrity. Work in coastal wetlands involves the need to engineer against mishaps. We need to balance these two factors in our design, and evaluating technology in the field allows us to determine whether we have successfully engineered for rapid input and against mishaps. A final benefit in early focus on the interface is that it allows us to begin to prioritize features in the application more effectively. We see how the application will be used, and evaluate the expected benefit of each feature in the interface.

The goal of the second stage is the evolution of a non-functional prototype to a functional application. With a user interface to design toward, the process of adding back-end data capture is relatively straightforward in mobile data collection tasks. However, care must be taken to preserve the performance of the application and to ensure data redundancy. While a high quality user interface has been designed in the first stage, the interface must evolve to match the application logic.

We separate application logic from interface development for two reasons. First, the application logic is a secondary concern to front-end system design in mobile fieldworker environments. The goal of the application is to replace paper as a data collection paradigm for field ecologists. Given that fieldwork is expensive and occurs in harsh conditions, the success of the application is determined by the user's ability to quickly and accurately record data. The ability of the application to archive that data once recorded is necessary but not sufficient for the success of the project. Where usability is the key determining factor in project failure, focusing on the user interface first allows us to manage risk. By focusing first on interface design and second on application logic, we maintain the primacy of the user interface in successful application design. Second, beyond the management of risk, application logic naturally occurs at a different stage in development. We use high-fidelity user interfaces to both elicit and validate our understanding of requirements, while application logic, instead, instantiates the requirements in a functioning software application. By explicitly separating these stages, we maintain a focus on *what* the system should do (first stage), followed by a focus on *how* the system should accomplish its goals.

The final stage allows us to tune the application during deployment in the field. The projects we seek to design applications for are, as noted earlier, limited term fieldwork projects. As a result, deployment occurred early in the project's lifespan, typically after approximately three weeks. One result of early, rapid, deployment it that the application that is deployed is a work-in-progress. The application continues to be tailored to the data collection task our users performed.

4   UCRAD in Practice

In this section, we briefly describe the evolution of our target software system. We first describe the sequence of development tasks. We then describe in brief the development of our software system for field biology to show how we elicit, validate, and then implement the system requirements.

Figure 4 depicts the development process over the four week period resulting in a deployed software application. The target ecology project continued for approximately two months after the completion of development, and we continued

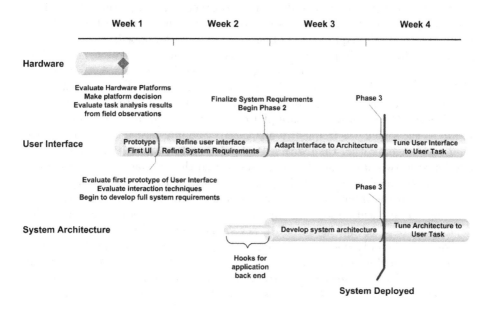

Fig. 4. In our methodology, software is designed from the front end to the back end

refining our application during deployment. As shown, we begin by selecting a platform, then design and implement the user interface. Back-end application logic is gradually developed and integrated into the application after validation of the user interface.

During the ini tial stages of user interface engineering, we worked with the biologists to understand exactly what the data collection process involved. In our development process, planning begins as a simple process of first interviewing the fieldworker about their data collection task and then observing that task in the field. Our initial planning involved a design meeting where the project goals were outlined, and hardware options were explored by the designers and users. Particularly during the first iteration, developers traveled to the field with the ecologists. This allowed the development team to evaluate different hardware platforms and to begin to develop a complete picture of the data collection task.

During the initial fieldwork with the ecologists, we spent two days working in the field. During this initial field outing, we validated the Pocket PC as an appropriate development platform. We considered other options, including Logitech electronic pens and tablet and laptop computers. Tablet and laptop computers are too expensive and to awkward for use by mobile fieldworkers, and electronic pens, while appropriate for fieldwork, work best for qualitative, not quantitative, data recording tasks. For quantitative data capture, handheld computers are the most effective application platform. During this initial fieldwork, observations of paper-based data collection tasks were also performed. We developed hierarchical task models, which we then validated with the ecologists during our evaluation meeting following our initial deployment. Being in the field watching the data collection process allowed us to develop a rich picture of the data collection task, the primary use case of our system. In validating this with the biologists, the basic requirements of the system were developed.

Using a drag and drop graphical user interface editor, we prototyped an initial user interface with no supporting back-end logic. The interface was designed to follow, as closely as possible, the specific actions involved in the ecologists' data collection task. During hardware evaluation, we also noted that, although the Pocket PC was an appropriate platform, stylus-based input was not appropriate as the stylus was frequently misplaced. The interface was designed to be used with fingers rather than with a Pocket PC stylus. The initial interface was developed in two days, and the biologists carried the interface with them when they went to the field and tested the interface for their data collection task.

We refined the interface over two additional iterations, and then began developing the application logic to support the interface components. During the deployment of a high-fidelity interface, several non-functional requirements came to light. For example, one of the ecologists noted during a design meeting, *"During our last field outing, someone fell and a GPS system got wet and stopped functioning. Many lessons were learned, [and we are even more nervous about technology in the field] ... Will that data persist even if we drop it in the water?"*

Fig. 5. Final user interface for our application

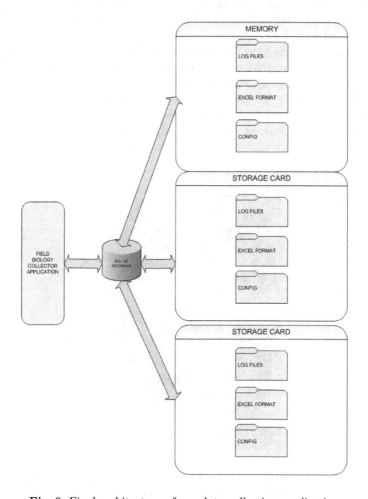

Fig. 6. Final architecture of our data collection application

In Figure 5, we show the final, functional application. The first two screens support data entry. Numerical entry is performed using a 10-key numeric keypad screen (not shown), while commonly found species are entered by selecting from a customizable screen that lists the species biologists expect to find at a given location. Another screen, not shown, lists over ninety-five species that are found in San Francisco wetlands. As we began to implement the back-end architecture, the need to support data collection came to light, and we added that functionality to our interface. When biologists select a previously entered data point from a list, they are presented with a screen that allows them to edit values associated with that data point.

After developing the core functionality in our interface, we designed and implemented a back-end architecture. The back-end architecture and hardware is designed to support data preservation in spite of submersion and other environmental hazards. In our system, we are using Dell Axim X50v Pocket PCs. These devices have random access memory (RAM) typical of Pocket PCs. They also have persistent internal storage in the form of 128MB of internal, writeable ROM. Finally, the Axims have both CompactFlash and Secure Digital (SD) Card slots. To protect the integrity of data, our system does several things. First, all data is stored in a SQL CE database. Second, each action by the user is added to a log file stored on persistent internal storage. Third, after each data point is added, the data is written to the database and a comma separated value (csv) file is written to the CompactFlash or SD cards if present or to persistent storage if these cards are not present. Typically, the ecologists we work with use SD

Fig. 7. Pocket PC application in use in the field in its waterproof case. In spite of the glare from the sun, the application can be seen faintly running through the waterproof membrane that permits interaction while protecting the Pocket PC device.

cards in all the Pocket PCs. Thus, even if the device falls out of its case and is submerged in water, the data collected by the ecologists is secure, and can be obtained either from the SD card or by reading the internal ROM in the Pocket PC. Figure 6 depicts the final architecture of our software system. To further protect the device, a waterproof case is used (Figure 7).

Modifications continued during the third phase. At one point, the data collection task changed slightly, requiring modifications to the interface. The storage format for data also changed several times, requiring a readjustment of the back-end architecture. By continually evaluating the software application, the system maintained a tight fit with the data collection task being performed.

5   Broader Lessons from Design

5.1   Successful Characteristics of Design

We continue designing field applications for use by biologists. From this design and early design of new applications, we note several characteristics of our design that assisted in its success. These include:

- Keeping features simple and data capture fluid.
- Deploying early.
- Rapid iteration.
- Over-engineering.

Simple features, as advocated by Extreme Programming, RAD, and other iterative methodologies, are an important consideration in design. Pen and paper are very successful in the field, and some biologists argue that it is because pen and paper only support the most basic interaction. As one user noted early in design: *"I can always transcribe in lab. I just need the data collected and I don't know how a computer will help."* Keeping features simple in the application allowed us to get an application into the field early, which is a second advantage. Many features that were planned prior to our design process were eliminated during our rapidly iterating cycle. As one example, early in design we proposed a set of web services to upload data. However, the use of a secure digital card in the Pocket PC proved sufficient. Our application currently saves two days of transcription time associated with each day spent collecting data in the field. Saving an additional ten minutes was a much lower priority. Plugging an SD card into a card reader connected to a PC and opening the CSV file in a spreadsheet program was sufficiently fast.

Early deployment, even of an imperfect interface, is not something to fear as long as the interface is solely for testing. To test our application in the field, we noted for biologists that it wasn't stable, that they should continue to use paper, and that all we wanted was what worked and what didn't for collecting data. Taking care in the design process to understand the task was important. The results of careful task analysis allowed us to develop and deploy a usable interface quickly. Small glitches in interaction were addressed through iterative refinement.

Rapid iteration through prototypes was another positive aspect of design in this domain. It is true that rapid prototyping results in initial applications that need significant improvement. However, in our case, as noted, getting software to the field quickly is a benefit in the limited term projects typical of field biology. As fixes are identified, correcting the software improves the effectiveness of technology in the field. Rapid iteration can continually improve prototypes, making technology even more useful over the course of the target project.

As well, early deployment, in our case, improved the transition of the ecologists we work with from informants to analysts and even to beginning designers. Once they understood how technology could be designed for the field, they were more able to engage actively in the design and evaluation process.

As a final comment, as designers in the field we noted that we underestimated how hostile the environment is. During one outing, a member of the design team was trapped in thick mud. On returning to the lab, he noted that he *"almost didn't make it back. I was sinking in mud, trapped, and I couldn't move..."* Data redundancy, protective cases, and other aspects of fault tolerant design are especially essential in biological fieldwork. Losing hardware is not critical. Losing time sensitive data is much more costly. Our rapid iterations and early deployment of semi-functional prototypes allowed us to develop an appreciation of the non-functional requirements of the system prior to full deployment.

5.2   Less Successful Design Processes

Paper prototyping, wireframes, or other low fidelity prototyping processes are one of the primary vehicles for cooperative and participatory design. It is a typical stage in many design processes, and some researchers have presented the results of low fidelity prototype testing as the validation for design guidelines in various domains [9].

The challenge with paper prototyping is that feedback on a design is suspect for highly mobile, context sensitive environments such as ecology. This is not a novel observation; Rudd et al. note that low-fidelity prototyping is not appropriate for evaluation, but is more appropriate for requirements elicitation [14]. Typical wireframe walkthroughs occur far from the context of use of software artefacts. While we did use wireframes in support of design meetings, we were careful to focus our evaluation and design planning on experiences with higher fidelity prototypes with functional graphical user interfaces that could execute in limited ways on the specific hardware platforms in the field.

Another common tool in interactive application design is participatory design, but it is a tool that must be used with caution. Our design process evolved out of a failure in participatory design. Researchers note that using participatory design is not straightforward. For example, Taxen notes that, in introducing participatory design into a museum environment there is a need to constantly validate products with respect to current work practice [17]. Carroll et al., in their work with schoolteachers, note a transition from Practitioner-Informants through Analysts to Designers over a five year period [3]. To participate in design, users need some experience with the technology in its use context. Rapid prototyping allowed our users to experiment with technology in the field and this improved their ability to identify positives and negatives in requirements and early designs.

6   Broader Applicability of UCRAD

In analyzing the problems with RAD, Howard notes two different forms of RAD: Rapid program development, where a detailed software specification is quickly implemented in code; and Rapid System Development, where a kernel of an idea for a project is evolved into a functional piece of software [8]. Our goal, in introducing our three-stage RAD model, has been to support Rapid System Development. However, as Howard notes, Rapid System Development requires extensive user involvement to describe what the system needs to do, to react to proposals, and to validate prototypes. He also comments on its "chaotic" nature [8].

Much of this paper focuses around our work in supporting the capture of quantitative data by mobile fieldworkers, specifically, in this case, ecologists using handheld computers. The process described in this paper was designed for the development of handheld computing applications, and handheld computers are particularly suited to quantitative data capture in mobile environments. Handheld computers are less suited to the capture of qualitative, observational data.

Although this development process has only been used to design systems for data capture for field biologists, it seems to hold promise for Rapid System Development tasks where user involvement is needed to simultaneously specify and validate both requirements and implementation. In this way, it is particularly suited to domains where the users have no prior experience using technology. In such domains, users find it challenging to work with designers to specify requirements as they have no pre-existing frame of reference. Participatory design breaks down, and even the specification of requirements with the users is challenging because they are unconvinced of the merits of technology. By first prototyping and implementing the interface, we can capture user requirements more effectively. Simultaneously, users become more informed about what the technology can accomplish and can see directly the benefits of using the technology. The result of using and experimenting with the technology aids users' transition from informants to co-designers.

The use of evolutionary prototyping in the process, coupled with continual evaluation of the prototype, allows the risk inherent in any development process to be managed. Systems evolve that suit user needs. If a suitable system cannot be implemented, this becomes obvious early in evaluation as the user interface will fail to support users' tasks. We noted this failure when working with qualitative data capture. The interface for handheld computers was not as efficient as pen and paper for capturing qualitative data in another ecology project we explored.

One advantage we had in our system design is that the back-end application logic was relatively simple. The requirements were that it captures specific data when entered in the interface and that it protects that data against environmental mishaps that would destroy the Pocket PC device. As the software architecture evolved, additional features were added to the user interface (e.g. a data grid that allowed direct manipulation of the database fields, a data correction screen that allowed users to select data points entered and correct values associated with them), but the core use-case could be fixed, validated, and supported immediately through user interface prototyping.

7   Conclusion

In this paper, we describe a modified form of Rapid Application Development called User Centred Rapid Application Development (UCRAD). Our development process is a three-stage process. We first focus on high-fidelity, semi-functional user interface prototyping with a drag and drop GUI editor to simultaneously elicit and validate requirements. We then evolve our limited prototype with its high quality user interface into a functional application. Finally, we deploy and continue to modify the application to tightly integrate with the appropriate task. Each stage in our process follows a Rapid Application Development methodology where implementations are tested in the field and evaluation is performed via joint meetings between developers and users. Our methodology has proved useful in the design of mobile, quantitative data collection applications for limited term biological fieldwork projects.

Acknowledgements

The work described in this paper is supported by National Science Foundation Award #0448540.

References

1. Ritu Agarwal, Jayesh Prasad, Mohan Tanniru, and John Lynch, "Risks of Rapid Application Development", CACM 43:11, November 2000, pp. 177–188.
2. V. Bellotti, N. Ducheneaut, M. Howard, I. Smith, and C. Neuwirth, "Innovation in extremis: evolving an application for the critical work of email and information management", Symposium on Designing Interactive Systems, London, June 2002, pp. 181–192.
3. J. Carroll, G. Chin, M. Rose and E. Neal, "The Development of Cooperation: Five Years of Participatory Design in the Virtual School", Proceedings of the Conference on Designing Interactive Systems 2000, New York, August 2000, pp. 239–251.
4. Ciavarella, C. and Paterno, F. The Design of a Handheld, Location-Aware Guide for Indoor Environments. Personal and Ubiquitous Computing 8 (2004) 82–91.
5. Chin, G. and Lansing, C. Capturing and Supporting Contexts for Scientific Data Sharing via the Biological Sciences Collaboratory. In Proceedings of the ACM Conferences on Computer Supported Cooperative Work, CSCW 2004, ACM Press (2004), pp. 409–418.

6. Griswold, W., et al. ActiveCampus: Experiments in Community-Oriented Ubiquitous Computing. IEEE Computer 37, 10 (2004), 73–81.

7. Hammontree, M., Weiler P. and Hendrich, B. PDA-Based Observation Logging. in Proceedings of the ACM Conference on Human Factors in Computer Systems, CHI 2004, ACM Press (1995), 25–26.

8. Alan Howard, "Rapid Application Development: Rough and Dirty or Value-for-Money Engineering?", CACM 45:10, October 2002, pp. 27–29.

9. Jiang, X., Hong, J., Takayama, L., and Landay, J. "Ubiquitous Computing for Firefighters: Field Studies and Prototypes of Large Displays for Incident Command", in Proceedings of the ACM Conference on Human Factors in Computer Systems, CHI 2004, Vienna, pp. 679–686.

10. P. Kruchten, The Rational Unified Process – an Introduction, Addison-Wesley, Reading, MA, 1998.

11. James Martin, *Rapid Application Development*. Macmillan, New York, 1991.

12. Pascoe, J., Ryan, N. and Morse, D. Using While Moving: HCI Issues in Fieldwork Environments. ACM TOCHI 7, 3 (2000), 417–437.

13. Rogers, Y., Price, S., Fitzpatrick, G., Fleck, R., Harris, E., Smith, H., Randell, C. Muller, H., O'Malley, C., Stanton, D., Thompson, M., and Weal, M. "Ambient Wood: Designing New Forms of Digital Augmentation for Learning Outdoors." in Proceeding of the Third Interation Conference for Interaction Design and Children, IDC 2004, ACM Press (2004), pp. 3–10.

14. Jim Rudd, Ken Stern, Scott Isensee, "Low vs. high-fidelity prototyping debate", *Interactions*, 3:1, January 1996, pp. 76–85.

15. Nick Ryan, Jason Pascoe and David Morse, "FieldWorker Advanced 2.3.5 and FieldWorker Pro 0.91", *Internet Archaelogy*, Issue 3, Autumn 1997.

16. Sawyer, S., Tapia, A., Pesheck, L. and Davenport, J. Mobility and the First Responder. CACM 47, 3 (2004), 62–65.

17. Taxen, G., "Cases and experiences: Introducing participatory design in museums", Proceedings of the eighth conference on Participatory design, Toronto, July 2004, pp. 204–213.

Software Testing with Evolutionary Strategies

Enrique Alba and J. Francisco Chicano

Departamento de Lenguajes y Ciencias de la Computación,
University of Málaga, Spain
eat@lcc.uma.es, chicano@lcc.uma.es

Abstract. This paper applies the Evolutionary Strategy (ES) meta-heuristic to the automatic test data generation problem. The problem consists in creating automatically a set of input data to test a program. This is a required step in software development and a time consuming task in all software companies. We describe our proposal and study the influence of some parameters of the algorithm in the results. We use a benchmark of eleven programs that includes fundamental algorithms in computer science. Finally, we compare our ES with a Genetic Algorithm (GA), a well-known algorithm in this domain. The results show that the ES obtains in general better results than the GA for the benchmark used.

1   Introduction

Automatic test data generation consists in proposing automatically a "good" set of input data for a program to be tested. This is a very important, time consuming, and hard task in software development [1]. But, what is a good set of input data? Intuitively, we can state that a good set of test data will allow a large amount of faults in a program to be discovered. For a more formal definition we have to resort to the *test adequacy criteria* [2].

The automatic generation of test data for computer programs has been tackled in the literature since many years ago [3, 4]. A great number of paradigms has been applied to the test data generation. In the next paragraphs we mention some of these techniques.

A first paradigm is the so-called *random test data generation*. The test data are randomly created until the test adequacy criterion is satisfied or a maximum number of program inputs is generated. We can find some experiments with random test data generators in [5] and more recently in [2].

Symbolic test data generation [3] consists in using symbolic values for the variables instead of real values to get a symbolic execution. Some algebraic constraints are obtained from this symbolic execution and these constraints are used for finding test cases. Godzilla [6] is an automatic test data generator that uses this technique.

A third and widely spread paradigm is *dynamic test data generation*. In this case, the program is instrumented to pass information to the test generator. The test generator checks whether the test adequacy criterion is fulfilled or not. If the criterion is not fulfilled it prepares new test data to serve as input for the

N. Guelfi and A. Savidis (Eds.): RISE 2005, LNCS 3943, pp. 50–65, 2006.

program. The test data generation process is translated into a function minimization problem, where the function is some kind of "distance" to an execution where the test criterion is fulfilled. This paradigm was presented in [4] and there are many works based on it [1, 2, 7, 8].

Following the dynamic test data generation paradigm, several metaheuristic techniques have been applied to the problem in the literature. Mantere and Alander in [9] present a recent review on the applications of the evolutionary algorithms to software testing. Most of the papers included in their discussion use GAs to find test data. In fact, only a few works listed in the review include other techniques such as cultural algorithms [10] (a special kind of GA), hill climbing [11], and simulated annealing [12].

We have found other recent works applying metaheuristic algorithms to software testing. In [13] the authors explain how a Tabu Search algorithm can be applied to generate test data obtaining maximum branch coverage. Sagarna and Lozano tackle the problem by using an Estimation of Distribution Algorithm (EDA) in [14] and they compare a Scatter Search (SS) with EDAs in [15].

In this work we propose the ES for finding input data sets in software testing. To our knowledge, this is the first work applying ES to this domain. This technique has some advantages such as self-adaptability, and real number representation of the problem variables. The former reduces the human effort in tuning the algorithm. The last makes possible to explore a wide region of the input values.

The rest of the paper is organized as follows. We detail the construction of our test data generator in the next section. Section 3 gives a description of the Evolutionary Strategy. Then, in Sect. 4 we analyze the experiments on the benchmark. Finally, Sect. 5 addresses the final conclusions and future work.

2   The Test Data Generator

In this section we describe the test data generator proposed and the whole test generation process. We are interested in testing the functional requirements of the software, that is, the relationship between input and output. Some other works apply evolutionary techniques in software testing to check non-functional requirements like temporal constraints [16]. As we said in the previous section, in order to formalize the problem we must define a test adequacy criterion. There exist many of them. For example, in the *statement coverage* we require all the statements in the program to be executed. On the other hand, *branch coverage* requires taking all the branches in the conditional statements. We choose in this work the same test adequacy criterion as in [2]: *condition-decision coverage*. To fulfill this criterion all conditions must be true and false at least once after executing all the set of test data on it. A condition is an expression that is evaluated during the program execution to a boolean value (true or false) with no other nested conditions. All the comparison expressions are conditions. On the contrary, a decision is a boolean expression whose value affects the control flow. The boolean expression following an if keyword in C is a decision. It is important to note that full condition-decision coverage implies full branch coverage but not vice versa. That is, if we find a set of test inputs that makes true and false all the program conditions at least once we can ensure that all the decisions will take values true and false and, in consequence, that all branches will be taken; but taking all branches does not ensure that all conditions take the two boolean values. We call *test program* to the program being tested.

Our proposal is a white-box test data generator, so the first step is to instrument the test program itself. To do this, we add some neutral statements to all the conditions in order to inform about the boolean value of the condition and the fitness value needed in the ES (see below). The previous process is done automatically by an application that parses the C source program and generates a modified C source program with the same original behavior. The modified code is compiled and linked with an object file to create the executable file used in the experiments. The process is summarized in Fig. 1.

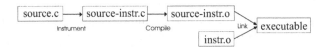

Fig. 1. The instrumentation process

In the instrumentation process each condition is transformed into an expression that is evaluated to the same value as the original condition. This expression has a side effect: it informs about the condition reached and the value it takes. Our actual version of the instrumentor software is able to transform all non-empty conditions appearing in a decision of a `for` loop, a `while` loop, a `do while` loop, and an `if` statement. At present, we must transform by hand all the `switch` sentences and the `(a?b:c)` expressions into one of the supported kinds.

The object file `instr.o` of Fig. 1 implements some functions that are called by the new added statements to inform about the conditions reached. The final executable file must be executed by using a special program: the *launcher*. This program acts as a bridge between the modified program and the test data generator (see Fig. 2). It writes to the standard output all the information about the conditions executed in the test program.

When the test data generator executes the modified test program with a given input, a report of the condition values is computed and transmitted to the launcher. The launcher writes this report to the standard output and the generator captures it. With this information the generator builds a coverage table where it stores, for each condition, the set of test data that makes the condition true and false along the process. That is, for each condition the table stores two sets: the true set and the false set. This table is an important internal data structure that is looked up during the test generation. We say that a condition is *reached* if at least one of the sets associated with the condition is non-empty. On the other hand, we say that a condition is *covered* if the two sets are non-empty.

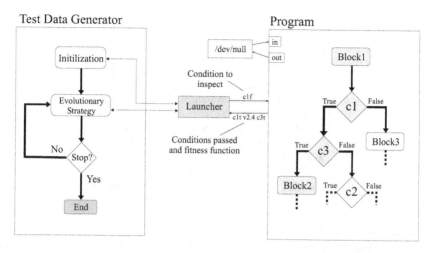

Fig. 2. The test data generation process. The launcher communicates with the test data generator by means of the standard input/output. The communication between the program and the launcher is carried out by using pipes.

The outline of the test generator is as follows. First, it generates some random test data (10 in this work) and executes the test program with these data. As a result, some entries of the coverage table will be filled. Then, it looks up in the coverage table for a condition reached but not covered. When found, it uses the ES to search a test data making that condition to take the value not covered yet. During this search the ES can find test data covering other conditions. These test data are also used for updating the condition table. If the ES does not fulfill its objective another reached and not covered condition is chosen and the ES is executed again. The loop stops when all the conditions are covered or when there is no insertion in an empty set of the coverage table during a predefined number of steps (10 steps in this work). Fig. 2 summarizes the test data generator scheme. We have implemented the test data generator in Java. In the next section we will detail the evolutionary strategy.

3   Evolutionary Strategy

An Evolutionary Strategy is a kind of Evolutionary Algorithm (EA). EAs [17] are heuristic search techniques loosely based on the principles of natural evolution, namely adaptation and survival of the fittest. These techniques have been shown to be very effective in solving hard optimization tasks. They are based on a set of solutions (individuals) called *population*. The problem knowledge is usually enclosed in a function, the so-called *fitness function*, that assigns a quality value to the individuals. In Fig. 3 we show the pseudocode of a generic EA. Initially, the algorithm creates a population of μ individuals randomly or by using a seeding algorithm. At each step, some individuals of the population are selected, usually according to their fitness values, and used for creating new λ

```
t := 0;
P(0) = Generate ();
Evaluate (P(0));
while not StopCriterion do
    P¹(t) := Select (P(t));
    P²(t) := VariationOps (P¹(t));
    Evaluate (P²(t));
    P(t+1) := Replace (P(t),P²(t));
    t := t+1;
endwhile;
```

Fig. 3. Pseudocode of an Evolutionary Algorithm (EA)

individuals by means of *variation operators*. Some of these operators only affect to one individual (mutation), but others generate a new individual by combining components of several of them (recombination). These last operators are able to put together good solution components that are distributed in the population, while the first one is the source of new different components. The individuals created are evaluated according to the fitness function. To end a step of the algorithm, a replacement operator decides what individuals will form part of the new population. This process is repeated until a stop criterion, such as a maximum number of evaluations, is fulfilled. Depending on the representation of the solutions and the variation operators used we can distinguish four main types of EAs: genetic algorithm, evolutionary strategy, evolutionary programming, and genetic programming.

In an Evolutionary Strategy [18] each individual is composed of a vector of real numbers representing the problem variables ($\mathbf{x}$), a vector of standard deviations (σ) and, optionally, a vector of angles (ω). These two last vectors are used as parameters for the main operator of this technique: the Gaussian mutation. They are evolved together with the problem variables themselves, thus allowing the algorithm to self-adapt the search to the landscape. For the recombination operator of an ES there are many alternatives: each of the three real vectors of an individual can be recombined in a different way. However, this operator is not so important as the mutation. In fact, we do not use recombination in our algorithm. The mutation operator is governed by the three following equations:

$$\sigma'_i = \sigma_i \exp(\tau N(0,1) + \eta N_i(0,1)) \ , \tag{1}$$

$$\omega'_i = \omega_i + \varphi N_i(0,1) \ , \tag{2}$$

$$\mathbf{x}' = \mathbf{x} + \mathbf{N}(\mathbf{0}, C(\sigma', \omega')) \ , \tag{3}$$

where $C(\sigma', \omega')$ is the covariance matrix associated to σ' and ω', $N(0,1)$ is the standard univariate normal distribution, and $\mathbf{N}(\mathbf{0}, C)$ is the multivariate normal distribution with mean $\mathbf{0}$ and covariance matrix C. The subindex i in the standard normal distribution indicates that a new random number is generated anew for each component of the vector. The notation $N(0,1)$ is used for indicating that the same random number is used for all the components. The parameters

τ, η, and φ are set to $(2n)^{-1/2}$, $(4n)^{-1/4}$, and $5\pi/180$, respectively, as suggested in [19]. With respect to the replacement operator, there is a special notation to indicate wether the old population is taken into account or not to form the new population. When only the new individuals are used, we have a (μ, λ)-ES; otherwise, we have a $(\mu + \lambda)$-ES.

The input values of a test program can only be real or integer numbers. Each of these number values is a problem variable in the ES and, thus, is represented with a real value. This value is rounded in the case of integer arguments when the test program is executed. In this way, the ES can explore the whole solution space. This contrasts with other techniques such as genetic algorithm with binary representation that can only explore a limited region of the space.

The test generator communicates the objective of the search to the modified test program (that is, the condition and its boolean value) by means of the launcher and the program computes the fitness value when it reaches the condition (regardless of the boolean value it takes). The fitness function is designed to be minimized and depends on the kind of target condition and the boolean value it should take. When the objective condition is not reached the fitness function takes a predefined high value (100000). Table 1 summarizes the fitness expressions for each kind of condition and boolean value desired.

Table 1. Fitness expressions for different kinds of conditions and desired boolean values. The variables a and b are numeric variables (integer or real).

Condition type	*true* fitness	*false* fitness
$a < b$	$a - b + 1$	$b - a$
$a <= b$	$a - b$	$b - a + 1$
$a == b$	$(b - a)^2$	$(1 + (b - a)^2)^{-1}$
$a \;!= b$	$(1 + (b - a)^2)^{-1}$	$(b - a)^2$
a	$(1 + a^2)^{-1}$	a^2

The population of the evolutionary strategy is partially seeded with some test data that is known to reach the objective condition. These data are taken randomly from the non-empty set associated to the objective condition in the condition table. The rest of the population is generated randomly.

4   Experiments

We present in this section the experiments performed over a benchmark of eleven test programs in C covering some practical and fundamental computer science aspects. The programs range from numerical computation (such as Bessel functions) to general optimization methods (such as simulated annealing). Most of the source codes have been extracted from the book "C Recipes" available on-line at http://www.library.cornell.edu/nr/bookcpdf.html. The programs are listed in Table 2, where we inform about the number of conditions, the lines of code

Table 2. Programs tested in the experiments. The *source* column presents the name of the function in C-Recipes.

Program	Conds.	LOC	Args.	Description	Source
triangle	21	53	3	Classify triangles	Ref. [2]
gcd	5	38	2	Greatest Common Denominator	Authors
calday	11	72	3	Calculate the day of the week	julday
crc	9	82	13	Cyclic Redundant Code	icrc
insertion	5	47	20	Sort by insertion method	piksrt
shell	7	58	20	Sort by shell method	shell
quicksort	18	143	20	Sort by quicksort method	sort
heapsort	10	72	20	Sort by heapsort method	hpsort
select	28	200	21	kth element of an unordered list	selip
bessel	21	245	2	Bessel J_n and Y_n functions	bessj*,bessy*
sa	30	332	23	Simulated Annealing	anneal

(LOC), the number of input arguments, a brief description of their goal, and the way of accessing them.

The first test program, triangle, receives three integer numbers and decides the kind of triangle they represent: equilateral, isosceles, scalene, or no triangle. The next program, gcd, computes the greatest common denominator of the two integer arguments. The calday test program computes the day of the week given a date as three integer arguments. In crc the cyclic redundant code is computed from 13 integer numbers given in the arguments. The next four test programs (insertion, shell, quicksort, heapsort) sort the 20 real arguments using well-known sorting algorithms. The select program gets the kth element from an unsorted list of real numbers. The first argument is k and the rest of the arguments forms the unsorted list. The next program computes the Bessel functions given an order n and real argument. Finally, the sa program solves an instance of the Travelling Salesman Problem with 10 cities by using Simulated Annealing. The three first arguments are seed parameters for the pseudorandom number generator. The rest of the arguments contains real numbers representing the two-dimensional position of each city.

In the following section we present the results with an evolutionary strategy. In Sect. 4.2 we perform a parametric study by changing the number of offsprings and the population size of the ES. Finally, in Sects. 4.3 and 4.4 we compare our ES with a GA and with previous results in the literature, respectively.

4.1   Results of the Evolutionary Strategy

Our ES has a population size of $\mu = 10$ individuals and the 10% of this population (that is, one individual) is seeded by using the mechanism explained in Sect. 2. The number of offsprings is $\lambda = 1$ and the maximum number of iterations of the ES main loop is 100 (110 evaluations). We perform 30 independent runs of the test data generator and we show in Table 3 some coverage measures, the average number of evaluations, and the average time used.

Table 3. Results obtained with the (10+1)-ES for the eleven programs. Average values over 30 independent runs.

Program	Cov.(%)	Corr. Cov.(%)	Max. Corr.(%)	Std. Dev.	Evals.	Time(s)
triangle	97.54	99.92	100.00	0.0044	1975	10.6
gcd	100.00	100.00	100.00	0.0000	21	0.0
calday	91.82	91.82	100.00	0.0246	1182	6.8
crc	94.44	100.00	100.00	0.0000	1114	28.7
insertion	100.00	100.00	100.00	0.0000	10	0.0
shell	100.00	100.00	100.00	0.0000	10	0.0
quicksort	88.89	94.12	94.12	0.0000	1110	8.4
heapsort	90.00	100.00	100.00	0.0000	1110	9.4
select	53.57	83.33	83.33	0.0000	1120	8.9
bessel	95.08	97.40	97.56	0.0061	1306	7.6
sa	97.06	98.70	100.00	0.0072	1329	5082.1

Analyzing the solutions, we found that a 100% of condition-decision coverage is impossible to reach in some test programs because there are conditions that can not be true or false in certain situations. For example, an infinite loop has a condition that is always true (Fig. 4 left). Another example is the condition (sign(x)>2), where the function sign can only return three values: -1, 0, $+1$. Thus, there can be pairs condition-value that are *unreachable*. In the previous cases the test generator can not reach the 100% of coverage due to the test program itself (code-dependent coverage loss), but we can find other reasons that can explain the absence of a perfect coverage: the inaccuracy of the test data generator and the environment in which it executes. One example of the second effect is related to the dynamic memory allocation. Suppose that a program allocates some dynamic memory and then checks if the memory allocation failed. Most probably it succeed and the check condition gets only one value. In this case we have an environment-dependent coverage loss (Fig. 4 right).

The code-dependent coverage loss is always present, no test data generator can get test data to cover the unreachable condition-value pairs. For this reason,

```
while(1)                        char *a;
{                               p = (char *)malloc (4);
/* The previous condition       if (!p)
is always true */               {
  :                                     fprintf("Error");
  :                                     exit(0);
}                               }
```

Fig. 4. Two pieces of code that prevent from reaching 100% of condition-decision coverage. The left one produces a code-dependent coverage loss, while the right one produces an environment-dependent coverage loss.

we have used another parameter, in addition to the condition-decision coverage, to measure the quality of the test data generator in a more reliable way. This parameter, that we call *corrected coverage*, appears in the third column of Table 3, and it is defined as the ratio between the condition-value pairs reached with the test data and all the potentially reachable condition-value pairs. The difference with the coverage is that the corrected coverage does not take into account the unreachable condition-value pairs. In the rest of this section we use the word coverage for referring to the corrected coverage. The fourth and fifth columns of the table show the maximum and the standard deviation of the corrected coverage for each test program.

Observing the values of Table 3 we can notice a result that justifies the need of the corrected coverage measure. According to the second column, the test data generator gets a higher coverage in the `calday` program than in the `quicksort` program. However, the third column seems to report the opposite: the corrected coverage for `quicksort` is higher than that for `calday`. If we focus on the maximum corrected coverage, the generator reaches a 100% of coverage with `calday` against the 94.12% of `quicksort`. From this result we conclude that the generator is very stable for the `quicksort` program but has an imprecise behavior with the `calday` program (standard deviation above zero). In summary, we can say that our test data generator is better for `quicksort` (more stable and precise) than for `calday`.

Comparing all the test programs with respect to the maximum corrected coverage we can see that only three out of eleven are below 100%. From these "more difficult" programs, `quicksort` and `select` have dynamic memory allocation sentences that never failed in the environment where they are executed.

With respect to the average number of evaluations, we observe that two programs got the very minimum number of them: `insertion` and `shell`. The ten evaluations correspond to the initial random test data generated. In these cases the test data generator gets full coverage with these random data. They are followed by `gcd`, that only needs one iteration of the evolutionary strategy loop to ensure a perfect coverage. This does not mean that it is straight-forward for a human programmer to test them. It just means that they are easy for our algorithm. For the test programs where the corrected coverage does not coincide with the condition-decision coverage (all test programs but `gcd`, `calday`, `insertion`, and `shell`) we expect a large number of evaluations in the results (confirmed by Table 3 and the tables below). The reason is that the algorithm tries to get 100% of non-corrected coverage, what is impossible due to the unreachable condition-value pairs.

To end this analysis we now focus on the running times. For most of the test programs the evaluation time is very low, as we can deduce comparing the two last columns of Table 3. However, `sa` is very time consuming, followed by `crc`.

4.2   Influence of λ and μ on the Results

In a second set of experiments we perform a study on the influence of several parameters of the ES in the results. In particular, we will change the num-

Table 4. Results after changing the number of offsprings λ

Test Programs	(10+1)-ES Cor.(%)	Evals.	(10+2)-ES Cor.(%)	Evals.	(10+3)-ES Cor.(%)	Evals.
triangle	99.92	1975	100.00	3329	100.00	4501
gcd	100.00	21	100.00	21	100.00	21
calday	91.82	1182	95.76	1994	95.91	3004
crc	100.00	1114	100.00	2124	100.00	3120
insertion	100.00	10	100.00	10	100.00	10
shell	100.00	10	100.00	10	100.00	10
quicksort	94.12	1110	94.12	2110	94.12	3110
heapsort	100.00	1110	100.00	2110	100.00	3110
select	83.33	1120	83.33	2119	83.33	3119
bessel	97.40	1306	97.48	2489	97.48	3577
sa	98.70	1329	99.15	2923	99.10	4115

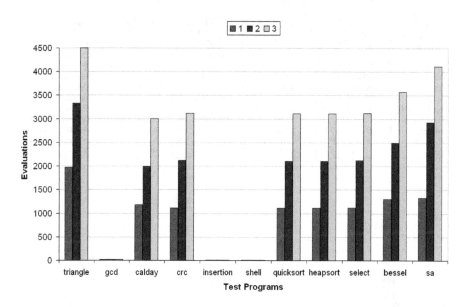

Fig. 5. Number of evaluations for $\lambda=1,2,3$. The value of μ is set to 10.

ber of offsprings generated at each iteration and the size of the population, that is, the parameters λ and μ. For each program we perform a Student t-test between the different parameterizations of the algorithm. We consider a statistically confidence of 95% (p-value below 0.05). First, we maintain the value of $\mu = 10$ and we try three values of λ: 1, 2, and 3. Table 4 and Fig. 5 summarize the results obtained when varying the number of offsprings λ.

As we can observe in Table 4, the influence of the number of offsprings in the coverage is negligible, only `triangle`, `calday`, `bessel`, and `sa` get a slightly higher coverage by increasing λ. In fact, there is statistical significance (p-value below 0.05) only in the case of `calday` and `sa`. This small influence can be due to the intrinsic high coverage obtained by the ES in all the test programs. The number of evaluations (and the time) is, in general, increased with the number of offsprings, because in each step of the ES there are more individuals to evaluate. The number of evaluations and the time are statistically significant for all the test programs except for `gcd`, `insertion`, and `shell`. From the results we conclude that $\lambda = 1$ seems to be the best number of offsprings.

Let us now turn to study the influence of the population size μ. We fix the number of offsprings to the best previous value $\lambda = 1$. In Table 5 and Fig. 6 we present the results.

In this case the coverage is approximately the same for a population size larger than one. In all the test programs the corrected coverage of the $(1+1)$-ES

Table 5. Results after changing the size of the population μ

Test	$(1+1)$-ES		$(5+1)$-ES		$(10+1)$-ES		$(20+1)$-ES		$(30+1)$-ES	
Programs	Cor.(%)	Evals.	Cor.(%)	Evals.	Cor.(%)	Evals.	Cor.(%)	Evals.	Cor.(%)	Evals.
triangle	35.77	1020	100.00	2010	99.92	1975	99.76	2178	99.84	2468
gcd	81.33	1020	100.00	21	100.00	21	100.00	30	100.00	39
calday	78.48	1020	93.03	1070	91.82	1182	91.52	1268	91.36	1386
crc	99.61	1020	100.00	1064	100.00	1114	100.00	1243	100.00	1330
insertion	100.00	10	100.00	10	100.00	10	100.00	10	100.00	10
shell	100.00	10	100.00	10	100.00	10	100.00	10	100.00	10
quicksort	94.12	1020	94.12	1060	94.12	1110	94.12	1210	94.12	1310
heapsort	100.00	1020	100.00	1060	100.00	1110	100.00	1210	100.00	1310
select	76.21	1020	83.33	1065	83.33	1120	83.33	1226	83.33	1338
bessel	80.16	1020	97.56	1233	97.40	1306	97.48	1446	97.56	1535
sa	96.61	1020	98.81	1309	98.70	1329	98.98	1513	99.04	1683

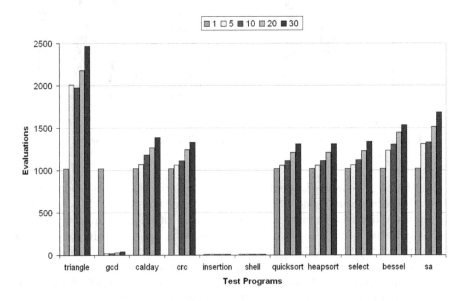

Fig. 6. Number of evaluations for μ=1,5,10,20,30. The value of λ is set to 1.

is statistically significant with the obtained by the other ESs. However, there is no statistical significance in the corrected coverage among the rest of the ESs except for `calday` in (5+1)-ES versus (30+1)-ES. With respect to the number of evaluations, it increases with the population size because there are more individuals in the initial population to evaluate. However, we observe an exception in (1+1)-ES for `gcd`: with a population of 1 individual the ES can not get 100% coverage and this explains the high number of evaluations needed.

As a global conclusion, we can state that the number of offsprings (λ) has a small influence in the coverage, but an important influence in the number of evaluations and, as a consequence, in the time. With respect to the population size (μ), we observe that the coverage is approximately the same when the population size is above a few individuals. The use of a single individual in the population must be avoided if the coverage is an important factor in the optimization. In general, the number of evaluations is increased with the size of the population. However, the growth is moderate in comparison with that provoked by changing λ. In order to end this discussion, we conclude that the best parameterization of ES for this benchmark is $\mu = 5$ and $\lambda = 1$.

4.3   A Comparison Between ES and GA

In this section we compare our (10+1)-ES with a Genetic Algorithm. A GA is another kind of evolutionary algorithm that usually represents the solutions by means of a binary string (chromosome). However, other representations have been employed with GAs, so we can not use this feature as a distinguishing difference. In fact, the individuals we use in our GA are not binary strings, they are strings of numeric values and they can be integer or real numbers. These numbers are the test program inputs. This algorithm does not use any self-adaptive parameter in the individual as the ES does, the individual contains only the representation of a solution. In opposite to the ES, the recombination operator has a great importance in GAs. We use here the double point crossover (DPX) that works as follows: it chooses two points in the parent strings and swaps all the numeric values between them. The mutation operator perturbs all numbers by adding a random value. The probability distribution of these random values is a normal distribution with mean zero and standard deviation one. The GA has ten individuals in the population and generates one only offspring by recombination and mutation (steady state GA). The maximum number of iterations is 100 (110 evaluations), like in the ES. The 10% of the initial population (one individual) is seeded by using the mechanism explained in Sect. 2. Results are summarized in Table 6. We highlight in boldface the best results.

We observe in Table 6 that the coverage is higher for the ES than the GA in the `triangle` program. This difference is statistically significant (p-value $\approx 10^{-9}$). For the `gcd` program the two algorithms get the maximum coverage. However, the GA needs 252 evaluations (that is, several iterations of the main loop) to get this coverage while the ES only needs 21 evaluations (that is, one iteration). In this case the ES has reached the objective very fast while the GA needs a larger effort. The observed advantage of the ES for the `calday` program with

Table 6. Comparison between ES and GA

Test	(10+1)-ES		GA	
Programs	Cor. cov. (%)	Evals.	Cor. cov. (%)	Evals.
triangle	**99.92**	**1975**	95.20	2009
gcd	**100.00**	**21**	100.00	252
calday	**91.82**	**1182**	90.91	1217
crc	**100.00**	**1114**	100.00	1121
insertion	**100.00**	**10**	100.00	10
shell	**100.00**	**10**	100.00	10
quicksort	**94.12**	**1110**	94.12	1110
heapsort	**100.00**	**1110**	100.00	1110
select	**83.33**	**1120**	83.33	1339
bessel	**97.40**	**1306**	96.91	1557
sa	**98.70**	1329	96.61	**1110**
Average	96.84	935	96.10	986

respect to the coverage is almost statistically significant (p-value 0.051, what means a 94.9% of confidence).

For the next six test programs (from crc to select) the two algorithms get the same coverage and similar number of evaluations with a slight advantage of the ES in two of them. At this point we can also conclude that insertion and shell are the easiest programs for the two test generators (with ES and GA). They only need 10 program executions to reach the objective.

The ES gets higher coverage than the GA for the two last programs (bessel and sa). However, the difference is statistically significant only in the case of sa. With respect to the number of evaluations, the sa program is the only test program in the table requiring a higher number of evaluations from the ES with respect to the GA.

As a global consideration, we observe from Table 6 that there is only a single value not highlighted in the ES columns, that is, all the results obtained with the ES are equal or better than those obtained by the GA. In addition, the ES has less parameters to fix than the GA (only population size and number of offsprings) and, for this reason, ES is easier to use than GA.

4.4   Previous Results

The task of comparing our results against previous works is very hard. First, we need to find works tackling the same test programs. There is a test program very popular in the domain of software testing: the triangle classifier. However, there are several different implementations in the literature and, usually, the source code is not provided. In [2] the source code of the triangle classifier is published in the paper. In this work, we use that implementation for making performance comparisons. We have two other test programs in common with [2]: the computation of the greatest common denominator and the insertion sort. However, we use different implementations for these algorithms. In order to ease future comparisons we have indicated in Table 2 how to get the source code of the test programs (available at URL http://tracer.lcc.uma.es/problems/testing).

A second obstacle to compare different techniques is that of the measurements. We use the average condition-decision coverage and a corrected coverage to measure the quality of the solutions. In [7, 14, 15] the authors report only on the branch coverage. On the other hand, the coverage measurement used in [2] is obtained by using a proprietary software: DeepCover. We can not directly compare all these results in a quantitative manner because all the works use different measurements. Another obstacle is the number of independent runs, that may affect the results. A low number of independent runs is not enough to obtain a clear idea about the behavior of the technique employed. It is not our case, but some papers perform a low number of independent runs.

In spite of all the previous considerations we include in Table 7 the best average coverage results reported for the triangle classifier algorithm in [2, 7, 14, 15] and their needed number of evaluations (program tests). We show in the same table the results of our (5+1)-ES, the best in coverage percentage.

Table 7. Previous results of coverage and number of evaluations for triangle

triangle	Ref. [7]	Ref. [2]	Ref. [14]	Ref. [15]	(5+1)-ES (here)
Coverage (%)	100.00[a]	94.29[b]	100.00[a]	100.00[a]	100.00[c]
Evaluations	18000	≈ 8000	608	3439	2010

[a] Branch coverage.
[b] DeepCover coverage.
[c] Corrected condition-decision coverage.

If we focus on the coverage of the Table 7 our (5+1)-ES has the best behavior at the same time as the algorithms of [7, 14, 15]. Comparing the number of evaluations we find the best (lowest) value in the work of Sagarna and Lozano [14] followed by our (5+1)-ES. However, we must recall that the condition-decision coverage (used in this work) is a test adequacy criterion harder than the branch coverage used in [14] (see Sect. 2).

5 Conclusions

In this article we have proposed the use of an Evolutionary Strategy to solve the test data generation problem in computer software. We employed a benchmark with eleven test programs implementing some fundamental algorithms in computer science.

We have studied different parameterizations for the ES, in particular we have analyzed the influence of the number of offsprings and the population size in the canonical algorithm. The former does not affect significatively the coverage, but the number of evaluations. The population size has a negligible influence in the coverage when it is larger than one individual, but the number of evaluations increases with it. We therefore propose the (5+1)-ES as the clear best algorithm in this study from the points of view of accuracy (coverage) and efficiency (evaluations). In fact, our (5+1)-ES outperforms the results of other works in coverage percentage and number of evaluations.

Comparing the (10+1)-ES with the GA we observe a clear advantage of the ES in accuracy and efficiency. Furthermore, ES has less algorithmic parameters to fix than GA, what means that the user can tune the system faster and does not require too much knowledge about it. This is a very good feature for those people interested in automatic software testing but with a little knowledge about Evolutionary Computation.

As future work, we plan to apply the ES-based test generator to other programs. We are specially interested in telecommunication software such as protocols, routing algorithms, and so on. In addition, we want to perform deeper improvements and use other metaheuristic techniques.

Acknowledgements

This work has been partially funded by the Ministry of Science and Technology (MCYT) and Regional Development European Found (FEDER) under contract TIC2002-04498-C05-02 (the TRACER project, http://tracer.lcc.uma.es). F. Chicano is supported by a grant from the Junta de Andalucía.

References

1. Korel, B.: Automated software test data generation. IEEE Transactions on Software Engineering **16** (1990) 870–879
2. Michael, C.C., McGraw, G., Schatz, M.A.: Generating software test data by evolution. IEEE Transactions on Software Engineering **27** (2001) 1085–1110
3. Clarke, L.A.: A system to generate test data and symbolically execute programs. IEEE Transactions on Software Engineering **2** (1976) 215–222
4. Miller, W., Spooner, D.L.: Automatic generation of floating-point test data. IEEE Trans. Software Eng. **2** (1976) 223–226
5. Bird, D., Munoz, C.: Automatic generation of random self-checking test cases. IBM Systems Journal **22** (1983) 229–245
6. Offutt, J.: An integrated automatic test data generation system. Journal of Systems Integration **1** (1991) 391–409
7. Jones, B.F., Sthamer, H.H., Eyres, D.E.: Automatic structural testing using genetic algorithms. Software Engineering Journal **11** (1996) 299–306
8. Wegener, J., Sthamer, H., Jones, B.F., Eyres, D.E.: Testing real-time systems using genetic algorithms. Software Quality Journal **6** (1997) 127–135
9. Mantere, T., Alander, J.T.: Evolutionary software engineering, a review. Applied Soft Computing **5** (2005) 315–331
10. Ostrowski, D.A., Reynolds, R.G.: Knowledge-based software testing agent using evolutionary learning with cultural algorithms. In: Proceedings of the Congress on Evolutionary Computation. Volume 3. (1999) 1657–1663
11. Tracey, N.: A search-based automated test-data generation framework for safety-critical software. PhD thesis, University of York (2000)

12. Tracey, N., Clark, J., Mander, K., McDermid, J.: An automated framework for structural test-data generation. In: Proceedings of the 13th IEEE Conference on Automated Software Engineering. (1998) 285–288
13. Díaz, E., Tuya, J., Blanco, R.: Automated Software Testing Using a Metaheuristic Technique Based on Tabu Search. In: Proceedings of the 18th IEEE International Conference on Automated Software Engineering (ASE'03), Montreal, Quebec, Canada (2003) 310–313
14. Sagarna, R., Lozano, J.A.: Variable search space for software testing. In: Proceedings of the International Conference on Neural Networks and Signal Processing. Volume 1., IEEE Press (2003) 575–578
15. Sagarna, R., Lozano, J.A.: Scatter search in software testing, comparison and collaboration with estimation of distribution algorithms. European Journal of Operational Research (2005) (in press).
16. Sthamer, H., Wegener, J., Baresel, A.: Using evolutionary testing to improve efficiency and quality in software testing. In: Proceedings of the 2nd Asia-Pacific Conference on Software Testing Analysis & Review, Melbourne, Australia (2002)
17. Bäck, T.: Evolutionary Algorithms in Theory and Practice: Evolution Strategies, Evolutionary Programming, Genetic Algorithms. Oxford University Press, New York (1996)
18. Rechenberg, I.: Evolutionsstrategie: Optimierung technischer Systeme nach Prinzipien der biologischen Evolution. Fromman-Holzboog Verlag, Stuttgart (1973)
19. Rudolph, G.: 9. In: Evolutionary Computation 1. Basic Algorithms and Operators. Volume 1. IOP Publishing Lt (2000) 81–88

A Technique to Represent Product Line Core Assets in MDA/PIM for Automation*

Hyun Gi Min and Soo Dong Kim

Department of Computer Science, Soongsil University,
511 Sangdo-Dong, Dongjak-Ku, Seoul 156-743, Korea
hgmin@otlab.ssu.ac.kr, sdkim@ssu.ac.kr

Abstract. A Product Line (PL) is a set of products (applications) that share common assets in a domain. Product line engineering (PLE) supports the systematic development of a set of similar software systems by common and distinguishing characteristics. Core assets, the common assets, are created and instantiated to make products in PLE. Model Driven Architecture (MDA) emphasizes its feasibility with an automatically developing product. Therefore, we can get the advantages of two paradigms, PLE and MDA, as core assets are represented as PIM in MDA with a predefined automatic mechanism. The PLE framework in the PIM level has to be interpreted by MDA tools. However, we do not have a standard UML profile for representing core assets. The research representing the PLE framework is not enough to automatically make core assets and products. We represent core assets in the PIM level in terms of architecture, components, and decision models. Core assets are specified with our profile at the level of PIM, where they can be automatically transformed and instantiated. The method of representing the framework with PLE and MDA is used to improve productivity, applicability, maintainability and quality of products.

1 Motivation

MDA is a new software development paradigm where a model plays a key role in automatic software development [1]. It provides a systematic framework to understand, design, operate, and evolve all aspects of an enterprise system, using engineering methods and tools. The goals of MDA are portability, interoperability, and reusability by the architectural separation of concerns. A very common technique for achieving platform independence is to target a system model for a technology-neutral virtual machine. A model in PIM is reusable over different platforms.

A product line is a set of products (applications) that share common assets in a domain. Product Line Engineering is a set of principles, techniques, mechanisms, and processes that enables the realization of produce lines [2]. Core assets, the common assets, are created and instantiated to make products in PLE. The concepts in the

---

* This work was supported by the Korea Research Foundation Grant funded by the Korean Government (MOEHRD). (KRF-2004-005-D00172).

N. Guelfi and A. Savidis (Eds.): RISE 2005, LNCS 3943, pp. 66–80, 2006.

application domain are analyzed and used to build a product line architecture, which includes reference architecture for the systems in the domain. Applications can then be constructed largely by instantiating this product line architecture.

Therefore, if main constructs and mechanisms of the MDA are combined with the core mechanisms and characteristics of PLE, we can expect to have an effective software development approach. PLE supports this by reusing common assets derived through core asset engineering, and MDA supports this by generating applications on diverse platforms through a model transformation. However, previous researches about representing assets are not enough to automatically make core assets and products.

In this paper, we suggest techniques to improve the advantage of PLE and MDA. We define the elements of core assets and PIM. We compare the needing of core assets and supporting PIM to present. We suggest a UML profile for PLE to present the gaps that can not be presented by a general PIM. Product line architecture, components, decision models, and resolution models are designed by our proposed method in MDA. The design can be automatically transformed to a source code implementation by using MDA transformation mappings. Eventually application engineering of PLE can be automated using MDA tools. We also believe that the productivity, applicability, maintainability, reusability, and quality of an application can be greatly increased.

2 Foundation

2.1 Model Driven Architecture (MDA)

MDA is an approach to using models in software development. The essence of MDA is making a distinction between Platform Independent Models (PIMs) and Platform Specific Models (PSMs). To develop an application using MDA, it is necessary to first build a PIM of the application, then transform this using a standardized mapping into a PSM, and finally map the latter into the application code by automation.

The goals of MDA are portability, interoperability and reusability through architectural separation of concerns [1]. Some of the motivations of the MDA approach are: reduce the time of adoption of new platforms and middleware, primacy of conceptual design, and interoperability. The MDA approach makes it possible to save the conceptual design, and helps to avoid duplication of effort and other needless waste [3][4].

2.2 Product Line Engineering (PLE)

PLE supports the systematic development of a set of similar software systems by understanding and controlling their common and distinguishing characteristics. Thus it is an approach for software reuse driven by the concepts from the real-world domain of software products, which are used to tackle main reuse challenges. The concepts in the application domain are analyzed and used to build a product line infrastructure, which includes reference architecture for the systems in the domain.

Concrete applications can then be constructed largely by instantiating and reusing this product line infrastructure [5].

2.3 UML Profile

A UML profile defines standard UML extensions that combine and/or refine existing UML constructs to create a dialect that can be used to describe artifacts in a design or implementation model. It defines a set of UML extensions that define several standard extension mechanisms, including stereotypes, constraints, tagged values and icons [6]. When one defines a profile, it is common MDA practice to also define mappings that specify how to transform models conforming to the profile into artifacts appropriate to the specific kinds of systems. If a model is not specified by a particular UML profile, the model can not be transformed automatically by the MDA mechanism.

The OMG has adopted a MOF metamodel of Java and EJB to complement the UML profile for EJB [7], a UML profile for modeling enterprise application integration [8] and a UML profile for CORBA [9] as well. However, there support implementation levels. The profiles do not present the component of a PIM level.

2.4 Gomaa's PLUS

Product Line UML-Based Software Engineering (PLUS) method extends the UML-based modeling methods that are used for single systems to address software product lines [10]. With PLUS, the objective is to model the commonality and variability in a software product line. Gomaa suggest stereotypes «kernel», «optional», «alternative», and «variant» to be used in UML diagrams. However, the elements are not explicitly identified in this model and no precise definition for the elements is suggested. These stereotypes about representing PLE framework are not enough to automatically make core assets and products.

2.5 Muthig's PLE Metamodel

The metamodel for the product line assets describes an information model for the assets capturing the explicit and integrated product line information [5]. The metamodel for product line assets consists of three packages. The *Asset* package contains the metamodel for general assets including assets used for single-system development.

The *GenericAsset* package depends on the *Asset* package and defines genericity as an add-on characteristic for any asset. The main concepts in the *GenericAsset* package are variant asset elements, which are variation points concerned with variant information at local points in an asset.

The *DecisionModel* package builds on generic assets and extends the variation point concept to decisions. Decisions are variation points that typically constrain other variation points and provide a question that must be answered during application engineering. These questions and the constraints among them support application engineering by guiding the instantiation of generic assets. The constraint network of decisions is the decision model.

3 Elements of Core Assets

In this section, we define elements of core assets and each element is elaborated in detail. A core asset plays a key role in PLE. It consists of product line architecture (PLA) which is generic to products, a component model capturing components and interfaces, and a decision model defining variability realization, as shown in Fig. 1. PLA and component model can be represented to architecture specifications, component specifications, and interface specifications. Like the C&V (Commonality and Variability) model, the variability should especially be specified to decision description.

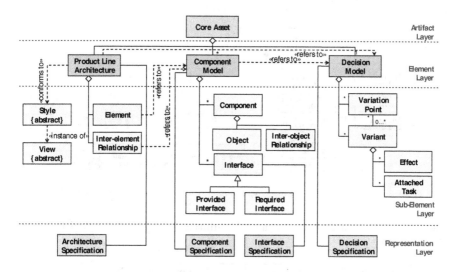

Fig. 1. Meta Model for Core Asset

Architecture specification effectively designs architecture. It is important that architecture specification include style, view, element and inter-element relationships. It describes the composition of software components and their functionalities in a conceptual level, while the component specification specifies objects and inter-object relationships.

Component specification specifies software components and their relationships with text or graphical notations such as UML diagrams [11]. The models can be represented by use case diagrams, class diagrams, and sequence diagrams in UML. Expression of Variability on the models has generally been proposed by using stereotypes. Interface specification specifies public interface through which two components communicate each other, and which consists of method signatures and semantics. In this specification, two types of the interfaces may exist, provided interface and required interface [11].

Decision specification is a realization of the variability of the C&V specification, and it consists of variation points, their associated variants, effects, and attached tasks. Several variants exist in one variation point, and each variant may have several effects and attached tasks.

4   Gap Analysis Between Core Asset and PIM Artifacts

MDA specification [12] and MDA guide [13] suggest the concept of PIMs. The PIM provides formal specifications of the structure and function of the system in a platform-independent manner using UML, MOF, and so on. We define the key elements of PIM in Fig. 2 to compare needing of core assets and supporting PIM to present.

The gaps that are differentiated between core asset artifacts and PIM are covered by UML profile for specifying PLE in section 5. If the gaps are covered by PIM with UML profile for PLE, the core asset contents can be designed by PIMs. Applications

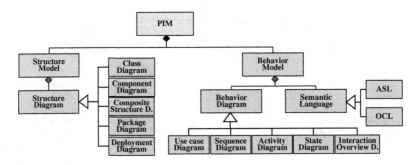

Fig. 2. Metamodel of PIM

Table 1. Gaps between Core Assets and PIM Artifacts (O: Support, △: Partially Support, −: Not supported)

Needed by Core Assets			Supporting by PIM (UML and ASL)	Gap
Element	Sub Element			
PLA Model	Module		Class, Component, Composite Structure, Package Diagram	△
	Relationship		Dependency, Association, Generalization, Realization, etc.	O
Component Model	Compo-nent	Intra-Object	Class, Composite Structure Diagram	O
		Relationship	Relationship	O
	Interface		Provided and Required Interface	O
	Functional View		Use case and activity Diagram Action Semantic Language	△
	Static View		Class, Component Diagram	O
	Dynamic View		Sequence Diagram Communication Diagram Interaction Overview Diagram	O
Decision Model	Variation Point		−	−
	Variant		−	−
	Effect		−	−
	Task		−	−

can be generated by the PIM using automation. We identify the gaps of PLA, components, and decision model as Table 1.

Product line architecture must provide a link between the standard organization, or communications protocols, and the individual components to permit clients to understand easily how the components will fit into their respective architecture [2]. The product line architecture model that consists of module and relationship between modules needed by core assets is covered by PIM, such as UML and ASL. However, the detailed types for the module are not specified by them.

The component model represents a design of components themselves which are represented with structural and behavioral models of objects, inter-object relationships, and interfaces. The component model of core assets is nearly supported by class, composite structure, and a component diagram.

The decision model is a specification of variations in core assets and includes variation points, variants, effects, and the attached task. Core assets are instantiated for an application by the decision model and resolution model. However, the elements of the decision model are not supported by PIM.

5   Method to Present the Core Asset in PIM

In this section, we specify methods to represent the core asset in PIM of MDA. The PIMs that are specified by our methods can be transformed into PSM and code sources using the automation of MDA. The method to present core assets consists of product line architecture, components, variations, and decision models. The method is showed by examples about core assets for rental application.

5.1   Method to Present Product Line Architecture

Software architecture realizes both functional and non-functional requirements. With the requirements and product line analysis model derived from the requirements, several kinds of views are proposed and used such as module view, C&C (Component and Connector) view and deployment view [14]. Several *styles* of a view can be applied to PLA. Architecture design begins with choosing the most appropriate architectural styles which can realize both types of requirements.

Element and *inter-element relationships* in PLA are directly derived from the requirements and especially inter-element relationships are guided by styles. Therefore, it is fair to state that elements and the relationships effectively implement functional and non-functional requirements. Hence the style is not a constituent of product line architecture, but an abstract element to which the architecture conforms.

The UML profile for specifying PLA can be described as shown in Table 2. The profile can specify module views and C&C views [14]. Conceptual components have conceptual relationships between each other. Relationships are abstracted interfaces between units. The styles of the C&C viewtype consist of the pipe-filter, shared-data, publish-subscribe, client-server, peer to peer, and communicating-processes styles.

Types of messages are control, data, and uses from QADA which are methods of standing for Quality-Driven Architecture Design Analysis method [15]. Passing *control* means, that one component controls a given aspect of the system. Passing *data* means, that one component inputs data to another component, but is still able to continue processing without waiting for a reply or return value. The situation is reversed when talking about *uses* relationships, where a component has a kind of subcontract with the component it uses [15]. Fig. 3 is an example of PIM for

Table 2. Elements of UML Profile for Specifying PLA

Element	Presentation	Applies to	Remarks
Unit	«module»	Class, Component, Package	
Connector	«connector»	Class, relationship	
Use Dependency	«use»	Relationship	Use UML2.0
Control Relationship	«control»	Relationship	
Data Relationship	«data»	Relationship	
Layer	«layer»	Package and class	
Filter	«filter»	Class, Component	
Pipe	«pipe»	Relationship	
Repository	«repository»	Class, Component	
Publish	«publish»	Relationship	
Subscribe	«subscribe»	Relationship	
Client	«client»	Class, Component	
Server	«server»	Class, Component	

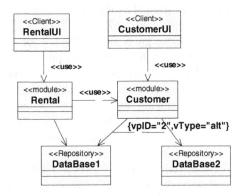

Fig. 3. Example of PLA PIM Design for Rental Application

specifying PLA. This unit and its relationships can have variation and can be instantiated.

5.2 Method to Present Components

The component model represents component designs themselves which are represented with structural and behavioral models of objects, inter-object relationships, and interfaces as Table 3. Generally, component-base development (CBD) is based on object-oriented development (OOD) and in this section we assume that functionality of the core asset is realized by its components. The component model is based on PLA.

Table 3. Elements of UML Profile for Specifying Components

Element	Presentation	Applies to	Remarks
Component	«component»	Component, Package	Use UML 2.0
Transient Class	«Transient»	Class	
Persistence Class	«Persistence»	Class	Default
Primary key filed	«UniqueId»	Attribute	
Synchronous Message	«Sync»	Operation	Default
Asynchronous Message	«Async»	Operation	
Relationships Between Components	Dependency, Association, Generalization, Realization, etc.	Relationship	Use UML 2.0
Interface	«Interface»	Interface	Use UML 2.0
Provided Interface	«ProvidedInterface»	Interface	Use UML 2.0
Required Interface	«RequiredInterface»,	Interface	Use UML 2.0
Signature	name (param : Type): return type	Operation	Use UML 2.0
Constraints	{ }, pre:, post:, inv:	Class, Method, Relationship, etc.	OCL
Algorithms	Use Text	Method	OCL, ASL

The components are identified by architecture models. The components are nearly described by UML 2.0. The structural model of the components can be represented by the composite structure diagram of UML 2.0. The behavior can be represented by sequence, communication, activity, state machine diagrams, and Action Semantic Language (ASL).

Components are the fundamental units of packaging related objects [16], hence we need to specify the related objects in a component in core asset PIM. A port is a connection point between a classifier and its environment. Connections from the outside world are made to ports according to what is provided and required.

Persistency objects that should be stored in the database or file systems are represented by a stereotype «Persistence». If some objects such as value objects [17]

for transforming data are not persistent, a stereotype «Transient» is used. Asynchronous messages use the stereotype «Async» that are described at methods in class, sequence, and communication diagrams. Constraints and algorithms can be expressed by Object Constraints Language (OCL), and ASL.

A component provides its component-level interface, i.e. the protocol for accessing the service of the component. An interface is clearly separated from the component implementation to increase the maintainability and replaceability [16]. Hence, we need to specify some interfaces as well as component units.

Two types of interfaces can be modeled; *provided* and *required* interfaces. The *provided* interface specifies the services provided by a component and it is invoked by other components or client programs at runtime. The stereotype «ProvidedInterface» is used to denote this interface, and the name *provided* interface is defined by using 'Ip' prefix name. The *required* interface specifies external services invoked by the current component, i.e. a specification of external services required by the current component [10]. By specifying the *required* interface for a component, we can precisely define the services invoked by the current component.

This information can later be used in integrating related components into core assets. The *required* interface can be specified with a stereotype «RequiredInterface». An interface consists of operation signatures and their semantics. The semantics can

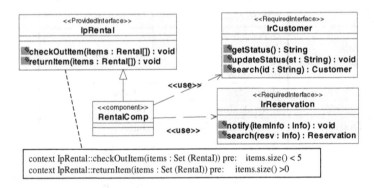

Fig. 4. Example of Components PIM Design for Rental Application

Table 4. Elements of Action Semantic Language

Semantics	Usage
Creating Object	**create object instance** <object reference> **of** <class>;
Deleting Object	**delete object instance** <object reference>;
Searching Object	**select [one|any|many]** <object reference set> **from instances of** <class> **where** <where clause>;
Writing Attribute	<object reference>.<attribute name> = <expression>;
Reading Attribute	...<object reference>.<attribute name>;
Sending Message	**generate** signal action to <class>

be expressed in terms of pre- and post-conditions and invariants using OCL. Fig. 4 is an example of component PIM design of a component RentalComp.

Behavior can be represented by behavior diagrams, ASL such as Executable UML [18], and OCL. The action semantic is described in Table 4. The behavior can generate source code using automation of MDA because the syntax can be read by MDA tools.

Fig. 5 is an algorithm of returnItem( ). If a customer should pay a penalty fee, the penalty fee is deducted from his or her mileage. If customers return items early, points are added to his or her mileage.

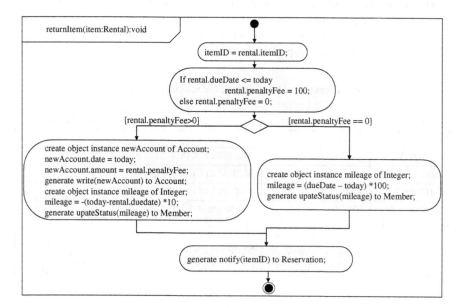

Fig. 5. Example of Behavior Modeling using ASL for Rental Application

5.3 Method to Present Variation and Decision Model

The instantiation of components in core assets of PLE differs from the customization of components in CBD. Binary components include customization mechanisms to set variation [19]. The variation is chosen by the component consumer after the transition. The core assets are instantiated by the resolution of the decision model in the application engineering before the transition. The unnecessary elements are removed or deselected for target application by the decision models. The decision model is a specification of variations in core assets and includes variation points, variants, effects, and the attached task [20].

A variation point is a place where slight differences among members may occurr. The variation point may be exposed in the architectural style, architectural elements and relationships, and component internals. *Variants* are valid values which can appropriately fill in a variation point. As the types of variation points and variability types such as optional and alternative, the variants may be designed into various formats.

The *effect* means a range of relationships among variations points, and is represented with dependencies and constraints. For example, some variations should be selected with some variations, but some variations are not. The relationships are an essential problem which should be specified and resolved in product line engineering [21]. Therefore, for one variant of a variation point, the effect can be represented as the post-conditions of setting the variant. The *Attached Task* is a set of activities to resolve a variation point for one selected variant, that is, to instantiate. Through the attached tasks, post-conditions of the instantiated variation point should satisfy defined effects for the variation point.

Table 5. Elements of UML Profile for Specifying Components

Element	Presentation	Applies to	Remarks
Variation Point	«VP»	Attribute, Method	Default
Attribute VP	«VP-A»	Attribute in Class	
Logic VP	«VP-L»	Method in Class, Sequence, etc.	
Workflow VP	«VP-W»	Method in Class, Sequence, etc.	
Interface VP	«VP-I»	Operation in Class Diagram	
Persistency VP	«VP-P»	Operation in Class Diagram	
Variation Scope	{vScope = value}	Variation Point	Close, Open, Unknown
ID of VP	{vpID = value }	Variation Point	Unique ID
Type of VP	{vpType = value }	Variation Point	opt, alt
Constraints	{ }, pre:, post:, inv:	Class, Method, Relationship, etc.	OCL
Algorithms	Use Text	Method	OCL, ASL

We define types of variation as attribute variability, logic, workflow, persistency and interface variability [22]. To express variation points of core assets, we propose stereotypes that are «VP-A», «VP-L», «VP-W», «VP-P» and «VP-I». The *attribute variability* denotes occurrences of *variation points* on attributes. Logic describes an algorithm or a procedural flow of a relatively fine-grained function. *Logic variability* denotes occurrences of *variation points* on the algorithm or logical procedure. *Workflow variability* denotes occurrences of *variation points* on the sequence of method invocations. Persistency is maintained by storing attribute values of a component in a permanent storage so that the state of the component can alive over system sessions. *Persistency variability* denotes occurrences of *variation points* on the physical schema or representation of the persistent attributes on a secondary storage.

We present two kinds of variation point scopes. The *open* scope variation point has any number of variants which are already known and additional variants which are currently unknown but can possibly be found later at the customization or deployment time. In constraint, the *close* scope variation point has two or more variants which are already known. The types of variation points consist of *opt* and *alt*. The *opt* is an optional selection of variants at the variation point. The variation cannot be used. The a*lt* is one of which could be selected at the variation point. Stereotype variation points have a tagged value about variation scope, ID of a variation point, and Type of a variation point.

The decision model for the returnItem ( ) in Fig. 6 is shown as Table 6. Decision models may be described using the table form in the tool. It is easily read by people. However, the table form cannot be read by tools for instantiation. Therefore, if the decision models are saved as XML, the file is easily read by tools.

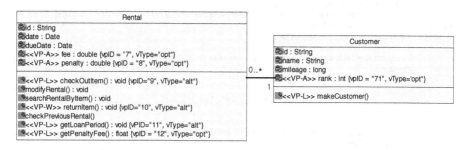

Fig. 6. Example of Variation Design for Rental Application

Table 6. Example of Decision Model of returnItem()

VP ID	Variant ID	Effect	Task
10	1	While returning items, points are assigned by each customer rank.	{if vpID==71 then varID == 1} //customer object should have an attribute rank generator notifyReservation() to Reservation; Point = 10 * customer.rank; generator IncPoint() to Member;
	2	While returning items, 100 points are assigned to each customer.	Point = 100; generator IncPoint() to Member; generator notifyReservation() to Reservation;

Decision specification can be represented to UML extensions and XML as Fig. 7. While variability occurs in components of a component-based development, it can occur in the component model or PLA of PLE. A variability listed in the decision specification is eventually reflected and realized in the architecture specification, component specification and interface specification.

```
<?xml version="1.0" encoding="UTF-8"?>
<DecisionModel xmlns:xsi=http://www.w3.org/2001/XMLSchema-instance
        xsi:noNamespaceSchemaLocation=". \DecisionModel.xsd">
    <VariationPoint ID="10">
      <Variant ID="1">
          <Effect> While returning items, points are assigned by each customer rank.</Effect>
          <AttachedTask>{if vpID==71 then varID == 1}</AttachedTask>
          <AttachedTask>generator notifyReservation() to Reservation;</AttachedTask>
          <AttachedTask>Point = 10 * customer.rank;</AttachedTask>
          <AttachedTask>generator IncPoint() to Member;</AttachedTask>
      </Variant>
      <Variant ID="2">
          <Effect> While returning items, 100 points are assigned to each customer.</Effect>
          <AttachedTask>Point = 100;</AttachedTask>
          <AttachedTask>generator IncPoint() to Member;</AttachedTask>
          <AttachedTask>generator notifyReservation() to Reservation;</AttachedTask>
      </Variant>
    </ VariationPoint>
</DecisionModel>
```

```
<?xml version="1.0" encoding="UTF-8"?>
<xs:schema xmlns:xs="http://www.w3.org/2001/XMLSchema" elementFormDefault="qualified"
attributeFormDefault="unqualified">
    <xs:element name="DecisionModel">
      <xs:annotation>
        <xs:documentation>Comment describing your root element</xs:documentation>
      </xs:annotation>
      <xs:complexType>
        <xs:sequence>
          <xs:element name="VariationPoint" minOccurs="0" maxOccurs="unbounded">
          <xs:complexType>
            <xs:sequence>
            <xs:element name="Variant" minOccurs="0" maxOccurs="unbounded">
            <xs:complexType>
             <xs:sequence>
              <xs:element name="Effect" minOccurs="0"/>
              <xs:element name="AttachedTask" minOccurs="0" maxOccurs="unbounded"/>
             </xs:sequence>
             <xs:attribute name="ID" type="xs:string " use="required"/>
            </xs:complexType>
            </xs:element>
            </xs:sequence>
            <xs:attribute name="ID" type="xs:string" use="required"/>
          </xs:complexType>
          </xs:element>
          </xs:sequence>
        </xs:complexType>
      </xs:element>
    </xs:schema>
```

Fig. 7. Decision Model and XMI Schema for Decision Model

6   Assessment

The UML 2.0 and Gomaa's PLUS do not sufficiently detail the profile for specifying architecture, components, and decision models. These stereotypes about the representing PLE framework are not enough to automatically make core assets and products. We suggest a UML profile that supports them. The core asset PIM can be present by our UML profile. The core asset PIM can be instantiated by MDA mapping rules for instantiation.

As shown in Fig. 8, the MDA transformation mechanism can be used to map a core asset to an instantiated core asset if the decision models and application specific decisions including variants are expressed in XMI. To automate the instantiation process, mapping rules that map elements of the core asset to the elements of the instantiated core asset are required, as in Fig. 8.

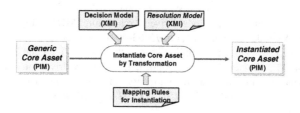

Fig. 8. Instantiation by MDA Transformation

7 Conclusion Remarks

Both PLE and MDA are emerging as effective paradigms for building a family of applications in a cost effective way. PLE supports this by reusing common assets derived through core asset engineering, and MDA supports this by generating applications on diverse platforms through model transformation. However, previous researches about representing the PLE framework are not enough to automatically make core assets and products.

In this paper, we propose the UML profile for specifying PLE. Our UML profile consists of UML extensions, notations, and related instructions to specify elements of PLE in MDA PIM models, which can be presented by general UML and MDA design tools. We introduce a concept of integrating MDA and PLE in software engineering. Once core assets are specified with our profile at the level of PIM, they can be automatically transformed and instantiated. Eventually, the application engineering of PLE is automated by MDA tools. We also believe that the productivity, applicability, maintainability, reusability, and quality of the application can be greatly increased.

References

[1] OMG, "MDA Guide Version 1.0.1," *omg/2003-06-01*, June 2003.
[2] Clements P, Northrop L, Software Product Lines, Addison Wesley, 2002.
[3] Flater., D., "Impact of Model-Driven Architecture," *In Proceedings of the 35th Hawaii International Conference on System Sciences*, January 2002.
[4] Frankel, D. and Parodi, *The MDA Journal, Model Driven Architecture Straigth from the Masters*, Meghan-Kiffer Press, 2004.
[5] Muthig, D. and Atkinson, C., "Model-Driven Product Line Architectures," *SPLC2 2002, LNCS Vol. 2379*, pp. 110–129, 2002.
[6] Frankel, D., *Model Driven Architecture™:Applying MDA™ to Enterprise Computing*, Wiley, 2003.
[7] Java Community Process , "UML Profile For EJB_Draft," 2001.

[8] OMG, "UML™ Profile and Interchange Models for Enterprise Application Integration(EAI) Specification," 2002.

[9] OMG, "UML Profile for CORBA Specification V1.0, OMG," Nov. 2000.

[10] Gomaa, H., Designing Software Product Lines with UML from Use Cases to Pattern-based Software Architectures, Addison-Wesley, 2004.

[11] Rumbaugh, J., Jacobson, I, and Booch, G., The Unified Modeling Language Reference Manual Second Edition, Addison-Wesley, 2004.

[12] Object Management Group, Model Driven Architecture (MDA), July 2001.

[13] OMG, MDA Guide Version 1.0.1, omg/2003-06-01, June 2003.

[14] Clements, P., et al., Documenting Software Architectures Views and Beyond, 2003.

[15] Matinlassi, M., Niemela, E., and Dobrica, L., "Quality-driven architecture design and quality analysis method: A revolutionary initiation approach to a product line architecture," *VTT publication 456, VTT Technical Research Center of Finland, ESPOO2002, 2002.*

[16] Heineman, G. and Councill, W., *Component-Based Software Engineering*, Addison Wesley, 2001.

[17] Roman, E., *Mastering Enterprise JavaBeans™ and the Java™2 Platform*, Enterprise Edition, WILEY, 1999.

[18] Mellor, S. and Balcer, M., Executable UML: A Foundation for Model-Driven Architecture, Addison Wesley, 2002.

[19] Kim, S., Min, H., and Rhew, S., "Variability Design and Customization Mechanisms for COTS Components," *Proceedings of The 2005 International Conference on Computational Science and its Applications (ICCSA 2005), LNCS Vol. 3480*, pp. 57–66, 2005.

[20] Kim, S., Chang, S., and Chang, C., "A Systematic Method to Instantiate Core Assets in Product Line Engineering," *Proceedings of Asian-Pacific Software Engineering Conference 2004*, Nov. 2004.

[21] Sinnema, M., Deelstra, S., Nijhuis, J., and Bosch, J., "COVAMOF: A Framework for Modeling Variability in Software Product Families," *Proceedings of the Third Software Product Line Conference (SPLC 2004), LNCS Vol. 3154*, August 2004.

[22] Kim, S., Her, J., and Chang, S., "A Theoretical Foundation of Variability in Component-based Development," *Information and Software Technology*, Vol. 47, pp. 663–673, July 2005.

Modeling Safety Case Evolution – Examples from the Air Traffic Management Domain

Massimo Felici

LFCS, School of Informatics, The University of Edinburgh,
Edinburgh EH9 3JZ, UK
mfelici@inf.ed.ac.uk
http://homepages.inf.ed.ac.uk/mfelici/

Abstract. In order realistically and cost-effectively to realize the ATM
(Air Traffic Management) 2000+ Strategy, systems from different suppli-
ers will be interconnected to form a complete functional and operational
environment, covering ground segments and aerospace. Industry will be
involved as early as possible in the lifecycle of ATM projects. EURO-
CONTROL manages the processes that involve the definition and validation of new ATM solutions using Industry capabilities (e.g., SMEs). In
practice, safety analyses adapt and reuse system design models (produced
by third parties). Technical, organisational and cost-related reasons often
determine this choice, although design models are unfit for safety analysis. This paper is concerned with evolutionary aspects in judging safety
for ATM systems. The main objective is to highlight a model specifically
targeted to support evolutionary safety analysis. The systematic production of safety analysis (models) will decrease the cost of conducting
safety analysis by supporting reuse in future ATM projects.

1 Introduction

The future development of Air Traffic Management (ATM), set by the ATM
2000+ Strategy [11], involves a structural revision of ATM processes, a new ATM
concept and a systems approach for the ATM network. The overall objective
[11] is, *for all phases of flight, to enable the safe, economic, expeditious and
orderly flow of traffic through the provision of ATM services, which are adaptable
and scalable to the requirements of all users and areas of European airspace.*
This requires ATM services to go through significant structural, operational
and cultural changes that will contribute towards the ATM 2000+ Strategy.
Moreover, from a technology viewpoint, future ATM services will employ new
systems forming the emergent ATM architecture underlying and supporting the
European Commission's Single European Sky Initiative.

ATM services, it is foreseen, will need to accommodate an increasing traffic,
as many as twice the number of flights, by 2020. This challenging target will
require the cost-effective gaining of extra capacity together with the increase of
safety levels [31, 32]. Enhancing safety levels affects the ability to accommodate
increased traffic demand as well as the operational efficiency of ensuring safe

N. Guelfi and A. Savidis (Eds.): RISE 2005, LNCS 3943, pp. 81–96, 2006.
© Springer-Verlag Berlin Heidelberg 2006

separation between aircraft. Suitable safety conditions shall precede the achievement of increased capacity (in terms of accommodated flights). Therefore, it is necessary to foreseen and mitigate safety issues in aviation where ATM can potentially deliver safety improvements.

In particular, there are *complex interactions* [34] between aircrafts and ATM safety functions. Unfortunately, these complex interactions may give rise to catastrophic failures. For instance, the accident (1 July 2002) between a BOEING B757-200 and a Tupolev TU154M [5], that caused the fatal injuries of 71 persons, provides an instance of unforeseen complex interactions. These interactions triggered a catastrophic failure, although all aircraft systems were functioning properly [5]. Humans [17, 33] using complex languages and procedures mediate these interactions. It is necessary further to understand how humans use external artifacts (e.g., tools) to mediate complex interactions. This would allow the understanding of how humans adopt technological artifacts and adapt their behaviours in order to accommodate ATM technological evolution. Unfortunately, the evolution of technological systems often corresponds to a decrease in technology trust affecting work practice [8]. Work practices and systems evolve rapidly in response to demand and a culture of continuous improvements [34]. A comprehensive account of ATM systems would allow the modeling of evolution. This will enhance strategies for deploying new system configurations or major system upgrades. On the one hand, modeling and understanding system evolution support the engineering of (evolving) ATM systems. On the other hand, modeling and understanding system evolution allow the communication of changes across different organisational levels [37]. This would enhance visibility of system evolution as well as trust in transition to operations.

Introducing safety relevant systems in ATM contexts requires us to understand the risk involved in order to mitigate the impact of possible failures. Safety analysis involves the activities (i.e., system identification and definition, risk analysis in terms of tolerable severity and frequency of hazards, definition of mitigation actions) that allow the systematic identification of hazards, risk assessment and mitigation processes in safety-critical systems [28, 41]. These general activities are deemed acceptable in diverse safety-critical domains (e.g., nuclear and chemical plants), which allow the unproblematic application of conventional safety analysis [28, 41]. Some safety-critical systems (e.g., nuclear or chemical plants) are well-confined entities with limited predictable interactions with the surroundings. Physical design structures constrain system interactions and stress the separation of safety related components from other system parts. This ensures the independence of failures. Therefore, in some safety-critical domains it is possible to identify acceptable tradeoffs between completeness and manageability during the definition and identification of the system under analysis. In contrast, ATM systems operate in open and dynamic environments. Hence, it is difficult to identify the full picture of system interactions in ATM contexts.

Recent safety requirements, defined by EUROCONTROL (European organization for the safety of air navigation), imply the adoption of a similar safety analysis for the introduction of new systems and their related procedures in the

ATM domain [10]. Unfortunately, ATM systems and procedures have distinct characteristics (e.g., openness, volatility, etc.) that expose limitations of the approach. In particular, the complete identification of the system under analysis is crucial for its influence on the cost and the effectiveness of the safety analysis. Therefore, safety analysis has to take into account complex interaction mechanisms (e.g., failure dependence, reliance in ATM, etc.) in order to guarantee and even increase the overall ATM safety as envisaged by the ATM 2000+ Strategy.

This paper is concerned with limitations of safety analysis with respect to evolution. The paper is structured as follows. Section 2 describes safety analysis in the ATM domain. Section 3 proposes a framework that enhances evolutionary safety analysis. Section 4 uses the ASCE™ tool for the analysis of safety case changes. Section 5 introduces a logical framework for modeling and capturing safety case changes. The framework enhances the understanding of safety case evolution. Finally, Section 6 draws some conclusions.

2   Safety Analysis in ATM

ATM services across Europe are constantly changing in order to fulfil the requirements identified by the ATM 2000+ Strategy [11]. Currently, ATM services are going through a structural revision of processes, systems and underlying ATM concepts. This highlights a systems approach for the ATM network. The delivery and deployment of new systems will let a new ATM architecture emerge. The EUROCONTROL OATA project [38] intends to deliver the concepts of operation, the logical architecture in the form of a description of the interoperable system modules, and the architecture evolution plan. All this will form the basis for common European regulations as part of the *Single European Sky*.

The increasing integration, automation and complexity of ATM systems requires a systematic and structured approach to risk assessment and mitigation, including hazard identification, as well as the use of predictive and monitoring techniques to assist in these processes. Faults [27] in the design, operation or maintenance of ATM systems or errors in ATM systems could affect the safety margins (e.g., loss of separation) and result in, or contribute to, an increased hazard to aircrafts or a failure (e.g., a loss of separation and an accident in the worst case). Increasingly, ATM systems rely on the reliance (e.g., the ability to recover from failures and accommodate errors) and safety (e.g., the ability to guarantee failure independence) features placed upon all system parts. Moreover, the increased interaction of ATM across state boundaries requires that a consistent and more structured approach be taken to the risk assessment and mitigation of all ATM System elements throughout the ECAC (European Civil Aviation Conference) states [9]. Although the average trends show a decrease in the number of fatal accidents for Europe, the approach and landing accidents are still the most safety pressing problems facing the aviation industry [35, 36, 42]. Unfortunately, even maintaining the same safety levels across the European airspace would be insufficient to accommodate an increasing traffic without affecting the overall safety of ATM Systems [7].

The introduction of new safety relevant systems in ATM contexts requires us to understand the risk involved in order to mitigate the impact of possible failures. The EUROCONTROL Safety Regulatory Requirement [10], ESARR4, requires the use of a risk based-approach in ATM when introducing and/or planning changes to any (ground as well as onboard) part of ATM systems. This concerns the human, procedural and equipment (i.e., hardware or software) elements of ATM systems as well as its environment of operations at any stage of the life cycle of the ATM System. The ESARR4 [10] requires that ATM service providers systematically identify any hazard for any change into ATM systems. Moreover, they have to assess any related risk and identify relevant mitigation actions. In order to provide guidelines for and standardise safety analysis EUROCONTROL has developed the EATMP Safety Assessment Methodology (SAM) [12] reflecting best practices for safety assessment of Air Navigation Systems.

The SAM methodology provides a means of compliance to ESARR4. The objective of the methodology is to define the means for providing assurance that an Air Navigation System is safe for operational use. The SAM methodology describes a generic process for the safety assessment of Air Navigation Systems. This process consists of three major steps: *Functional Hazard Assessment (FHA), Preliminary System Safety Assessment (PSSA)* and *System Safety Assessment (SSA)*. The process covers the complete lifecycle of an Air Navigation System, from initial system definition, through design, implementation, integration, transfer to operations and maintenance. Although the SAM methodology describes the underlying principles of the safety assessment process, it provides limited information how to apply these principles in specific projects.

3   Evolutionary Safety Analysis

Evolutionary Safety Analysis [15] relies on a logical framework that captures cycles of discoveries and exploitations. The underlying idea involves the identification of mappings between socio-technical solutions and problems. The proposed framework [15] exploits these mappings in order to construct an evolutionary model that enhances safety analysis. This section briefly recalls the proposed framework for evolutionary safety analysis. The remainder of the paper shows a particular aspect of the framework, which captures safety case evolution. The examples drawn from the ATM domain emphasise how evolutionary safety analysis supports work practice. Figure 1 shows the framework for evolutionary safety analysis. The framework captures these evolutionary cycles at different levels of abstraction and on diverse models. This paper explicitly develops the evolution of safety cases. The framework consists of three different hierarchical layers: *System Modeling Transformation (SMT), Safety Analysis Modeling Transformation (SAMT)* and *Operational Modeling Transformation (OMT)*. The remainder of this section describes the three hierarchical layers.

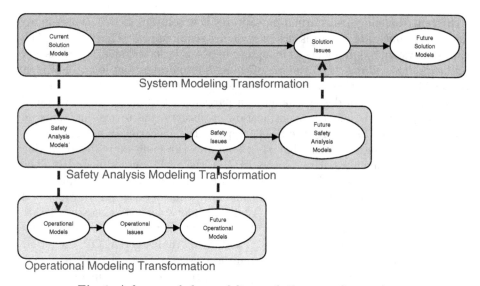

Fig. 1. A framework for modeling evolutionary safety analyses

3.1   System Modeling Transformation

The definition and identification of the system under analysis is extremely critical in the ATM domain. System models defined during the design phase are adapted and reused for safety and risk analysis. Organisational and cost-related reasons often determine this choice, without questioning whether models are suitable for the intended use. System models capture characteristics that may be of primary importance for design, but irrelevant for safety analysis. The main drawback is that design models are tailored to support the work of system designers. Models should be working-tools that, depending on their intended use, ease and support specific activities and cognitive operations of users.

Heterogeneous engineering [29] provides a comprehensive viewpoint, which allows us to understand the underlying mechanisms of evolution of socio-technical systems. Heterogeneous engineering involves both the systems approach [22] as well as the social shaping of technology [30]. According to heterogeneous engineering, system requirements specify mappings between problem and solution spaces. Both spaces are socially constructed and negotiated through sequences of mappings between solution spaces and problem spaces [3, 4]. Therefore, system requirements emerge as a set of consecutive solution spaces justified by a problem space of concerns to stakeholders. Requirements, as mappings between socio-technical solutions and problems, represent an account of the history of socio-technical issues arising and being solved within industrial settings. The formal extension of these mappings (or solution space transformations) identifies a framework to model and capture evolutionary system features (e.g., requirements evolution, evolutionary dependencies, etc.) [14].

System Modeling Transformation captures how solution models evolve in order to accommodate design issues or evolving requirements. Therefore, a SMT captures system requirements as mappings between socio-technical solutions and problems. This allows the gathering of changes into design solutions. That is, it is possible to identify how changes affect design solution. Moreover, this enables sensitivity analyses of design changes. In particular, this allows the revision of safety requirements and the identification of hazards due to the introduction of a new system. Therefore, the SMT supports the gathering of safety requirements for evolving systems. That is, it supports the main activities occurring during the top-down iterative process FHA in the SAM methodology [12]. The FHA in the SAM methodology then initiates another top-down iterative approach, i.e., the PSSA. Similarly, the framework considers design solutions and safety objectives as input to Safety Analysis. Safety analysis assesses whether the proposed design solution satisfies the identified safety objectives. This phase involves different methodologies (e.g., Fault Tree Analysis, HAZOP, etc.) that produce diverse (system) models. System usage or operational trials may give rise to unforeseen safety issues that invalidate (parts of) safety models. In order to take into account these issues, it is necessary to modify safety analysis. Therefore, safety analysis models evolve too.

3.2 Safety Analysis Modeling Transformation

The failure of safety-critical systems highlights safety issues [23, 28, 34, 41]. It is often the case that diverse causes interacted and triggered particular unsafe conditions. Although safety analysis (i.e., safety case) argues system safety, complex interactions, giving rise to failures, expose the limits of safety arguments. Therefore, it is necessary to take changes into account in safety arguments [18]. Greenwell, Strunk and Knight in [18] propose an enhanced safety-case lifecycle by evolutionary (safety-case) examples drawn from the aviation domain. The lifecycle identifies a general process for the revision of safety cases.

Figures 2 and 3 show subsequent versions of a safety case. The graphical notation that represents the safety cases is the Goal Structuring Notation (GSN) [24]. Although GSN addresses the maintenance of safety cases, the approach provides limited support with respect to complex dependencies (e.g., external to the safety argument) [25]. Moreover, it lacks any interpretation of the relationships between subsequent safety cases. Figure 2 shows the initial safety case arguing: *"Controller aware of altitude violations"*. Unfortunately, an accident invalidates the justification J1. The satisfaction of the subgoal G2 is insufficient for the satisfaction of the goal G1. Figure 3 shows the revised safety case that addresses the issue occurred. Unfortunately, another accident, again, invalidates the second safety case [18]. Hence, the safety argument needs further revision in order to address the safety flaw uncovered by the accident. Safety Analysis Modeling Transformation, similarly to the SMT, captures how safety analysis models evolve in order to accommodate emerging safety issues. Although design models serve as a basis for safety models, they provide limited support to capture unforeseen system interactions. Therefore, SAMT supports those activities

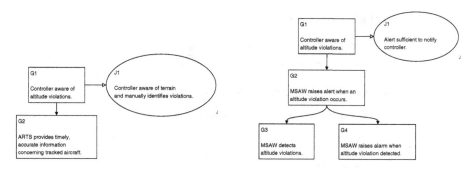

Fig. 2. Initial safety argument   **Fig. 3.** Revised safety argument

involved in the PSSA process of the SAM methodology [12]. Note that although the SAM methodology stresses that both FHA and PSSA are iterative processes, it provides little support to manage process iterations as well as system evolution in terms of design solutions and safety requirements. The framework supports these evolutionary processes.

3.3   Operational Modeling Transformation

Operational models (e.g., structured scenarios, patterns of interactions, structured procedures, workflows, etc.) capture heterogeneous system dynamics. Unfortunately, operational profiles often change with system usage (in order to integrate different functionalities or to accommodate system failures). The main problems areas (e.g., ATC Human Performance, Flight Crew Human Performance, Aircraft, etc.) identified in Controller Reports [1] and TCAS II Incidents [2] highlight the complexity and the coupling within the ATM domain [34]. The analysis [15] of the reports is in agreement with other studies [39, 43] that analyse human errors as organisational failures [20, 28, 37].

Capturing operational interactions and procedures allows the analysis of *"human reliability"* [20]. In a continuously changing environment like ATM, adaption enhances the coupling between man and machine [21]. Hollnagel in [21] identifies three different adaption strategies: *Adaption Through Design, Adaption through Performance* and *Adaption through Management*. Operational Modeling Transformation captures how operational models change in order to accommodate issues arising. The evolution of operational models informs safety analyses of new hazards. Therefore, OMT supports the activities involved in the SSA process of the SAM methodology.

4   Safety Case Changes

This section uses the (Assurance and Safety Case Environment) ASCE™ tool (see Appendix A) for the analysis of safety case changes. The ASCE Difference Tool v1.1 supports the analysis of differences between two ASCE networks (i.e., safety cases). Note that this functionality has been recently released with ASCE™

Node differences

> **Please note:** When analysing changes in Node narratives (HTML Content), only new and deleted sentences are shown. Formatting changes, moved sentences and copied/duplicated sentences are **not shown**.

Node N7737803 (N7737803 - J1) was changed

Node HTML narrative content was changed/edited.

Removed sentences	Inserted sentences
Controller aware of terrain and manually identifies violations. (approx 0% into document)	Alert sufficient to notify controller. (approx 0% into document)

Node N1813777 (N1813777 - G2) was changed

Node HTML narrative content was changed/edited.

Removed sentences	Inserted sentences
ARTS provides timely, accurate information concerning tracked aircraft. (approx 0% into document)	MSAW raises alert when an altitude violation occurs. (approx 0% into document)

Supporting Link (type = [1]) from Node [N7822475 - G3] was added.
Supporting Link (type = [1]) from Node [N8116556 - G4] was added.

Node N7822475 (N7822475 - G3) was added.

Node N8116556 (N8116556 - G4) was added.

Fig. 4. Analysing differences between two ASCE networks

v3.0. Although it is possible to analyse safety case changes in small and simple examples, the tool supports the automation of safety case management and analysis. This further stresses how capturing safety case evolution would support safety case judgement and safety analysis practice. Figure 4 shows a report from the ASCE™ Difference Tool.

The report consists of the comparison of the two subsequent safety cases, i.e., Figure 2 and Figure 3. The analysis points out the differences (i.e., safety case changes) between the subsequent safety cases. It clearly points out the safety case changes: changing the nodes J1 and G2; adding the two new nodes G3 and G4. The ASCE™ Difference Tool detects and reports on structural and content differences between two networks, such as: General configuration changes (e.g., project name, version, author, description); Added new and deleted nodes; Modified node attributes (e.g., type, id, title, status fields), Modified node content, and optionally new and deleted sentences in the node narratives; Structural changes (i.e. new, deleted and modified links).

The identification of differences between two ASCE networks relies on the comparison between safety case structures. This further highlights the importance of comparing and representing structured safety cases. Related research [26] highlights the role of structured safety cases in the analysis of the whole ATM airspace. The findings of comparing different structured safety cases [26] stress the importance of understanding how structured safety cases change [26]. Hence, capturing safety case changes supports safety case judgement and evolutionary safety analysis.

5   Modeling Safety Case Changes

This section shows that it is possible to capture safety case changes in a logical framework. The logical framework is similar to the one underlying System Modeling Transformations (SMTs) for modeling requirements evolution [14]. Requirements, as mappings between socio-technical solutions and problems, represent an account of the history of socio-technical issues arising and being solved within industrial settings [3, 4]. These mappings identify a *Functional Ecology* model that defines requirements as emerging from solution space transformations. The Functional Ecology model describes solution-problem iterations of the form: *solution → problem → solution* . A solution space solves some highlighted problems. The contextualization of the selected problems into the initial solution space identifies the system requirements as mappings between solution and problem spaces. The resolution of these problems identifies a future solution. The mappings between the solved problems and the future solution define further system requirements. This heterogeneous account of requirements is convenient to capture requirements evolution [14]. This implies that requirements engineering processes consist of solutions searching for problems, rather than the other way around (that is, problems searching for solutions) [3, 4].

This section extends the use of evolutionary modeling [14] to safety case evolution, hence *safety space transformation*. Modeling safety case changes relies on a formal extension of solution space transformations [14]. The basic idea is to provide a formal representation of solutions (i.e., safety cases) and problems. The aim of a formal representation is twofold. On the one hand the formalisation of safety cases and problems supports *model-driven judgement*. On the other hand it allows us to formally capture *safety space transformations*, hence *safety case evolution*. The formalisation represents safety cases and problems in terms of modal logic [6, 16]. Propositional modal logic provides enough expressiveness in order to formalise safety space transformations. The formal representation relies on logic bases: syntax, semantics and proof systems[1]. All definitions can be naturally extended in terms of other logics (e.g., [13, 40]) bases (i.e., syntax, semantics and proof systems). The definitions still remain sound and valid due to construction arguments.

Intuitively, a *Safety Space* is just a collection of safety cases, which represent the organisational knowledge acquired by the social shaping of technical systems. The *Current Safety Space*, denoted as $\mathcal{S}_t$, embodies the history of solved

---

[1] Note that there exist different logics (e.g., **K, D, K4, S4, S5**, etc.) that correspond to different proof systems [6, 16]. Any specific proof system implies particular features to the models that can be proved. It is beyond the scope of this work to decide which proof system should be used in any specific case.

social, technical, economic and procedural problems (i.e., socio-technical problems) that constitute the legacy of previously solved organisational problems at current time t. The Current Safety Space exists within a *Local Safety Space*. That is, $\mathcal{S}_t$ is a subspace of $\mathcal{S}$. The Current Safety Space therefore captures the knowledge acquired by organisational learning (i.e., the previously solved organisational problems). In other words, the Current Safety Space consists of the adopted solutions due to organisational learning. This definition further supports the assumption that safety space transformations capture organisational learning and system safety judgement, hence safety case evolution. Safety goals therefore are *accessible possibilities* or *possible worlds* in safety spaces available in the production environment. This intentionally recalls the notion of possible world underlying *Kripke models* [13]. Thus, safety cases are Kripke models. It is moreover possible to model the Current Safety Space in terms of Kripke models. $\mathcal{S}_t$ is a collection of Kripke models. Note that Kripke models enable reasoning about knowledge [13] and uncertainties [19].

Let us briefly recall the notion of a Kripke model. A Kripke model, $\mathcal{M}$, consists of a collection G of *possible worlds*, an *accessibility relation* R on possible worlds and a mapping $\Vdash$ between possible worlds and propositional letters. The $\Vdash$ relation defines which propositional letters are true at which possible worlds. Thus, $\mathcal{S}_t$ is a collection of countable elements of the form

$$\mathcal{M}_i^t = \langle G_i^t, R_i^t, \Vdash_i^t \rangle . \tag{1}$$

Each Kripke model then represents an available safety case. Thus, a Kripke model is a system of worlds in which each world has some (possibly empty) set of alternatives. The accessibility relation (or alternativeness relation), denoted by R, so that $\Gamma R \Delta$ means that Δ is an alternative (or possible) world for Γ. For every world Γ, an atomic proposition is either true or false in it and the truth-values of compound non-modal propositions are determined by the usual truth-tables. A modal proposition $\Box \varphi$ is regarded to be true in a world Γ, if φ is true in all the worlds accessible from Γ. Whereas, $\Diamond \varphi$ is true in Γ, if φ is true at least in one world Δ such that $\Gamma R \Delta$. In general, many safety cases may address a given problem. The resolution of various problems, hence the acquisition of further knowledge, narrows the safety space by refining the available safety cases.

Problems are formulae of (propositional) modal logic. Collections of problems (i.e., problem spaces) are issues (or believed so) arising during system production. Kripke models (i.e., solutions) provide the semantics in order to interpret the validity of (propositional) modalities (i.e., problems). Note that it is possible to adopt different semantics of the accessibility relations in Kripke models. For instance, the accessibility relation can capture information like safety case dependencies (or dependencies between safety goals). Using different semantics for interpreting the accessibility relation highlights and captures diverse evolutionary information. On the one hand, the use of different semantics highlights the flexibility of the given framework. On the other hand, it requires careful considerations when used in practice to capture diverse evolutionary aspects of safety cases. Based on the syntax of Kripke models, proof systems (e.g., *Tableau systems*) consist of procedural rules (i.e., inference rules) that allow us to prove formula validity or to find counterexamples (or countermodels).

The mappings between the Current Safety Space $\mathcal{S}_t$ and the *Proposed Safety Problem Space* $\mathcal{P}_t$ identify safety requirements (demands, needs or desires of stakeholders) that correspond to problems as contextualised by a current safety case. These mappings represent the *safety arguments*. Let $\mathcal{S}_t$ be the Current Safety Space and $\mathcal{P}_t$ be the Proposed Safety Problem Space. The safety arguments $\mathbf{SC}_a^t$ consists of the mappings (i.e., pairs) that correspond to each problem P_j^t in $\mathcal{P}_t$ contextualised by a safety case $\mathcal{M}_i^t$ in $\mathcal{S}_t$. Thus, for any possible world Γ in a Kripke model $\mathcal{M}_i^t \in \mathcal{S}_t$ and for any problem $P_j^t \in \mathcal{P}_t$ such that $(\mathcal{M}_i^t, \Gamma) \not\Vdash_i^t P_j^t$, the pair $\langle \Gamma, P_j^t \rangle$ belongs to $\mathbf{SC}_a^t$. In formula,

$$\mathbf{SC}_a^t = \left\{ \langle \Gamma, P_j^t \rangle | (\mathcal{M}_i^t, \Gamma) \not\Vdash_i^t P_j^t \right\} . \tag{2}$$

The final step of the Safety Space Transformation consists of the reconciliation of the Safety Space $\mathcal{S}_t$ with the Proposed Safety Problem Space $\mathcal{P}_t$ into a Proposed Safety Space $\mathcal{S}_{t+1}$ (i.e., a subspace of a *Future Safety Space* $\mathcal{S}'$). The Proposed Safety Space $\mathcal{S}_{t+1}$ takes into account (or solves) the selected problems. The resolution of the selected problems identifies the proposed future safety cases.

The reconciliation of $\mathcal{S}_t$ with $\mathcal{P}_t$ involves the resolution of the problems in $\mathcal{P}_t$. In logic terms, this means that the proposed solutions should satisfy the selected problems (or some of them). Note that the selected problems could be unsatisfiable as a whole (that is, any model is unable to satisfy all the formulae). This requires stakeholders to compromise (i.e., prioritise and refine) over the selected problems. The underlying logic framework allows us to identify model schemes that satisfy the selected problems. This requires to prove the validity of formulae by a proof system. If a formula is satisfiable (that is, there exist a model in which the formula is valid), it would be possible to derive by the proof system a model (or counterexample) that satisfies the formula. The reconciliation finally forces the identified model schemes into future solutions.

The final step of the Safety Space Transformation identifies mappings between the Proposed Safety Problem Space $\mathcal{P}_t$ and the Proposed Safety Space $\mathcal{S}_{t+1}$. These mappings of problems looking for solutions represent the *safety constraints*. Let $\mathcal{S}_t$ be the Current Safety Space, $\mathcal{P}_t$ be the Proposed Safety Problem Space and $\mathcal{S}_{t+1}$ be a Proposed Safety Space in a Future Safety Space $\mathcal{S}'$. The safety constraints in $\mathbf{SC}_c^t$ consist of the mappings (i.e., pairs) that correspond to each problem P_j^t in $\mathcal{P}_t$ solved by a safety case $\mathcal{M}_i^{t+1}$ in $\mathcal{S}_{t+1}$. Thus, for any $\langle \Gamma, P_j^t \rangle \in \mathbf{SC}_a^t$, and for any Kripke model $\mathcal{M}_i^{t+1} \in \mathcal{S}_{t+1}$ that solves the problem $P_j^t \in \mathcal{P}_t$, the pair $\langle P_j^t, \Gamma \rangle$ belongs to $\mathbf{SC}_c^t$. In formula,

$$\mathbf{SC}_c^t = \{ \langle P_j^t, \Gamma \rangle | (\Gamma, P_j^t) \in \mathbf{SC}_a^t \text{ and } (\mathcal{M}_i^{t+1}, \Gamma) \Vdash_i^{t+1} P_j^t \} . \tag{3}$$

Figure 5 shows a safety space transformation. The safety case transformation captures the changes from the initial safety case $\mathcal{M}_i^t$ (see Figure 2) to the revised safety case $\mathcal{M}_i^{t+1}$ (see Figure 3).

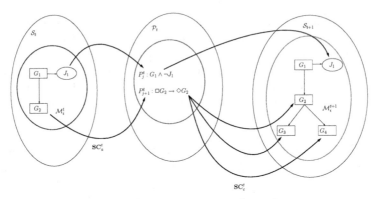

Fig. 5. A safety space transformation

An accident invalidates the justification J1. The satisfaction of the subgoal G2 is insufficient for the satisfaction of the goal G1. The proposed safety problem space, $\mathcal{P}_t$, contains these problems, i.e., P_j^t and P_{j+1}^t. The safety space transformation addresses the highlighted problems into the proposed safety case $\mathcal{M}_i^{t+1}$. In order to address the highlighted problems, it is necessary to change the initial safety case. The proposed changes are taken into account in the proposed safety case. Note that there might be different proposed safety cases addressing the proposed safety problem space.

The safety space transformation identifies the safety case construction and judgement in terms of safety arguments and constraints. The safety case consists of the collections of mappings between safety cases and problems. The first part of a safety case consists of the safety arguments, which capture the relationship that comes from safety cases looking for problems. The second part of a safety case consists of the safety constraints, which capture how future safety cases address given problems. Safety cases at any given time, t, can be represented as the set of all the arcs, that reflect the contextualised connections between the problem space and the current and future safety space. In formula,

$$\mathbf{SC}^t = (\mathbf{SC}_a^t, \mathbf{SC}_c^t) \tag{4}$$

The definition of safety case transformation enables us further to interpret and understand safety case changes, hence safety case evolution [14].

6   Conclusions

This paper introduces a logical framework for modeling safety case evolution. The framework extends the use of evolutionary modeling [14] to *safety space transformation*, hence *safety case evolution*. Modeling safety case changes relies on a formal extension of solution space transformations [14]. The underlying idea is to provide a formal representation of safety cases and problems. On the one hand, the formalisation of safety cases and problems supports *model-driven judgement*. On the other hand, it allows us to formally capture *safety space transformations*, hence *safety case evolution*. The modeling of safety case evolution provides new insights in safety case judgement and safety analysis.

Modeling Safety Case Evolution. The framework captures how safety cases evolve in order to accommodate arising safety problems. The safety space transformation identifies the safety case construction and judgement in terms of safety arguments and constraints. The safety case consists of the collections of mappings between safety cases and problems. The first part of a safety case consists of the safety arguments, which capture the relationship that comes from safety cases looking for problems. The second part of a safety case consists of the safety constraints, which capture how future safety cases address given problems. The definition of safety case transformation enables us further to interpret and understand safety case changes, hence safety case evolution. Therefore, the framework enables the implementation of evolutionary safety analysis [15].

Formal Tool Extensions. The framework provides a formal extension of the ASCE Difference Tool. The tool relies on the comparison between two structured safety cases. Therefore, the logical framework provides a formal support for interpreting and capturing safety case changes.

Support for Guidelines and Work Practice. The framework supports industry guidelines (e.g., SAM methodology [12]), which emphasise the iterative nature of safety analysis [12, 15]. Moreover, the framework supports safety judgement as well as evolutionary safety analysis [15]. The underlying evolutionary aspects characterise work practice in the safety analysis of continuously evolving industry domain (e.g., ATM).

Organisational Knowledge and Safety Judgement. The framework relies on basic logic models (i.e., Kripke models) that enable reasoning about knowledge [13] and uncertainty [19]. This highlights safety judgement (that is, the construction of safety cases) as an organisational process. That is, the safety judgement consists of gathering organisational knowledge about the system. This further highlights how organisational (knowledge) failures affect safety [28, 34, 37].

In conclusion, this paper introduces a framework for modeling safety case evolution. The framework supports safety judgement and evolutionary safety analysis. Future work intends to implement an ASCE plugin that supports safety case evolution. This would enhance and support the dissemination of safety case evolution practice among safety case users.

Acknowledgments. I would like to thank George Cleland and Luke Emmet of Adelard - http://www.adelard.com/ - for their help and comments on the Assurance and Safety Case Environment, ASCE™. ASCE™ is free for non commercial teaching and research purposes. ASCE™ V3.0 is available for download - http://www.adelard.com/software/asce -. This work has been supported by the UK EPSRC Interdisciplinary Research Collaboration in Dependability, DIRC - http://www.dirc.org.uk - grant GR/N13999.

References

1. Aviation Safety Reporting System. *Controller Reports*, 2003.
2. Aviation Safety Reporting System. *TCAS II Incidents*, 2004.
3. M. Bergman, J. L. King, and K. Lyytinen. Large-scale requirements analysis as heterogeneous engineering. *Social Thinking - Software Practice*, pages 357–386, 2002.
4. M. Bergman, J. L. King, and K. Lyytinen. Large-scale requirements analysis revisited: The need for understanding the political ecology of requirements engineering. *Requirements Engineering*, 7(3):152–171, 2002.
5. BFU. *Investigation Report, AX001-1-2/02*, 2002.
6. A. Chagrov and M. Zakharyaschev. *Modal Logic*. Number 35 in Oxford Logic Guides. Oxford University Press, 1997.
7. J. H. Enders, R. S. Dodd, and F. Fickeisen. Continuing airworthiness risk evaluation (CARE): An exploratory study. *Flight Safety Digest*, 18(9-10):1–51, September-October 1999.
8. EUROCONTROL. *Human Factor Module - Human Factors in the Development of Air Traffic Management Systems*, 1.0 edition, 1998.
9. EUROCONTROL. *EUROCONTROL Airspace Strategy for the ECAC States, ASM.ET1.ST03.4000-EAS-01-00*, 1.0 edition, 2001.
10. EUROCONTROL. *EUROCONTROL Safety Regulatory Requirements (ESARR). ESARR 4 - Risk Assessment and Mitigation in ATM*, 1.0 edition, 2001.
11. EUROCONTROL. *EUROCONTROL Air Traffic Management Strategy for the years 2000+*, 2003.
12. EUROCONTROL. *EUROCONTROL Air Navigation System Safety Assessment Methodology*, 2.0 edition, 2004.
13. R. Fagin, J. Y. Halpern, Y. Moses, and M. Y. Vardi. *Reasoning about Knowledge*. The MIT Press, 2003.
14. M. Felici. *Observational Models of Requirements Evolution*. PhD thesis, Laboratory for Foundations of Computer Science, School of Informatics, The University of Edinburgh, 2004.
15. M. Felici. Evolutionary safety analysis: Motivations from the air traffic management domain. In R. Winther, B. Gran, and G. Dahll, editors, *Proceedings of the 24th International Conference on Computer Safety, Reliability and Security, SAFECOMP 2005*, number 3688 in LNCS, pages 208–221. Springer-Verlag, 2005.
16. M. Fitting and R. L. Mendelsohn. *First-Order Modal Logic*. Kluwer Academic Publishers, 1998.
17. Flight Safety Fundation. *The Human Factors Implication for Flight Safety of Recent Developments In the Airline Industry*, number (22)3-4 in Flight Safety Digest, March-April 2003.
18. W. S. Greenwell, E. A. Strunk, and J. C. Knight. Failure analysis and the safety-case lifecycle. In *Proceedings of the IFIP Working Conference on Human Error, Safety and System Development (HESSD)*, pages 163–176, 2004.
19. J. Y. Halpern. *Reasoning about Uncertainty*. The MIT Press, 2003.
20. E. Hollnagel. *Human Reliability Analysis: Context and Control*. Academic Press, 1993.
21. E. Hollnagel. The art of efficient man-machine interaction: Improving the coupling between man and machine. In *Expertise and Technology: Cognition & Human-Computer Cooperation*, pages 229–241. Lawrence Erlbaum Associates, 1995.

22. A. C. Hughes and T. P. Hughes, editors. *Systems, Experts, and Computers: The Systems Approach in Management and Engineering, World War II and After.* The MIT Press, 2000.

23. C. W. Johnson. *Failure in Safety-Critical Systems: A Handbook of Accident and Incident Reporting.* University of Glasgow Press, Glasgow, Scotland, Oct. 2003.

24. T. P. Kelly. *Arguing Safety - A Systematic Approach to Managing Safety Cases.* PhD thesis, Department of Computer Science, University of York, 1998.

25. T. P. Kelly and J. A. McDermid. A systematic approach to safety case maintenance. In M. Felici, K. Kanoun, and A. Pasquini, editors, *Proceedings of the 18th International Conference on Computer Safety, Reliability and Security, SAFECOMP'99*, number 1698 in LNCS, pages 13–26. Springer-Verlag, 1999.

26. S. Kinnersly. Whole airspace atm system safety case - preliminary study. Technical Report AEAT LD76008/2 Issue 1, AEA Technology, 2001.

27. J.-C. Laprie et al. Dependability handbook. Technical Report LAAS Report no 98-346, LIS LAAS-CNRS, Aug. 1998.

28. N. G. Leveson. *SAFEWARE: System Safety and Computers.* Addison-Wesley, 1995.

29. D. A. MacKenzie. *Inventing Accuracy: A Historical Sociology of Nuclear Missile Guidance.* The MIT Press, 1990.

30. D. A. MacKenzie and J. Wajcman, editors. *The Social Shaping of Technology.* Open University Press, 2nd edition, 1999.

31. S. Matthews. Future developments and challenges in aviation safety. *Flight Safety Digest*, 21(11):1–12, Nov. 2002.

32. M. Overall. New pressures on aviation safety challenge safety management systems. *Flight Safety Digest*, 14(3):1–6, Mar. 1995.

33. A. Pasquini and S. Pozzi. Evaluation of air traffic management procedures - safety assessment in an experimental environment. *Reliability Engineering & System Safety*, 2004.

34. C. Perrow. *Normal Accidents: Living with High-Risk Technologies.* Princeton University Press, 1999.

35. H. Ranter. Airliner accident statistics 2002: Statistical summary of fatal multi-engine airliner accidents in 2002. Technical report, Aviation Safety Network, Jan. 2003.

36. H. Ranter. Airliner accident statistics 2003: Statistical summary of fatal multi-engine airliner accidents in 2003. Technical report, Aviation Safety Network, Jan. 2004.

37. J. Reason. *Managing the Risks of Organizational Accidents.* Ashgate Publishing Limited, 1997.

38. Review. Working towards a fully interoperable system: The EUROCONTROL overall ATM/CNS target architecture project (OATA). *Skyway*, 32:46–47, Spring 2004.

39. S. A. Shappell and D. A. Wiegmann. The human factors analysis and classification system - HFACS. Technical Report DOT/FAA/AM-00/7, FAA, Feb. 2000.

40. C. Stirling. *Modal and Temporal Properties of Processes.* Texts in Computer Science. Springer-Verlag, 2001.

41. N. Storey. *Safety-Critical Computer Systems.* Addison-Wesley, 1996.

42. G. W. van Es. A review of civil aviation accidents - air traffic management related accident: 1980–1999. In *Proceedings of the 4th International Air Traffic Management R&D Seminar*, New-Mexico, Dec. 2001.

43. D. A. Wiegmann and S. A. Shappell. A human error analysis of commercial aviation accidents using the human factors analysis and classification system (HFACS). Technical Report DOT/FAA/AM-01/3, FAA, Feb. 2001.

A   ASCE™

The Assurance and Safety Case Environment, ASCE™, is a graphical hypertext tool which allows the development, review, analysis and dissemination of safety and assurance cases. It is based on the concept that a safety or assurance case should show the argument structure as well as providing evidence to support that argument. A safety case is *"a documented body of evidence that provides a demonstrable and valid argument that a system is adequately safe for a given application and environment over its lifetime"*. ASCE represents the underlying models/networks in XML (.axml files). This allows full programmatic access to the underlying content in order to implement any kind of required analysis. One major new functionality in ASCE™ V3.0 is the availability of *plugins*. Implementing analysis functionality as a plugin provides a way to analyse the safety case's structure. Figure 6 shows an example application domain for ASCE™, i.e., the range of processes and activities that ASCE™ can support.

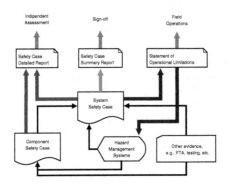

Fig. 6. An application domain for ASCE™

The ASCE™ Difference Tool is a simple standalone tool for comparing two ASCE networks, and is very useful in supporting reviewing or auditing activities over some period whilst the ASCE network has been edited. It generates a report that summarises differences between any two ASCE networks.

Type-Driven Automatic Quotation of Concrete Object Code in Meta Programs

J.J. Vinju

Centrum voor Wiskunde en Informatica,
P.O. Box 94079, NL-1090 GB, Amsterdam, The Netherlands
Jurgen.Vinju@cwi.nl

Abstract. Meta programming can be facilitated by the ability to represent program fragments in concrete syntax instead of abstract syntax. The resulting meta programs are more self-documenting. One caveat in concrete meta programming is the syntactic separation between the meta language and the object language. To solve this problem, many meta programming systems use quoting and anti-quoting to indicate precisely where level switches occur. These "syntactic hedges" can obfuscate the concrete program fragments. This paper describes an algorithm for inferring quotes, such that the meta programmer no longer needs to explicitly indicate transitions between the meta and object languages.

1 Introduction

Programs that manipulate programs as data are called *meta programs*. Examples of meta programs are compilers, source-to-source translators, type-checkers, documentation generators, refactoring tools, and code generators. We call the language that is used to manipulate programs the *meta language*, and the manipulated language the *object language*. Meta programming is the method for implementing automated software engineering tools.

Any general purpose programming language can be used to write meta programs. The object program fragments are represented using the data type constructs available in the meta language. An old idea to facilitate meta programming is the use of *concrete syntax* to represent program fragments [1]. Using concrete syntax, as opposed to abstract syntax, all program fragments in a meta program are represented in the syntax of the object language [2, 3]. Concrete syntax combines the readability of the string representation with the structural and type-safe representation of abstract syntax trees. The meta programmer embeds the actual program fragments literally in his meta program, but the underlying representation of these fragments is an abstract syntax tree. The resulting meta programs are more self-documenting because "what you see is what you manipulate".

One caveat in concrete meta programming is the syntactic separation between the meta language and the object language. Conventional scanning and parsing technologies have a hard time distinguishing the two levels. To solve this problem, many meta programming systems use quoting and anti-quoting to indicate

N. Guelfi and A. Savidis (Eds.): RISE 2005, LNCS 3943, pp. 97–112, 2006.

precisely where level switches are made. To further guide the system, the user is sometimes obliged to explicitly mention the type of the following program fragment. These "syntactic hedges" help the parser, but they can obfuscate the concrete program fragments. In practice, it leads to programmers avoiding the use of concrete syntax because the benefit becomes much less clear when it introduces more syntactic clutter than it removes. We would like to *infer* the transitions between the object and meta languages automatically without asking the user to express the obvious.

Contributions and Road-Map. This paper contributes by removing the technical need for quotes and anti-quotes. We first explore meta programming with concrete syntax in some detail by describing a number of existing systems that implement it (Section 2). We then introduce an algorithm that automatically detects transitions from meta language to object language (Section 3). The architecture around this algorithm is based on scannerless generalized parsing and a separate type-checking phase that both have been described earlier [4, 5]. By making the transitions between meta language and object language invisible we introduce parsing challenges: ambiguous and cyclic grammars. In Section 4 we address these issues. Sections 5 and 6 describe experience and conclusions respectively.

2   The Syntax of Program Fragments in Meta Programming

Plain Java. Suppose we use Java as a meta programming language to implement a Java code generator. Consider the following method that generates a Java method.

```
String buildSetter(String name, String type) {
  return "public void set" + name + "(" + type + " arg)\n"
      + "  this." + name + " = arg; }\n"
}
```

The string representation is unstructured, untyped and uses quotes and anti-quotes. There is no guarantee that the output of this method is a syntactically correct Java method. However, the code fragment is immediately recognizable as a Java method. The following Java code applies a more structured method to construct the same fragment:

```
String buildSetter(String name, String type) {
  Method method = method(
      publicmodifier(), voidType(), identifier("set" + name),
      arglist(formalarg(classType(type),identifier("arg"))),
      statlist(stat(assignment(
          fieldref(identifier("this"),identifier(name)),
          expression(identifier("arg"))))));
  return method.toString();
}
```

This style uses a number of methods for constructing an abstract syntax tree in a bottom-up fashion. If the used construction methods are strictly typed, this style exploits the Java type system to obtain a syntactically correct result. That means that if all `toString()` methods of the abstract representation are correct, then the new expression will also generate syntactically correct Java code.

The Jakarta Tool Suite. This is the first system we describe that employs concrete syntax. JTS is designed for extending programming languages with domain specific constructs. It implements and extends ideas of intentional programming and work in the field of syntax macros [6].

The parser technology used in JTS is based on a separate lexical analyzer and an LL parser generator. This restricts the number of language extensions that JTS accepts. The program fragments in JTS are quoted with *explicit typing*. For selected non-terminals there is a named quoting and anti-quoting operator, like mth{...} and $id(...) in the following example:

```
public FieldDecl buildSetter(String name, String type) {
    QualifiedName methodName = new QualifiedName("set" + name);
    QualifiedName fieldName = new QualifiedName(name);
    QualifiedName typeName = new QualifiedName(type);
    return mth{public void $id(methodName) ($id(typeName) arg) {
            this.$id(fieldName) = arg; } } }
```

Concrete Syntax in ML. In [7] an approach for adding concrete syntax to ML is described. This system also uses quotation operators. It employs scannerless parsing with Earley's generalized parsing algorithm. Disambiguation of the meta programs with program fragments is obtained by the following:

- Full integration of the parser and type-checker of ML: a context-sensitive parser. All type information can be used to guide the parser. Only type correct derivations are recognized, such that quoting operators do not often need explicit types like in JTS.
- In case the type-checking parser cannot decide, the user may explicitly annotate quoting operators with types, like in JTS.

This system is able to provide typing error messages instead of parse errors. Both the level of automated disambiguation, and the level of the error messages are high. The following example shows how anonymous quoting ([| ... |]) and anti-quoting (^...) are used to indicate transitions:

```
fun buildSetter name type =
          [| public void ^(concat "set" name) (^type arg) {
              this.^name = arg; } |]
```

Meta-Aspect/J. This is a tool for meta programming Aspect/J programs in Java [8]. It employs context-sensitive parsing, in a manner similar to the approach taken for ML. As a result, this tool also does not need explicit typing.

```
MethodDec buildSetter(String name, String type) {
   String methodName = "set" + name;
   return '[public void #methodName (#type arg) {
                this.#name = arg; } ]; }
```

Note that Meta Aspect/J offers a fixed combination of one meta language (Java) with one single object language (Aspect/J), while the other systems combine one meta language with many object languages.

ASF+SDF. This is a specialized language for meta programming with concrete syntax. The implementation of ASF+SDF is based on scannerless generalized LR parsing (SGLR) [4] and conditional term rewriting [9]. The syntax of the object language is defined in the SDF formalism. Then rewrite rules defined in ASF implement appropriate transformations, using concrete syntax. The SGLR algorithm takes care of a number of technical issues that occur when parsing concrete syntax:

- It accepts all context-free grammars, which are closed under composition. This allows the combination of any meta language with any object language.
- Due to scannerless parsing, there are no implicit global assumptions like longest match of identifiers, or reserved keywords. Such assumptions would influence the parsing of meta programs. The combined language would have the union set of reserved keywords, which is incorrect in both separate languages.
- Unlimited lookahead takes care of local conflicts in the parse table.

The following rephrases the examples of the introduction in ASF+SDF:

```
context-free syntax
   buildSetter(Identifier, Type) -> Method
variables
  "Name"    -> Identifier
  "Type"    -> Type
equations
[] buildSetter(Name, Type) =
   public void set ++ Name (Type arg) {
     this.Name = arg; }
```

ASF+SDF does not have quoting, or anti-quoting. There are two reasons for this. Firstly, within program fragments no nested ASF+SDF constructs occur that might overlap or interfere. Secondly, the ASF+SDF parser is designed in a very specific manner. It only accepts type correct programs because a specialized parser is generated for each ASF+SDF module. The type system of ASF+SDF requires that all equations are *type preserving*. To enforce this rule, a special production is generated for each user-defined non-terminal X: X "=" X -> Equation. So instead of having one Term "=" Term -> Equation production, ASF+SDF generates specialized productions to parse equations. After this syntax generation, the fixed part of ASF+SDF is added. That part contains the skeleton grammar in which the generated syntax for `Equation` is embedded.

The ASF+SDF example shown above has some syntactic ambiguity. For example, the meta variable `Type` may be recognized as a Java class name, or as a meta variable. Another ambiguity is due to the following user-defined *injection* production: `Method -> Declaration`. Thus, the equation may range over the `Declaration` type as well as over the `Method` type. To disambiguate, ASF+SDF prefers to recognize declared meta variables over object syntax identifiers, and shorter derivations over longer derivations. We call these two preferences the *meta disambiguation rules* of ASF+SDF. This design offers the concrete syntax functionality we seek, but the assumptions that are made limit its general applicability:

- The type system of the meta language must be expressible as a context-free grammar. Consequently, higher-order functions or parametric polymorphism are not allowed.
- Typing errors are reported as parsing errors which makes developing meta programs difficult.

Stratego. This is a meta programming language based on the notion of rewrite rules and strategies [10]. The concrete object syntax feature of Stratego is also based on SGLR, but the separation between the meta language and the object language is done by quoting and anti-quoting. The programmer first defines quotation and anti-quotation notation syntax herself, and then the object language is combined with the Stratego syntax. After parsing, the parse tree of the meta program is mapped automatically to normal Stratego abstract syntax [11]. This is natural for Stratego, since it has no type system to guide parsing, and nested meta programs are allowed in object fragments.

The following example defines the syntax of quotation operators for some Java non-terminals, with and without explicit types:

```
context-free syntax
          "|[" Method "]|" -> Term          {cons("toMetaExpr")}
   "Method |[" Method "]|" -> Term          {cons("toMetaExpr")}
   "~" Term                -> Identifier    {cons("fromMetaExpr")}
   "~id" Term              -> Identifier    {cons("fromMetaExpr")}
variables
   "type" -> Type
strategies
builderSetter(|name, type) =
    !|[public void ~<conc-strings> ("set", name)(type arg) {
        this.~name = arg; } ]|
```

The productions' "cons" attributes are used to guide the automated mapping to Stratego abstract syntax. The ambiguities that occur in ASF+SDF due to injections also occur in Stratego, but the user can always use the explicitly typed quoting operators. In the example, we used both Stratego syntax, like the ! operator and the `conc-strings` library strategy, and Java object syntax.

To indicate the difference, we also used an implicit meta variable for the type argument, and an explicitly anti-quoted variable for the field name that we set.

Stratego leaves part of implementing concrete syntax, namely combining the meta language with the object language, to the user. The use of quoting operators makes this job easier, but the resulting meta programs contain many quoting operators. Questions the user must be able to answer are:

- For which non-terminals should quotation operators be defined.
- When should explicit typing be used.
- What quotation syntax would be appropriate for a specific non-terminal.

If not carefully considered, the answers to these questions might differ for different meta programs that manipulate the same object language. The solution to this problem is to let an expert define the quotation symbols for selected object languages, and put these definitions in a library.

TXL. TXL [12] is a meta programming language that uses backtracking to generalize over deterministic parsing algorithms. TXL has a highly structured syntax, which makes extra quoting unnecessary. Every program fragment is enclosed by a certain operator. The keywords of the operators are syntactic hedges for the program fragments:

```
function buildMethod Name [Identifier] Type [Type]
  replace M [Method]
    construct MethodName [Identifier]
        set [+ Name]
  by
    public void MethodName (Type arg) {
        this.Name = arg; }
end function
```

The example shows how code fragments and the first occurrence of fresh variables are explicitly typed. The [...] anti-quoting operator is used for explicit typing, but it can also contain other meta level operations, such as recursive application of a rule or function. Keywords like construct, replace, and by cannot be used inside program fragments, unless they are escaped.

Although technically TXL does use syntactic hedging, the user is hardly aware of it due to the carefully designed syntax of the meta language. Compared to other meta programming languages, TXL has more keywords.

Discussion. Table 1 summarizes the concrete meta programming systems just discussed. The list is not exhaustive, there are many more meta programming systems, or language extension systems available. Clearly the use of quoting and anti-quoting is a common design decision for meta programming systems with concrete syntax. Explicit typing is also used in many systems. Type-safety is implemented in most of the systems described. From studying the above systems, we draw the following conclusions:

Table 1. Concrete syntax in several systems

	ASF	Stratego	ML	JTS	TXL	MAJ
Typed	+	–	+	+	+	+
Implicit quoting	+	Opt.	–	–	+	–
No type annotations	+	Opt.	–	–	–	+
Nested meta code	–	+	+	–	+	–

- The more *typing context* provided by the meta programming language, the less explicit quoting operators are necessary.
- It is hard to validate the claim that less quotation and anti-quotation is better in all cases. Possibly, this boils down to a matter of taste. Evidently *unnecessary* syntactic detail harms programmer productivity, but that argument just shifts the discussion to what is necessary and what is not. A hybrid system that employs both quote inferencing and explicit quoting would offer the freedom to let the user choose which is best.
- A shortcoming of many systems that employ concrete syntax is that the error messages that they are able to provide are not very informative.

Our goal is to design a parsing architecture that can recognize code fragments in concrete syntax, without syntactic hedges, embedded in meta programming languages with non-trivial expression languages with strict type systems. As an aside, we note that *syntax highlighting* object code differently and the use of *optional quoting operators* are very practical features, but we consider them to be orthogonal to our contribution.

3   Architecture

We start with a fixed syntax definition for a meta language and a user-defined syntax definition for an object language. In Fig. 1 the general architecture of the process starting from these two definitions and a meta program, and ending with an abstract syntax tree is depicted. The first phase, the syntax merger, combines the syntax of the meta language with the syntax of the object language.

The second phase parses the meta program using SGLR [4]. Generalized parsing algorithms do not complain about ambiguities or cycles. In case of ambiguity

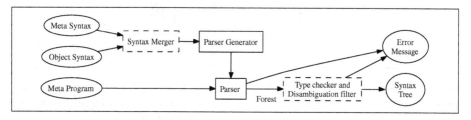

Fig. 1. Overview: parsing concrete syntax using type-checking to disambiguate

they produce a compact representation of a "forest" of trees. This enables this architecture in which the disambiguation process is merged with the type checking algorithm of the meta language rather than integrated in its parsing algorithm.

The final phase type-checks and disambiguates the parse forest, filtering out type-incorrect trees. This architecture is consistent with the idea of disambiguation by filtering as described by [13], which has been applied earlier [5, 4, 14].

3.1 Syntax Transitions

The syntax merger creates a new syntax module, importing both the meta syntax and the object syntax. We assume there is no overlap in non-terminals between the meta syntax and the object syntax, or that renaming is applied to accomplish this. It then adds productions that link the two layers automatically. For every non-terminal X in the object syntax the following productions are generated: X -> `Term` and `Term` -> X, where `Term` is a unique non-terminal selected from the meta language. For example, for Java, the `Term` non-terminal would be `Expression`, because expressions are the way to build data structures in Java.

We call these productions the *transitions* between meta syntax and object syntax. They replace any explicit quoting and unquoting operators. For clarity we will call the transitions to meta syntax the *quoting transitions* and the transitions to object syntax the *anti-quoting transitions*. Figure 2 illustrates the intended purpose of the transitions: nesting object language fragments in meta programs, and nesting meta language fragments again in object language fragments.

The collection of generated transitions from and to the meta language are hazardous. They introduce many ambiguities, including cyclic derivations. An *ambiguity* arises when more than one derivation exists for the same substring with the same non-terminal. Intuitively, this means there are several interpretations possible for the same substring. A *cycle* occurs in derivations if and only if a non-terminal can produce itself without consuming terminal symbols. To get a correct parser for concrete meta programs without quoting, we must

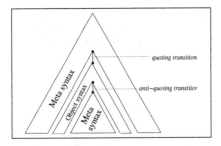

Fig. 2. A parse tree may contain both meta and object productions, where the transitions are marked by quoting and unquoting transition productions

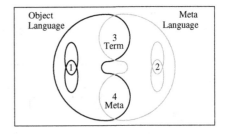

Fig. 3. Classification of ambiguities after joining a meta language with an object language

resolve all ambiguities introduced by the transitions between meta and object syntax. Figure 3 roughly classifies the ambiguities that may occur. Note that ambiguities from different classes may be nested.

Class 1: Ambiguity in the object language itself. This is an artifact of the user-defined syntax of the object language. Such ambiguity must be ignored, since it is not introduced by the syntax merger. The C language would be a good example of an ambiguous object language, with its overloaded use of the * operator for multiplication and pointer dereference.

Class 2: Ambiguity of the meta language itself. This is to be ignored too, since it is not introduced by the syntax merger. Usually, the designer of the meta language will have to solve such an issue separately.

Class 3: Ambiguity directly via syntax transitions. The   Term   nonterminal accepts all sub languages of the object language. Parts of the object language that are nicely separated in the object grammar, are now overlaid on top of each other. For example, the *isolated* Java code fragment i = 1 could be a number of things including an assignment statement, or the initializer part of a declaration.

Class 4: Object language and meta language overlap. Certain   constructs in the meta language may look like constructs in the object language. In the presence of the syntax transitions, it may happen that meta code can also be parsed as object code. For example, this hypothetical Java program constructs some Java declarations: Declarations decls = int a; int b;. The int b; part can be in the meta program, or in the object program.

4   Disambiguation Filters

We will explicitly ignore ambiguity classes 1 and 2, such that the proposed disambiguation filters do not interfere with the separate definitions of the meta language and the object language. We will analyze ambiguity classes 3 and 4, and explain how a disambiguating type-checker will either resolve these ambiguities.

4.1   Disambiguation by Type-Checking

Type-checking is a phase in compilers where it is checked if all operators are applied to compatible operands. Traditionally, a separate type-checking phase takes an abstract syntax tree as input and one or more symbol tables that define the types of all declared and built-in operators. The output is either an error message, or a new abstract syntax tree that is decorated with typing information [15]. Other approaches incorporate type-checking in the parsing phase [7, 16] to help the parser avoid conflicts. We do the exact opposite, the parser is kept simple while the type-checker is extended with the ability to deal with alternative parse trees [5].

Figure 4 shows the internal organization of a disambiguating typechecker. Type-checking forests to filter them is a natural extension of normal type-checking of trees. A forest may have several sub-trees that correspond to different interpretations of the same input program. Type-checking a forest is the process of selecting the single type correct tree. If no single type correct tree is available then we deal with the following two cases:

- No type correct abstract syntax tree is available; present the collection of error messages corresponding to all alternative trees.
- Multiple type correct trees are available; present an error message explaining the alternatives.

Note that resolving the ambiguities caused by syntax transitions resembles type-inference for polymorphic functions [17]. The syntax transitions can be viewed as overloaded (ad-hoc polymorphic) functions. There is one difference: the forest representation already provides the type-inference algorithm with the set of instantiations that is locally available, instead of providing one single abstract tree that has to be instantiated.

Regarding the feasibility of this architecture, recall that the amount of nodes in a GLR parse forest can be bounded by a polynomial in the length of the input string [18, 19]. This is an artifact of smart sharing techniques for parse forests produced by generalized parsers. Maximal sub-term sharing [20] helps to lower the average amount of nodes even more by sharing all duplicated sub-derivations that are distributed across single and multiple derivations in a parse forest. However, the scalability of this architecture still depends on the size of the parse forest, and in particular the way it is traversed. A maximally shared forest may still be traversed in an exponential fashion. Care must be taken to prevent visiting unique nodes several times. We use *memoization* to make sure that each node in a forest is visited only once.

4.2   Class 3. Ambiguity Directly Via Syntax Transitions

We further specialize this class intro four parts:

Class 3.1: Cyclic derivations. These are derivations that do not produce any terminals and exercise syntax transitions both to and from the meta grammar. For example, every X has a direct cycle by applying X -> `Term` and `Term` -> X.

Class 3.2: Meaningless coercions. These are derivations that exercise the transition productions to cast any X from the object language into

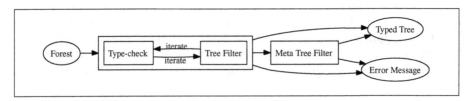

Fig. 4. The organization of the type-checking and disambiguation approach

another Y. Namely, every X can be produced by any other Y now by applying `Term -> ` X and Y ` -> Term`.

Class 3.3: Ambiguous quoting transitions. Several X ` -> Term` are possible from different Xs. The ambiguity is on the `Term` non-terminal. For any two non-terminals X and Y that produce languages with a non-empty intersection, the two productions X ` -> Term` and Y ` -> Term` can be ambiguous.

Class 3.4: Ambiguous anti-quoting transitions. Several `Term -> ` X are possible, each to a different X. For any two productions of the object language that produce the same non-terminal this may happen. A ` -> ` X and B ` -> ` X together introduce an anti-quoting ambiguity with a choice between `Term -> ` A and `Term -> ` B.

In fact, classes 3.1 and 3.2 consist of degenerate cases of ambiguities that would also exist in classes 3.2 and 3.3. We consider them as a special case because they are easier to recognize, and therefore may be filtered with less overhead. The above four subclasses cover all ambiguities caused directly by the transition productions. The first two classes require no type analysis, while the last two classes will be filtered by type checking.

Class 3.1. Dealing with Cyclic Derivations. The syntax transitions lead to cycles in several ways. The most direct cycles are the immediate application of an anti-quoting transition after a quoting transition. Any cycle, if introduced by the syntax merger, always exercises at least one production X ` -> Term`, and one production `Term -> ` Y for any X or Y [21].

Solution 1. The first solution is to filter out cyclic derivations from the parse forest. With the well known `Term` non-terminal as a parameter we can easily identify the newly introduced cycles in the parse trees that exercise cyclic applications of the transition productions. A single bottom-up traversal of the parse forest that detects cycles by marking visited paths is enough to accomplish this. With the useless cyclic derivations removed, what remains are the useful derivations containing transitions to and from the meta level.

We have prototyped solution 1 by extending the ASF+SDF parser with a cycle filter. Applying the prototype on existing specifications shows that for ASF+SDF such an approach is feasible. However, the large amount of meaningless derivations that are removed later do slow down the average parse time of an ASF+SDF module significantly. To quantify, for smaller grammars with ten to twenty non-terminals we witnessed a factor of 5, while for larger grammars with much more non-terminals we witnessed factors of 20 times slow down.

Solution 2. Instead of filtering the cycles from the parse forest, we can prevent them by filtering reductions from the parse table. This technique is based on the use of a disambiguation construct that is described in [4]. We use *priorities* to remove unwanted derivations, in particular we remove the reductions that complete cycles. The details of this application of priorities to prevent cycles are described in a technical report [21]. The key is to automatically add the following priority for every object grammar non-terminal X: X ` -> Term > Term -> ` X.

Because priorities are used to remove reductions from the parse table the cyclic derivations do not occur at all at parsing time.

Prototyping the second scheme resulted in a considerable improvement of the parsing time. The parsing time goes back to almost the original performance. However parse table generation time slows down significantly. So when using solution 2, we trade some compilation time efficiency for run time efficiency. In a setting with frequent updates to the object grammar, it may pay off to stay with solution 1.

Class 3.2. Dealing with Meaningless Coercions. For every pair of non-terminals X and Y of the object language that produce languages that have a non-empty intersection, an ambiguity can be constructed by applying the productions `Term -> ` X and Y ` -> Term`. Effectively, such a derivation casts an Y to an X, which is a meaningless coercion.

These ambiguities are very similar to the cyclic derivations. They are meaningless derivations occurring as a side-effect of the introduction of the transitions. Every direct nesting of an unquoting and a quoting transition falls into this category. As such they are identifiable by the structure of the tree, and a simple bottom-up traversal of a parse forest is able to detect and remove them. No type information is necessary for this. As an optimization, we can again introduce *priorities* to remove these derivations earlier in the parsing architecture.

Class 3.3. Dealing with Ambiguous Quoting. So far, no type checking was needed to filter the ambiguities. This class however is more interesting. The X ` -> Term` productions allow everything in the object syntax to be `Term`. If there are any two non-terminals of the object language that generate languages with a non-empty intersection, and a certain substring fits into this intersection we will have an ambiguity. This happens for example with all injection productions: X ` -> ` Y, since the language produced by X is the same as the language produced by Y.

An ambiguity in this class consists of the choice of nesting an X, or an Y object fragment into the meta program. So, either by X ` -> Term` or by Y ` -> Term` we transit from the object grammar into the meta grammar. The immediate typing context is provided by the surrounding meta code. Now suppose this context enforces an X. Disambiguation is obtained by removing all trees that do not have the X ` -> Term` production at the top.

The example in Fig. 5 is a forest with an ambiguity caused by the injection problem. Suppose that from a symbol table it is known that `f` is declared to be a function from `Expression` to `Identifier`. This provides a type-context that selects the transition to `Expression` rather than the transition to `Identifier`.

Class 3.4. Dealing with Ambiguous Anti-quoting. This is the dual of the previous class. The `Term -> ` X productions cause that at any part of the object language can contain a piece of meta language. We transit from the meta grammar into the object grammar. The only pieces of meta language allowed are produced by the `Term` non-terminal. The typing context is again provided by

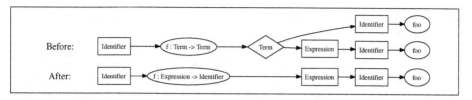

Fig. 5. An abstract syntax forest (drawn from left to right) is disambiguated by using a type declaration for the function **f**

the meta language, but now from below. Suppose the result type of the nested meta language construct is declared X, then we filter all alternatives that do not use the `Term -> ` X transition.

Discussion. To implement the above four filters a recursive traversal of the forest is needed. It applies context information on the way down and brings back type information on the way back. Note that the typing contexts necessary for the above may be inconclusive. For example, with *overloaded* methods in Java a type-checker may not be able to decide which is which. In general, when several ambiguities remain, a disambiguation type-checker may either choose to precisely report the conflict, or continue and use some of the filters discussed in the following.

4.3   Class 4. Object Language and Meta Language Overlap

The most common example in this class is how to separate meta variables from normal identifiers in the object syntax (Section 2). Other examples are more complex: the meta and object program fragments must accidentally have exactly the same syntax, and both provide type-correct interpretations. The following example illustrates this. The meta language is ASF+SDF, and the object language is Java:

```
equations
[] int[] foo = int[]
[] foo = bar
```

```
equations
[] int[] foo = int[][] foo = bar
```

The overlapping language constructs are the fragments: "[]" and "=". For ASF+SDF, the "[]" is an empty equation tag and "=" is the equation operator, while in Java "[]" is a part of an array declarator and "=" is the initializer part. The parser returns two alternative interpretations. The first has two equations, the second only one. By using suggestive layout, and printing the ASF+SDF symbols in *italics*, we illustrate how the right-hand side of the first rule can be extended to be a two dimensional array declarator that is initialized by **bar**: the combination of "[]" overlapping with array declarators and "=" overlapping with variable initializers leads to the ambiguity. Both interpretations are syntactically correct and type-correct. Note that the above example depends on a particular Java object grammar.

To solve this class of rare and hard to predict ambiguities we introduce a separate meta disambiguation phase (Fig. 4). A number of implicit but obvious rules will provide a full separation between meta and object language. The rules are not universal. Each meta programming language may select different ones applied in different orders. Still, the design space can be limited to a number of choices:

Rule 1: Prefer/avoid declared meta identifiers over object identifiers.
Rule 2: Prefer simpler/more complex object language derivations.
Rule 3: Maximize/minimize the number of meta language productions.
Rule 4: Propose explicit quoting to the user.

Rule 1 is a generalization of the variable preference rule (Section 2). All meta level identifiers, such as function names and variables are preferred. This rule may involve counting the number of declared meta identifiers in two alternatives and choosing the alternative with the least or most meta identifiers.

Rule 2 is needed only when the type context is not specific down to a first order type, but does impose some constraints. This can happen in systems with polymorphic operators, like Haskell functions, or the overloaded methods of Java, or the equations of ASF+SDF. For example: a function with type $f: a \rightarrow a \rightarrow b$ maps two objects of any type a to another object of type b. Even though the function is parameterized by type, the first two arguments must be of the same type. In the presence of injections like $X \rightarrow Y$, any X can also be a Y. If the first argument of the function f can be parsed as an X, it could also be parsed as a Y. Rule 2 then decides whether the "simpler" X or the more "complex" Y interpretation is picked.

Rule 3 expresses that object language fragments should be either as short, or as long as possible. The more meta productions are used, the shorter object fragments become. This takes care of our earlier example involving the "[]" and "=".

Rule 4. If Rule 3 fails, Rule 4 provides the final fail-safe to all ambiguities introduced by merging the meta and object syntax.

Discussion. The above rules have a heuristic nature and their semantics depend on the order in which they are applied. They should always be applied after the type-checker, such that only degenerate cases are subject to these rules. Another viewpoint is to avoid the application of these heuristics altogether, and propose explicit disambiguations to the user when necessary.

5   Experience

Parsing. This work has been applied to parsing ASF+SDF specifications. First the syntax of ASF+SDF was extended to make the meta language more complex: a generic expression language was added that can be arbitrarily nested with object language syntax. Before there were only meta variables in ASF+SDF, now we can nest meta language function calls at arbitrary locations into object language patterns, even with parametric polymorphism. Then a syntax merger was developed that generates the transitions, and priorities for filtering cycles. The generated parsers perform efficiently, while producing large parse forests.

Type Based Disambiguation. Both experience with post-parsing disambiguation filters in ASF+SDF [14], and the efficient implementation of type-inference algorithms for languages as Haskell and ML suggests that our cycle removal and type-checking disambiguation phase can be implemented efficiently. Knowing the polynomial upper-bound for the size of parse forests, we have implemented a type-checker for ASF+SDF that applies the above described basic disambiguation rules. Note that the equation operator of ASF+SDF can be viewed as a parametric polymorphic operator, but we have not yet experimented with user-defined polymorphic parameters.

Furthermore, in [5] we described a related disambiguation architecture that also employs disambiguation by type checking. In this approach we show how such an architecture can remove the need for explicitly typed quotes, but not the need for explicit quoting in general. We applied the disambiguation by type checking design pattern to Java as a meta programming language. A Java type checker is used to disambiguate object language patterns. As reported, such an algorithm performs very well. We further improve on these results in this paper, removing the need for explicit quotes altogether.

6 Conclusion

An architecture for parsing meta programs with concrete syntax was presented. By using implicit transitions syntactic hedges are avoided. We offered a "quote inference" algorithm, that allows a programmer to remove syntactic hedges if so desired. Inferring quotes is a feasible algorithm due to sharing and memoization techniques of parse forests. We use a three-tier architecture, that efficiently detects syntax transitions and then resolves ambiguities, including cycles, or returns precise error messages. Resolving ambiguities occurs either on simple structural arguments, or on typing arguments, or optionally based on heuristics.

References

1. McCarthy, J., Abrahams, P.W., Edwards, D.J., Hart, T.P., Levin, M.I.: LISP 1.5 Programmer's Manual. The MIT Press, Cambridge, Mass. (1966)
2. Sellink, M., Verhoef, C.: Native patterns. In Blaha, M., Quilici, A., Verhoef, C., eds.: Proceedings of the Fifth Working Conference on Reverse Engineering, IEEE Computer Society Press (1998) 89–103
3. Heering, J., Hendriks, P., Klint, P., Rekers, J.: The syntax definition formalism SDF - reference manual. SIGPLAN Notices **24** (1989) 43–75

4. Brand, M.v.d., Scheerder, J., Vinju, J., Visser, E.: Disambiguation Filters for Scannerless Generalized LR Parsers. In Horspool, R.N., ed.: Compiler Construction (CC'02). Volume 2304 of LNCS., Springer-Verlag (2002) 143–158

5. Bravenboer, M., Vermaas, R., Vinju, J., Visser, E.: Generalized type-based disambiguation of meta programs with concrete object syntax. In: Generative Programming and Component Engineering (GPCE). (2005) to appear.

6. Leavenworth, B.M.: Syntax macros and extended translation. Commun. ACM **9** (1966) 790–793

7. Aasa, A., Petersson, K., Synek, D.: Concrete syntax for data objects in functional languages. In: Proceedings of the 1988 ACM conference on LISP and functional programming, ACM Press (1988) 96–105

8. Zook, D., Huang, S.S., Smaragdakis, Y.: Generating AspectJ programs with MetaAspectJ. In Karsai, G., Visser, E., eds.: Generative Programming and Component Engineering: Third International Conference, GPCE 2004. Volume 3286 of Lecture Notes in Computer Science., Vancouver, Canada, Springer (2004) 1–19

9. Brand, M., Deursen, A., Heering, J., Jong, H., Jonge, M., Kuipers, T., Klint, P., Moonen, L., Olivier, P.A., Scheerder, J., Vinju, J., Visser, E., Visser, J.: The ASF+SDF Meta-Environment: a Component-Based Language Development Environment. In Wilhelm, R., ed.: CC'01. Volume 2027 of LNCS., Springer-Verlag (2001) 365–370

10. Visser, E.: Stratego: A language for program transformation based on rewriting strategies. System description of Stratego 0.5. In Middeldorp, A., ed.: RTA'01. Volume 2051 of LNCS., Springer-Verlag (2001) 357–361

11. Visser, E.: Meta-programming with concrete object syntax. In Batory, D., Consel, C., eds.: Generative Programming and Component Engineering (GPCE'02). Volume 2487 of LNCS., Springer-Verlag (2002)

12. Cordy, J., Halpern-Hamu, C., Promislow, E.: TXL: A rapid prototyping system for programming language dialects. Computer Languages **16** (1991) 97–107

13. Klint, P., Visser, E.: Using filters for the disambiguation of context-free grammars. In Pighizzini, G., San Pietro, P., eds.: Proc. ASMICS Workshop on Parsing Theory, Milano, Italy, Tech. Rep. 126–1994, Dipartimento di Scienze dell'Informazione, Università di Milano (1994) 1–20

14. Brand, M., Klusener, S., Moonen, L., Vinju, J.: Generalized Parsing and Term Rewriting - Semantics Directed Disambiguation. In Bryant, B., Saraiva, J., eds.: Third Workshop on Language Descriptions Tools and Applications. Volume 82 of Electronic Notes in Theoretical Computer Science., Elsevier (2003)

15. Aho, A., Sethi, R., Ullman, J.: Compilers. Principles, Techniques and Tools. Addison-Wesley (1986)

16. Paakki, J.: Attribute grammar paradigms: a high-level methodology in language implementation. ACM Comput. Surv. **27** (1995) 196–255

17. Milner, R.: A theory of type polymorphism in programming. Journal of Computer and System Sciences **17** (1978) 348–375

18. Johnson, M.: The computational complexity of GLR parsing. In Tomita, M., ed.: Generalized LR Parsing. Kluwer, Boston (1991) 35–42

19. Billot, S., Lang, B.: The structure of shared forests in ambiguous parsing. In: Proceedings of the 27th annual meeting on Association for Computational Linguistics, Morristown, NJ, USA, Association for Computational Linguistics (1989) 143–151

20. Brand, M., Jong, H., Klint, P., Olivier, P.: Efficient Annotated Terms. Software, Practice & Experience **30** (2000) 259–291

21. Vinju, J.: A type driven approach to concrete meta programming. Technical Report SEN-E0507, CWI (2005)

Dynamic Imperative Languages for Runtime Extensible Semantics and Polymorphic Meta-programming

Anthony Savidis

Institute of Computer Science, Foundation for Research and Technology – Hellas,
GR-70013, Heraklion, Crete, Greece
as@ics.forth.gr

Abstract. Dynamically typed languages imply runtime resolution for type matching, setting-up an effectible ground for type-polymorphic functions. In statically typed object-oriented languages, operator overloading signifies the capability to statically extend the language semantics in the target program context. We show how the same can be accomplished dynamically in the Delta dynamic language, through simple member-function naming contracts. Additionally, we provide a software-pattern for dynamically extensible function semantics, something that cannot be accommodated with static function overloading. We demonstrate how meta-programming, i.e. crafting of parametric program capsules solving generic problems known as meta-algorithms or meta-components, become truly polymorphic, i.e. can accept an open set of parameter values, as far as those dynamically bind to eligible elements compliant to the meta-program design contract. In Delta, inheritance is dynamically supported as a runtime function, without any compile-time semantics, while all member function calls are resolved through late binding. We employ those features to show how Delta supports the imperative programming of polymorphic higher-order functions, such as generic function composers or the map function.

1 Introduction

Statically typed compiled languages have been widely deployed for the implementation of typical stand-alone software applications, while interpreted dynamically typed languages became mostly popular as a means to support web application development. Dynamic languages not only enable rapid development, but also facilitate far more flexible and open component reuse and deployment. The lack of static type matching enables truly polymorphic programming templates, relying on late binding and conformance to predefined design contracts, in the deployment program context. A superset of key features met in existing imperative dynamic languages like Python (http://www.python.org/), Lua (Ierusalimschy et al., 1996), and ECMA Script (ECMA, 2004), encompasses: dynamically typed variables, prototype-based runtime classes, functions as first-class values, support for unnamed functions, dynamic handling of actual arguments, and extensible operator semantics.

We extend this set of features, in the context of the Delta language, by introducing: (a) prototypes with member functions being independent callable first-class values, as

N. Guelfi and A. Savidis (Eds.): RISE 2005, LNCS 3943, pp. 113 – 128, 2006.

atomic pairs holding both the function address and the alterable owner instance; (b) dynamic inheritance, having entirely runtime semantics, in comparison to the traditional compile-time inheritance operators; (c) a programming recipe for runtime extensible function semantics; and (d) an enhanced operator overloading technique. We also show how polymorphic programming of software patterns is possible, relying on the dynamic language features. The latter is only partially accommodated in statically typed OO languages, for types conforming to predefined super-types, once the LSP (Liskov, 1988) design contract is not broken. Finally, we demonstrate the way polymorphic higher-order functions, such as function generators, are implementable through functor object instances.

1.1 Link to Rapid Integration of Software Engineering Techniques

The key contribution of dynamic languages in the context of rapid integration of software engineering techniques concerns their genuine capability to accommodate quickly advanced software patterns like: extensible semantics, higher-order functions, coupling-relieved dynamic inheritance, and polymorphic pattern programming. Due to the inherent type-dynamic nature of such languages, the transition from generic design capsules to concrete algorithmic meta-programs is straightforward, as there are no syntactic constructs that introduce unnecessary type-domain restrictions, like typed arguments, typed function signatures, or compile-time base classes.

It is argued that software engineering is by no means independent of the adopted programming language, as languages may severely affect, infect, advance, or define the particular software engineering code of practice. For instance, Eiffel (Meyer, 1997) by semantically and syntactically reflecting an innovative software design recipe requires explicitly programmers to assimilate and apply the Design by Contract method. This way, the language itself provides an effective safety net ensuring developers cannot deviate from the design prescription itself.

Dynamic languages make it implementationally easier, while syntactically more economic, to practice the implementation of generic functions and directly programmable program patterns, thus leading to easily manageable reusable code units. But in the mean time, due to complete lack of compile-time safety, they require algorithmic type-check safeguards, that, when implemented in a less than prefect manner, may unnecessarily compromise both code quality and runtime performance.

2 Prototypes as Instance Factories

In the Delta language, prototypes are runtime class values, from which instances are dynamically produced through *replication*. In this context, following the recipe of existing dynamic languages, object classes never appear within the source code in the form of compile-time manifested types, but only as first-class runtime values called *prototypes*. The characteristics of prototypes in the Delta language are:

❑ They are associative table objects, having no prototype-specialized compile-time or runtime semantics; prototypes are normal object instances, chosen by programmers to play the role of class-instance generators, thus prototypes are effectively a design pattern combined with a deployment contract;

❏ There are no reserved constructor functions; construction is implemented through programmer-decided *factory* member functions, primarily relying on instance cloning.

Associative tables constitute the sole object model in the Delta language, offering indexed member access through late binding; *member* functions are allowed inside associative-table construction expressions, i.e. enumeration of member elements between [and]. Such table construction expressions are called *prototype definition* expressions. Member functions have the following key properties:

❏ They are typical table members, associated by default to the constructed table instance; however, the owner instance of a member function can be dynamically altered, while it is not required to be an instance of the original prototype, i.e. the prototype whose definition syntactically encompasses the member function definition;

❏ New member functions can be also installed to a table instance dynamically, i.e. outside the syntactic context of the respective prototype definition;

❏ Within member function definitions, the keyword *self* always resolves dynamically to the runtime owner table instance;

❏ The value of a member function itself is directly callable, internally, being an atomic pair of the owner instance and function address; upon call, members will resolve *self* references to their owner instance value. This way, member function calls do not syntactically require an object instance expression, as it is the case with C++, Java, ECMA Script or Lua.

The dotted syntax, e.g. p.x is syntactically equivalent to p["x"], where member x binding within p always takes place during runtime. This is similar to name-based late binding in Lua methods and ECMA Script member functions. This dynamic form of late-binding can be openly deployed for any object instance, once the object caters to dynamically resolve to the referred named members. However, this behavior is not accomplishable in statically typed languages, as compile-time conformance of the object instance and the referenced member is required to a specific type inheritance hierarchy and function signature, respectively. Moreover, late binding in dynamic languages is straightforward for data members too, something that is not accommodated in statically typed languages. A *member* function in Delta is an unnamed value; it is referenceable through the programmer decided index value. A function definition inside parenthesis, like for instance (member() {return copy(self);}), is a function value expression, internally carrying the function address; the same form is applicable to non-member functions as well.

In Fig. 1, one of the possible ways to implement prototypes in Delta is outlined. Following this method, prototypes are stored in static local variables, inside their respective prototype-returning function, e.g. PointProto(). The prototype is constructed as a model-instance, offering a set of members chosen by the programmer. It should be noted that none of the following member function names appearing in Fig. 1, like clone instance production function, new constructor function, and class reflecting the prototype name, is enforced by the Delta semantics, but those are freely chosen by the programmer.

```
function PointProto() { // Prototype extraction function
        static proto;
        if (typeof(proto)=="Undefined") // First time called.
            proto = [
                    {"x", "y" : 0 },
                    {"class"  : "Point" },
                    {"clone"  : (member(){return copy(self);})}
                    {"new"    : (member(x,y) { // Constructor.
                                 p = self.clone();
                                 p.x = x, p.y = y;
                                        return p;
                                 } ) }
                    ];
        return proto;
}
p1 = PointProto().new(30, 40);    // Via prototype constructor
p2 = p1.clone();                  // By instance replication
fc = p1.clone;                    // Getting p1 "clone" member
p2 = fc();                        // Calls p1 "clone" member
```

Fig. 1. Examples of simple prototype implementation and use

2.1 Details on Object Oriented Extensions to Deployment of Associative Tables

Associative tables (or tables) play a key role in the Delta language: (a) they are the only built-in aggregate type; and (b) they provide the ground for object-oriented programming. Tables are stored in variables by reference, so assignment or parameter passing semantics does not imply any kind of copy, while comparison is also done by reference. Within a table, indexing keys of any type may be used to store associated values of any type. Tables grow dynamically; they can be constructed through a table constructor expression, while individual elements can be easily added or removed. The expression [] constructs an empty table, while [{"x":0}] makes a table with a single element, with value 0, indexed by the *string* key "x". Table instance elements can be removed by setting the corresponding value to *nil*, implying that *nil* cannot be stored within a table. Hence, t.x = nil; causes the entry indexed by key "x" within t to be directly removed. Finally, the following library functions are provided:

➢ *tabindices(t₁)*, returning a new constructed table t_2 where: $\forall$ pair of index and associated value $(K_j, V_j) \in t_1$, $j \in [0, N)$, N being the total stored values in t_1, the pair (j, K_j) is added in t_2. That is, a table with all keys indexed by ordered consecutive integer values is returned. The way the ordering of keys is chosen is implementation dependent (i.e. undefined).

➢ *tablength(t₁)*, returning N being the total stored values in t_1.

➢ *tabcopy(t₁)*, returning a new constructed table t_2 where: $\forall$ pair of index and associated value $(K_j, V_j) \in t_1$, $j \in [0, N)$, N being the total stored values in t_1, the pair (K_j, V_j) is added in t_2. That is, an exact copy of t_1 is returned. The *tabcopy* function is implemented by using *tabindices* and *tablength* as follows:

```
function tabcopy(t1) {
    for (t2=[], ti=tabindices(t1), n=tablength(ti)-1; n>=0;
--n)
        t2[ti[n]] = t1[ti[n]];
    return t2;
}
```

In prototype definitions through associative tables, there is no support for a built-in destructor function in the Delta language. Although Delta is a language supporting automatic garbage collection, it was decided to separate memory disposal, taking place when tables can no longer be referenced via program variables, from the particular application-specific object destruction or clean-up logic. This decision is backed-up by the following remark:

➢   Application objects need to be cancelled exactly when the application logic decides that the relevant destruction conditions are met. In such cases, all corresponding cancellation actions, which actually implement the application-specific policy for the internal reflection of the cancellation event, are performed as needed. Once application-specific actions are applied, memory disposal takes place only at the point there is no program variable assigned to particular the subject object instance. Hence, it is clear that memory disposal is semantically thoroughly separated from application-oriented object lifetime control and instance cancellation (i.e. destruction).

It should be noted that the use of *tabcopy* should be avoided when there are member functions in tables, since their internal owner table reference is not changed but is copied as it is. Instead, the *copy(t₁)* should be employed, which in addition to *tabcopy*, performs the following:

➢   Let t_2 be the returned copy of t_1. Then, $\forall$ member function value $(F,T) \in t_1$, if $T = t_1$, then add (F, t_2) in t_2 else add (F, t_1) in t_2. In other words, member function values of the original table become member function values of the table copy. The functioning of *copy* is not recursive, meaning in case of member instances programmers have to take care for proper instance *copy* as well.

3 Dynamic Inheritance

Inheritance is based on dynamic associations of the form $\alpha \swarrow \beta$ (α derived from β) and $\beta \nearrow \alpha$ (β inherits to α), to reflect that table instance α inherits directly from table instance β. This association defines an inheritance tree, where, if γ is a predecessor of δ, then we define that δ is derived from γ, symbolically $\delta \leftarrow \gamma$, while γ is also said to be a *base* instance for δ. The establishment of an inheritance association $\alpha \swarrow \beta$ is regulated by the precondition:

$$\alpha \neq \beta \wedge \neg \beta \leftarrow \alpha \wedge \neg (\exists \gamma : \gamma \neq \beta \wedge \gamma \swarrow \beta)$$

This precondition formalizes the fact that an instance: (a) cannot inherit from its self; (b) cannot inherit from any of its derived instances; and (c) can inherit to at most one instance. In the Delta language, the following basic library functions are provided for dynamic management of inheritance associations among table instances:

❑ *inherit(t$_\alpha$, t$_\beta$)*, which establishes the associations $t_\alpha \swarrow t_\beta$ and $t_\beta \nearrow t_\alpha$
❑ *uninherit(t$_\alpha$, t$_\beta$)*, which cancels the association $t_\alpha \swarrow t_\beta$ and $t_\beta \nearrow t_\alpha$
❑ *isderived(t$_\alpha$, t$_\beta$)*, returning, *true* if $t_\alpha \leftarrow t_\beta$, else *false*

In Delta, inheritance is a runtime function applied on instances, establishing an augmented member-binding context for derived instances. The metaphoric *isa* connotation of base and derived classes are not entirely adopted in Delta, since *inherit(x, y)* doesn't state that *x isa y*, neither that *x* depends implementationally on *y*; it only defines augmented member binding for both *x* and *y*, i.e. if a member requested for *x* or *y* is not found in *x* (derived), then try to find it in *y* (base).

3.1 Dynamic Virtual Base Classes

In a given inheritance hierarchy *I* with most derived class *C*, a virtual base class *B* is a class required to be inherited only *once* by *C*, irrespective of how many times *B* appears as a base class in *I*. In statically typed OOP languages, compilers "know" the static inheritance hierarchy, so they construct appropriate memory models for derived classes having a single constituent instance per virtual base class. In the context of dynamic inheritance, the same behavior is accomplished with the special form of virtual inheritance programmed as shown in Fig. 2.

```
function virtually_inherit(derived, base) {
        t = allbaseinstances(derived);
        for (n = tablength(t) - 1; n >= 0; --n)
              if (t[n].class == base.class)
                    return;
        inherit(derived, base);
}
```

Fig. 2. Implementation of virtual dynamic inheritance

Its implementation uses the allbaseinstances(x) library function, returning a numerically indexed table encompassing references to all base instances of x. The function virtually_inherit is actually supplied as a library function in Delta for convenience. In the implementation of Fig. 2, we need only seek for a base instance whose class name matches the supplied base instance argument. If such an instance is found, i.e. derived already inherits from base, inheritance is not reapplied. However, we have also extended the virtually_inherit library function to enable dynamically the conditional update of the current virtual base instance with the supplied base argument.

3.2 Member Resolution in Dynamic Inheritance Chains

Inheritance associations define an augmented way for late binding of instance members, reflecting the fundamental priority of member versions in *derived* instances over the member versions of *base* instances, within inheritance hierarchies. Additionally, programmers may qualify member bindings as *bounded*, when there is a need to employ the original member versions of base instances, as opposed to the refined ones. The member-binding algorithm is a tree search algorithm, as shown in Fig. 3.

```
bind (t, x, bounded) {
        if (bounded = true and x ∈ t ) then
                return t.x
        V = {}                  /* V holds visited base instances */
        r = resolve({ t.root }, x)  /*'root' denotes the most derived instance */
        if ( r ≠ nil ) then
                return r.x
        else
                return nil
}
resolve (S, x) {
        L = {}    /* Set of all base instances for the instances of S*/
        for ( each t ∈ S where t ∉ V ) do {
                if ( x ∈ t ) then
                        return t
                V = V ∪ { t }
                L = L ∪ t.base     /* 't.base' is a set of 't' base instances */
        }
        if ( L ≠ ∅ ) then
                return resolve(L, x)
        else
                return nil
}
```

Fig. 3. Member binding logic within instance inheritance chains; notice that *root* denotes the most derived instance in an instance inheritance hierarchy

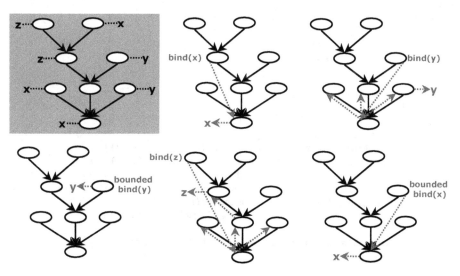

Fig. 4. Examples of member search paths (dotted arrows) for late binding of different members in an instance inheritance hierarchy; the shaded tree indicates the real member storage, while the most derived instance is actually the *root* instance

Following Fig. 3 (left), in case the *bounded* flag (i.e. bounded use) of the *bind* function is *true*, resolution of *x* directly in instance *t* is performed. Otherwise, i.e. ¬ *bounded* ∨ *x* ∉ *t*, the resolution function *resolve* is called, which performs a breadth-first search starting from the root, i.e. the most derived instance in the runtime inheritance tree. This search always returns the first member resolution closest to the inheritance root (most derived instance). In Fig. 4, a few examples are provided regarding the alternative search paths, to resolve particular members within an instance inheritance hierarchy. The distinction of table instances into either object prototypes or object instances is a semantic separation in the context of the program design, not reflecting any particular built-in language semantics for associative tables. Similarly, the semantics of the inheritance-association management functions concern table instances in general, without any operational differentiation for either object prototypes or object instances. This feature allows:

❑ *Dynamically installable/removable inheritance*, facilitated by connecting/disconnecting a complete instance inheritance sub-hierarchy to/from the target instance, through a call to *inherit/uninherit* library function.

4 Function Overloading Pattern

The deployment of unnamed functions, dynamic manipulation of actual arguments, runtime type identification, and associative storage, allows the implementation of a

```
function sig(t) {
    for (s = "", n = tablength(t), i = 0; i < n; ++i)
        s += typeof(t[i]);
    if (s == "")    return "void";
    else            return s;
}
function overloaded() {
    static dispatcher;
    if (typeof(dispatcher) == "Undefined")
        dispatcher = [
            {"NumberNumber" : ( function(x,y) {...}) },
            {"StringString" : ( function(a,b) {...}) },
            {"Table"        : ( function(t)   {...}) },
            {"void"         : ( member() { return self; })},
            {"install"      : ( member(sig, f) {
                                  self[sig] = f; })}
        ];
    return dispatcher[sig(arguments)] (|arguments|);
}
function added (x, s) {...}
overloaded().install("NumberString", added);
```

Fig. 5. Dynamic function overloading for extensible function semantics

dynamic function-overloading pattern, relying on runtime management of alternative function versions through string-based signatures. It is a software pattern in the sense that it is not a built-in language mechanism, but an accompanying language-specific programming recipe for dynamically extensible function semantics. The programming pattern for function overloading is illustrated in Fig. 5, with an example function supporting three alternative signatures. As it is shown, overloaded functions encapsulate a static local dispatch table, named dispatcher, storing the alternative

```
function sig(t) {
       for (s = "", n = tablength(t), local i = 0; i < n; ++i)
              if (typeof(t[i])=="table" and t[i].class != nil)
                     s += t[i].class;
              else
                     s += typeof(t[i]);
       return s=="" ? "void" : s;
}


function metaconstructor() {
       return [
              {"construct" : (member() {
                     f = self.constructors[sig(arguments)];
                     return f(|arguments|);
              })}
       ];
}
proto = [
    {  "constructors" : [
       { "void" : (function(){ return copy(proto); }) },
       { "numbernumber" :   // Parameterized constructor
         (function(x,y){
             p = copy(proto); p.x = x; p.y = y; return p; }) },
       { "Point" :          // Copy constructor
         (function(pt){ return proto.construct(pt.x, pt.y); })}
       ]
    }
];
inherit(proto, metaconstructor());

function midpointconstructor(p1,p2) {
       p = copy(PointProto());      // Instantiate from prototype
       p.x = (p1.x+p2.x)/2;         // Initialize members
       p.y = (p1.y+p2.y)/2;
       return p;                    // Return the new instance
}

// Installing the constructor at the prototype
PointProto().constructors.PointPoint = midpointconstructor;
```

Fig. 6. The meta-constructor pattern for dynamic constructor overloading. Notice that to allow dynamically installed constructors, those are turned to non-member functions.

implemented versions as embedded unnamed functions. The actual argument expression |*table*| unrolls all elements of *table*, as if those where supplied by distinct actual expressions (i.e. "pushed" on the arguments' stack); this is similar to the ∗ operator for sequences in Python. Also, arguments is a reserved local variable (of table type) carrying all actual arguments of the current call (numerically indexed). Thus, |arguments| propagates the actual arguments of the present call to an encapsulated delegate function invocation.

If overloaded is called without arguments, it returns a handle to the internal dispatcher table, offering the install member function to dynamically add / remove / update a function version for arguments signature sig (in Delta, removal of a table element is equivalent to setting nil as the element value).

4.1 Dynamic Constructor Overloading

Overloaded constructors basically follow the dynamic function-overloading pattern previously discussed (see Fig. 5). Additionally, such alternative constructors can be dynamically extensible, meaning argument conversion and instance initialization functions can be installed on the fly as needed, either at an instance or prototype level.

We will slightly modify the sig function which extracts the type-signature of the actual argument list to cater for object-instance arguments in the following manner: if an argument is of type "table", then if it has a "class" member, its value is asserted to be of "string" type and its content is returned as the type value; else, the "table" type is returned. As it is shown in Fig. 6, all constructors are dynamically collected in one member-table of the object prototype named "constructors", while the dynamic installation of a particular constructor requires the provision of a unique signature and a corresponding constructor function. Also, the meta-construction functionality is named "construct", internally dispatching to the appropriate signature-specific constructor, is implemented as an inherited member function, meaning it can be directly re-used. One important modification of this overloaded constructor in comparison to the function-overloading pattern is that the overloaded constructor functions are now non-member functions. The latter is necessary once we decide to allow dynamically installable constructors, effectively requiring that such constructor functions can be defined externally to table constructor definitions, i.e. being non-member functions.

5 Operator Overloading Contract

In Delta the semantics of all binary operators are dynamically extensible for table object instances through the following implementation technique:

❑ *eval*(t_1 *op* ^{binary} t_2). If there is a t_1 member named *op* being actually a function *f*, the result of evaluation is $f(t_1, t_2)$. Otherwise, the original semantics for t_1 *op* t_2 are applied.
❑ *eval*(*op* ^{unary} t_1). If there is a t_1 member named *op* being actually a function *f*, the result of evaluation is $f(t_1)$. Otherwise, the original semantics for t_1 *op* t_2 are applied.

In the current implementation, this method applies to most binary operators in Delta, like arithmetic and associative operators, as well as the function call () and the table

member access operators. For prefix and postfix unary operators -- and ++, the +
and - binary operators need to be only overloaded. Boolean operators are excluded as
short-circuit boolean evaluation diminishes boolean operators from the target code.
However, different Delta implementations may override short-circuit code and introduce boolean instructions in the virtual machine, meaning overloading can be also
supported in this case. Regarding table member access, we distinguish among read /
write access through "[]" (read access) and "[]=" (write access), also covering the
use of "." supplied in place of "[]" for syntactic convenience. Once table member
access is overloaded, the native operator is hidden unless the member is temporarily
removed and reinstalled again; this is possible with the explicit non-overloaded member access functions tabget and tabset. Finally, for unary operators: **not** requires
overloading of !=, and unary minus requires overloading of multiplication operator
with numbers (-x it is calculated as x*-1).

To make binary operators more efficient we distinguish the position of the primary
table argument with a dot, so there are two member versions; e.g. ".+" and "+.".
The operator overloading approach in Delta is very simple, yet very powerful. *Overloaded operators constitute normal members distinguishable uniquely through a
naming contract being part of the language semantics.* This makes operators directly
derivable through dynamic inheritance, since, as normal object members, they are
also subject to late binding; finally, operator functions as first-class values are dynamically extractable, removable or substitutable. An example showing operator
overloading is provided in Fig. 7.

```
function Polygon() {
    static proto = [
        {"area"         : (member(){...})},
        {".<="          : (function(p1,p2) {
                              return p1.area() <= p2.area(); })},
        {".+"           : (function(p,x)   {
                              p[".+dispatch"][sig(x)](p,x); })},
        {".+dispatch" : [
                    {"Point"  : (function(a,b){…})},
                    {"Number" : (function(a,b){…})},
                    ]},
    ];
}

p1 = Polygon().new();
p2 = Polygon().new();
if (p1 <= p2)
        p1 = p2 + 10;
```

Fig. 7. Dynamic operator overloading for dynamically extensible language-operator semantics

6 Polymorphic Pattern Programming

Software patterns are defined as recurring solutions to common design problems
mostly provided as recipes having a standardised documentation, rather than as

directly reusable code. Since software patterns constitute meta-solutions, the capability to turn their documentation to an equally generic programmed artefact is really a matter of appropriate abstraction choices in the context of pattern implementation, and effective support for polymorphism in the context of pattern deployment. Theoretically, patterns are meta-programs, where *meta* accounts to type abstraction and polymorphism for constituent content or logic elements. Arguably, once the necessary type-abstraction and type-polymorphism support is provided, polymorphic pattern programming is directly accomplishable. It is clear that to enable generic polymorphism, the compile-time matching barrier needs to be effectively bypassed.

```
// Returns an instance of the 'State' pattern.
function StatePattern() {
    return [
        { "setstate" : (member(newState) {
            uninherit(self, self.State);
            inst = prototypes[self.class].States[newState].new();
            inherit(self, self.State = inst);
        })}
    ];
];

inherit(a, StatePattern());
a.setstate("foo");
```

Fig. 8. The reusable polymorphic *State* pattern implementation

We demonstrate the capability for polymorphic pattern programming for the *State* pattern (Gamma *et al.*, 1995), concerning classes supporting runtime updateable behaviors, the latter implemented as distinct classes. It is interesting to note that the *State* pattern implicitly exposes the need to support dynamic inheritance, since the *State* pattern was born as a design recipe to craft classes conditionally reflecting, during runtime different behavioral pictures. The implementation of a directly deployable polymorphic *State* pattern is shown in Fig. 8. Following Fig. 8, we choose to store at runtime any state-related prototype named *S*, for class-specific prototype named *A*, within prototypes[A].States[S]. The State pattern logic is actually consolidated in a single function performing the following actions:

❑ Cancels the inheritance association with the current base *State* instance self.State;
❑ Makes a new instance corresponding to the prototype of the new state, that is prototypes[self.class].States[newState];
❑ Establishes an inheritance association with the new base *State* instance, while setting the current *State* name, i.e. inherit(self, self.State = inst);

The runtime associations for the *State* pattern are shown in Fig. 9. The *"owns"* label indicates the instance in which members are actually stored, *"binds"* denotes members resolved via late-binding to a base / derived instance, while *"refers"* signifies members being instance references.

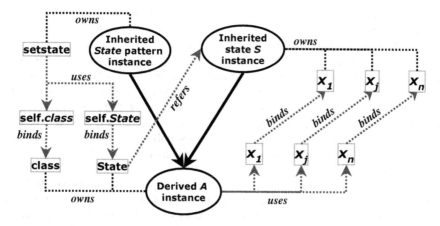

Fig. 9. The runtime associations for the *State* pattern and the way the various members are dynamically resolved; notice that the state-specific instance constitutes a dynamic base instance, rather than a delegate local instance as it is in the original implementation recipe (Gamma *et al.*, 1995)

7 Polymorphic Higher-Order Functions

Higher-order functions are functions taking functions as arguments and / or delivering functions as results; the most challenging case concerns function generators. Functional programming languages like Haskell (Peyton Jones, 2003) or Scheme (Abelson *et al.*, 1998) genuinely support the definition of generic (polymorphic) higher-order functions through the λ-lambda operator. Although dynamically typed languages easily overpass the signature-checking barrier, they only manage to allow polymorphic function generators once functions are treated as object instances by the underlying implementation, with their own call-persistent data members. In Python this is possible with an interpreted implementation, however compiled dynamically typed languages like Lua (Ierusalimschy et al., 1996) fail in this respect because they do not provide a truly object-oriented model for functions. In Delta, the implementation of

```
function compose(f, g) {
    return [
        { "f"  : f },
        { "g"  : g },
        { "()" : (member(){
                return self.f(|self.g(|arguments|)|); })}
    ];
}
mul           = function(x,y){ return x*y; });
sqrpair       = function(x,y){ return [ sqr(x), sqr(y) ]; });
mulsquares    = compose(mul, sqrpair);
x             = mulsquares(3, 7));
```

Fig. 10. A polymorphic function composer

function generators is straightforward: *they are functions returning table instances overloading the function call* () *operator; the latter are commonly called functors.* In Fig. 10, the implementation of a generic function composer is shown.

The compose function returns a table object instance which stores in local members the two functions (those need not be "normal" functions, but can be functors as well), while also overloading the call operator (), binding to a an appropriate member function. This member function performs firstly a call to *g*, propagating to it the actual arguments of the composed function via the |arguments| expression. Then, the return values of this call, collected in a table, are supplied as actual arguments to the *f* call, as |self.g(…)|. The result of *f* invocation is by definition the correct result of the composition.

Next we present the imperative implementation of three additional key polymorphic higher-order functions in the Delta language (see Fig. 11): (a) the *mapping* function, applying an argument function to all entries of a table; (b) the *const* function, transforming a value parameter to a mathematical constant function (i.e. always returning this value when called); and (c) the *delayed call* function, which accepts a function and its actual arguments, returning a function which is equivalent to this call.

```
function map(f, t) {
    for (ti = tabindices(t), n = tablength(ti)-1; n >= 0; --n)
        t[ti[n]] = f(t[ti[n]]);
}
function sqr(x) {
        if (typeof(x)=="number") return x*x; else return x;
}
t = [0, 1, 2, 3, 4, {"x", "y" : 4}, {"name" : "t"} ];
map(sqr, t); // Affects only numeric values, for all indices
function const(c) {
        t = [ {"c" : c}, {"f" : (member(){ return self.c; })} ];
        return t.f;
}
c_10 = const(10);
print(c_10());          // Prints "10"
c_hello = const("hello");
c_hello();              // Prints "hello"

function call(f) {
        for (args=[], n=tablength(arguments) - 1; n > 0; --n)
            args[n-1] = arguments[n]; // Shift indices left
        t = [ { "args" : args }, { "f" : f },
            { "call" : (member(){
                        return self.f (|self.args|); })}
            ];
        return t.call;
}
c = call(compose, mul, sqrpair);
print(c()(3, 2));    // Prints "36"
```

Fig. 11. Examples of additional polymorphic higher-order functions, with an imperative implementation in the Delta language

The programming of such higher-order functions in the Delta language is enabled by the deployment of two key features: (i member functions as distinct first-order values internally carrying both the member function address and the associated table instance; and (ii) late binding of actual arguments, supporting "transit" actual argument passing in a functional programming style. For instance, every call to the `const` higher-order function (see Fig. 11) constructs a table encompassing both the supplied value indexed by `"c"`, and a member function indexed by `"f"`, the latter returning the `"c"` member of its associated runtime table; effectively, the `const` function returns the member function value of the newly constructed table, i.e. a pair of the function address and constructed table instance.

8 Discussion and Conclusions

The benefits of introducing enhanced dynamic-language features, towards directly deployable polymorphic program capsules, can be argued and demonstrated, however, they cannot be largely predicted and projected. Since we lack theoretical frameworks to assess the computational necessity of constructs like polymorphic higher-order functions, dynamically extensible function semantics, or dynamic inheritance hierarchies, in an imperative programming context, it is hard to formally prove that their introduction always leads to an enhanced code of programming practice. Intuitively, truly dynamic languages enable a more natural and convenient mapping of abstract designs to source code units, while effectively enabling the accommodation of computable design decisions injected in the runtime logic, as static invariant associations and dependencies are diminished. This remark implies that there is a very strong impact of truly dynamic imperative languages on the software engineering of meta-programs and polymorphic code capsules. Practically, the main implications lay on the fact that meta-elements and parametric polymorphism become directly implementable, turning design patterns and software recipes to concrete program units. However, increased flexibility is usually paid by decreased safety. This is also true for the Delta language, as the programming flexibility offered by dynamic typing has to be eventually paid by the manual embedding of runtime type checking logic. This implies that all potential type conflicts are only detectable during runtime, meaning that the test units have to be designed in a way ensuring the exhaustive execution of all type safety guards. In this context, the dynamic function-overloading pattern provides a standard entry point to attack type conflicts, as well as potential functional extensions, either during development (manually encapsulating functions) or during runtime (signature-based installation of overloaded functions). While at present the object-oriented support offered by the Delta language is primarily focused on re-usability and polymorphism, the language misses the ingredients to facilitate encapsulation and information hiding. Although programmers currently follow the software pattern of accessing member variables only through member functions, language extensions may need to be introduced to support typical member access qualifiers such as `private` or `const`, to guard pattern conformance during execution. However, considering the semantics of Delta tables, such guards can be only accommodated in the form of runtime member-access check-points, meaning that more testing code is needed, to ensure that "information hiding" related qualifiers are always respected.

References

H. Abelson, R.K. Dybvig, C.T. Haynes, G.J. Rozas, N.I. Adams IV, D.P. Friedman, E. Kohl-becker, G.L. Steele Jr., D.H. Bartley, R. Halstead, D. Oxley, G.J. Sussman, G. Brooks, C. Hanson, K.M. Pitman, M. Wand (1998). *Revised Report on the Algorithmic Language Scheme*. Journal of Higher-order and Symbolic Computation, 11(1), pp. 7–105.

ECMA (2004). ECMA Script Language Specification. Available electronically from: http://www.ecma-international.org/publications/files/ECMA-ST/Ecma-262.pdf.

Gamma, E., Helm, R., Johnson,R., Vlissides, J. (1995). Design Patterns: Elements of Re-Usable Object-Oriented Software. Addison-Wesley.

Ierusalimschy, R., Henrique de Figueiredo, L., Celes Filho, W. (1996). Lua – an extensible extension language. Journal of Software Practice & Experience 26(6), pp. 635–652.

Liskov, B. (1988). Data Abstraction and Hierarchy, *SIGPLAN Notices*, 23,5 (May, 1988).

Meyer, B. (1997). *Object-Oriented Software Construction - Second Edition*. Prentice Hall, Santa Barbara, CA.

Peyton Jones, S. (2003). *Haskell 98 Language and Libraries*, Cambridge University Press.

Context-Aware Service Composition in Pervasive Computing Environments

Sonia Ben Mokhtar, Damien Fournier, Nikolaos Georgantas, and Valérie Issarny

INRIA Rocquencourt 78153 Le Chesnay, France
{Sonia.Ben_Mokhtar, Damien.Fournier, Nikolaos.Georgantas,
Valerie.Issarny}@inria.fr
http://www-rocq.inria.fr/arles/

Abstract. A major challenge in pervasive computing environments is to provide users with complex, context-sensitive applications, dynamically composed
from networked services. In this paper, we present an approach to the dynamic,
context-aware composition of services to perform user tasks, i.e., software applications abstractly described on the user's handheld device. Both networked
services and user tasks are modeled as semantic Web services in OWL-S extended
with context information. The distinctive feature of our solution is the ability to
compose Web services that expose complex behaviors (conversations) to realize
a user task that itself has a complex behavior. Furthermore, the context-related
requirements of the task are met by aggregating the context-sensitive behaviors
of the individual services.

1 Introduction

The user-centric view promoted by the pervasive computing paradigm advocates placing
less demand on user attention [25]. Thus, pervasive computing applications need to be
more autonomous and sensitive to context. In this domain, one of most challenging objectives to be achieved is to automatically enable software applications by dynamically
composing services of the pervasive environment. In this direction, our work presented
herein aims at enabling users to perform tasks (i.e., abstract user applications modeled as
workflows) on the fly by composing various networked service capabilities provided in
the pervasive environment. While service composition allows some degree of autonomy
to be achieved, context-awareness allows user applications to be more sensitive to the
environment's changes, leading to a higher level of autonomy and adaptation.

A number of research effort have been conducted in the area of context-aware
systems. In particular, various models have been proposed to represent context information, among which attributes and values models, object oriented models and ontologies.
Ontologies have proved to be the most suitable model for representing and reasoning on context information for the following reasons [5] : (i) ontologies enable knowledge sharing in open, dynamic systems; (ii) ontologies with well defined declarative
semantics allow efficient reasoning on context information; and (iii) ontologies enable
service interoperability and provide the means for networked services to collaborate
in a non-ambiguous manner. The Ontology Web Language (OWL[1]) is a recent W3C

---

[1] OWL: Ontology Web Language. http://www.w3.org/TR/owl-ref/

N. Guelfi and A. Savidis (Eds.): RISE 2005, LNCS 3943, pp. 129–144, 2006.

recommendation for formally specifying ontologies. A number of context ontologies proposed in the literature are based on OWL.

Most existing approaches to context-aware systems propose either a user-centric or a service-centric view of context. User-centric approaches promote applications that move with the users and follow their preferences [20]. Service-centric approaches promote service adaptability to the context changes [12]. We propose a solution that combines both views. Indeed, both users-related and services-related contextual requirements are taken into account in our approach to service composition. This leads us to extend the Ontology Web Language for Services (OWL-S[2]) for modeling services-related context but also user tasks contextual requirements. Our OWL-S-based model for services and user tasks has various advantages. First, our model captures both services-related and user-related context enabling service composition to effectively be context-sensitive. Second, as our model is based on OWL-S, it is easily extensible. Third, our model can employ any existing context ontology to describe context information.

We present in this paper a solution for context-aware service composition based on workflow integration. More precisely, both networked services and user tasks have workflow descriptions in OWL-S enriched with context, and our aim is to integrate services' workflows to realize a target user task, further enabling context-awareness.

The remainder of this paper is structured as follows. The next section introduces definition of context and context awareness and presents effort on modeling context. In Section 3, we present our context model extending OWL-S for modeling context-aware services and tasks. Then, we present our approach to context-aware service discovery and composition in Section 4. Further in Section 5, we employ a scenario inspired from the networked home environment, as investigated in the IST Amigo project[3], that we adopt in our work to illustrate our solution. Finally, in Section 6 we review related research effort in the area of context-aware service composition and conclude with a summary of our contribution and future work.

2 Background

In this section, we present our adopted definition of context and context-awareness (§2.1). We also survey various efforts that have been undertaken for modeling context (§2.2).

2.1 Context-Awareness

Definitions of context and context-awareness are rather subjective in the literature. We adopt the generic definitions proposed by Dey et al. [6]:

*"**Context** is any information that can be used to characterize the situation of an entity. An entity is a person, place, or object that is considered relevant to the interaction between a user and an application, including the user and application themselves."*

---

[2] OWL-S: Semantic Markup for Web Service. http://www.daml.org/services/owl-s

[3] Amigo: Ambient intelligence for the networked home environment.
http://www.extra.research.philips.com/euprojects/amigo/

*"**Context-awareness** is a property of a system that uses context to provide relevant information and/or services to the user, where relevancy depends on the user's task."*

Different categories of context can be distinguished. For example, Schilit defines three categories of context [21]: (i) *Device context*, which is contextual information related to devices, such as available CPU, memory, reachable networks etc.; (ii) *User context*, including the user's profile and preferences, but also information about the user's applications; and (iii) *Physical context* such as location, weather, light etc. All these contextual information coming from various entities in the environment (e.g., sensors, applications, devices) are heterogeneous and have to be represented in a well defined shared model in order to be understandable by user applications.

2.2   Context Modeling

Context modeling defines how context data are structured and maintained which play a key role in supporting efficient context management. Context modeling mainly relies on two important features [29]. First, it is essential to adopt a flexible structure with explicit concepts and associations to model knowledge, define semantic relations and enable data sharing and reuse. Second, logic reasoning or inference mechanisms on raw data are necessary to deduce high-level contextual information from low-level context data (e.g., sensed data). Choosing an adequate context model is crucial to enable context-aware services. We survey below, proposed approaches to model context information.

The most simple way to model and maintain context information is to define a set of context attributes and associated values. The most known system using this kind of model, is the PARC's mobile computing environment, proposed by Schilit *et al.* in [22]. This is an easy solution to enable sharing of context information among applications. But, although it is fast and easy to set and update context modeled with such a data structure, context-awareness is only possible if applications use attributes with the given names. Moreover, such a model is not sufficient for describing concepts and associations between them, and for making abstraction of raw data. Markup languages are another way to model contextual knowledge. Flexibility and structural properties are strong advantages of this approach. In context-aware systems, markup languages are commonly used to describe profiles. For example, CC/PP (Composite Capabilities / Preferences Profile) is an RDF-based language designed for describing user preferences and hardware capabilities, well suited for mobile computing. A number of research effort have been made to adapt CC/PP to define context (e.g., [9]). Markup languages are simple, flexible, structured, and seem to be suitable for pervasive computing. But, data ambiguity must be solved by applications, complex relationships between data can not be defined, and a more formal definition of context can not be expressed. Another approach to model context, lies in using object-oriented concepts [26]. Object-oriented modeling allows defining a structured and scalable context model. Object implementation further uses aggregation mechanisms for abstraction, retrieving high-level concepts and solving data ambiguity and consistency. But, object-oriented models are often defined for a specific context domain. Sharing data and interoperability between different context applications may be difficult. Ranganathan *et al.* [19], and Seng W. Loke [11] have tried to model context with predicates and logic deduction. Modeling context using first order logic allows higher-level context retrieval. However, this model lacks defining structures and relations between context information and does not resolve ambiguity between context data.

The last modeling approach that we consider in this section is the use of ontologies. Ontology-based models are very close to the requirements of context modeling. While the overall objective of using ontologies is to define common vocabularies, context modeling in pervasive computing uses ontology models to represent relevant information for users. Like many recent approaches, we choose to define context using ontologies built upon the Ontology Web Language (OWL) for the following reasons:

- Ontologies allow defining concepts, entities, properties and also relationships between concepts.
- Since OWL is based on RDF Schema, OWL ontologies can be validated with tools as Jena[4] or OWLP[5].
- OWL is dynamic and flexible, allowing context data to be easily added, deleted, and updated with programming interfaces for OWL (e.g., Jena, OWL API[6]).
- Many tools have been developed for reasoning on OWL ontologies to deduce abstract concepts (e.g., Racer[7], Jena).
- Knowledge sharing can be achieved between heterogeneous context sources.

Among recent approaches to ontology-based context modeling, SOUPA [5] and CONON [29] define two-level ontologies for context modeling. A core ontology defines generic concepts that are usually modeled in context such as platform or users, while more specific ontologies introduce concepts for a particular application domain such as characteristics of users and devices, and location (vertical extensions), or the definition of intelligent environments such as home or office (horizontal extensions). SOUPA also addresses security and privacy with the protection of users' personal information, and proposes a set of policies to restrict data access. CONON focuses on characterizing user situation with a set of user-defined first order logic rules. More generic, Preuveneers *et al.* in [17] define a simple context ontology which is easily extensible and allows the description of semantic Web services. Interoperability is also studied in [3], which proposes an approach for mapping concepts between different ontologies.

3   Modeling Context-Aware Services and Tasks

Our objective is to allow a user to perform a task any where and at any time, on the fly, without any previous knowledge about the services available in the environment. Moreover, accounting for both the user's actual context and the services' contextual requirements, but also ensuring a QoS that fulfills the requirements specified by the user. In our approach, we consider as QoS all context information related to resource consumption such as the device context (§2.1). In this paper, we focus on managing the remaining context information, such as user context and physical context, while QoS management has been described in [2].

---

[4] Jena: A Semantic Web Framework for Java. http://jena.sourceforge.net/

[5] OWLP: http://www-db.research.bell-labs.com/user/pfps/owlp/

[6] OWL API: sourceforge.net/projects/owlapi

[7] Racer: http://www.sts.tu-harburg.de/ r.f.moeller/racer/

3.1   OWL-S Based Context Model for Pervasive Services

Semantic Web services results from the combination of the Semantic Web and Web
Services. A number of research effort have been conducted in order to bring semantics to Web services [16, 7, 24]. These effort aim at the semantic specification
of Web Services towards automating Web services discovery, invocation, composition and execution monitoring. In this area, the Ontology Web Language for Services
(OWL-S) is the most complete effort for describing semantic Web services. Besides
describing high-level capabilities of services, OWL-S allows the description of services' behaviors using conversations. OWL-S defines Web services capabilities in
three parts: the Service Profile, the Process Model and the Service Grounding. The
Service Profile gives a high-level description of a service and its provider. It is generally used for service publication and discovery. The Process Model describes the
service's behavior as a process. This description contains the specification of a set
of sub-processes coordinated by a set of control constructs. These control constructs
are: Sequence, Split, Split + Join, Choice, Unordered, If-Then-Else, Repeat-
While, and Repeat-Until. The sub-processes can be either composite or atomic.
Composite processes are decomposable into other atomic or composite processes,
while atomic ones correspond to WSDL[8] operations. The Service Grounding specifies the information necessary for service invocation, such as underlying communication protocols, message formats, serialization, transport and addressing information.
The Service Grounding defines mapping rules to link OWL-S atomic processes to
WSDL operations.

In our approach, networked services are described in OWL-S extended with context information. This information decomposes to: (i) high-level context attributes;
and (ii) contextual preconditions and effects. A high-level context attribute makes a
service aware of some context information, such as location or physical conditions.
Then, the service may use this context information to provide the user with appropriate context-sensitive responses. Contextual preconditions are conditions to be fulfilled for the valid execution of a service, while contextual effects result from this execution and affect the current context. For example the operation Turn_On_The_Light
of a Light_Management_Service requires as preconditions that there is some one in
the room, the light level is low, and nobody is sleeping; this operation has as effect the
lighting of the corresponding room.

OWL-S allows the description of non-functional properties of services by extending the Service Profile ontology. Thus we extend the Service Profile to allow service
providers to specify context attributes that characterize a service (see Figure 1). In addition to this, as our composition approach involves services' atomic processes (operations) [1], further context information is needed at the atomic process level. This
context information is provided in the form of contextual preconditions and effects.
Thus, we propose to extend OWL-S to allow atomic processes to provide contextual
preconditions and effects. As shown in Figure 1, contextual preconditions and effects
are subclasses of the Condition and Expression classes defined in the OWL-S specification. These classes allow the description of logical expressions in the form of literals

---

[8] WSDL: Web Services Description Language. http://www.w3.org/TR/wsdl

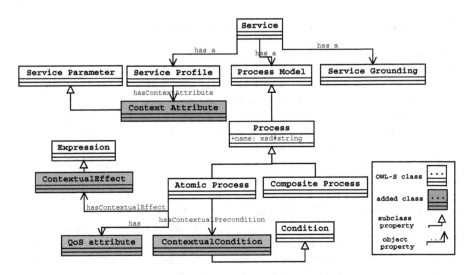

Fig. 1. Context-Aware Service Description

encoded in XML by using existing logic languages such as SWRL[9], KIF[10] and PDDL[11]. Another extension that we have introduced to OWL-S is the specification of QoS attributes at the atomic process level. This allows specifying, among others, resource consumption due to the invocation of a service operation. For example, based on execution histories a service can publish for each operation the latency induced by the invocation on this operation. This information can be further exploited to compose services in a way that fulfills the QoS requirements specified by the user task [2].

3.2   OWL-S Based Context Model for User Tasks

As for networked services, the description of the user task is given in the form of an abstract OWL-S process. Furthermore, we extend the OWL-S process description in order to allow the specification of non-functional requirements, such as QoS requirements and contextual conditions (see Figure 2). QoS requirements correspond to global requirements that have to be fulfilled by the resulting service composition (e.g., $latency < 2sec$, $availability > 80\%$). On the other hand, contextual conditions can be either global or local. A global contextual requirement has to be fulfilled by the resulting service composition. For example, a global contextual requirement can be: "the commission of a travel reservation composite service < 10 euros" or "the distance to be covered by the user wishing to use a printer and a scanner < 300 m". These global requirements have to be checked during the service composition, by aggregating contextual information provided by the individual services. Local contextual requirements

---

[9] SWRL: A Semantic Web Rule Language Combining OWL and RuleML.
  http://www.daml.org/2003/11/swrl/

[10] KIF: Knowledge Interchange Format. http://logic.stanford.edu/kif/kif.html

[11] PDDL: Planning Domain Definition Language. http://planning.cis.strath.ac.uk/competition/
  pddl.html

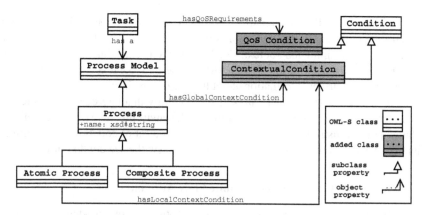

Fig. 2. User task description

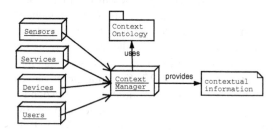

Fig. 3. Context manager service

are associated to a part of the task's description (some of the task's atomic processes) and have to be fulfilled by services' operations. For example, if the user task involves looking for a movie theater, the operation that will be selected will have to take into account the user's actual location and return to the user the nearest movie theater. Thus, the service providing this operation should have as a context attribute the physical distance awareness. Other examples of local contextual requirements can be the selection of the least loaded printer, or the selection of the road with least traffic. The main difference between user task descriptions and service descriptions is that in contrast to the atomic processes involved in the services processes, those involved in user task processes are not bound to any service, since services to be invoked are dynamically discovered. Thus the OWL-S Grounding corresponding to a task's process is generated at runtime from the Groundings of the composed services.

Context management associated with context-sensitive services relies on a context manager, which provides on demand contextual information in terms of a specific ontology as depicted in Figure 3. We do not enforce the use of a specific context ontology, any existing OWL-based context ontology can be used (e.g., [18, 5, 29, 17]). What we define is a model for services and tasks enabling context-aware service composition. This model can easily be used in conjunction with any OWL context ontology. In Figure 3, the context manager collects information from different entities that affects context (e.g., sensors, users, devices, etc.). Then, it uses a context ontology to provide contextual information formatted in this ontology. The context manager has two modes. A normal running mode in which it returns the actual context, and a simulation mode in which it returns a simulated context. The latter mode is used during the composition process in which we need to know what will be the new context if a specific operation is performed. Further information about the use of the simulation mode is given in Section 4.2. The context manager can be a central entity that aggregates the heterogeneous information provided by various entities in the environment [5], but it can also be distributed [14]. A distributed context manager can be a set of collaborating intelligent agents that exchange context knowledge fragments to synthesize context information.

3.3   Modeling OWL-S Processes as Finite State Automata

Towards dynamic composition of services, we introduce formal modeling of OWL-S processes as finite state automata. Other approaches for formalizing Web services conversations and composition have been proposed in the literature based on Petri nets [27], process algebras [10] or finite state machines [8]. Our objective in using finite state automata is to translate the problem of integrating complex processes to an automata analysis problem. Figure 4 describes the mapping rules that we have defined for translating an OWL-S Process Model to a finite state automaton. In this model, automata symbols correspond to the OWL-S atomic processes (the services operations) involved in the OWL-S process. The initial state corresponds to the root OWL-S composite process, and a transition between two states is performed when an atomic process is executed. Each process involved in the OWL-S Process Model, either

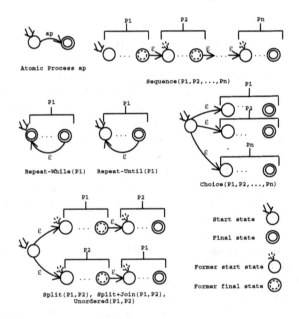

Fig. 4. Modeling OWL-S processes as finite state automata

atomic or composite, is mapped to an automaton and linked together with the other automata in order to build the OWL-S process automaton. This is achieved by following the OWL-S process description and the mapping rules shown in Figure 4. Further details about modeling OWL-S processes as automata can be found in [1].

4   Context-Aware Dynamic Service Composition

Our approach to context-aware service composition is performed in two steps. First, context-aware service discovery provides a set of services that are candidate to the composition (§4.1). Second, starting from the automata descriptions of the selected services and user task, context-aware process integration provides a set of composition schemes that conform to the task's behavior further meeting all the context requirements (§4.2).

4.1   Context-Aware Service Discovery

In this section, we present our semantic- and context-aware service discovery, which aims at selecting a set of services providing atomic processes that are semantically equivalent in terms of provided capabilities to the atomic processes involved in the user task. Additionally, during the discovery of services, the contextual requirements of the task are matched against the context attributes of services. This discovery algorithm compares semantically the atomic processes of the user task with those of the networked services.

Semantic-aware service discovery is based on the matching algorithm proposed by Paolucci *et al.* in [15]. This algorithm is used to match a requested service with a set of advertised ones. The requested service has a set of provided inputs in_{Req}, and a set of expected outputs out_{Req}, whereas each advertised service has a set of expected inputs in_{Adv} and a set of provided outputs out_{Adv}. This matching algorithm defines four levels of matching between two concepts in an ontology, a requested concept C_{Req} and an advertised concept C_{Adv}.

- *Exact*: if $C_{Req} = C_{Adv}$ or C_{Req} is a direct subclass of C_{Adv}
- *Plug in*: if C_{Adv} subsumes[12] C_{Req}, in other words, C_{Adv} could be used in the place of C_{Req}
- *Subsumes*: if C_{Req} subsumes C_{Adv}, in this case, the service does not completely fulfill the request. Thus, another service may be needed to satisfy the rest of the expected data.
- *Fail*: failure occurs when no subsumption relation between the advertised concept and the requested one is identified.

We have introduced a number of modifications to adapt the above algorithm to our composition approach:

- We match atomic processes rather than high level service capabilities.
- The previous algorithm recognizes an *exact* match between two concepts C_{Req} and C_{Adv} if $C_{Req} = C_{Adv}$ or C_{Req} is a direct subclass of C_{Adv}. For the latter case, our algorithm recognizes a *plug in* match.

---

[12] Subsumption means the fact to incorporate something under a more general category.

- We are not interested in *subsumes* matches as we consider that this degree of match cannot guarantee that the required functionality will be provided by the advertised service. Moreover, as we match operations we do not want to split them between two or more services.
- We do not define priorities between matching inputs and outputs. Thus, we consider that a match between an advertised atomic process and a requested atomic process is recognized when all outputs of the request are matched against all outputs of the advertisement; and all the inputs of the advertisement are matched against all the inputs of the request.

In order to optimize semantic service discovery, we assume that services are classified according to their context-attributes. This classification is done off-line (not during the composition process) by the service discovery protocol each time a new service appears in the network. This classification allows minimizing the number of semantic matches performed during the composition. Specifically, we propose to classify services' descriptions by using the context attributes specified in the service descriptions (§3.1). For example, location-aware services, i.e., services that provide information according to the user's location, will be put together. Thus, when looking for an operation involved in the user task, which has a contextual requirement such as physical distance awareness, we will only perform semantic matching within the above group of services. Once a set of services that provide semantically equivalent operations with those of the user task, further meeting the contextual requirements of the task, is selected, the next step is to compose those services in a way that meets the task's conversation structure. This service composition involves the integration of the selected services' processes, as described in the following section.

4.2 Context-Aware Process Integration

Our context-aware process integration algorithm aims at integrating the processes of services, selected by semantic service discovery, to reconstruct the process of the target user task. To perform such an integration, we employ the finite state automata model that we have defined earlier. Thus, we consider the automaton representing the process of the user task and the automata representing the processes of the selected services. In a first stage, we connect the automata of selected services to form a global automaton. This global automaton contains a new start state, empty transitions that connect this state with the start states of all selected automata, and other empty transitions that connect final states of each selected automata with the new start state. This allows the use of the selected services more than once in the same service composition. The next stage of our process integration algorithm is to parse each state of the task's automaton starting with the start state and following the automaton transitions. Simultaneously, a parsing of the global automaton is carried out in order to find for each state of the task's automaton an equivalent state of the global automaton. An equivalence is detected between a task's automaton state and a global automaton state when for each incoming operation[13] of the former, there is at least one semantically equivalent incoming operation of the latter. We recall that equivalence relationship between operations is

---

[13] Incoming operations are the set of symbols attached to a state's following transitions.

a semantic equivalence that have already been checked during the semantic discovery. Each state of the task's automaton is parsed just once.

In addition to checking for each state the equivalence between incoming operations, management of contextual information is performed. This management is composed of two parts. First, contextual preconditions and effects of service operations have to be taken into account, and second, global task's contextual requirements have to be checked. The first part implies the verification of the contextual preconditions of the selected operations. Furthermore, each time an operation is selected, its contextual effects have to be taken into account as a new parameter of the user's actual context. Thus, a simulation of the user's context based on the assumed contextual effects of the selected operations added to the current context, have to be done each time an operation is selected. This simulation is performed by the context manager (§3.2). Note that we assume that the user's context does not change during the composition process. This assumption is valid because we consider that the composition duration (in milliseconds [2]), is very short compared to a user activity that affects the context, such as moving to the button switch and turning on the light (may take a few seconds). The second part implies that each time an operation is selected, some context attributes from the above simulated context have to be compared to the task's global requirements.

During the composition process, various paths in the global automaton that represent intermediate composition schemes, are investigated. Some of these paths will be rejected during the composition while some others will be kept. A path can be rejected for one of the following reasons:

1. Starting from the actual state of the path, the task's following symbols cannot be reached in the global automaton;
2. The simulated context, i.e., the contextual effects of the path's operations added to the current context, does not fulfill the contextual preconditions of the incoming operations;
3. Some attributes of the simulated context do not meet the global contextual requirements of the user task.

The remaining paths, represent the possible composition schemes that can be performed to realize the user task, further meeting both the task's contextual requirements, and the contextual precondition and effects of the involved services.

The proposed process integration algorithm gives a set of sub-automata from the global automaton that behave like the task's automaton. The last step is then to select arbitrarily one of these automata as they all behave as the user task. Using the sub-automaton that has been selected, an executable description of the user task that includes references to existing environment's services is generated, and sent to an execution engine that executes this description by invoking the appropriate service operations.

5 Scenario

We present a simple example that illustrates how our context-aware composition algorithm can be used in a networked home environment. This example is inspired from one of the Amigo scenarios.

"...Robert, (Maria's and Jerry's son) is waiting for his best friend to play video games. Robert's friend arrives bringing his new portable DVD player. He proposes to watch a film rather than playing games, and asks Robert if he prefers to watch one of the films brought on his device or if he rather prefers to watch any films from his home databases. In order to use his friend's DVD player, Robert has asked the system to consider this device as a guest device and to authorize it to use the home's services. This player is quite complex as it takes into consideration some user's contextual and access rights information. The former is used to display the video streams according to the user's physical environment and preferences (for example by adapting the lighting and the sound volume or displaying the film on other devices more pleasant for the user, such as a plasma or a home cinema), while the latter is used to check whether the user is authorized to visualize a specific stream (for example some violent films may be unsuitable for children)..."

Robert's friend DVD player contains a Video Application that uses Web ontologies to describe its offered and required capabilities. The conversation that is published by this application is depicted in Figure 5 (left higher corner). This conversation is described as an OWL-S process that contains concrete offered operations (in white) and abstract required operations (in gray) that have to be bound to environment's operations. On the other hand, Robert's home environment contains a number of services among which a Digital Resource Database Service a Context Manager Service and a Location-Aware Display Service; all publish OWL-S conversations as shown in the same figure (on the right higher, left lower and right lower corners respectively). In this case, the context manager is a networked home service, which provides different kinds of context information, among which the user's location (using a network of cameras or radio receivers and a transmitter embedded on the user's device).

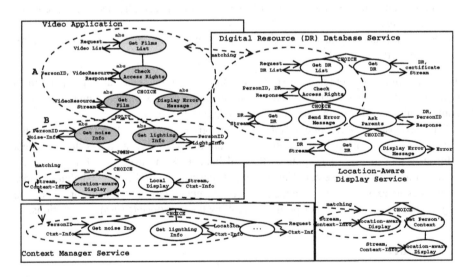

Fig. 5. Example of the context-aware process integration

At execution time, the DVD player will discover the missing abstract conversation fragments included in its description. The semantic discovery step will allow the selection of the three previous services as they contain operations that match the operations of the video application. Furthermore, the location-aware context condition specified in the operation Location-aware Display of the user task will lead to the selection of the display service which provides the location-awareness context attribute. The second step of the composition is the process integration step. In this step our algorithm attempts to reconstruct the abstract conversation of the Video Application by using the conversations of the selected services. The selected fragments after matching are shown in Figure 5. In this step, the fragment A of the task's conversation will be matched against a part of the DR Database service, while the fragments B and C will be matched against parts of the Context Manager Service and the Display Service respectively.

In addition to the composition of services' conversations, the fulfillment of the contextual preconditions of some operations have to be checked. For example, the operation Get Film may have as precondition that there is enough free disk on the user's device. On the other hand the operation Location-aware Display may have as precondition that nobody is sleeping in the current user's location.

6 Conclusion

Compared to existing work in the field of context-aware service composition, our composition approach is more flexible. Indeed, most existing approaches, such as [14, 28, 23] propose simple composition solutions based on planning techniques. Planning is an automated service composition approach, generally performed by a planner, that starts from a set of user's required outputs and provided inputs and performs a combinatorial service chaining based on signatural compatibility, i.e., compatibility between exchanged inputs/outputs. Then, the planner gives a set of plans (service compositions) that meets the user's request. In this area, Vukolvic *et al.* propose a syntactic model to represent context attributes [28]. The composition approach proposed in that work is based on HTN planning using the SHOP2 planner. In this approach, a description of a composition is given in BPEL4WS. Within this description, predefined actions are specified according to static context conditions. Then, this description is translated into SHOP2 goals, and the planner gives a plan meeting these goals. Finally, the returned plan is translated to BPEL4WS and sent to a BPEL execution engine. Mostefaoui *et al.* use an RDF-based model for describing context information [14]. The composition approach proposed in that work considers a complex service request that is decomposed into basic services. These services are discovered in the environment using context information and constraints specified in the service description such as "free memory > 128 KB". While composing the discovered services, additional constraints extracted from the user preferences are taken into account, such as "commission < 500 euros" for a travel reservation composite service. Sheshagiri *et al.* propose an approach for managing context information, in which context information sources are represented as semantic Web services [23]. This enables context information to be automatically discovered and accessed. In that approach context knowledge is represented in OWL, and services are represented as OWL-S atomic processes. A backward-chaining approach is then used to build a plan corresponding to a service composition. While planning allows an automated service composition, we argue that it presents the following limitations: (i) the resulting service compositions are based on service signatural compatibility; however, this does not guarantee that the resulting composition will really meet the user's intended semantics; and (ii) since it is a combinatorial solution, planning is a costly computational approach, and we argue that it is not well suited for resource-constrained devices.

Coming from the software engineering community, complex composition approaches have been proposed in the literature [4, 13]. Compared to these approaches our composition approach deals with a higher level of flexibility. More precisely, the distinctive feature of our solution is the ability to compose Web services that expose complex behaviors (i.e., workflows) to realize a user task that itself has a complex behavior. Existing approaches generally assume that either the services or the task have a simple behavior (i.e., services are described as a list of provided operations, and/or tasks are described as a single or a set of required operations), thus leading to simple integration solutions. In our case, we assume complex behaviors for both services and tasks described as OWL-S processes, and we propose a matching algorithm that attempts to integrate the services' processes to realize the user task.

In the last few years, context-awareness and dynamic composition of services have been very active fields of research. However, there is a little work combining both efforts. Researchers working on context-aware systems generally focus on modeling context knowledge and defining software architectures for the perception and aggregation of context information from heterogeneous sources in the environments. Thus, most service composition approaches proposed in this area are simple composition approaches, generally based on planning techniques. On the other hand, researchers from the software engineering domain have been very active in the field of dynamic service composition, and very interesting approaches have been proposed in this area. However, most of these approaches poorly deal with context-awareness.

Based on a flexible service composition approach, our solution deals at the same time with context information, combining both user-centric and service-centric views. We are developing a prototype for evaluating our approach to context- and QoS-aware service composition. Currently, the prototype contains only an implementation of our QoS- aware service composition approach. The preliminary results show that the run-time overhead of our algorithm is reasonable, and further, that QoS-awareness improves its performance [2]. Finally, our ongoing research effort aims at introducing context-awareness to our prototype and at evaluating the efficiency and performance of our solution to context-awre service composition.

References

1. Sonia Ben Mokhtar, Nikolaos Georgantas, and Valerie Issarny. Ad hoc composition of user tasks in pervasive computing environments. In *Proceedings of the 4th Workshop on Software Composition (SC 2005). Edinburgh, UK, April 2005. LNCS 3628.*
2. Sonia Ben Mokhtar, Jinshan Liu, Nikolaos Georgantas, and Valerie Issarny. QoS-aware dynamic service composition in ambient intelligence environments. Submitted for publication.

3. Paolo Bouquet, Fausto Giunchiglia, Frank van Harmelen, Luciano Serafini, and Heiner Stuckenschmidt. C-owl: Contextualizing ontologies. In *International Semantic Web Conference*, pages 164–179, 2003.

4. A. Brogi, S. Corfini, and R. Popescu. Composition-oriented service discovery. In *Proceedings of the 4th Workshop on Software Composition (SC 2005). Edinburgh. UK. LNCS 3628.*

5. Harry Chen, Filip Perich, Timothy W. Finin, and Anupam Joshi. Soupa: Standard ontology for ubiquitous and pervasive applications. In *MobiQuitous*, pages 258–267. IEEE Computer Society, 2004.

6. A. Dey, D. Salber, and G. Abowd. A conceptual framework and a toolkit for supporting the rapid prototyping of context-aware applications. In *Human-ComputerInteraction*, volume 16, pages 97–166, 2001.

7. Andreas Eberhart. Ad-hoc of invocation semantic web services. In *IEEE International Conference on Web Services (San Diego, California ICWS 2004)*, pages 116–124, June 2004.

8. Howard Foster, Sebastian Uchitel, Jeff Magee, and Jeff Kramer. Model-based verification of web service compositions. In *IEEE International Conference on Automated Software Engineering*, 2003.

9. Jadwiga Indulska, Ricky Robinson, Andry Rakotonirainy, and Karen Henricksen. Experiences in using cc/pp in context-aware systems. In Ming-Syan Chen, Panos K. Chrysanthis, Morris Sloman, and Arkady B. Zaslavsky, editors, *Mobile Data Management*, volume 2574 of *Lecture Notes in Computer Science*, pages 247–261. Springer, 2003.

10. M. Koshkina and F. van Breugel. Verification of business processes for web services. Technical report, York University, 2003.

11. Seng Wai Loke. Logic programming for context-aware pervasive computing: Language support, characterizing situations, and integration with the web. In *Web Intelligence*, pages 44–50. IEEE Computer Society, 2004.

12. Zakaria Maamar, Soraya Kouadri, and Hamdi Yahyaoui. A web services composition approach based on software agents and context. In *SAC '04: Proceedings of the 2004 ACM symposium on Applied computing*, pages 1619–1623, New York, NY, USA, 2004. ACM Press.

13. Shalil Majithia, David W. Walker, and W. A. Gray. A framework for automated service composition in service-oriented architecture. In *1st European Semantic Web Symposium*, 2004.

14. Soraya Kouadri Mostéfaoui, Amine Tafat-Bouzid, and Béat Hirsbrunner. Using context information for service discovery and composition. In *iiWAS*, 2003.

15. Massimo Paolucci, Takahiro Kawamura, Terry R. Payne, and Katia Sycara. Semantic matching of Web services capabilities. *Lecture Notes in Computer Science*, 2342:333–347, 2002.

16. Joachim Peer. Bringing together Semantic Web and Web services. *The Semantic Web - ISWC 2002: First International Semantic Web Conference, Sardinia, Italy, 2002.*, 2342:279, 2002.

17. Davy Preuveneers, Jan Van den Bergh, Dennis Wagelaar, Andy Georges, Peter Rigole, Tim Clerckx, Yolande Berbers, Karin Coninx, Viviane Jonckers, and Koenraad De Bosschere. Towards an extensible context ontology for ambient intelligence. In Panos Markopoulos, Berry Eggen, Emile H. L. Aarts, and James L. Crowley, editors, *EUSAI*, volume 3295 of *Lecture Notes in Computer Science*, pages 148–159. Springer, 2004.

18. Davy Preuveneers, Jan Van den Bergh, Dennis Wagelaar, Andy Georges, Peter Rigole, Tim Clerckx, Yolande Berbers, Karin Coninx, Viviane Jonckers, and Koenraad De Bosschere. Towards an extensible context ontology for ambient intelligence. In *EUSAI*, pages 148–159, 2004.

19. Anand Ranganathan, Roy H. Campbell, Arathi Ravi, and Anupama Mahajan. Conchat: A context-aware chat program. *IEEE Pervasive Computing*, 1(3):51–57, 2002.

20. Manuel Roman and Roy H. Campbell. A user-centric, resource-aware, context-sensitive, multi-device application framework for ubiquitous computing environments. Technical report, Department of Computer Science, University of Illinois at Urbana-Champaign, 2002.

21. B. Schilit, N. Adams, and R. Want. Context-aware computing applications. In *IEEE Workshop on Mobile Computing Systems and Applications*, 1994.

22. Bill N. Schilit, Norman Adams, Rich Gold, Michael M. Tso, and Roy Want. The parctab mobile computing system. In *Workshop on Workstation Operating Systems*, pages 34–39, 1993.

23. Mithun Sheshagiri, Norman Sadeh, and Fabien Gandon. Using semantic web services for context-aware mobile applications. In *MobiSys 2004 Workshop on Context Awareness*.

24. Kaarthik Sivashanmugam, Kunal Verma, Amit P. Sheth, and John A. Miller. Adding semantics to web services standards. In *Proceedings of the International Conference on Web Services, ICWS '03, 2003, Las Vegas, Nevada, USA*, pages 395–401, June 2003.

25. João Pedro Sousa and David Garlan. Aura: an architectural framework for user mobility in ubiquitous computing environments. In *Proceedings of the IFIP 17th World Computer Congress - TC2 Stream / 3rd IEEE/IFIP Conference on Software Architecture*, pages 29–43. Kluwer, B.V., 2002.

26. Maria Strimpakou, Ioanna Roussaki, Carsten Pils, Michael Angermann, Patrick Robertson, and Miltiades E. Anagnostou. Context modelling and management in ambient-aware pervasive environments. In Thomas Strang and Claudia Linnhoff-Popien, editors, *LoCA*, volume 3479 of *Lecture Notes in Computer Science*, pages 2–15. Springer, 2005.

27. W.M.P. van der Aalst and A.H.M. ter Hofstede. Yawl: Yet another workflow language. *Accepted for publication in Information Systems*, 2004.

28. Maja Vukovic and Peter Robinson. Adaptive, planning-based, web service composition for context awareness. In *International Conference on Pervasive Computing, Vienna, April 2004*.

29. Xiao Hang Wang, Da Qing Zhang, Tao Gu, and Hung Keng Pung. Ontology based context modeling and reasoning using owl. In *PerCom Workshops*, pages 18–22, 2004.

Can Aspects Implement Contracts?

Stephanie Balzer*, Patrick Th. Eugster, and Bertrand Meyer

ETH Zurich (Swiss Federal Institute of Technology),
Department of Computer Science,
CH-8092 Zürich, Switzerland
{first_name.last_name}@inf.ethz.ch

Abstract. Design by Contract[TM] is commonly cited as an example of
the "crosscutting" concerns that aspect-oriented programming can address. We test this conjecture by attempting to implement contracts
through aspects and assessing the outcome. The results of this experiment cast doubt on the validity of the conjecture, showing that aspects
appear unable to capture contracts in a way that retains the benefits of
the Design by Contract methodology.

1 Introduction

Aspect-oriented programming (AOP) [1] emerged from a criticism of earlier programming approaches, which it blames for focusing on just one dimension of
design. Object-oriented languages, for example, focus on the dimension of *data
abstraction* [2]. According to the AOP analysis, this prevents capturing other dimensions and results in tangled code, where code fragments representing dimensions not supported by the programming language are replicated throughout the
code, defeating the advertised benefits of reuse and economy. Such dimensions,
or *aspects*, are said to "crosscut" the basic decomposition units of the software.
AOP instead supports multiple dimensions of design by turning such aspects
into first-class programming concepts, to be directly supported by the programming language. Aspects, in the AOP view [3], allow programmers to capture
crosscutting concerns in a concise and modular way.

As an example of a crosscutting concern, the AOP literature frequently cites
[4, 5, 6, 7, 8] *Design by Contract*[TM](DbC)[1]. DbC [9] is a methodology to guide
many aspects of software development including in particular analysis, design,
documentation and testing. It is based on the specification of contracts that gov-
ern the cooperation between components of a system by specifying each party's
expectations and guarantees.

In the DbC view [9], contracts should appear in the components themselves.
Replacing contracts by aspect-based techniques would contradict this view since
aspects, by definition, appear separately from the program units they "crosscut".

---

* Contact address: Stephanie Balzer, Chair of Software Engineering, Clau-
siusstrasse 59, 8092 Zürich, Switzerland.
[1] Design by Contract is a trademark of Eiffel Software.

N. Guelfi and A. Savidis (Eds.): RISE 2005, LNCS 3943, pp. 145–157, 2006.

We will start from this contradiction and investigate whether it can be resolved; for this purpose we will take the assertion that "aspects can emulate contracts" at face value and attempt to build such an emulation in practice.

The analysis uses a simple example that we first implement in *Eiffel* [10], the "mother tongue" of Design by Contract, and then in *AspectJ*^{TM}, a general-purpose aspect-oriented extension to Java and the most prominent realization to date of AOP ideas.

We illustrate through this example the loss of some of the principal benefits of Design by Contract when emulating contracts with aspects, in particular documentation and support for inheritance-based refinement. We further show that contracts are not crosscutting by nature, and that aspectizing them risks creating interactions with other aspects.

The remainder of this discussion is organized as follows. Section 2 provides a short introduction to AOP. Section 3 illustrates the concepts of DbC and introduces the running example of this paper. Section 4 studies, on the basis of the running example, how to aspectize contracts in AspectJ. Section 5 — the core of our comparative analysis — assesses whether and how this aspect-based emulation achieves the goals of the original contract-based design. Section 6 draws from this analysis to discuss the general question of whether aspects can emulate DbC. Section 7 provides our conclusion.

2   Aspect-Oriented Programming

This section provides an overview of *Aspect-oriented programming* (AOP) [1] and introduces its underlying terminology.

2.1   Overview

AOP promises improved separation of design concerns by modeling aspects separately from components. Typical applications of AOP include [11, 4] logging, concurrency/synchronization, change propagation, security checking, and — the claim examined in this paper — DbC enforcement. The announced benefits of aspect-oriented techniques include [4, 12, 13]:

- *Explicitness.* Aspects explicitly capture the structure of crosscutting concerns.
- *Reusability.* Since aspects can apply to multiple components, it is possible through a single aspect to describe crosscutting concerns common to several components.
- *Modularity.* Since aspects are modular crosscutting units, AOP improves the overall modularity of an application.
- *Evolution.* Evolution becomes easier since implementation changes of crosscutting concerns occur locally within an aspect and save the need to adapt existing classes.
- *Stability.* Special AOP language support ("property-based aspects" in AspectJ), make it possible to express generic aspects, which will remain applicable throughout future class evolution.

– *Pluggability.* Since aspects are modular, they can be easily plugged in and out of an application.

2.2   Terminology

In discussing aspects, we will use the terminology of AspectJ as it is the best known variant. AspectJ is an extension of Java enabling the specification of aspects and their crosscutting with classes. AspectJ expresses crosscutting through *join points* and *pointcuts*. Joint points are well-defined points in the execution of a program. Pointcuts are distinguished selections of join points that meet some specified criteria. In addition to pointcuts, aspects allow specifying *advice*: method-like constructs defining complementary behavior at join points. To become effective, a given advice has to be attached to a specific pointcut. Depending on the declaration, advice bodies are executed *before* or *after* a specified join point, or they can surround (*around*) that join point. Besides pointcuts and advice, aspects can list ordinary Java member declarations such as attributes, methods, and constructors.

3   Design by Contract

In this section we present the concepts of *Design by Contract* (DbC) [9] and introduce a running example.

3.1   Overview

DbC is a methodology to guide analysis, design, documentation, testing and other tasks of software development.

The application of DbC to software design requires the developer to build software systems based on precisely defined contracts between cooperating components. Contracts, similar to real-life contracts, define the relationship between two cooperating components — the client and the supplier — by expressing each party's expectations and guarantees. A general characteristic of contracts is that they turn the obligation for one of the parties into a benefit of the other. Contracts are expressed through *preconditions*, *postconditions*, and *class invariants*.

– *Preconditions* are conditions that the client must fulfill for the supplier to carry out its task properly. Preconditions are an obligation for the client and a benefit for the supplier.
– *Postconditions* are properties satisfied at the end of the task's execution, assuming the preconditions were met at the beginning. Postconditions are an obligation for the supplier and a benefit for the client.
– *Class invariants* capture the deeper semantic properties and integrity constraints of a class and its instances. Class invariants must be satisfied by every instance of a class whenever the instance is externally accessible: after creation; before and after any call to an exported routine (function or procedure) of the class.

Applying DbC to software analysis and design helps build correct software. By providing preconditions, postconditions and class invariants, programmers explicitly specify the assumptions on which they rely to ensure the correctness of every software element.

Besides providing analysis and design guidance, DbC improves the documentation of software systems. Preconditions describe to client programmers which conditions they must achieve before calling a routine. Postconditions describe what the routine will then do for them. Class invariants make it possible to reason abstractly and statically on the objects of a system's execution. The "contract view" of a class, retaining these elements but discarding implementations, provides a description of software components at just the right level of abstraction; it can be produced by tools of the environment, such as EiffelStudio, and serves as the fundamental form of documentation for DbC-based software, making it possible to use a component on the sole basis of its contract view. In the DbC view all this assumes — as noted above — that the contracts are an integral part of the software text.

DbC also plays a major role in the debugging and testing of software systems. As preconditions, postconditions and invariants are correctness conditions governing the correct functioning of software components and the relationship between components, a contract violation at run time always signals a bug: client bug for a precondition violation, supplier bug for a postcondition or invariant violation. A DbC development environment must provide a compilation option for enabling and disabling run-time contract monitoring. This provides crucial help during the testing and debugging process, making these activities more focused than in other approaches: only with explicit contracts can one explicitly compare the relationship between desired and actual behavior.

Among other advertised benefits of contracts is their support for the maintenance activity: when changing a class, the maintainer should be guided by the existing contracts, class invariants in particular, and generally maintain them even if the implementation changes.

Contracts also play a significant role, as detailed in section 5.4, in controlling the inheritance mechanism, including when used for analysis of software.

3.2   An Example

In this section we introduce the running example of this paper. The example is based on one presented in [4] and models points in the Cartesian coordinate system. To illustrate the basic DbC ideas we provide the example first in *Eiffel* [10]. Later, in section 4, we show the corresponding implementation in AspectJ.

Listing 1.1 shows the Eiffel class POINT implementing the example. This version does not contain any contracts yet (see Listing 1.2 for the version including contracts). The class declares the following five features[2]: the attributes x

---

[2] Features are the basic constituents of Eiffel classes and are either attributes or routines.

```
class
    POINT

feature -- Access

    x : DOUBLE
            -- Abscissa value of current point
    y : DOUBLE
            -- Ordinate value of current point

feature -- Element change

    change_point (new_x : DOUBLE; new_y : DOUBLE) is
            -- Overwrite coordinates of current point with provided values.
        do
            x := new_x
            y := new_y
        end

    move_by (delta_x : DOUBLE; delta_y : DOUBLE) is
            -- Move current point by provided values.
        do
            x := x + delta_x
            y := y + delta_y
        end

feature -- Output

    to_string : STRING is
            -- String representation of current point
        do
            Result := "(" + x.out + ", " + y.out + ")"
        end

end
```

Listing 1.1. Cartesian point implementation in Eiffel without contracts

and y, the procedures change_point and move_by, and the function to_string. The various feature clauses within the class text allow feature categorization.

All features in POINT are accessible by all clients of the class. Attributes x and y are public; this is the appropriate policy since attribute access in Eiffel is read-only for clients (any modification requires, in accordance with object-oriented principles, the provision of an associated "setter" procedure).

Listing 1.2 shows the complete point implementation with contracts. Due to the straightforwardness of the example there are only a few contracts, in this case only postconditions. In Eiffel, postconditions are introduced by the keyword **ensure** following the routine body. Preconditions are introduced by the keyword **require** and have to precede the routine body, that is they are placed before the **do** keyword. Class invariants are introduced by the keyword **invariant** and have to be mentioned after the last feature in the class text. It is possible, although not required, to *tag* individual assertion clauses for identification: the example uses this possibility, as with the y_correctly_moved tag for the last assertion of the procedure move_by.

The class in listing 1.1 appears satisfactory in some general and fairly vague sense — vague precisely because in the absence of contracts it is impossible to know for sure what it is really supposed to do, and hence to talk about its

```
class
    POINT

feature  --  Access

    x:  DOUBLE
            --  Abscissa  value  of  current  point
    y:  DOUBLE
            --  Ordinate  value  of  current  point

feature  --  Element change

    change_point  (new_x:  DOUBLE;  new_y:  DOUBLE)  is
            --  Overwrite  coordinates  of  current  point  with  provided  values.
        do
            x  :=  new_x
            y  :=  new_y
        ensure
            x_correctly_updated:  x = new_x
            y_correctly_update:  y = new_y
        end

    move_by  (delta_x:  DOUBLE;  delta_y:  DOUBLE)  is
            --  Move  current  point  by  provided  values.
        do
            x  :=  x + delta_x
            y  :=  y + delta_y
        ensure
            x_correctly_moved:  x = old x + delta_x
            y_correctly_moved:  y = old y + delta_y
        end

feature  --  Output

    to_string:  STRING  is
            --  String  representation  of  current  point
        do
            Result  :=  "(" + x.out + ", " + y.out + ")"
        end

end
```

Listing 1.2. Cartesian point implementation in Eiffel with contracts

"correctness" or absence thereof. The new variant of POINT in listing 1.2 keeps the implementation — so that in non-erroneous cases at least the new class will "function" like the previous one — but makes it possible to talk about correctness since it now includes contracts.

The postcondition of procedure move_by, for example, uses old x to denote the value attribute x had on routine entry, that is before the assignment was executed. Such "old expressions", permitted only in postconditions, are essential to express the effect of a routine by stating how the final state differs from the original state.

Listing 1.2 demonstrates the power of having contracts embedded within the class text. Although contracts are clearly distinguishable from the actual routine bodies, they are still part of their declaration. This encourages programmers to update contracts when changing implementations. If they forget, run-time contract monitoring will help spot the mistake quickly.

4   Aspectizing Contracts

In an interview [5] Kiczales cites DbC as an example of a crosscutting concern:

"[...] there are many other concerns that, in a specific system, have cross-cutting structure. Aspects can be used to maintain internal consistency among several methods of a class. They are well suited to enforcing a Design by Contract style of programming."

Other authors [4, 6, 7, 8] share that opinion. The idea has also been patented [6]. Let us pursue this idea and attempt to aspectize the preceding example using AspectJ.

Listing 1.3 displays a Java counterpart of the original, uncontracted Eiffel class POINT of listing 1.1. Except for syntactical differences, the two versions most notably differ in the handling of attributes (fields in Java terminology). Since attribute access in Java is not restricted by default, Java programmers typically declare attribute values to be private and, additionally, provide appropriate "getter" methods.

Listing 1.4 displays the aspectized version of listing 1.3 that emulates the contracted Eiffel version of listing 1.2 within an aspect using AspectJ. For simplicity, we only list the aspectized postcondition of procedure move_by(); the other contract clauses would be amenable to the same treatment.

The aspect PointMoveByContract defines a pointcut, which denotes all calls of moveBy(), and an associated after advice for the postcondition enforcement. In case the postcondition is violated, the advice throws an exception. In addition, the aspect declares auxiliary constructs for recording the attribute values before

```java
public class Point {

    private double x;
    private double y;

    public double getX(){
        return x;
    }

    public double getY(){
        return y;
    }

    public void changePoint(double x, double y){
        this.x = x;
        this.y = y;
    }

    public void moveBy(double deltaX, double deltaY){
        this.x += deltaX;
        this.y += deltaY;
    }

    public String toString(){
        return "(" + getX() + ", " + getY() + ")";
    }
}
```

Listing 1.3. Cartesian point implementation in Java

```
public aspect PointMoveByContract {

    private double Point.oldX;
    private double Point.oldY;
    private double Point.newX;
    private double Point.newY;

    public pointcut checkContract(Point p, double dx, double dy):
        call(void Point.moveBy(double, double))
        && args(dx, dy)
        && target(p);

    before(Point p, double dx, double dy): checkContract(p, dx, dy){
        p.oldX = p.getX();
        p.oldY = p.getY();
    }

    after(Point p, double dx, double dy): checkContract(p, dx, dy){
        p.newX = p.getX();
        p.newY = p.getY();
        if ((p.newX != p.oldX + dx) || (p.newY != p.oldY + dy))
            throw new ContractViolationException("p not correctly moved");
    }
}
```

Listing 1.4. Aspect implementing the postcondition of moveBy()

and after the method moveBy() was executed. To this end, the aspect includes the inter-type declarations Point.oldX, Point.oldY, Point.newX, and Point.newY and a before advice.

Although other techniques might be available, this seems to be the most direct and effective way to "aspectize" contracts as suggested by the AOP literature.

5   Analysis

To compare the original contracted version (listing 1.2) and its aspect-based emulation, we examine it in the light of some of the benefits of contracts listed in section 3.1 — analysis and design, documentation, testing and debugging — and two other important criteria: reusability and ease of use.

5.1   Analysis and Design Guidance

Both approaches provide design guidance by requiring developers to build software systems based on precisely defined contracts. In AOP, however, one tends to impose aspects on classes once the classes are developed, which clearly contradicts the DbC methodology.

5.2   Documentation Aid

As Eiffel includes preconditions, postconditions, and invariants directly in the class text, contracts become part of the class specification and thus increase system documentation. In AspectJ, contracts are separated from the class they describe and thus force the programmer to switch back and forth between classes and aspects. Appropriate tool support, such as the AspectJ Development Tools (AJDT) project for the Eclipse development environment, alleviates the problem by highlighting the places where advice are injected.

5.3   Testing Assistance

Eiffel relies on run-time contract monitoring, which can be enabled or disabled by setting a respective compilation option. AspectJ too, facilitates "pluggable" run-time contract monitoring since aspectized contracts can be added or removed from classes. Once an aspectized contract is removed, however, its documentation is lost.

5.4   Contract Reuse

The application of wildcards in pointcuts makes aspects applicable to many classes. In this way, AspectJ facilitates contract reuse. Eiffel too, allows contract reuse, but restricts it to classes related by inheritance (see section 6.4).

5.5   Ease of Use

Eiffel promotes ease of contract application. Programmers declare contracts directly within the class text, at the place where they want them to apply. Moreover, Eiffel provides several constructs, such as the old notation (see section 3.2), to facilitate the expressing of assertions. In AspectJ, programmers specify the code places, where to inject the contracts, indirectly by means of pointcuts.

6   Discussion

In this section, we attempt to generalize from the example and assess whether aspects are suited for emulating DbC.

6.1   Support of DbC Methodology

The analysis in section 5 implies that aspect-based DbC implementations do not support the DbC methodology to the same extent as implementations in contract-enabled languages. An aspect-based emulation ignores the documentation mechanisms made possible by DbC. Since contracts are separated from classes, the risk of introducing inconsistencies between classes and contracts is increased; as programmers become aware of contracts only when using special tools for browsing the spread application structure, they are more likely to forget adapting the contracts when changing the classes. This issue can get worse after system deployment, once the aspectized contracts are removed. How will a client, of a library component for example, know under which conditions it may call a service?

Such removal of contracts also raises questions of maintainability. One of the benefits of contracts mentioned in section 3.1 is to guide the evolution of classes; but this assumes that the contracts are in the software.

Aspectized contracts promote a different focus on software design than DbC. Whereas AOP aims at separating concerns, DbC fosters the explicit specification of inter-module cooperation, in the modules themselves.

6.2   Are Contracts Crosscutting?

Contracts are *recurrent* in DbC-based code. Are they also *crosscutting*?

We can assess this conjecture by examining its consequences. If contracts were crosscutting, an aspectized contract implementation would yield the benefits presented in section 2.1. For example, the improved *modularity* requires aspectized contracts to be modular. According to Parnas [14] modularity is, besides the existence of explicit interfaces, defined by the possibility to create a module with little knowledge of the code in other modules and the expectation that drastic changes within one module will not require adaptations in other modules. Contracts do not meet that definition: Since they semantically depend on their classes, they can only be created with detailed knowledge of the associated classes, and are likely to be affected by modifications of these classes. Aspectization is unlikely to change that situation.

Similar reasoning applies to other benefits listed: *evolution* and *stability*. Separating contracts from classes does not isolate the changes.

The remaining benefits mentioned in section 2.1 — *explicitness, reusability, pluggability* — are achieved, at least partially, by an aspectized contract implementation. They would, however, also exist without aspectization. Implementing contracts in Eiffel (see listing 1.2) makes contracts explicit, offers pluggability of run-time contract monitoring, and allows contract reuse through genericity and multiple inheritance (see also section 6.4 below).

The preceding considerations suggest that although contracts appear repeatedly within the class text — before and after each routine and at the end of the class — they are not crosscutting by nature.

6.3   Aspect Interactions

Hannemann et al. [15] and Bergmans [16] have pointed out the existence of aspect interactions in AOP. Such interactions can result in conflicts between classes and aspects or between aspects and aspects. Aspects intended to emulate contracts seem to create many such interactions.

To illustrate that problem, we extend our running example and assume that we want to scale points transparently to the clients of class Point. This is typical of the kind of incremental, seamless addition that aspects are intended to permit. Listing 1.5 presents an aspect achieving this extension for scaling points according to a specified scale factor. Whenever we attempt to change the coordinates of a point, the around advice of aspect ScalePoint will multiply the new

```
public aspect ScalePoint {

    private static double scaleFactor = 10;

    public pointcut change(Point p, double x, double y):
        target(p) &&
        args (x, y) &&
        (execution(void Point.changePoint(double, double)) ||
                execution(void Point.moveBy(double, double)));

    void around(Point p, double x, double y): change(p, x, y){
        proceed(p, scaleFactor * x, scaleFactor * y);
    }
}
```

Listing 1.5. Aspect allowing to scale points by a specified scale factor

coordinates we provide by scaleFactor. Such an aspect could be useful for displaying points when the display device requires a special formatting.

Adding such an aspect breaks the contract of class Point. Both the new aspect and the aspectized contract advise method moveBy. The problem is that they work on the same method in a nested fashion without being aware of each other. As soon as one aspect changes the state of the object on which the routine operates, or changes the value of an argument of the routine, it compromises any assumptions by the other aspect on object state or argument values.

The interleaved advice execution sequence in the example is as follows:

1. Before advice of aspect PointMoveByContract.
2. Around advice of aspect ScalePoint.
3. After advice of aspect PointMoveByContract.

Since the around advice of aspect ScalePoint changes the point coordinates invisibly to the aspectized contract, the postcondition ceases to be ensured. With contract monitoring on, the after advice will raise a ContractViolationException. The aspect ScalePoint interferes with the contract.

The example suggests that no module in a system — class or aspect — can be oblivious of the presence of contracts.

6.4   Contracts and Inheritance

A key property of DbC is its connection with the inheritance mechanism and, as a consequence, software reuse. When a class inherits from one or more others, the following rules apply to its contracts [9]:

- *Parent's invariant rule:* The invariants of all the parents of a class apply to the class itself.
- *Assertion redeclaration rule:* A routine redeclaration may only replace the original precondition by one equal or weaker, and the original postcondition by one equal or stronger. This applies both to *redefinition* (overriding an inherited implementation) and *effecting* (providing a first implementation of a feature inherited as *deferred*, that is to say, without an implementation);

the second application is particularly useful in the transition from analysis (which uses deferred classes) to design and implementation.

Ideally, the development environment should enforce these rules. With aspectized contracts, however, there seems to be no clear way of achieving this. It is left to the programmer to make sure that the pointcuts for injecting invariants also apply to descendant classes and that the refinement of preconditions and postconditions in descendant classes follows the assertion redeclaration rule. Intended revisions on the AspectJ join point model aiming at increasing the expressiveness of pointcut definitions [17] might abate the problem in future. For the moment, however, programmers must live with the pure syntactical mechanisms of the AspectJ join point model, and take care of consistent contract refinement themselves.

7   Conclusion

Our investigation of whether aspects are suited for implementing Design by Contract suggests that such an emulation fails to provide some of the principal benefits of Design by Contract, in particular documentation and support for inheritance-based refinement. We have further observed that contracts are not crosscutting by nature, and that aspectizing them risks creating interactions with other aspects.

These conclusions are of course dependent on the context of our study: it may be — although we have no evidence of either possibility — that using another AOP environment than AspectJ, the current flagship and reference for AOP, would yield better results; and that we used the wrong techniques for aspectizing contracts, missing more effective solutions.

Based on the current state of our aspectizing efforts, however, the conclusion seems clear: the widely repeated AOP claim that aspects can emulate contracts does not appear to stand.

References

1. Kiczales, G., Lamping, J., Mendhekar, A., Maeda, C., Lopes, C., Loingtier, J.M., Irwin, J.: Aspect-oriented programming. In Aksit, M., Matsuoka, S., eds.: ECOOP '97 - Object-Oriented Programming: 11th European Conference. Volume 1241 of Lecture Notes in Computer Science., Springer-Verlag GmbH (1997) 220–242
2. Lieberherr, K.J., Lorenz, D.H., Mezini, M.: Building modular object-oriented systems with reusable collaborations (tutorial session). In: ICSE, ACM Press (2000) 821
3. Lopes, C.V., Kiczales, G.: Improving design and source code modularity using AspectJ (tutorial session). In: ICSE, IEEE-CS : Computer Society and SIGSOFT: ACM Special Interest Group on Software Engineering and Irish Comp Soc : Irish Computer Society, ACM Press (2000) 825
4. Kiczales, G., Hilsdale, E., Hugunin, J., Kersten, M., Palm, J., Griswold, W.G.: Getting started with AspectJ. Commun. ACM **44** (2001) 59–65

5. TheServerSide.COM: Interview with Gregor Kiczales, topic: Aspect-oriented programming (AOP).   http://www.theserverside.com/talks/videos/GregorKiczalesText/interview.tss (2003)
6. Lopes, C.V., Lippert, M., Hilsdale, E.A.: Design by contract with aspect-oriented programming. U.S. Patent No. 6,442,750 (2002)
7. Diotalevi, F.: Contract enforcement with AOP.
   http://www-128.ibm.com/developerworks/library/j-ceaop/ (2004)
8. Skotiniotis, T., Lorenz, D.H.: Cona: aspects for contracts and contracts for aspects. In: OOPSLA Companion, ACM Press (2004) 196–197
9. Meyer, B.: Object-Oriented Software Construction. Second edn. Prentice Hall Professional Technical Reference (1997)
10. Meyer, B.: Eiffel: The Language. Prentice Hall Professional Technical Reference (1991)
11. Kiczales, G.: AspectJ: Aspect-oriented programming in Java. In Aksit, M., Mezini, M., Unland, R., eds.: NetObjectDays. Volume 2591 of Lecture Notes in Computer Science., Springer-Verlag GmbH (2002) 1
12. Kiczales, G., Hilsdale, E., Hugunin, J., Kersten, M., Palm, J., Griswold, W.G.: An overview of AspectJ. In Knudsen, J.L., ed.: ECOOP. Volume 2072 of Lecture Notes in Computer Science., Springer-Verlag GmbH (2001) 327–353
13. Lopes, C.V., Kiczales, G.: Recent developments in aspect. In Demeyer, S., Bosch, J., eds.: ECOOP Workshops. Volume 1543 of Lecture Notes in Computer Science., Springer-Verlag GmbH (1998) 398–401
14. Parnas, D.L.: On the criteria to be used in decomposing systems into modules. Commun. ACM **15** (1972) 1053–1058
15. Hannemann, J., Chitchyan, R., Rashid, A.: Analysis of aspect-oriented software. In Buschmann, F., Buchmann, A.P., Cilia, M.A., eds.: ECOOP Workshops. Volume 3013 of Lecture Notes in Computer Science., Springer-Verlag GmbH (2003) 154–164
16. Bergmans, L.: Towards detection of semantic conflicts between crosscutting concerns. In Hannemann, J., Chitchyan, R., Rashid, A., eds.: Workshop on Analysis of Aspect-Oriented Software. ECOOP 2003 (2003)
17. Kiczales, G., Mezini, M.: Aspect-oriented programming and modular reasoning. In: ICSE, ACM Press (2005) 49–58

Aspects-Classes Integration Testing Strategy:
An Incremental Approach

Philippe Massicotte, Linda Badri, and Mourad Badri

Software Engineering Laboratory,
Department of Mathematics and Computer Science,
University of Quebec at Trois-Rivières,
C.P. 500, Trois-Rivières, Québec, Canada G9A 5H7
{Philippe.Massicotte, Linda.Badri, Mourad.Badri}@uqtr.ca

Abstract. Aspect-Oriented Programming is an emerging software engineering paradigm. It provides new constructs and tools improving separation of crosscutting concerns into single units called aspects. In fact, existing object-oriented programming languages suffer from a serious limitation in modularizing adequately crosscutting concerns. Many concerns crosscut several classes in an object-oriented system. However, new dependencies between aspects and classes result in new testing challenges. Interactions between aspects and classes are new sources for program faults. Existing object-oriented testing methods (unit and integration testing) are not well adapted to the aspect technology. Thus, new testing techniques must be developed for aspect-oriented software. We present, in this paper, a new aspects-classes integration testing strategy. The adopted approach consists of two main phases: (1) static analysis: generating test sequences based on the dynamic interactions between aspects and classes, (2) dynamic analysis: verifying the execution of the selected sequences. We focus, in particular, on the integration of one or more aspects in the control of collaborating classes.

Keywords: AOST, Aspects, Classes, Interactions, Sequences, Criteria, Generation, Verification, Testing Coverage.

1 Introduction

Existing object-oriented programming languages suffer from a serious limitation to adequately modularize crosscutting concerns in software. The code related to these concerns is often duplicated within several classes. Aspect-Oriented Software Development (AOSD) [3] introduces new abstractions dealing with separation of crosscutting concerns in software development. By using this new technique, the code corresponding to crosscutting concerns may be separated into modular units called aspects [4]. This reduces the dispersion of the code related to crosscutting concerns and tends to improve programs modularity as stated in many papers [12, 17, 19]. In spite of the many claimed benefits that the aspect paradigm seams offering, it remains that it is not yet mature. Consequently, testing aspect-oriented software is a huge challenge. Aspect-Oriented Programming (AOP) introduces new dimensions in terms of control and complexity to software engineering. As a consequence, AOP generates

N. Guelfi and A. Savidis (Eds.): RISE 2005, LNCS 3943, pp. 158–173, 2006.

new types of faults as mentioned in [2]. Aspects' features are not covered by existing testing approaches as mentioned by several authors [2, 21, 22].

Testing process is an important issue in software development. It represents an essential task to ensure software quality [9]. Existing object-oriented testing methods are not well adapted to the aspect technology. The code related to aspects as well as the introduced abstractions and constructs are prone to cause new faults as stated in [2, 12]. Moreover, aspects are not complete code units and their behavior often depends on the woven context as mentioned in [2]. In aspect-oriented programs, integration is more fine grained and occurs as stated in [2] with respect to the intra-method control and data flow. As a consequence, new integration testing techniques must be developed to deal with the new dimensions introduced by aspects. The main difficulty comes from the relationship between aspects and classes. A link between an aspect and a class is not identifiable when analyzing classes [2, 12, 19, 22]. One of the major forms of dependencies between aspects and classes comes from the specific relationship (*caller/called*). Most of object-oriented testing techniques are based on this type of relationship between classes [7]. In object-oriented systems, the caller and the called, at a high level, are classes. In such systems, a caller specifies the different calls that it carries out as well as the control related to these calls. In an aspect-oriented system, something different occurs since integration rules are defined in aspects and it is done without consideration to classes. An aspect describes, using various constructs, how this integration will be done. This additional level of abstraction, and its consequences in terms of control and complexity, must be taken in consideration in order to make sure that dependencies between aspects and classes are tested adequately as mentioned in [22].

We present, in this paper, a new aspects-classes integration testing strategy. The adopted approach consists of two main phases: (1) static analysis: generating testing sequences based on interactions between aspects and classes, (2) dynamic analysis: verifying the execution of the selected sequences. We focus, in particular, on the integration of one or more aspects in the control (interactions) of collaborating classes. The proposed approach follows an iterative process. The first main phase of the strategy consists in the generation of testing sequences corresponding to the various scenarios of the collaboration between the objects including weaved aspects. Interactions between collaborating classes are specified using UML collaboration diagrams. Aspects are integrated to the original sequences (collaboration) in an incremental way. The second main phase of the strategy supports the verification process of the executed sequences. We focus in our work on AspectJ programs. The proposed technique is, however, general and may be adapted to others aspect implementations. The present work represents an extension of a previous work that focused on a general presentation of the test sequences generation technique [11].

The rest of the paper is organized as follows: in section 2, we present a survey on related works. Section 3 gives the basic concepts of AspectJ. The main steps of our strategy are discussed in section 4. Section 5 introduces collaboration diagrams. The proposed testing criteria are discussed in section 6. Section 7 presents the testing sequences generation technique and its illustration on a real case study. Section 8 presents the verification process that we implemented and the used fault-based model. Finally, section 9 gives a general conclusion and some future work directions.

2 Related Work

Alexander et al. discuss in [2] various types of faults that could occur in aspect-oriented software. They consider the new dimensions introduced by the integration of aspects into an object code. They propose a fault model including six types of potential sources of errors in an aspect-oriented software. This model constitutes, in our believe, an interesting first basis for developing testing strategies and tools for aspect-oriented software. Mortensen et al. [12] present an approach combining two traditional testing techniques: structural approach (*white box coverage*) and mutation testing. Aspects are classified according to whether they modify or not the state of a system. This technique mainly consists in discovering faults that are related to the code introduced by advice. The mutation operators are applied to the process that weaves advice to the object code.

Zhou et al. [22] suggest a unit testing strategy for aspects. Their approach is presented in four phases. The first step consists in testing classes to eliminate errors that are related to aspects. Each aspect is integrated and tested individually in a second step. All aspects are integrated and tested in an incremental way. Finally, the system is entirety re-tested. This approach is based on the source code of the program under test. Moreover, a *framework* is proposed by Xie et al. [19] to generate automatically a set of unit tests by using the compiled AspectJ *bytecode*. In the same context, Zhao [21] proposes an approach based on control flow graphs. Three testing levels are applied to aspects and classes. The strategy proposed by Zhao focuses on unit testing of aspect-oriented programs.

The presented approaches are rather based on the source code (aspects and classes) of the programs under test. Moreover, other approaches focused on generating test sequences using state diagrams [20]. Such approaches focus on the behavior of a class where an aspect is weaved. Our research is related to the behavior for a group of collaborating objects where one or more aspects are integrated. The collaboration between several objects specifies how the objects interact dynamically in order to realize a particular task. The problem in this context comes from the aspects integration while they can affect the behavior of the collaboration. We must thus ensure that aspects are integrated correctly into the collaboration. When integrated to the control, aspects have the possibility to change the state of the system as stated in [12]. Concerns implemented in aspects have the potential to extend the original behavior of a given collaboration.

3 AspectJ: Basic Concepts

AspectJ is an aspect-oriented extension for Java [5]. Eclipse (with *AJDT*) [4] is a compiler as well as a platform supporting the development of AspectJ programs. AspectJ achieves modularity with aspect abstraction mechanisms, which encapsulate behavior and state of a crosscutting concern. It introduces several new language constructs such as introductions, jointpoints, pointcuts and advice. Aspects typically contain new code fragments that are introduced to the system. Aspects make it explicit where and how a concern is addressed, in the form of jointpoints and advice. An aspect gathers pointcuts and advice to form a regrouping unit [5, 8, 19]. An aspect is similar to a Java or C++ class in the way that it contains attributes and methods. Jointpoints are used to define concerns structure. AspectJ makes it possible to define jointpoints in relationship to a method call or a class constructor [8]. A pointcut is a set of jointpoints. An advice is a mechanism (method like abstraction) used to specify the code to execute when a jointpoint is reached. It can also expose some of the values in the execution of these jointpoints. Pointcuts and advice define integration rules. For more details see [4].

4 Integration Strategy: Main Phases

The proposed methodology consists in two main steps (Figure 1). The first one is related to the generation of the basic test sequences corresponding to the collaboration between classes. Each generated sequence corresponds to a particular scenario of the collaboration diagram. Those sequences represent the main scenario (*happy path*) [10] and its various extensions. We use XML to describe collaboration diagrams and aspects. The proposed strategy consists, in a first step, to generate test sequences corresponding to all scenarios without aspects integration. This will support the testing process of the collaboration. The main goal of this step is to verify the collaboration (without aspects) for the realization of a given task and to eliminate faults that are not related to aspects. Aspects are integrated in a second step, in an iterative way. This process is based on the testing criteria presented in section 6. We assume that this will reduce the complexity of the testing process. We focus on the impact of aspects integration on the original scenarios of the collaboration. We formally identify the sequences that are affected by the integration of aspects. Aspects are automatically integrated, in an incremental way, to the original sequences and tested during the verification process. Finally, all aspects are integrated to the

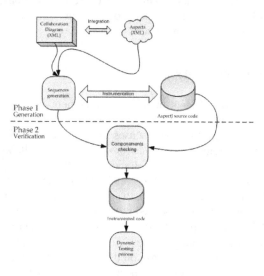

Fig. 1. Testing process

collaboration diagram to ensure that the original behavior is not affected in one hand and that aspects are correctly integrated in the collaboration in the other hand.

The second main step of our strategy consists of a dynamic analysis that allows verifying whether the implementation of each collaboration (including aspects) is in accordance with the corresponding specification. This process is supported by a source code instrumentation of the program under test. The following algorithm represents important steps of our strategy.

1. Generating control flow graphs corresponding to the methods implied in the collaboration.
2. Generating messages tree of the collaboration.
3. Generating basic sequences (based on the collaboration between objects).
4. Testing the collaboration between classes based on the various scenarios.
5. Integrating aspects: While there is non integrated aspects
   a. Integrating one aspect.
   b. Identifying sequences that are affected by this integration (following the aspect's control).
   c. Re-testing the affected sequences.
   d. If there are no problems, return to step 5.
6. Testing entirely the collaboration including aspects.
7. End

To instrument the software under test we do use an aspect (generated by our tool) for every sequence that we want to test to capture dynamically all invoked methods in the collaboration (aspects and classes). This particular aspect verifies dynamically, among others, if the executed sequence conforms to the selected one (sequence of messages, conditions). The complete sequences, after aspects integration, take into consideration not only the original collaboration between objects including aspects, but several aspects related to their control as well (pre conditions, post conditions, sequencing, control structures associated to the interactions, etc.). This allows supporting formally the verification process.

5   Collaboration Diagrams

In object-oriented systems, objects interact to implement behavior. Object-oriented development describes objects and their collaborations [10, 16]. Behavior can be described at two levels. The first one focuses on the individual behavior of objects while the second one is related to the behavior of a group of collaborating objects [1]. The collective behavior of a group of collaborating objects, for the realization of a specific task, can be specified using UML collaboration diagrams. UML collaboration diagrams [18] illustrate the interactions between objects in the form of graphs. Each scenario of the collaboration is represented by a specific sequence.

We are interested, in our approach, to the impact of the integration of one or more aspects to a group of collaborating classes. According to the faults model presented by Alexander et al. in [2], two situations could be at the origin of faults. The first one is related to the link that weaves an aspect with its primary abstraction while it introduces new dependencies. The second level is related to the fact that several aspects are integrated to a single class. In that case, it becomes difficult to localize the source of a fault when failures occur. The various control permutation between aspects may complicate the localization of the origin of an error. To reduce this complexity, we adopted an iterative approach for aspects integration. The following criteria aim to cover the new dimensions introduced by the integration of aspects to a group of collaborating classes.

6 Testing Criteria

A testing criterion is a rule or a set of rules that impose conditions on testing strategies [12, 15, 19]. It also specifies the required tests in terms of identifiable coverage of the software specification used to evaluate a set of test cases [12]. Testing criteria are used to determine what should be tested without telling how to test it. Testing engineers use those criteria to measure the coverage of a test suite in terms of percentage [14]. They are also used to measure the quality of a test suite. The first two criteria are based on collaboration diagrams [1, 6, 15, 18]. We extend these criteria to take into account the new dimensions related to the integration of aspects in a collaboration diagram.

Transition Coverage Criterion

A transition represents an interaction between two objects in a collaboration diagram. Each interaction must be tested at least once [13]. According to Offutt et al. [15], a tester should also test every pre-condition in the specification at least once to ensure that it will always be possible to execute a given scenario (some scenarios might never be executed if a pre-condition is not well-formed). A test will be executed only when the pre-condition related to the transition is true.

C1: Every transition in a collaboration diagram must be tested at least once.

Sequence Coverage Criterion

The previous criterion relates to testing transitions taken individually. It does not cover transitions sequences [13]. A sequence is a logical suite of several interactions. It represents, in fact, a well-defined scenario in the collaboration that has the possibility to be executed at least once during the program execution. By testing sequences with their control (pre and post condition), we verify all possibilities based on the collaboration diagram (main scenario and its various extensions). In certain cases, the number of sequences is unlimited (presence of iterations). The test engineer has to select the most relevant sequences.

C2: Every valid sequence in a collaboration diagram must be tested at least once.

The first two criteria are related to collaboration diagrams. They do not cover aspects dependencies. Thus, we need to develop new criteria. The following criteria cover the news dimensions introduced by aspects. They are based on the faults model presented by Alexander et al. in [2].

Modified Sequences Coverage Criterion

The collaboration between objects is first tested without aspects in order to make sure that the various scenarios are implemented correctly. This is possible since an aspect, from its nature, should not modify the semantic of a class [22]. Aspects depend on classes' context concerning their identity as mentioned by Alexander et al [2]. Therefore, aspects are bounded to classes and they cannot exist by themselves. However, aspects introduce new fragments of code that must be integrated to the collaboration. Those fragments can modify the state of a system [12] and change the behavior of a group of collaborating classes. It is imperative to adequately test sequences affected by aspects.

C3: Every sequence that is modified by aspects in the collaboration diagram must be re-tested.

Simple Integration Coverage Criterion

Simple integration occurs when only one aspect is introduced to a given class. We need, in this case, to determine formally the affected sequences and test them again. We focus here on the link between the aspect and the class without context consideration.

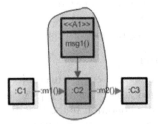

Fig. 2. Simple integration

C4: If a method of a given class is affected by an advice and if that method is used in the collaboration diagram, all sequences that include the execution of that method must be re-tested.

Multi-aspects Integration Coverage Criterion

It is possible that several aspects come to be weaved to a method of a given class. In this situation, several conflicts may arise. In spite of certain mechanisms making it possible to specify the execution order, it is always possible to be confronted to a random sequencing. The context is important since executing an aspect before another can change the state of a system. Especially, when the aspects are *stateful* or *altering* [12].

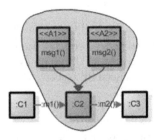

Fig. 3. Multi-aspects integration

C5: If a method of a given class is affected by several advice and if that method is used in the collaboration diagram, all sequences that include the execution of that method must be re-tested. This test will have to be executed with all possible advice permutation after aspects integration.

7   Automated Test Sequences Generation

7.1   Approach

Test sequences generation process takes into consideration the control described in the collaboration diagram. Each valid sequence in the collaboration diagram corresponds to a possible scenario that may be executed. Our strategy takes into consideration the two levels of integration: classes-classes and aspects-classes integration. It follows an iterative process. The following example has been modeled from a real AspectJ application. This example illustrates some ways that dependent concerns can be encoded with aspects. It uses an example system comprising a simple model of telephone connections to which timing and billing features are added using aspects, where the billing feature depends upon the timing feature. It constitutes, in our opinion, an interesting concrete example to present our approach. We have generated the corresponding collaboration diagram (figure 4) by analyzing the classes implied in the example. For more details about the example see AspectJ web site [5].

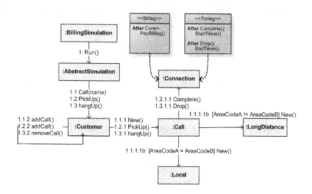

Fig. 4. Collaboration diagram

The following figure 5 shows an adapted version of the source code of the *Timing* aspect implied in the collaboration.

We start by creating the messages tree corresponding to the collaboration diagram. By analyzing the messages tree, we generate the original sequences, which will make it possible to test the collaboration between classes in order to check if the implementation of the various scenarios is in accordance with the specification. This will allow thereafter, according to the introduced criteria, to determine and visualize the scenarios modified by aspects. Aspects integration is done incrementally. When all aspects are successfully integrated, we test the whole collaboration diagram to

```
1 public aspect Timing {
2     /**
3      * Start the timer when call completed
4      */
5     after (Connection c): target(c) && call(void Connection.complete())(
6          StartTimer(c);
7     )
8     private void StartTimer(Connection c){
9        getTimer(c).start();
10    }
11    /**
12     * When to stop the timer
13     */
14    pointcut endTiming(Connection c): target(c) &&
15         call(void Connection.drop());
16    /**
17     * Stop the timer when call dropped and update the involved parties
18     */
19    after(Connection c): endTiming(c){
20       EndTimer(c);
21    }
22    private void EndTimer(Connection c){
23        getTimer(c).stop();
24        c.getCaller().totalConnectTime += getTimer(c).getTime();
25        c.getReceiver().totalConnectTime += getTimer(c).getTime();
26    }
27 }
```

Fig. 5. Source code for the aspect *Timing*

ensure that aspects and collaborating classes are working together correctly. This step is also used to determine the possible conflicts, which can be generated by the aspects. By integrating incrementally aspects, the faults related to the interactions between aspects and classes are relatively easy to identify. The sequences are generated by considering all the possible combinations, for a multi-aspects integration, in order to detect the errors related to the possible random behavior in this case.

7.2   Control Graphs

Control graphs are used in order to modularize the control of the methods involved in the collaboration. They are at the basis of the complete control graph of the collaboration. This later presents a global overview of the control present in the collaboration diagram. Figure 6 shows the control graph of the collaboration described in Figure 4.

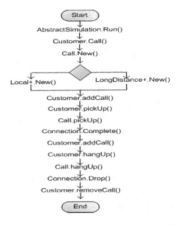

Fig. 6. Messages control flow graph

7.3 Messages Tree

The control graph related to each method implied in the collaboration is, in fact, translated into a principal sequence (*regular expression*). The objective at this stage consists in generating the principal sequence of each method. To this end, we use the following notations: The notation {*sequence*}, expresses zero or several executions of the sequence. The notation (*sequence 1/sequence 2*) expresses a mutual exclusion during the execution between sequence 1 and sequence 2. The notation [*sequence*] expresses that the sequence can be executed or not. Once methods sequences are created, we use those as a basis for the construction of the main sequence (corresponding to the collaboration) and to generate the corresponding messages tree. Each message is replaced by its own sequence. The substitution process stops when messages are at the leaf levels of the tree. At this step, we do not consider aspects. Figure 7 illustrates the principal sequence of the considered collaboration.

AbstractSimulation.Run(),   Customer.Call(),Call.New(),
(*Local.New()/LongDistance.New()*), Customer.addCall(), Customer.pickUp(), Call.pickUp(),
Connection.Complete(),   Customer.addCall(),   Customer.hangUp(),
Call.hangUp(),Conneciton.Drop(), Customer.removeCall()

Fig. 7. Main sequence

7.4 Main Test Sequences

The technique consists of generating, using the messages tree, all possible paths starting from the root and taking into account the control. Each path will correspond to a particular test sequence. Every generated sequence represents, in fact, a specific scenario of the collaboration. In order to simplify the notation, we assign a node number to the methods involved in the collaboration. Table 1 shows messages with their assigned node. Table 2 illustrates the generated sequences based on the main sequence presented in figure 7. Our initial tests use those sequences to ensure that the collaboration is working correctly.

Table 1. Messages number

Node	Classes' Messages
1	AbstractSimulation.Run()
2	Customer.Call()
3	Call.New()
4	Local.New()
5	LongDistance.New()
6	Customer.addCall()
7	Customer.pickUp()
8	Call.pickUp()
9	Connection.Complete()
10	Customer.hangUp()
11	Call.hangUp()
12	Conneciton.Drop()
13	Customer.removeCall()

Table 2. Generated basic sequences

Scenario	Test	Sequences
1	#1	$1 \rightarrow 2 \rightarrow 3 \rightarrow 4 \rightarrow 6 \rightarrow 7 \rightarrow 8 \rightarrow 9 \rightarrow 6 \rightarrow 10 \rightarrow 11 \rightarrow 12 \rightarrow 13$
2	#2	$1 \rightarrow 2 \rightarrow 3 \rightarrow 5 \rightarrow 6 \rightarrow 7 \rightarrow 8 \rightarrow 9 \rightarrow 6 \rightarrow 10 \rightarrow 11 \rightarrow 12 \rightarrow 13$

7.5 Aspects Integration

When all basic sequences related to the collaboration between classes are generated and tested, we proceed to aspects integration. Aspects are integrated in an incremental way, as mentioned previously, to facilitate errors detection. We adopted an iterative strategy by starting with the most complex aspect. According to the criteria established in section 6, we determine the sequences to which the aspects are weaved. These sequences will be re-tested. When all aspects are entirely integrated, we re-test all sequences one more time to ensure that the collaboration, including the aspects, works correctly. According to the collaboration diagram given by figure 4, the aspect *Timing* introduces two methods to the main sequences. Consequently, advice integration starts with this aspect. The proceeding order to introduce advice does not have importance. We begin with *StartTimer* and *EndTimer*. Table 3 shows the methods introduced by the *Timing* aspect with their associated node number. The obtained sequences are presented in tables 4 and 5.

Knowing that each advice is being integrated individually, we test the whole aspect. We integrate all the messages in the basic sequences and we re-test them (table 6).

Table 3. Messages number for Timing aspect

Node	Aspect's Methods
14	StartTimer ()
15	EndTimer()

Table 4. With *StartTimer()*

Scenario	Test	New sequences
1	#3	$1 \rightarrow 2 \rightarrow 3 \rightarrow 4 \rightarrow 6 \rightarrow 7 \rightarrow 8 \rightarrow 9 \rightarrow 14 \rightarrow 6 \rightarrow 10 \rightarrow 11 \rightarrow 12 \rightarrow 13$
2	#4	$1 \rightarrow 2 \rightarrow 3 \rightarrow 5 \rightarrow 6 \rightarrow 7 \rightarrow 8 \rightarrow 9 \rightarrow 14 \rightarrow 6 \rightarrow 10 \rightarrow 11 \rightarrow 12 \rightarrow 13$

Table 5. With *EndTimer()*

Scenario	Test	New sequences
1	#5	$1 \rightarrow 2 \rightarrow 3 \rightarrow 4 \rightarrow 6 \rightarrow 7 \rightarrow 8 \rightarrow 9 \rightarrow 6 \rightarrow 10 \rightarrow 11 \rightarrow 12 \rightarrow 15 \rightarrow 13$
2	#6	$1 \rightarrow 2 \rightarrow 3 \rightarrow 5 \rightarrow 6 \rightarrow 7 \rightarrow 8 \rightarrow 9 \rightarrow 6 \rightarrow 10 \rightarrow 11 \rightarrow 12 \rightarrow 15 \rightarrow 13$

Table 6. Integration of aspect *Timing*

Scenario	Test	New sequences
1	#7	1 → 2 → 3 → 4 → 6 → 7 → 8 → 9 → **14** → 6 → 10 → 11 → 12 → **15** → 13
2	#8	1 → 2 → 3 → 5→ 6 → 7 → 8 → 9 → **14** → 6 → 10 → 11 → 12 → **15** → 13

After that we integrate the aspect *Billing*. This aspect is particular because its poincut point on a class constructor. The main problem comes from the fact that this class is an abstract class. The advice related to that pointcut will be triggered when one of the sub-classes will be instantiated. The implementation for the connection class is done in two sub-classes: *Local* and *Longdistance*. Thus, every instance of those two classes will trigger the poincut defined in the aspect *Billing*. Table 7 presents the method introduced by the *Billing* aspect. The new sequences are shown in the table 8.

Once the integration of all aspects is done, we test the system entirely by integrating all aspects to the collaboration diagram. Knowing that we have two scenarios, the last two tests need be applied (table 9).

Table 7. Message number for *Billing* aspect

Node	Aspect's Methods
16	PayBilling()

Table 8. Integration of aspect *Timing*

Scenario	Test	New sequences
1	#9	1 → 2 → 3 → 4 → **16**→ 6 → 7 → 8 → 9 → 6 → 10 → 11 → 12 → 13
2	#10	1 → 2 → 3 → 5 → **16**→ 6 → 7 → 8 → 9 → 6 → 10 → 11 → 12 → 13

Table 9. Global integration

Scenario	Test	New sequences
1	#11	1 → 2 → 3 → 4 → **16** → 6 → 7 → 8 → 9 → **14** → 6 → 10 → 11 → 12 → **15** → 13
2	#12	1 → 2 → 3 → 5→ **16** → 6 → 7 → 8 → 9 → **14** → 6 → 10 → 11 → 12 → **15** → 13

8 Testing Process

The testing process that we implemented aims essentially to verify if the executed sequences conform to the selected ones in one hand and if the obtained results conform to the specifications in the other hand. We present, in what follows, the main phases of the testing process. For each generated sequence S_i:

1. Instrumenting the program under test.
2. Executing the program under test.
3. Analyzing the results.

8.1 Instrumentation

When all sequences are generated, we can start the testing process. In opposition to traditional instrumentation techniques, we do use aspects to capture dynamically a trace of the executed methods in a given sequence. The advantage of our approach is that we don't modify in any way the original source code of the program we are testing. Traditional instrumentation techniques consist generally in introducing many lines of source code in the program under test. Those fragments of code may introduce involuntary faults [9]. We generate an aspect for each sequence that we want to test. When we want to test a specific sequence, we compile the software with the corresponding aspect. The tracking aspects are automatically build using the tool we developed and are functional with any AspectJ [5] program. In fact, our strategy is general and would be easily adaptable to another aspect implementation. When a method involved in a sequence is executed, the tracking aspect will keep information about that execution. This information will be used in the following steps (verification process, testing coverage).

8.2 Executing the Program Under Test

When the instrumentation phase is completed, we can execute the program. It mainly consists to run the program and test a specific sequence. It remains to the tester to provide testing entries to ensure the execution of the selected sequence. When the inputs have been provided we can launch the program with the selected testing sequence.

8.3 Analyzing the Results

When a sequence has been successfully executed, an analyzer compares the executed methods with the expected ones. Our strategy essentially consists to discover three types of faults.

1. Specifications based faults.
2. Pre-condition based faults.
3. Source code based faults (java exceptions).

Specification Based Faults
This kind of fault occurs when some parts of the specification are not well transposed in the application. A missing method, an invalid method signature could be source of this type of fault. This level mainly consists to verify if an executed sequence is in accordance with the expected one. To test the potential source of fault, we voluntary omitted to call a method in the class *Call*. The line 60 in figure 8 has been inserted as a commentary which will cause the method being not called.

```
57    public void pickup()
58    {
59      Connection connection = (Connection)connections.lastElement();
60      //Connection.complete();
61    }
```

Fig. 8. Example of a specification fault

Pre-condition Based Faults

This step verifies all pre-conditions defined in a collaboration diagram. In the considered collaboration diagram (figure 4), two sequences are possible. The pre-conditions related to the message *New* of the classes *Local* and *LongDistance* determine if the selected scenario concern a local phone call or a long distance call. The tester can voluntary throws a pre-condition based fault by applying wrong entries when testing a specific sequence. For example, let's suppose we want to test the first scenario (local call). We will intentionally execute the second scenario (long distance call). The program under test will simulate a long distance call while our analyzer expects a local call. The precondition *AreaCodeA = AreaCodeB* won't be respected and an error will be thrown.

Source Code Based Faults (Java Exceptions)

One of the best features about java is its capacity to handle errors when they occur. However, it is possible with AspectJ [5] to collect those errors. While we automatically create aspects to track the executed messages, we also generate *pointcuts* that will watch all exceptions thrown by java. In our example (*Telecom*), we inserted some code that will produce an IOException in the *Timing* aspect.

```
45      private void StartTimer(Connection c)
46      {
47        getTimer(c).start();
48
49        /**
50        * Do an exception fault
51        */
52        BufferedReader in;
53        String f = "c:\\NonExistantFile.txt";
54        try
55        {
56           in = new BufferedReader(new FileReader(f));
57        } catch (FileNotFoundException e){
58           System.out.println("Can't open the file : " + f);
59           return;
60        }
61
62        /**
63        *End of fault code
64        */
65      }
```

Fig. 9. Inserting an exception fault

The introduced code (lines 49 to 64), in figure 9, aims to open a non existing file (*NonExistantFile.txt*). Since the file does not exist, java will throw an IO exception. The tracking aspect will find the error and a message will inform the tester where exactly the fault has been detected. Moreover, the implemented approach allows computing the testing coverage according to the tested sequences. The sequence coverage (SC) is calculated as following:

$$SC = \frac{Number\ of\ Executed\ Sequences\ (NES)}{Number\ of\ Generated\ Sequences\ (NGS)}$$

9   Conclusion and Future Work

Aspect-oriented programming introduces new abstractions and dimensions in terms of control and complexity. Existing object-oriented testing techniques do not cover the characteristics of aspects and their consequences in terms of control. We focus, in this paper, in an important dimension of aspect-oriented programs. This dimension is related to the behavior of a group of collaborating objects to which are weaved one or several aspects. Our methodology is based on the specifications described in a collaboration diagram. It offers, compared to the code based approaches, the advantage of preparing the testing process early in a software development.

The adopted approach consists of two main phases. The first one (1) is a static analysis. We generate test sequences based on the dynamic interactions between aspects and classes. It consists in generating the test sequences based on the various scenarios from a given collaboration between a group of objects without any aspects consideration. This step verifies if the collaboration is working correctly and errors that are not aspect-related are eliminated. The second phase (2) is a dynamic analysis, which mainly consists to verify the execution of the selected sequences. Aspects are integrated incrementally to the collaboration diagram. New sequences are generated according to the defined testing criteria. The fragments of code introduced by aspects are integrated to the basic sequences. The new sequences take into consideration the collaboration between objects in terms of messages, control related to these inter-actions and weaved aspects. The second phase of our strategy consists to verify the execution of the generated sequences. This phase is supported by an instrumentation of the AspectJ code of the program under test. This makes it possible to check if the implementation conforms to the specification. A tool supporting this phase has been implemented based on a three levels fault model. The first one is concerning specification faults, the second one focuses on discovering pre-condition faults while the last step is about java source code faults (exceptions). We plan to experiment our approach and the developed tool using real AspectJ programs.

References

[1]   A. Abdurazik and J. Offutt, Using UML Collaboration Diagrams for Static Checking and Test Generation, *In Third Internationl Conference on The Unified Modeling Language (UML '00)*, York, UK, October 2000.

[2]   R. Alexander, J. Bieman and A. Andrews, Towards the Systematic Testing of Aspect-Oriented Programs, *Technical Report CS-4-105,* Colorado State University, Fort Collins, Colorado, USA, March 2004.

[3]   Aspect-Oriented Software Development Web Site (AOSD), http://.aosd.net/

[4]   T. AspectJ, The AspectJ™ Programming Guide, 2002.

[5]   AspectJ Web Site, http://eclipse.org/aspectj/

[6]   M. Badri, L. Badri, and M. Naha, A use Case Driven Testing Process: Toward a Formal Approach Based on UML Collaboration Diagrams, Post-Proceedings of FATES *(Formal Approaches to Testing of Software) 2003*, in LNCS (Lecture Notes in Computer Science) 2931, Springer-Verlag, January 2004.

[7]   T. Ball, On the Limit of Control Flow Analysis for Regression Test Selection, *In Proceedings of ACM SIGSOFT International Symposium on Software Testing and Analysis (ISSTA-98), volume 23,2 of ACM Software Engineering Notes*, New York, March 1998.

[8]   J. Baltus, La Programmation Orientée Aspect et AspectJ : Présentation et Application dans un Système Distribué, *Mini-Workshop: Systèmes Coopératifs. Matière Approfondie*, Institut d'informatique, Namur, 2001.

[9]   B. Beizer, Software Testing Techniques, International Thomson Comuter Press, 1990.

[10] C. Larman, UML et les Design Patterns,*2e édition*, CampusPress 2003.

[11] P. Massicotte, M. Badri and L. Badri, Generating Aspects-Classes Integration Testing Sequences: A Collaboration Diagram Based Strategy. *3rd ACIS International Conference on Software Engineering Research, Management & Applications (SERA2005)*, IEEE CSP, Central Michigan University, Mt. Pleasant, Michigan, USA, August 2005.

[12] M. Mortensen and R. Alexander, Adequate Testing of Aspect-Oriented Programs, *Technical report CS 04-110*, Colorado State University, Fort Collins, Colorado, USA, December 2004.

[13] J. Offutt and A. Abdurazik, Generating Tests from UML Specications, *In Second International Conference on the Unified Modeling Language (UML '99)*, Fort Collins, CO, October 1999.

[14] J. Offutt and J. Voas, Subsumption of Condition Coverage Techniques by Mutation Testing, *ISSE-TR-96-01*, January 1996.

[15] J. Offutt, Y. Xiong and S. Liu, Criteria for Generating Specification-based Tests, *In Engineering of Complex Computer Systems, ICECCS '99*, Fifth IEEE International Conference, 1999.

[16] Rational Software Corporation. Rational Rose 98: Using Rational Rose, Rational Rose Corporation, Cupertino CA, 1998.

[17] R. Walker, E. Baniassad and G. Murphy, An initial assessment of aspect-oriented programming, *In Proceedings of the 21st International Conference on Software Engineering*, Los Angeles, CA, May 1999.

[18] Ye Wu, Mei-Hwa Chen and Jeff Offutt, UML-based Integration Testing for Component-based Software, *In Proceedings of the Second International Conference on COTS-Based Software Systems*, September 2002.

[19] T. Xie, J. Zhao, D. Notkin, Automated Test Generation for AspectJ Programs, *In Proceedings of the AOSD '05 Workshop on Testing Aspect-Oriented Programs (WTAOP 05)*, Chicago, March 2005.

[20] D. Xu, W. Xu and K. Nygard, A State-Based Approach to Testing Aspect-Oriented Programs, *Technical report*, North Dakota University, Department of Computer Science, USA, 2004.

[21] J. Zhao, Tool support for unit testing of aspect-oriented software, *In Proceedings OOPSLA' 2002 Workshop on Tools for Aspect-Oriented Software Development*, November 2002.

[22] Y. Zhou, D. Richardson, and H. Ziv, Towards a Practical Approach to test aspect-oriented software, *In Proc. 2004 Workshop on Testing Component-based Systems (TECOS 2004)*, Net.ObjectiveDays, September 2004.

Prototyping Domain Specific Languages with COOPN

Luis Pedro, Levi Lucio, and Didier Buchs

University of Geneva, Centre Universitaire d'Informatique,
24, rue du Général-Dufour CH-1211 Genève, Switzerland
{Luis.Pedro, Levi.Lucio, Didier.Buchs}@cui.unige.ch

Abstract. The work described in this article presents how we use COOPN in the context of the MDA (Model Driven Architecture) philosophy for prototyping Domain Specific Languages. With this principle we increase the abstraction of COOPN language representation enabling standard data interchange with other applications that use the same approach. In particular we will present the architecture of the transformation from Domain Specific Languages; its advantages concerning the ability to have COOPN models as a standard format for representing the semantics of Domain Specific Languages and to reuse software prototyping and testing techniques developped for this formalism. As example we will show how our work is proceeding towards transformation from UML to COOPN.

We also argue how our approach can be easily used in order to produce rapid system prototyping and verification for Domain Specific Languages (DSLs).

1 Introduction

This paper exposes how Concurrent Object-Oriented Petri Nets [2] (COOPN) language and COOPBuilder Integrated Development Environment (IDE) have been provided with Model Driven Architecture (MDA) concepts and functionalities with the aim of building a fully integrated solution for the prototyping of Domain Specific Languages (DSLs). In this particular subject, the main goal of our work is to achieve a full functional Model-Based test case generation and verification framework [7]. Our technique aims to create an infrastructure for providing translation semantics (and tools) to automate testing and verification for complex object oriented systems that can be specified in some Domain Specific Language (DSL). Up to now, our main targets are Fondue [11] (UML dialect), Critical Complex Control System Specification Language [10] (C^3S^2L) and Workflow Languages. Partial experiments have also been conducted on toy imperative language for teaching.

Expressing COOPN language by means of its Meta Model - defined as a Meta Object Facility [5] (MOF) model - it is possible to use Model Transformation from (and to) any other specification language (e.g. UML) that uses the same approach. The use of model-driven approaches as a requirement is emphasized by

N. Guelfi and A. Savidis (Eds.): RISE 2005, LNCS 3943, pp. 174–189, 2006.

the need of building reliable systems towards a solution based on modeling rather than on programing issues - model-driven development enables development at a higher level of abstraction by using concepts closer to the problem domain. Our goal is to achieve a level of abstraction that allows easy and intuitive system specifications providing at the same time an extremely accurate specification using concepts of a formal based specification language.

Taking into account that COOPN is a formal specification language allowing symbolic execution and state space exploration, it is our objective to provide COOPN a higher level of abstraction for its internal data description and format (the data that is responsible to handle the information of COOPN specifications). At the same time, keeping in mind the maximum standardization possible, we provide a set of interfaces which main goal is exactly to give access to COOPN data repositories for model transformation purposes. This procedure is the natural path for us to regulate access to COOPN data and being able to use a development methodology that encompasses *Analysis − Prototyping − Implementation*, as well as automated test case generation and verification. Using COOPN as the basis for prototyping and verification of DSLs is the natural step in our work: COOPN can be seen as an intermediate format for a DSL, giving it a formal and precise semantics.

Fig. 1 depicts the process of prototype generation and verification using COOPN as intermediate format. The process involves the specification of each DSL abstract syntax (UML Fondue and D^3S^2L as example in the figure) using its Meta-Model (an instance of MOF). A model transformation must be defined via a transformation language and transformation mapping in order to apply transformation from a DSL to obtain a COOPN model which will serve as

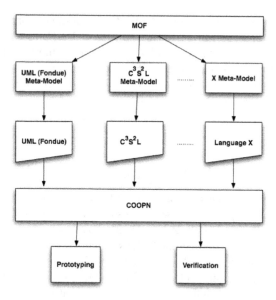

Fig. 1. Prototype generation and verification using CCOPN as an intermediary format

semantics. Transformations are composed of a series of rules which are applied to the source Fondue model. Each rule attempts to find some pattern in the source model and, if successful, generate some corresponding pattern in an target CO-OPN model. One see can the transformation mapping as a set of transformation rules consisting of two parts of a graph: a left-hand side (LHS); and a right-hand side (RHS).

Under some restrictions, the COOPN existing utilities allow to: a) generate a prototype for a given specification; b) enrich it with specific code; c) execute it or perform verification of implementations through testing. In this sense COOPN is both the intermediary semantic format for a given DSL and the instrument that consents the transformation from Platform Independent Model (PIM) to Platform Specific Models (PSM) allowing code generation.

There are various reasons why we argue that COOPN is suitable to be chosen as an intermediate format. Some of the more relevant are:

- It is modular specification language allowing to specify different DSL components and their relationships;
- The specifications are described in a completely abstract axiomatized fashion;
- The system states can be completely defined and explored.

Being able to describe COOPN data format within the MDA framework and integrating it in the COOPNBuilder IDE it is a very important step. It is fundamental towards a methodology that will allow full system specification and prototype generation using a formal language as core. This process will be detailed in section 3.

In this paper we will present:

- Some backgrounds on how to use COOPN for language prototyping;
- How we developed the infrastructure to take COOPN to the MDA level;
- Our ongoing work towards a complete development methodology in order to achieve Model Transformation for DSL prototyping;
- The tools that we are developing in our lab to support our methodology;
- Fondue as an example of DSL that we are working on.

2   Background

2.1   COOPN Specification Language

COOPN is a formal specification language built to allow the expression of models of complex concurrent systems. Its semantics is formally defined in [1], making it a precise tool not only for modeling, but, thanks to its operational semantics, also for prototyping and test generation. COOPN's richness gives us the possibility to specify in a formal fashion models of the systems. It groups a set of object-based concepts such as the notion of class (and object), concurrency, sub-typing and inheritance that we use to define the system specification coherently regarding notions used by other standard modeling approaches. An additional coordination

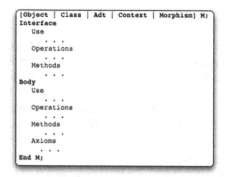

Fig. 2. General example of COOPN syntax

layer provides the designer with an abstract way of representing interaction between modeling entities and an abstract mapping to distributed computations.

Using COOPN we can profit from the advantages of having the system specified in a formal language: the unambiguous representation of the system; the easy reusability based on the fact that, usually, formal expressions are mathematically based and by definition more robust with respect to the evolution of the target systems; and also the fact that verification is more precise and more independent of the context. As such, with COOPN it is possible to completely define each state of the transition system - a requirement for model based test case generation.

The COOPN object oriented modeling language is based on Algebraic Data Types (ADT) and Petri Nets. It provides a syntax and semantics that allow using Heterogeneous Object Oriented (OO) concepts for system specification. The specifications are collections of *ADT*s, *classes* and *context* - the COOPN modules.

Syntactically speaking, each module encompasses the same overall structure including: *Name* - which represents the name of the module; *Interface* - that mainly comprises the types and elements accessible from the outside; *Body* - that includes the internal (private) information of the module. In addition, the *Body* section includes different parts like *Axioms* - operations' properties expressed by means of conditional equations; *Use* - field that indicates the list of dependencies of other modules. Class and context modules also have convenient graphical representations that denote its Petri net model. In figure 2 it is possible to see a general example from the COOPN syntax - detailed information about COOPN language can be found in [3].

2.2 The MDA Framework and DSL

The key of model-driven development is transforming high-level models into platform-specific models that can be used, for example, for automatically generating code or transforming models of the same level of abstraction. If, on one hand, it is possible to use the abstract syntax defined by a MOF model to store data in an XMI format that is coherent with that abstract syntax, on the other hand it is also possible to use the abstract definition of a language to define transformation rules. The general idea is to give part of the semantics using the transformation rules applied to the abstract syntax, being the other part provide directly and automatically by the fact that the transformation leads to a COOPN model. Using model-driven development with definition of MOF models for each language provides us with the necessary artifacts to perform transformations both at the PIM to PIM level and at the PIM to PSM one. We thus think the integration of MDA approach compliant techniques in COOPNBuilder plays a fundamental rule concerning the need of a fully automatic framework that goes from system specification in a DSL to system prototyping and verification.

2.3   System Prototyping with COOPN

Development using the COOPN language and in particular the COOPNBuilder IDE supports a general model based software development as well as various interactive development aspects at the specification level providing the possibility to deal with the high level of expressivity intrinsic to the COOPN language .

The life-cycle of a specification with COOPNBuilder it is composed by different steps going from writing a COOPN specification (step 1 in Fig. 3) using textual or graphical *editors*, to system simulation and deployment. In between, a checker tool (point 2 in Fig. 3) verifies that a COOPN specification is syntactically correct and well typed, being also possible to generate different prototypes of the system (e.g. in Java language). The code generation (prototype generation in Fig. 3) feature in COOPNBuilder is one of the approaches that enables execution of COOPN specifications. The generated Java code that corresponds to a COOPN specification includes algebraic data types, implementation of concurrency and the implementation of transactional mechanisms for the synchronizations between events. These artifacts can be used as a interpreted specifications within COOPNBuilder. This means that the generated code can be executed by using the Java reflexive mechanisms. In particular, the code generator can be used for simulation in order to allow an interactive follow up of the development methodology - implementation choices and their consequences are easily observed using the functionalities of the simulation provided by the IDE. COOPN prototypes are not rigidly defined, they can be enriched by manually written code either for particularising data structures or algorithms or by linking this code to external libraries.

3   Generalization of COOPN Data Format Using MDA Framework

This section concerns the basis of our work for performing transformations from any MDA compliant specification language into COOPN, and vice-versa.

We provide an overview of the technologies involved and how the export procedure from COOPN standard data format to XMI based data format is achieved. Although the text is focused on the particular transformation from COOPN standard data format to an XMI based format, it uses concepts and functionalities that we are exploring in other parts of the work being developed in our laboratory. We expect this work will provide the basis of the transformation we are currently working from a sub-set of UML. This methodology is named Fondue, uses a collection of UML diagrams with extensions of Object Constraint Language (OCL) and is our DSL example explored in section 6. Fondue can be seen as a Domain Specific Model (DSM) for reactive systems that includes a description of both the problem domain and of the functional requirements of the system.

The basis for the generalization of the COOPN data format using MDA concepts is to have a self described, accurate and standard way of storing COOPN specifications. At the same time we want to be able to achieve an abstraction level were transformations could be easily accomplished. The re-usablility of the work developed is one of the main concerns allowing, e.g. transformations to be performed redefining only the set of transformation rules and their algorithms. The re-usability is accomplished mainly by modularization of meta models and composition of transformation rules. The concepts behind the ideas of re-usability for easily perform transformation are detailed in section 6.1 and 6.3. As we are going further detail, even the process of exporting COOPN sources to XMI format uses general purpose techniques that are going to be re-used in other parts of our work.

The general approach includes the automatic generation of a set of Java interfaces that can be used both to populate a COOPN specification source file(s) or to browse existing ones. These interfaces are generated based on COOPN MOF model. The technology used is named Java Meta Data Interfaces [9] (JMI) that is a platform independent, vendor-neutral specification for modeling, creating, storing, accessing, querying, and interchanging metadata using UML, XML, and Java.

The Java APIs generated from the COOPN Meta-Model are used to interface with COOPNBuilder core in order to populate a COOPN specification source in XMI format. Steps 5 and 6 of figure 3 illustrate the process that concerns the operation of exporting a COOPN specification into a format based on XMI (XML Metadata Interchange) [6]. This process allows using COOPN data manipulation for transformation towards, for example, other specification languages. This procedure ill be detailed in this article and it is illustrated in point 6 of Fig. 3. At the same time, this procedure will be also used in the other direction: using the exact same technology (and base) framework a transformation from other DSLs to COOPN is possible to achieve defining a set of transformation rules.

According to the previous description what we do is to add to COOPNBuilder IDE the functionality to export data using a standard approach - this means that, if we combine the procedure illustrated by Fig. 1 and Fig. 3 we are able to, giving a system specification described in any DSM, transform it to COOPN. Using COOPN we can enhance DSLs with a formally and rigorous semantics. This allows to check the specification, generate a prototype, validate it.

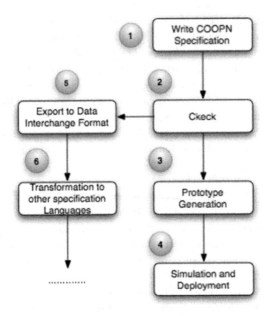

Fig. 3. COOPN Development Life-Cicle

4   Model Transformation for DSL Prototyping

The core elements for prototyping a DSL are the model transformation from the DSL to COOPN (PIM to PIM transformation) and the code generator in COOPN (PIM to PSM transformation). The DSL to COOPN transformation, although executed at a very abstract level, is responsible for giving to any DSL the semantics that are available in COOPN. This well defined semantics guarantees that a prototype generation and verification is possible and coherent with the principles given in the translation.

4.1   Semantics Enrichment of a DSL

No matter what is the semantics (or lack of it) of a DSL, when we transform it into COOPN it gains automatically COOPN semantics. This means that, if a transformation between a DSL and COOPN is possible, the DSL can be easily enriched with all the concepts and functionalities of COOPN language. Taking into account that COOPN can be seen is a General Propose Language (GPL) usually a mapping between a DSL and COOPN is possible but not always the reverse.

The gains of model transformation from a DSL to COOPN exist at various levels. Typical examples are the possibility of adding concurrent and transactional aspects to a language that, initially defined without such capabilities. Other examples might be pointed out but the big achievement of the transformation in

terms of giving precise semantics is to be able to use COOPN mechanisms for prototype generation, execution and state space exploration (verification). COOPN
has precise semantics that, after the transformation are *loaned* to the DSL.

4.2   Prototyping and Verification of a DSL Specification

Prototyping of a DSL can be achieved by using COOPNBuilder's prototyping
mechanisms. As was previously explained, COOPN has a precisely defined semantics allowing the automatic generation of Java code. As long as the translation algorithms into COOPN are semantically correct with respect to the DSL,
a prototype with the functionality described on the DSL can be automatically
produced. Obviously, the functionality of the produced prototype will be "raw"
in the sense that no interaction with the exterior can be modeled in COOPN.
This kind of functionality will have to be added by hand.

In what concerns verification issues, COOPNBuilder includes a test language
that allows building black-box tests for Class and Context modules of a COOPN
specification. These tests can be later applied to an implementation of that
specification. Given that COOPN specifications are hierarchical in the sense
that modules include other modules, producing black-box tests for a Class or a
Context module C implies producing integration tests for the modules $C1..Cn$
that compose C. There is however an open issue while testing DSL specifications:
where will the test intentions be defined? We can define them using the test
language editor included in COOPNBuilder, after having transformed the DSL
specification into COOPN. The problem with this approach is that some of the
clarity of the specification concepts defined in the DSL may be lost during the
translation into COOPN, making the test definition harder. A simple solution
for this problem would be to define test templates that would produce generic
tests with certain properties. Example properties for generated tests would be:
number of operations in the test inferior to a given number; all possible methods
called; all possible gates stimulated.

4.3   Architecture for Meta-Model Based Transformation

The detailed architecture of our process can be depicted in Fig. 4. The left
(darker side) of the picture shows how the process of data transformation works
interfacing with COOPN. The right side (in light grey) illustrates how the more
general process of transformation works.

From the left darker side of the picture we can see how the export procedure
to COOPN XMI data format is performed. A COOPN specification is furnished
and used by COOPN checker that verifies its integrity. The *Export Procedure*
task takes both the checked COOPN specification using the COOPN kernel
interfaces to parse it and the (already generated from the COOPN Meta-Model)
JMI interfaces. This tasks generates a COOPN XMI based specification fully
equivalent to the one that was supplied in the COOPN standard data format.

The right side of the figure 4 shows how the exact same technologies are
used to transform from any specification which Meta-Model is MOF based into

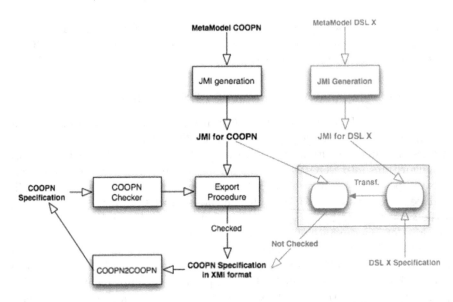

Fig. 4. General behavior of COOPN data format export and Model transformation

COOPN. This process is of course possible if a coherent mapping is provided. The mapping functions will intervene in what is performed by the *Transf.* arrow in the picture. Although the transformation process is completely dependent on what are the functionalities and concepts intrinsic to the *DSL X*, the technology and general procedure is the same whatever the *DSL X* is. The *Transf.* function can either be a simple mapping algorithm the uses source and target JMI or be based on transformation languages (like YATL [8] or MTL [12]) that make also use of MOF technologies. The cycle is complete once we use the *COOPN2COOPN* one to one mapping that transforms back to COOPN standard data format so that can be used by COOPN kernel, specially by the COOPN checker. This step is fundamental since the result from a direct transformation from a *DSL X* to COOPN, although syntactically correct, does not know anything about COOPN semantics - the XMI result of a transformation is a COOPN non-checked specification.

5 Meta-Modeling Utilities

By the time we are writing this paper, Meta-Modeling and transformation tools are being developed in our laboratory. A description of its functionalities and architecture follows:

The tool supports MOF models exploration, generic model browsing and JMI interfaces generation. The fact that transformations from a source to a target model are required is also foreseen. The tool is capable to cope with plugins (basically the definition of the transformation rules and their algorithms) that will use existing generated JMI interfaces (and consequently the Meta-Models of each language) to achieve transformation.

5.1   Functionalities

The tool being developed supports projects handling functionality. The user can create a new project or open an existing one. Each project has a pre-defined structure that is suitable to deal with:

- Meta-Model information in: XMI[UML] format (this is typically the format that results from the process of creating a Meta-Model using a given case tool that supports XMI type data manipulation); in XMI[MOF] format (this is the standard format for the Meta-Models);
- JMI interfaces both in source code and compiled;
- Different models of the language for which the project applies to - in XMI[*Language X*];
- Transformation algorithms that can be seen as plugins to the tool and that will relate (in terms of transformation) the Language that is represented by the project to other in other language also present in the project repository of the toll.

In terms of basic functionalities, and apart from the project handling functionality, the tool also supports:

- Automatic transformation from XMI[UML] to XMI[MOF];
- Generation and compilation of the JMI interfaces for the Meta-Model referent to project;
- Generic browsing of the Meta-Model structure via Java reflective interfaces. This provides the possibility to browse the elements (classes, associations, etc.) present in the Meta-Model;
- Generic browsing capabilities for the models present in the project repository. This is a kind of a *raw browse* in terms of a simple tree that represents the data in a model using the previously generated JMI interfaces;
- Specific model browsing capabilities. A configuration procedure is made available in order to support more than just a generic model browse;
- Transformation definitions in terms of algorithms written in Java. This functionality provides the possibility to add different *transformation programs* to the project repository that relate two models present in the repository.

With all this functionalities present in our tool we expect to be able to cover the full process of model transformation and model browsing from any predefined DSL to COOPN.

5.2   Browsing

The model browsing functionality (already pointed in the previous subsection), includes both generic and specific (specialized and configurable) model browsing.

This section concerns the specific model browsing functionality and the definition of the rules that will provide a visual syntax to the models.

This tasks includes providing the possibility to configure in terms of visual representation the elements (and associations between them) present in a Meta-Model of a *Language X*. The goal is to be able to specify a map between the elements of each language and the syntax of the Scalable Vector Graphics (SVG).

SVG is a language for describing two-dimensional graphics in XML. SVG allows different types of graphic objects like: vector graphic shapes (e.g., paths consisting of straight lines and curves), images and text. Graphical objects can be grouped, styled, transformed and composited into previously rendered objects. The feature set includes nested transformations, clipping paths, alpha masks, filter effects and template objects [13].

With SVG is used to create a definition between the elements available in a Meta-Model for a language and SVG elements: it is possible to access to SVG Document Object Model (DOM), which provides complete access to all elements, attributes and properties. A set of event handlers (such as *onmouseover* and *onclick*) can also be assigned to any SVG graphical object.

By providing the possibility to the user to define the map between his language and a standard like SVG the tool that we are developing goes in a direction of a complete utility that supports model transformation, browsing and interface creation for data access and manipulation.

5.3   Editing

In order to provide edition of DSL language at a general level, generic tools must be devised from the Abstract syntax contained in Meta level. We are currently implementing in our tool functionalities that allow edition of models of a given language. Although our tools are based in the Meta-Model of a language and the abstract syntax is available, the edition (as well as the creation) of a model from a given language must also be based on the verified abstract syntax - the type checked syntax.

The functionalities that provide access to DSL editing must combine knowledge from three different levels: 1) Concrete Syntax, provided by XMI but can be easily managed by special purpose Java interfaces; 2) Abstract Syntax, imposed by the Meta-Model and that can be accessed by JMI that also enforce its correctness - OCL constraints might be added to the Meta-Model in order to re-enforce some rules; 3) Type Checked Syntax.

The DSL edit operation can be seen as the composition of the browsing and modification functionalities. Where modification can both creation and destruction operations. We expect to provide general functionalities to perform this operation for any DSL.

6   Example of DSL: Fondue

In our approach, supporting Fondue is the result of providing Fondue Models with semantics in term of COOPN.

The transformation from Fondue to COOPN must be as automatic as possible. By basing the transformation rules in the two meta models (Fondue as the source model and COOPN as the target one) and developing tools to use them, it is possible to pass from Fondue to COOPN - the other components of the test case generation framework will take the COOPN model, generates and applies tests to the System implementation.

In terms of model analysis, the Fondue methodology provides two main artifacts: *Concept* and *Behavior* Models. The first one is represented as *UML class diagrams* and defines the static structure of the system information. The *Behavior Model* defines the input and output communication of the system, and is divided in three models: *Environment*, *Protocol* and *Operation* - represented respectively by *UML collaboration diagrams*, *UML state diagrams* and *OCL operations*.

6.1   Modularisation of the Meta Models

The abstract syntax of a formalism is usually factorized into several separated concepts aggregated together, for instance Algebraic abstract data types are the basis of class models expressed by Petri Nets in the COOPN formalism. According [4] it is possible to parameter language sub-models and consequently to be able to have full meta model seen as composition and instanciation of fragment of languages.

Give a language Meta-Model L based on a language(Meta-Model) P, we note $L(P)$ this parameterized view. If P is abstract enough to describe only the external definitions necessary for defining L, the instanciation process will described the concrete language P that can be used with L.

As an example, Horn logic is based on functional elements that can be for first order logic Herbrand functional terms $Horn(Terms)$ (corresponding to the prolog language) or for a simpler logic just propositional variables $Horn(Prop)$. In the modular approach Horn clauses will be defined independently of the functional terms $Horn(T)$, and later instanciated with specific elements.

- $Horn(T) = \{t_1 : -t_2, ..., t_n | t_1, t_2, ..., t_n \in T\}$;
- $Terms_{OP} = \{op \in OP_{s_1, s_2, ..., s_n} | \forall t_1, t_2, .., t_n \in Terms_{OP}, op(t_1, t_2, ..., t_n) \in Terms_{OP}\}$;
- T is a set of values.

This approach has a consequence on the way transformation can be defined. The idea is to define also abstract transformation and to instanciate them in a synchonous way with the instanciation of the modular parametrized meta models.

6.2   Composition of the Meta Models

Composing meta models is based on union of models and instanciation. The complete meta model that fully describes the abstract syntax of a language can be seen as the composition of smaller other meta models.

Taking Fondue as an example we can empathize that its complete meta model ($Fondue_{mm}$) is composed by four different ones:

$$Fondue_{mm} = E_{mm} + C_{mm} + P_{mm} + O_{mm}$$

being: E_{mm} the Fondue Environment meta model; C_{mm} the Fondue Concept meta model; P_{mm} the Fondue Protocol meta model and O_{mm} the Fondue Operation Schema meta model.

This does not means that relations between meta models do not exist, but rather that we can achieve full description of a specific domain using a DSL by means of composition of its different meta models. Each meta model can represent a part of the domain description and their relationships and combination allows complete characterization of the domain specific language.

6.3   Modularization of the Transformation Process

With this approach, Fondue models will have a unique COOPN equivalent element model (for instance a class in Fondue Concept Model is a class in COOPN). An association in Fondue is a class in COOPN and cardinalities in Fondue will become decoration in the COOPN axioms. The same approach is used for Fondue environment models and protocol - each environment model will have a Context and Petri-Net, receptively, as its equivalent in COOPN.

The modularization of the transformation process goes in the same line as the modularization of the meta models. A transformation from Fondue to COOPN is a function:

$$\forall M \in Fondue, \exists C \in COOPN : T_r(M) = C$$

At the same time, the transformation $T_r(M)$ is a composition of the transformation of each one of the Fondue models:

$$\forall M = < e, c, p, o > \in Fondue, e \in E, c \in C, p \in P, o \in O : T_r(M)$$
$$= T_r(e) + T_r(c) + T_r(p) + T_r(o)$$
$$\text{with,}$$

E the set of Fondue Environment diagrams, C the set of Fondue Concept diagrams, P the set of Fondue Protocol diagrams and O the set of Fondue Operation Schemas. The '+' operator is the disjoint union.

In particular, lets take the Fondue Environment diagrams and Operation Schemas:

Environment diagram: The Environment diagram in Fondue is composed of one System, messages going to the system and messages sent by the system to the outside. Being S, M_i, M_o the System, the set of input messages and the set output messages respectively we can formalize the trivial transformation of a Fondue Environment diagram as:

$$\forall s \in S, m_i \in M_i, m_o \in M_o \supset E, \exists Tr(E) : Tr(E) = Tr(s) + Tr(m_i) + Tr(m_o)$$

Taking into account that one system is transformed in a COOPN Context, the input messages into methods of the Context and the output messages into gates of the COOPN Context, and being C_{COOPN} the set of COOPN Contexts, M the set of COOPN Methods and G the set of COOPN gates:

$$\forall s \in S, m_i \in M_i, m_o \in M_o \supset E, \exists c_{coopn}, m, g \in C_{COOPN}, M, G : Tr(s)$$
$$= c_{coopn}; Tr(m_i) = m; Tr(m_o) = g \Rightarrow Tr(E) = c_{coopn} + m + g$$

Operation Schemas: The Fondue Operation Schemas are more complex models, they are basically composed by OCL expressions. The Fig. 5 shows the skeleton of a Fondue Operation Schema that we will base to define the transformation $T_r(o)$.

The composition of the transformation in what concerns the Operations Schemas can be defined as:

$$\forall op, message \in (M_i \cup M_o), pre \in PRE, post \in POST, \exists o \in O : T_r(o)$$
$$=< T_r(op), T_r(message), T_r(pre)..T_r(post) >$$

taking into account that: O is the set of Fondue Operation Schemas; PRE set of pre-conditions; $POST$ the set of post-conditions.

In fact, the transformations $T_r(op)$ ad $T_r(message)$ in this context are identities. They are just to express that the Operation Schema that is being transformed refers to input and output messages previously transformed from Fondue Environment diagram.

The pre- and post-conditions are based on control operators (if then... else ...), affectation based on OCL expressions. For simplicity we are not going to differentiate any $T_r(pre)$ and $T_r(post)$ since they are of the same nature. Given $expr \in FEXP$, with $FEXP$ being the set of Fondue expressions and $lexpr \in FLEXP$. We need also to define the following sets:

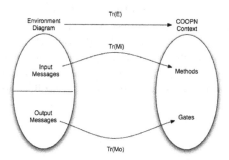

Fig. 5. Transformation of Fondue Environment diagram

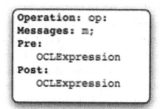

Fig. 6. Operation Schema skeleton

$FEXP = \{if\ lexpr\ then\ expr\ else\ expr | logicalvar := oclexpr | expr, expr\}$, and
$$FLEXP = \{oclexpr = oclexpr\}$$

For transformation, all these expressions will be transformed into only positive conditional axioms.

For example:

```
if cond1 then
  if cond2 then do1 else do2
  else
  do3
```

Will be transformed into 3 positive conditional axioms:

```
if cond1 and cond2 then do1;
if cond1 and not(cond2) then do2;
if not(cond1) then do3;
```

These axioms will be transformed as follows:

$$\forall expr \in FEXP, Tr(expr) = Tr(if\ lexpr\ then\ exp1, exp2, exp3) = $$
$$TrOCL(lexp) => Tr(exp1)..Tr(exp2)...$$

This transformation will produce several components in COOPN of format:

$$TrOCL(lexpr) =< logical\ expr, synchronisation >$$

We should note that, for logical expressions that are simple boolean conditions without access to elements in Class model, we will have $synchronization = \oslash$. Moreover, the .. operator is used to gather the result of each sub expressions. It means conjunction of logical expressionss and sequence of synchronizations. The result will be one COOPN axiom for each flatenned axioms.

Due to the complexity of the OCL language, describing its translation to COOPN is out of the scope of this paper. Abstractly, the transformation will mainly be a constructive semantic definition of the OCL operators in terms of COOPN.

7 Conclusion

In this paper we have presented our ideas on how to provide semantics to Domain Specific Languages by mapping them into our formal specification language COOPN. In order to do that we propose using techniques and tools from the Model Driven Architecture philosophy. In particular, we have used: MOF as a way of expressing in a common syntax metamodels of our source and target languages (respectively the DSL and COOPN); JMI as a way of interfacing with the metamodel repositories in XMI format. A side effect of our approach is that we need to provide our COOPN IDE (COOPNBuilder) a way of exporting and importing specifications in XMI format. This will not only make COOPNBuilder up to date with current standards for data interchange, but will also allow us to directly import into COOPNBuilder the products of an MDA transformation.

The final goal of our work will be to prototype and verify (by testing) a model expressed in any DSL. COOPNBuilder includes tools for prototyping and verification, so these activities will be possible in the measure of the correctness of the mapping of the DSL semantics in to COOPN. We are also working on generalizing these transformations by modularizing the metamodels and the transformation process itself.

References

1. Olivier Biberstein. *CO-OPN/2: An Object-Oriented Formalism for the Specification of Concurrent Systems*. PhD thesis, University of Geneva, 1997.
2. Olivier Biberstein, Didier Buchs, and Nicolas Guelfi. CO-OPN/2: A concurrent object-oriented formalism. In *Proc. Second IFIP Conf. on Formal Methods for Open Object-Based Distributed Systems, Canterbury, UK*, pages 57–72. Chapman and Hall, Lo, 1997.
3. Didier Buchs and Nicolas Guelfi. A formal specification framework for object-oriented distributed systems. *IEEE Transactions on Software Engineering*, 26(7):635–652, July 2000.
4. F. Fondement and R. Silaghi. Defining model driven engineering processes. Technical Report IC/2004/94, Swiss Federal Institute of Technology in Lausanne, Switzerland, November 2004.
5. Object Management Group. Meta-Object Facility. URL: http://www.omg.org/technology/documents/formal/mof.htm.
6. Object Management Group. XML Metadata Interchange. URL: http://www.omg.org/technology/documents/formal/xmi.htm.
7. Levi Lucio, Luis Pedro, and Didier Buchs. A Methodology and a Framework for Model-Based Testing. In N. Guelfi, editor, *Rapid Integration of Software Engineering techniques*, volume LNCS 3475, page 5770. LNCS, 2005.
8. Octavian Patrascoiu. YATL:Yet Another Transformation Language. In *Proceedings of the 1st European MDA Workshop, MDA-IA*, pages 83–90. University of Twente, the Nederlands, January 2004.
9. Java Comunity Process. Java Metadata Interface(JMI) Specification. Technical report, Sun, June 2002.
10. M. Risoldi and D. Buchs. Model-based prototyping of graphical user interfaces for complex control systems. Submited to MoDELS 2005 conference.
11. Alfred Strohmeier. Fondue: An Object-Oriented Development Method based on the UML Notation. In *X Jornada Técnica de Ada-Spain, Documentación, ETSI de Telecommunicación, Universidad Politécnica de Madrid,*, Madrid, Spain, November 2001.
12. Triskell team. MTL Documentation. URL: http://modelware.inria.fr/rubrique4.html.
13. W3C. Scalable Vector Graphics (SVG) 1.1. Technical Specification, January 2005.

An Improved Case-Based Approach to LTL Model Checking*

Fei Pu, Wenhui Zhang, and Shaochun Wang

Laboratory of Computer Science,
Institute of Software, Chinese Academy of Sciences,
P.O.Box 8718, 100080 Beijing, China
{pufei, zwh, scwang}@ios.ac.cn

Abstract. The state space explosion is the key obstacle of model checking. Even a relatively small system specification may yield a very large state space. The case-based approach based on search space partition has been proposed in [18, 19] for reducing model checking complexity. This paper extends the approach by considering wider ranges of case-bases of models and multiple case-bases such that it can be applied to more types of applications. The improved approach also combines the search space partition and static analysis or expert knowledge for guaranteeing the completeness of the cases. The case study demonstrates the potential advantages of the strategy and show that the strategy may improve the efficiency of system verification and therefore scale up the applicability of the verification approach.

1   Introduction

Designing and studying (software) systems using abstract behavioral models is becoming more and more feasible due to the increased capabilities of verification techniques developed lately. The most important of such techniques is model checking, where the validity of formally-specified requirements can be checked automatically on the model. As the state space explosion is the major bottleneck to model checking, much research is devoted to state space reduction techniques. It is crucial that such state space reduction preserves the properties under investigation. Related works can for instance be found in [2, 4–6, 8, 14]. The topics include compositional techniques [1, 16] for splitting verification tasks, bounded model checking [3] for checking satisfiability, symmetric reduction [10, 11] for applying symmetries, abstraction techniques [12] for reducing models and partial order reduction [13] for exploiting the partial order semantics for concurrent systems.

In addition to general techniques which can be used to a wide range of model, it is also important to develop techniques for special types of models in order

* This work is supported by the National Natural Science Foundation of China under Grant No. 60223005, 60373050, 60421001, and 60573012, and the National Grand Fundamental Research 973 Program of China under Grant No. 2002cb312200.

N. Guelfi and A. Savidis (Eds.): RISE 2005, LNCS 3943, pp. 190–202, 2006.

to enhance the applicability of model checking to these types of models. In previous works, we have investigated search space partition using case basis for the purpose of reduction in verification of models with non-deterministic choices and open environment. The reductions have been implemented, and show appropriate size on the subgoal, and therefore allowed for analysis of larger systems. The approach is to partition a model checking task into several cases and prove that the collection of these cases covers all possible cases, in which the former is done by model checking and the latter is done by using static analysis or by expert judgment to decide whether a model satisfies given criteria.

In [18, 19], the condition which the case-based approach can be used to model checking tasks is that there is some variable which is changed at most once during every execution of the model. Here, we extend the condition, so that we do not need to consider the number of the changes of the values of the variable during every execution of the model, as long as there is a corresponding variable satisfying some property when the variable does not take the given value. This is an extension of the condition of [18, 19], as it is a special case of the new condition. We further use multiple case-bases which can divide the task into a set of simpler tasks for reducing the need of memory in model checking. Hence, this work extends the capability of the approach such that it can be applied to wider ranges of models and to more types of applications. The modeling language of systems used in this paper is Promela – a high level specification language for system descriptions used by SPIN [7].

The paper is organized as follows. In section 2, we introduce the improved partition strategy. In section 3, we discuss static analysis of Promela models. In section 4, An application example is presented. Section 5 is concluding remarks and future work.

2   The Improved Partition Strategy

The motivation of the strategy is the verification of models with non-deterministic choice and open environment. The basic idea is to find a method for adequately representing different cases in such models, in order to reduce memory usage in model checking. The strategy partitions a model checking task into several cases and proves that the collection of these cases covers all possible case. We first give an introduction to the background of the basic strategy described in [18, 19] and then discuss the extensions of this strategy to wider ranges of case-bases and to multiple case-bases.

2.1   Basic Strategy

Let M be a system and $\vec{x}$ be the variable array of M. The system is in the state $\vec{v}$, if the value of $\vec{x}$ at the current moment is $\vec{v}$. A path of M is a sequence of states. The property of such a path can be specified by PLTL (propositional linear temporal logic) formulas [17].

- φ is a PLTL formula, if φ is of the form $z = w$ where $z \in \vec{x}$ and w is a value.
- Logical connective of PLTL include:
  $\neg(negation)$, $\wedge(conjunction)$, $\vee(disjunction)$ and $\rightarrow$ $(implication)$.
  If φ and ψ are PLTL formulas, then so are $\neg\varphi$, $\varphi \wedge \psi$, $\varphi \vee \psi$, and $\varphi \rightarrow \psi$.
- Temporal operations include:
  $X(nexttime)$, $U(until)$, $\Diamond(future)$ and $\Box(always)$.
  If φ and ψ are PLTL formulas, then so are $X\varphi$, $\varphi U\psi$, $\Diamond\varphi$, and $\Box\varphi$.

Let π be a path of M. Let $HEAD(\pi)$ be the first element of π and $TAIL^i(\pi)$ be the path constructed from π by removing the first i elements of π. For convenience, we write $TAIL(\pi)$ for $TAIL^1(\pi)$. Let $\pi \models \varphi$ denote the relation "π satisfies φ".

Definition 1. $\pi \models \varphi$ *is defined as follows:*

$\pi \models x = v$ *iff the statement $x = v$ is true in $HEAD(\pi)$.*
$\pi \models \neg\varphi$ *iff $\pi \not\models \varphi$.*
$\pi \models \varphi \wedge \psi$ *iff $\pi \models \varphi$ and $\pi \models \psi$.*
$\pi \models \varphi \vee \psi$ *iff $\pi \models \varphi$ or $\pi \models \psi$.*
$\pi \models \varphi \rightarrow \psi$ *iff $\pi \models \varphi$ implies $\pi \models \psi$.*
$\pi \models X\varphi$ *iff $TAIL(\pi) \models \varphi$.*
$\pi \models \varphi U\psi$ *iff $\exists k$ such that $TAIL^k(\pi) \models \psi$ and $TAIL^i(\pi) \models \varphi$ for $0 \leq i < k$.*
$\pi \models \Diamond\varphi$ *iff $\exists k$ such that $TAIL^k(\pi) \models \varphi$.*
$\pi \models \Box\varphi$ *iff $\pi \models \varphi$ and $TAIL(\pi) \models \Box\varphi$.*

Let τ be a set of paths.

Definition 2. $\tau \models \varphi$ *if and only if $\forall\pi \in \tau : \pi \models \varphi$.*

Definition 3. $\tau \not\models \varphi$ *if and only if $\exists\pi \in \tau : \pi \not\models \varphi$.*

Let $HEAD(\tau)$ be the set consisting of $HEAD(\pi)$ for all $\pi \in \tau$ and $TAIL(\tau)$ be the set consisting of $TAIL(\pi)$ for all $\pi \in \tau$. From the above definitions, we can derive the following:

$\tau \models x = v$ *iff the statement $x = v$ is true in s for all $s \in HEAD(\tau)$.*
$\tau \models \neg\varphi$ *iff $\tau \not\models \varphi$.*
$\tau \models \varphi \vee \psi$ *iff there are τ' and $\tau'' : \tau = \tau' \cup \tau''$ and $\tau' \models \varphi$ and $\tau'' \models \psi$.*
$\tau \models \varphi \wedge \psi$ *iff $\tau \models \varphi$ and $\tau \models \psi$.*
$\tau \models \varphi \rightarrow \psi$ *iff there are τ' and $\tau'' : \tau = \tau' \cup \tau''$ and $\tau' \not\models \varphi$ and $\tau'' \models \psi$.*
$\tau \models X\varphi$ *iff $TAIL(\tau) \models \varphi$.*
$\tau \models \varphi U\psi$ *iff there are τ' and $\tau'' :$*
$\qquad \tau = \tau' \cup \tau''$ and $\tau' \models \psi, \tau'' \models \varphi$ and $TAIL(\tau'') \models \varphi U\psi$.
$\tau \models \Diamond\varphi$ *iff there are τ' and $\tau'' :$*
$\qquad \tau = \tau' \cup \tau''$ and $\tau' \models \varphi$ and $TAIL(\tau'') \models \Diamond\varphi$.
$\tau \models \Box\varphi$ *iff $\tau \models \varphi$ and $TAIL(\tau) \models \Box\varphi$.*

Now let τ be the set of the paths of system M and φ be the propositional linear temporal logic formula. Let $M \models \varphi$ denote the relation "M satisfies φ".

Definition 4. $M \models \varphi$ *if and only if* $\tau \models \varphi$.

Suppose that there is a model M and a formula φ, and the task is to check whether φ holds in M, i.e. we would like to prove:

$$M \models \varphi.$$

The principle of case-based partition is to partition the search space of M, so the formula φ can be proved within each portion of the search space. The technique for this characterization is to attach formulas to φ, so that in the verification of $M \models \varphi$, only the paths relevant to the attached formulas are fully explored (or paths irrelevant to the attached formulas are discarded at an early phase of model checking).

Theorem 1. *Let* $\psi_1, \ldots, \psi_n$ *be formulas such that* $M \models \psi_1 \vee \cdots \vee \psi_n$. $M \models \varphi$ *if and only if*

$$M \models \psi_i \to \varphi$$

for all $i \in \{1, 2, \ldots, n\}$.

Proof. It is obviously that $M \models \varphi$ implies $M \models \psi_i \to \varphi$. We prove that $M \models \psi_i \to \varphi$ for all $i \in \{1, 2, \ldots, n\}$ implies $M \models \varphi$ as follows.

- Let τ be the set of paths of M. Since $M \models \psi_1 \vee \cdots \vee \psi_n$, there are $\tau_1, \ldots, \tau_n$ such that $\tau = \tau_1 \cup \cdots \cup \tau_n$ and $\tau_i \models \psi_i$ for all i.
- On the other hand, we have $\tau \models \psi_i \to \varphi$, hence $\tau_i \models \psi_i \to \varphi$ and $\tau_i \models \psi_i$ for all i. Therefore, $\tau \models \varphi$.   □

Remark 1. A similar strategy is the assume-guarantee paradigm in compositional reasoning. But they are different. The strategy of Theorem 1 partitions a model checking task into several cases (the verification of which is done separately by model checking), and proves that the collection of these cases covers all possible case, then establishes the correctness of the entire system. On the other hand, the assume-guarantee technique verifies each component process (or group of component processes) separately by combining the set of assumed and guaranteed properties of component processes in an appropriate manner, such that it can verify the correctness of the entire systems without constructing the global state-transition graph provided that the finite state system is composed of multiple processes running in parallel.

For a given model M, in order to be successful with this strategy, we have to be sure that the proof of $M \models \psi_i \to \varphi$ is simpler than the proof of $M \models \varphi$ for each i. Therefore τ (the set of paths representing the behavior of M) should have the following properties: τ can be partitioned into τ_i' and τ_i'' such that:

- $\tau_i' \not\models \psi_i$ and $\tau_i'' \models \varphi$;
- $\tau_i' \not\models \psi_i$ can be checked with high efficiency;
- τ_i'' is significantly smaller than τ.

For the selection of ψ_i (which determines τ_i' and τ_i''), it would be better to ensure τ_i'' $(i = 1, \ldots, n)$ be pair-wise disjoint, whenever this is possible. In addition, we shall discharge $M \models \psi_1 \vee \cdots \vee \psi_n$ by one of the following methods:

- Application of static analysis;
- Application of expert knowledge.

The reason for not verifying $M \models \psi_1 \vee \cdots \vee \psi_n$ with model checking is that the verification of this formula is not necessarily simpler than the verification of $M \models \varphi$. In order to be able to discharge $M \models \psi_1 \vee \cdots \vee \psi_n$ easily by the proposed methods, in [18, 19] the formula ψ_i is restricted to be of the form $\Box(x = v_0 \vee x = v_i)$ where x is a variable and v_0, v_i are constants. We call the variable x the basic case-basis of a partitioning. Consequently, we have the following theorem.

Theorem 2. [18, 19] *Let v be a variable, $\{v_0, v_1, \ldots, v_n\}$ be the range of v and v_0 be the initial value of v. Suppose that v is changed at most once during every execution of M. $M \models \varphi$ if and only if*

$$M \models \Box(v = v_0 \vee v = v_i) \rightarrow \varphi$$

for all $v_i \neq v_0$ in the range of variable v.

2.2   The Improved Strategy

In contrast to the case-based approach described above, the new approach is based on the new types of case-bases which is a generalization of basic case-bases.

Definition 5. *Let v be a variable of M, and $\{v_0, v_1, \ldots, v_n\}$ be the range of v, where v_0 is the initial value of v. If there exists a variable u satisfying: if variable v first takes value v_k after $v = v_0$, then $\Box((v \neq v_0) \rightarrow (v = v_k \vee \phi(u)))$ is true during the execution of M, where $v_k \in \{v_1, \ldots, v_n\}$ and $\phi(u)$ is a propositional formula related to u, then we call u a conjugate variable of v, and (v, u) the case-basis of M.*

Remark 2. The conjugate variable of v may be v itself. If v satisfies: v is changed at most once during each execution of M, and assume variable v first takes value v_k after $v = v_0$, where $v_k \in \{v_1, \ldots, v_n\}$, then $\Box((v \neq v_0) \rightarrow (v = v_k))$ is true during the execution of M, where $\phi(v) \equiv (v = v_k)$. Hence, the basic case-basis is the special case of the newly defined case-basis.

In order to make the analysis of the case-basis easy, the formula $\phi(u)$ is restricted to be of the form $(u = u_p)$ or $(u \neq u_p)$, where u_p is a value belonging to its range.

Lemma 1. *Let v be a variable of M and $\{v_0, v_1, \ldots, v_n\}$ be the range of v. Suppose u is a conjugate variable of v. Then we have*

$$M \models \bigvee_{i=1}^{n} \Box(v = v_0 \vee v = v_i \vee \phi(u)).$$

Proof. Let x be an arbitrary execution path of M, assume variable v first takes value v_i $(1 \leq i \leq n)$ in trace x after $v = v_0$. Since u is a conjugate variable of v, $\Box(v \neq v_0 \rightarrow (v = v_i \vee \phi(u)))$ is true during the execution of M. i.e. $\Box(v = v_0 \vee v = v_i \vee \phi(u))$ is true during the execution of M $(i \in \{1, \ldots, n\})$. Hence, $x \models \Box(v = v_0 \vee v = v_i \vee \phi(u))$. Then $M \models \bigvee_{i=1}^{n} \Box(v = v_0 \vee v = v_i \vee \phi(u))$.
$\qquad\qquad\qquad\qquad\qquad\qquad\qquad\qquad\qquad\qquad\qquad\qquad\qquad\qquad$ $\Box$

Theorem 3. *Let v be a variable of M and $\{v_0, v_1, \ldots, v_n\}$ be the range of v. Suppose u is a conjugate variable of v. $M \models \varphi$ if and only if*

$$M \models \Box(v = v_0 \vee v = v_i \vee \phi(u)) \rightarrow \varphi$$

for all $v_i \neq v_0$ in the range of variable v.

Proof. It follows from Lemma 1 and Theorem 1 by taking $\psi_i = \Box(v = v_0 \vee v = v_i \vee \phi(u))$.
$\qquad\qquad\qquad\qquad\qquad\qquad\qquad\qquad\qquad\qquad\qquad\qquad\qquad\qquad$ $\Box$

2.3 Multiple Case-Bases Strategy

A complicated (software) system may have multiple case-bases, i.e. there may be several (x_j, y_j) satisfying the condition that $M \models \psi_1 \vee \cdots \vee \psi_m$ where ψ_j is of the form $\Box(x_j = v_0 \vee x_j = v_j \vee \phi(y_j))$, and y_j is a conjugate variable of x_j. In case of two case-bases: (u_1, v_1) and (u_2, v_2), we have $M \models \psi_1^1 \vee \cdots \vee \psi_m^1$ for (u_1, v_1) and $M \models \psi_1^2 \vee \cdots \vee \psi_n^2$ for (u_2, v_2). For the model M, it can be divided in even smaller pieces τ_{ij}, where $\tau_{ij} \models \psi_i^1 \wedge \psi_j^2$. Then the verification task $\tau \models \varphi$ can be divided into a set of simpler verification tasks $\tau \models \psi_i^1 \wedge \psi_j^2 \rightarrow \varphi$. Generally, we have the following theorem.

Theorem 4. *Let $(x_i, y_i)(i = 1, \ldots, l)$ be a set of case-bases of M, where y_i is the conjugate variable of x_i, and let $\{v_{i0}, v_{i1}, \ldots, v_{in_i}\}$ be the range of x_i. Assume that $M \models \psi_1^i \vee \cdots \vee \psi_{n_i}^i$ holds, where $\psi_j^i = \Box(x_i = v_{i0} \vee x_i = v_{ij} \vee \phi(y_i))$ $(1 \leq i \leq l, 1 \leq j \leq n_i)$. Then $M \models \varphi$ if and only if*

$$M \models \psi_m^1 \wedge \psi_n^2 \wedge \cdots \wedge \psi_k^l \rightarrow \varphi$$

for $1 \leq m \leq n_1$, $1 \leq n \leq n_2$ and $1 \leq k \leq n_l$.

Proof. It can be proved with induction on the number of case-bases of M by applying Theorem 3.
$\qquad\qquad\qquad\qquad\qquad\qquad\qquad\qquad\qquad\qquad\qquad\qquad\qquad\qquad$ $\Box$

This theorem is an extension of Theorem 3, and also an extension of the basic case-basis in [18, 19].

3 Static Analysis

In order to successfully find the variables satisfying the conditions of Theorem 3, we should use static analysis to find the case-bases of models. We consider models of particular types with a situation where the non-deterministic choice is present. Let the non-deterministic choice be represented by $choice(\overrightarrow{x}, y)$, where $\overrightarrow{x} = \{v_0, v_1, \ldots, v_n\}$ is the set of possible values of variable x and v_0 is the initial value of x, y is the conjugate variable of x. We consider two types of the $choice(\overrightarrow{x}, y)$:

do ... if $:: x == v_1;$ ...; $\phi(y);$ ... $\vdots$ $:: x == v_n;$ ...; $\phi(y);$ ... fi; ... od;	do ... if $:: \text{run } p(\ldots, v_1, \ldots);$ ...; $\text{run } p(\ldots, v_m, \ldots);$... $\vdots$ $:: \text{run } p(\ldots, v_k, \ldots);$ ...; $\text{run } p(\ldots, v_n, \ldots);$... fi; ... od;

$\phi(y)$ is restricted to be a disjunction of terms like $(u = u_p)$ or $(u \neq u_p)$, where u_p is a value belonging to its range. We refer to the first type as $choice_1(\overrightarrow{x}, y)$ and the second type as $choice_2(\overrightarrow{x}, y)$. The set of paths of a model of these types has the potential (depending on the successfully static analysis) to be divided into subsets such that each subsets satisfies one of the following formulas:

$$\Box(x = v_0 \lor x = v_1 \lor \phi(y)), \ldots, \Box(x = v_0 \lor x = v_n \lor \phi(y)).$$

The purpose of the static analysis is to show that the partition of the search space into these cases is complete, i.e. to show

$$M \models \Box(x = v_0 \lor x = v_1 \lor \phi(y)) \lor \cdots \lor \Box(x = v_0 \lor x = v_n \lor \phi(y)).$$

Basically, we analyze the model in order to determine the set of cases and to ensure that (x, y) is the case-basis of a partition (in accordance with Theorem 1), i.e. checking the following conditions:

- the range of x is $\{v_0, v_1, \ldots, v_n\}$, and the range of y is $\{u_0, u_1, \ldots, u_m\}$.
- $\phi(y)$ is of the form $(y = u_p)$ or $(y \neq u_p)$, where $u_p \in \{u_0, u_1, \ldots, u_m\}$.
- during the execution of the model, if x first takes value v_k, $\Box(x \neq v_0 \rightarrow (x = v_k \lor \phi(y)))$ is true.

To locate $choice(\overrightarrow{x}, y)$, We analyze the structure of Promela programs to find out for a given pair (x, y), whether $choice(\overrightarrow{x}, y)$ satisfies all of the conditions, in order to determine whether (x, y) can be used as the case-basis of the verification task.

Summarizing the above discussion, we refine the steps of the verification strategy as follows:

- Use static analysis to analyze the model to get the case-basis (x, y) and their ranges $\overrightarrow{v}, \overrightarrow{u}$.
- For each $v_i \in \overrightarrow{v}$, construct $\varphi_i = \Box(x = v_0 \lor x = v_i \lor \phi(y)) \rightarrow \varphi$ as a subgoal for verification.

- Use the model checker SPIN to check whether $M \models \varphi_i$ holds for $i = 1, \ldots, n$.
- When find more than one case-bases, we pick some or all of them to construct subgoals according to Theorem 4.

Limitations. It is worth mentioning some limitations of our static analysis. The first drawback is that it is hard to trace the value in channel, such that we cannot analyze the accurate range of variable x, if there are communication processes like $ch?x$ or $ch!x$. For the second, it may not find all of the case-bases of the Promela model because the above mentioned types of $choice(\overrightarrow{x}, y)$ do not cover all the cases that may yield the case-bases of the model. Therefore, analysis techniques need to be improved in the future research. Even so, the strategy and static analysis are very useful to model checking large models which is shown in the next section by application example.

Parallel Computation. It is easy to take advantage of parallel and networked computing power when the problem can be decomposed in independent subproblems. One problem is how to fully exploit the available computing resources. It may not be possible (with the proposed strategy) to divide a problem in such a way that all subproblems require approximately the same amount of time. It could be better with respect to the utilization of the available computing power, if there are more subproblems than available computing units. In such cases, we may estimate the difficulty of the subproblem and make a schedule for the subproblems.

4   Case Study

We have chosen an application example from security protocol verification which is of the type $choice_2(\overrightarrow{x}, y)$. The verification of security protocols is the main application area for model checking techniques (e.g. [15]). We have chosen the Needham-Schroeder-Lowe Protocol. Needham-Schroeder-Lowe Protocol is a well known authentication protocol. It aims at establishing mutual authentication between an initiator A and a responder B, after which some session involving the exchange of messages between A and B can take place. We use the model of Needham-Schroeder-Lowe protocol (the fixed version) created to the principle presented in [9]. We first consider a simple version of the protocol, then the complicated version of this protocol. The following is a description of this protocol.

$$A \rightarrow B : \{n_a, A\}_{PK(B)}$$
$$B \rightarrow A : \{n_a, n_b, B\}_{PK(A)}$$
$$A \rightarrow B : \{n_b\}_{PK(B)}$$

Here A is an initiator who seeks to establish a session with responder B. A selects a nonce n_a, and sends it along with its identity to B encrypted using B's public key. When B receives this message, it decrypts the message to obtain the nonce n_a. It then returns the nonce n_a along with a new nonce n_b and its identity to A, encrypted using A's public key. When A receives this message, he should be assured that he is talking to B, since only B should be able to decrypt the first message to obtain n_a. A then returns the nonce n_b to B, encrypted using B's public key. Then B should be assured that he is talking to A.

The simple version of the protocol includes one initiator, one responder and one intruder. The property to be checked can be expressed as following PLTL formulas.

- $\psi_1 : \Box(\Box\neg IniCommitAB \lor (\neg IniCommitAB \; U \; ResRunningAB))$;
- $\psi_2 : \Box(\Box\neg ResCommitAB \lor (\neg ResCommitAB \; U \; IniRunningAB))$.

In which

- $IniRunningAB$ is true iff initiator A takes part in a session of the protocol with B;
- $ResRunningAB$ is true iff responder B takes part in a session of the protocol with A;
- $IniCommitAB$ is true iff initiator A commits to a session with B;
- $ResCommitAB$ is true iff responder B commits to a session with A.

We now consider a more complicated version of this protocol which includes two initiators, one responder, and one intruder, namely, $A1, A2, B$, and I. Similarly, the property to be checked can be represented as:

- $\psi_1 : \Box(\Box\neg IniCommitA1B \lor (\neg IniCommitA1B \; U \; ResRunningA1B))$;
- $\psi_2 : \Box(\Box\neg ResCommitA1B \lor (\neg ResCommitA1B \; U \; IniRunningA1B))$.

The Promela model includes the proctype $PIni$ which has the structure as follows:

```
proctype PIni(mtype self; mtype party; mtype nonce)
{
  mtype g1;
  atomic{
  g1=self;
  IniRunning(self, party);
  ca!self, nonce, self, party;
   }
  atomic{
  ca?eval(self), eval(nonce), g1, eval(self);
  IniCommit(self,party);
  cb!self, g1, party;
   }
}
```

Parameter $self$ represents the identity of the host where the initiator process is running, whereas $party$ is the identity of the host with which the $self$ host wants to run a protocol session. Finally, $nonce$ is the nonce that the initiator process will use during the protocol run.

In this proctype, Since $\Box((PIni : party \neq 0) \rightarrow (PIni : party = v \vee PIni : g1 \neq 0))$ is true provided that $PIni : party$ first takes value $v(v = I$ or $B)$ during the execution of the Promela model, and proctype $PIni$ is used in the following context:

```
if
:: run PIni(A1, I, Na1); run PIni(A2, I, Na2)
:: run PIni(A1, B, Na1); run PIni(A2, I, Na2)
:: run PIni(A1, I, Na1); run PIni(A2, B, Na2)
fi
```

thus the conditions of $choice_2(\overrightarrow{x}, y)$ are satisfied. We obtain a case-basis $(PIni : party, PIni : g1)$. Note that the range of $PIni : party$ is $\{0, B, I\}$ and $PIni : party$ is changed more than once (it may be changed twice) during an execution of the protocol. The strategy of search space partition in [18, 19] will not be applicable for this case. We also detect $(PIni : self, PIni : g1)$ and $(PIni : nonce, PIni : g1)$ as case-bases, however they have less cases than $PIni : party$ and may be used as a part of multiple base-cases. After choosing $(PIni : party, PIni : g1)$ as the case-basis, for each property ψ_i to be checked, two subgoals are constructed as follows:

- ψ_{i1}: $\Box(PIni : party = 0 \vee PIni : party = I \vee PIni : g1 \neq 0) \rightarrow \psi_i$,
- ψ_{i2}: $\Box(PIni : party = 0 \vee PIni : party = B \vee PIni : g1 \neq 0) \rightarrow \psi_i$.

Table 1. Verification of Needham-Schroeder-Lowe protocol using case-basis

Verification Task	States	Transitions
ψ_1	7179	32090
ψ_{11}	6285	28768
ψ_{12}	901	3329
ψ_2	7172	33740
ψ_{21}	6285	31332
ψ_{22}	894	2415

The verification results are shown in table 1. As shown, the maximum and minimum numbers of states during the verification have been reduced to about 87% and 12% of those of the original task respectively.

Remark 3. To illustrate how the case-based verification works, we arbitrarily choose a formula ψ_{i1}:

$$\Box(PIni : party = 0 \vee PIni : party = I \vee PIni : g1 \neq 0) \rightarrow \psi_i$$

the second term of the precondition of ψ_{i1}, namely, $PIni : party = I$ means that only those options which the first proctype $PIni(...)$ satisfying $PIni : party = I$ can be chosen to run. Thus, in the above context of $PIni$, the first and the third lines (options) can run. If $PIni : party = B$, then only the second line (option) can run. The third term of the precondition of ψ_{i1}, i.e. $PIni : g1 \neq 0$ guarantees that during the execution of the protocol, $\Box(PIni : party = 0 \vee PIni : party = I \vee PIni : g1 \neq 0)$ is true provided that PIni:party first takes value I after PIni:party=0.

We can also use multiple case-bases to verify this protocol. As previously discussed, $(PIni : self, PIni : g1)$ and $(PIni : nonce, PIni : g1)$ can also be used as case-bases, the ranges of $PIni : self$ and $PIni : nonce$ are $\{0, A1, A2\}$ and $\{0, Na1, Na2\}$ respectively. We take

$$\{(PIni : party, PIni : g1), (PIni : self, PIni : g1), (PIni : nonce, PIni : g1)\}$$

as multiple case-bases. Then for each property to be verified eight subgoals are constructed as follows:

- ψ_{i1}: $\Box((PIni : party = 0) \vee (PIni : party = I) \vee (PIni : g1 \neq 0)) \wedge$
    $\Box((PIni : self = 0) \vee (PIni : self = A1) \vee (PIni : g1 \neq 0)) \wedge$
    $\Box((PIni : nonce = 0) \vee (PIni : nonce = Na1) \vee (PIni : g1 \neq 0)) \rightarrow \psi_i$

- ψ_{i2}: $\Box((PIni : party = 0) \vee (PIni : party = I) \vee (PIni : g1 \neq 0)) \wedge$
    $\Box((PIni : self = 0) \vee (PIni : self = A1) \vee (PIni : g1 \neq 0)) \wedge$
    $\Box((PIni : nonce = 0) \vee (PIni : nonce = Na2) \vee (PIni : g1 \neq 0)) \rightarrow \psi_i$

$\vdots$

- ψ_{i8}: $\Box((PIni : party = 0) \vee (PIni : party = B) \vee (PIni : g1 \neq 0)) \wedge$
    $\Box((PIni : self = 0) \vee (PIni : self = A2) \vee (PIni : g1 \neq 0)) \wedge$
    $\Box((PIni : nonce = 0) \vee (PIni : nonce = Na2) \vee (PIni : g1 \neq 0)) \rightarrow \psi_i$

The verification results are shown in table 2. As shown, the maximum and minimum numbers of states during the verification have been reduced to about 99%, 12% of those of the original task respectively.

Table 2. Verification of Needham-Schroeder-Lowe protocol using multiple case-bases

Verification Task	States	Transitions	Verification Task	States	Transitions
ψ_1	7179	32090	ψ_2	7172	33740
ψ_{11}	6285	28768	ψ_{21}	6285	31332
ψ_{12}	7	7	ψ_{22}	7	7
ψ_{13}	7	7	ψ_{23}	7	7
ψ_{14}	7	7	ψ_{24}	7	7
ψ_{15}	901	3329	ψ_{25}	894	2415
ψ_{16}	7	7	ψ_{26}	7	7
ψ_{17}	7	7	ψ_{27}	7	7
ψ_{18}	7	7	ψ_{28}	7	7

From the above example, we have been assured that the maximum and minimum reduced numbers of states of subgoals using multiple case-bases are not less than any those of subgoals using only one case-basis. If there are several case-bases, it will be hard to determine which case-bases get the best reduction on the number of states of subgoals before verification of the model, then multiple case-bases are practical in model checking large (software) systems.

5   Concluding Remarks and Future Work

The results presented in this paper extend those achieved previously in [18, 19]. Firstly, the new case-bases which have wider ranges of applications are introduced such that the basic case-bases are the special case of the new case-bases. Secondly, the use of multiple case-bases for further reduction of potential high memory requirements has been considered. Since multiple case-bases can achieve better reduction on the state space than only one case-basis (in the sense of maximum and minimum reduced numbers of state space of subgoals), it may improve the efficiency of (software) system verification. Finally, the principle of static analysis for case-bases exploration is introduced.

With respect to [1], a similar strategy is proposed. The basic idea is to break the proof of temporal property $\Box\varphi$ into cases based on the value of a given variable v. However, there are two differences: first, it is only applicable to safety properties; second, when the strategy is used alone, it does not do well with the model checker SPIN, because the whole state space still have to be searched to check whether the safety property holds (in each of the subtask).

The approach presented here can also be used as the basis for utilizing parallel and networked computing power for model checking (software) systems, although, the complexity of each subgoal with respect to model checking memory (time) may be different.

Further improvement of this approach can be achieved by investigating static analysis techniques that can be used to detect the (multiple) case-bases automatically, and by using symmetric reduction for reducing the number of subgoals when multiple case-bases is used to verifying complicated (software) systems.

Acknowledgements

The authors wish to thank anonymous referees for detailed comments and very helpful suggestions.

References

1. K.L. McMillan. Verification of Infinite State Systems by Compositional Model Checking. In *Proceedings of 10th International Conference on Correct Hardware Design and Verification Methods(CHARME'99), LNCS 1703*, page 219–234. Springer, 1999.
2. R. Bloem, K. Ravi and F. Somenzi. Efficient Decision Procedures for Model Checking of Linear Time Logic Properties. In *Proceedings of 11th International Conference on Computer Aided Verification(CAV'99), LNCS 1633*. page 222–235. Springer, 1999.

3. N. Amla, R. Kurshan, K.L. McMillan, and R. Medel. Experimental Analysis of Different Techniques for Bounded Model Checking. In *Proceedings of 9th International Conference on Tools and Algorithms for the Construction and Analysis of Systems(TACAS'03), LNCS 2619.* page 34–48, Springer, 2003.
4. B.B. David, C. Eisner, D. Geist and Y. Wolfsthal. Model Checking at IBM. *Formal Methods in System Design,* 22:101–108, 2003.
5. K. Yorav, Ogumber. Static Analysis for Stats-Space Reductions Preserving Temporal Logics. *Formal Methods in System Design,* 25:67–96, 2004.
6. L.I. Millett, T. Teitelbaum. Issues in Slicing PROMELA and Its Application to Model Checking, Protocol Understanding, and Simulation. *International Journal on Software Tools for Technology Transfer.* 2(4): 343–349, 2000.
7. G.J. Holzmann. *The SPIN Model Checker: Primer and Reference Manual.* Addison-Wesley, 2004.
8. E.M. Clark, O. Grumberg and D. Peled. *Model Checking.* The MIT Press, 1999.
9. P. Maggi and R. Sisto. Using SPIN to Verify Security Properties of Cryptographic Protocols. In *Proceedings of 9th International SPIN Workshop on Model Checking of Software(SPIN'02), LNCS 2318,* pages 187–204. Springer, 2002.
10. P. Godefroid, A.P. Sistla. Symmetric and Reduced Symmetry in Model Checking. In *Proceedings of 13th International Conference on Computer Aided Verification(CAV'01), LNCS 2102.* page 91–103. Springer, 2001.
11. D. Bosnacki, D. Dams and L. Holenderski. Symmetric Spin. *International Journal on Software Tools for Technology Transfer.* 4:92–106, 2002.
12. E.M. Clarke, O. Grumberg and D.E. Long. Model Checking and Abstraction. *ACM Transactions on Programming Languages and Systems.* 16(5): 1512–1542, 1994.
13. D. Peled. Ten Years of Partial Order Reduction. In *Proceedings of 10th International Conference on Computer Aided Verification(CAV'99), LNCS 1427.* page 17–28. Springer, 1998.
14. G.J. Holzmann. *Design and Validation of Computer Protocols.* Prentice-Hall, 1991.
15. G. Lowe: Breaking and Fixing the Needham-Schroeder Public-Key Protocol Using FDR. In *Proceedings of 9th International Conference on Tools and Algorithms for the Construction and Analysis of Systems(TACAS'96), LNCS 1055.* page 147–166, Springer, 1996.
16. S. Berezin and S. Campos and E.M. Clarke. Compositional Reasoning in Model Checking. In *Proceedings of International Symposium on Compositionality: The Significant Difference(COMPOS'97), LNCS 1536,* page 81–102, Springer, 1997.
17. E.A. Emerson. *Temporal and Modal Logic.* Handbook of Theoretical Computer Science (B): 997–1072, 1990.
18. B. Su and W. Zhang. Search Space Partition and Case Basis Exploration for Reducing Model Checking Complexity. In *Proceedings of 2th International Symposium on Automated Technology on Verification and Analysis(ATVA'04), LNCS 3299,* page 34–48. Springer, 2004.
19. W. Zhang. Combining Static Analysis and Case-Based Search Space Partition for Reducing Peek Memory in Model Checking. *Journal of Computer Science and Technology.* 18(6): 762–770, 2003.

Synthesized UML, a Practical Approach to Map UML to VHDL

Medard Rieder, Rico Steiner, Cathy Berthouzoz, Francois Corthay,
and Thomas Sterren

Infotronics Unit (www.infotronics.ch),
University of applied Sciences Valais (www. hevs.ch),
Rte du Rawyl 47, 1950 Sion, Switzerland
{rim, sti, bet, cof, sth}@hevs.ch

Abstract. Embedded Systems are complex systems with limited resources such as reduced processor power or relatively small amounts of memory and so on. The real time aspect may also play an important role, but is definitely not a main consideration of this work. Complexity of recent embedded systems is growing as rapidly as the demand for such systems and only can be managed by the use of a model-driven design approach. Since modeling languages such as UML are semi-formal they allow the design of systems that can't be implemented using formal languages such as C/C++ or VHDL. This paper intends to show how the gap between model and formal language can be bridged. First of all a set of rules restricts the use of model elements in a way that the model will become executable. Furthermore a unique mapping between UML and formal language elements enables automatic code generation. Formal verification at model level is an important consideration and becomes possible by the fact that rules restrict the application of model elements. UML to software (C/C++) and UML to hardware (VHDL) mapping form the base for a practical codesign approach where a part of the system is realized through software and another part trough hardware. Mapping of UML to programming languages is well known today and realized in many tools. Mapping of UML to hardware description languages is less known and not realized in tools. This paper documents an attempt to define a set of rules and to implement UML to VHDL mapping in a practical code generator. It also shows parts of a real world sample that was realized to verify usability and stability of rules and mapping. Finally, an outlook on further developments, improvement of the UML to VHDL mapping and a simple codesign process called 6qx will be given.

1 Introduction

While Embedded Systems were not widespread before 1990, nowadays they have become very popular. Affordable prices of big sized memory and powerful processors form the ideal alchemy for the birth of numerous embedded systems. Another component of this alchemy is the fact that hardware has become programmable. Field Programmable Gate Arrays (FPGA) with sufficient number of gates at reasonable prices made the borderline between hardware and software vanish.

N. Guelfi and A. Savidis (Eds.): RISE 2005, LNCS 3943, pp. 203–217, 2006.

Even though there are a rising number of basic components for embedded systems, and new technologies appear in rapid succession, the system development cycle is still quite traditional as illustrated by figure 1.

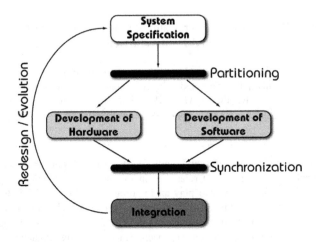

Fig. 1. Traditional Embedded System Development Cycle

2 Codesign

In such a traditional process, hardware and software are developed parallel, which brings up several issues, such as:

- Need of early hardware and software partitioning.
- Asynchronous development of hardware and software.
- Late integration with possible need of redesign.
- Missing hardware prevents testing the software before integration.

An important reason why development of hardware and software is not integrated is the lack of simple model-based approaches. Several reasons prevent the use of model-driven development.

Existing Codesign tools are very expensive and mostly dedicated: If codesign tools exist, these are almost certainly very expensive and dedicated to a specific thematic and platform. Readapting to other thematic and /or other platforms is practically impossible.

Developers think in terms of code and not model: Traditional thinking [1, 2, 3] and often also investments that have been made into some existing platform inhibit a change of attitude. Since formal descriptions are what they are and do not heal lack of methodic approach, first experiences in modeling are mostly disappointing and many hardware and software programmers therefore fall back into well-known territory, which means thinking either in hardware or in software code.

Therefore the HEVs approach of a codesign method was to use existing software modeling techniques already established on the market and to bridge the gap between software engineering and system engineering (codesign) by adding the hardware engineering part. How this was done will be described in detail in the following chapters and sections.

2.1 A Theoretical Codesign Approach

As a theoretical approach, we have developed a quite simple pyramid with the integrated system model as its top.

As underlying layer, we split up the model into a hardware model and a software model section. This process is called partitioning. The partitioning is done manually to give us the most flexibility to draw the boarder line (Figure 3) between hardware and software. However all needed interfaces between hardware and software are automatically created. Each of the models will then be translated into either hardware code (VHDL) [4] or software code (C/C++) [5]. Afterwards, the code will get synthesized or compiled and then uploaded into the target system. These last two steps are automated and require no user interaction. Figure 2 shows the theoretical model.

Finally there has to be a formal verification step. The produced code has to be verified against the model. Not only the software and the hardware code have to be verified, also the semantics of the overall system have to be tested. Timing constraints has to be tested to.

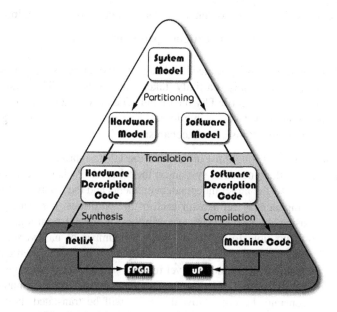

Fig. 2. Model Driven Codesign of Embedded Systems

It can easily be seen that integration problems will be minimized, since integration is already part of the model. It also can be seen that different degrees of partitioning are possible throughout this model. Figure 3 shows both, one hardware (a) and one software centric (b) partition (solution) of a given system.

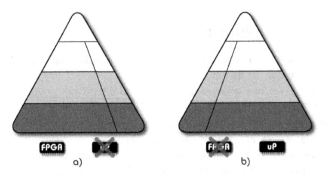

Fig. 3. Different Degrees of Partitioning

2.2 A Practical Codesign Approach

Theoretical approaches are nice to have a basic understanding, but to come to true results, practical models have to be developed out of the theoretical ones. We did this by instantiating a codesign model using realistic tools and targets. Figure 4 shows an overview of this practical approach.

To make complexity of this problem reasonable some constraints are introduced:

- Actually, we can do the two extreme partitions: either full hardware or full software.
- A formal verification of the produced code against the model is not yet possible.
- Real time aspects are only partially taken into account. The system has to reproduce the behavior specified by the model. The code is not able to handle hard-real-time situations. But it is possible to generate very compact and target specific code due to the flexible translation mechanism.

To understand figure 4, one must understand the UML approach we use to manage different partitions of the embedded system on model level. Packages, classes and state charts are used to model the target independent elements and the behavior of the system. Further on one component is defined for each of the partitions (hardware / software). Interfaces allow using the same system description for several partitions and targets. Doing so makes it possible to define an arbitrary number of hardware respectively software components for an arbitrary number of targets. A partition specific component holds all the information that is model-level related such as which packages or classes are part of this specific partition. It also holds all target specific information such as which tool will generate the code, how this code will be translated, how it will be synthesized or compiled and how it will be uploaded to the embedded system. In this way it is possible to automate the entire build and execute command chain.

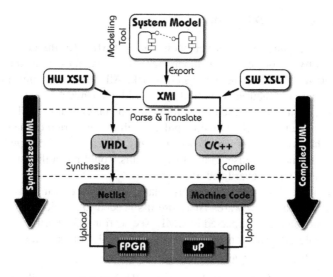

Fig. 4. A Practical Codesign Approach

Basically, the build command is run with the components name as parameter, the entire model will then be exported and either the hardware or software translator parses and translates information related to the specific component (partition) out of the exported model. It would also be possible to have a single translator, which receives one more parameter that determines whether to translate model information into hardware or software code. For reasons of simplicity (a translator is a quite complex matter) we decided to build two separated ones.

It has to be emphasized that the partitioning is done manually by defining components and assigning packages and classes to them. Also, components have to be equipped with target specific information. But it has also to be emphasized that partitioning is done after modeling the system and just before generating the code.

3 Translation

Correct translation of the UML elements into code is the core problem of any realistic codesign approach. Many researchers have already worked on this problem. The translation of UML to software code has been thoroughly researched and today offers good stability and performance. When it comes to translation of UML to hardware the papers of McUmber & Cheng [6, 7] are good examples. Unfortunately many of these works lead towards code that can't be compiled/synthesized because they have their main focus on the model level. For our work it is a main consideration that the generated code has to be compileable/synthesizable. To do real codesign, both, model and generated code have to be adapted to each other. Therefore the main effort of our research went towards this problem [8]. The next sections describe the main results of this work.

3.1 Hardware Thinks Differently

To communicate, using events is very common in UML. But the concept of events known from software doesn't exist in hardware. The one and only event in hardware is the continuous clock signal, the system clock. All other communication is done using signals that hold their value until they are told to change it.

In software, events can be used for communication tasks. But in hardware that isn't true. Even if one defines a signal with a pulse width of one period of the system clock as an event, this won't be an event, because only the value of the signal is taken in consideration and not the pulse width. In UML this would mean that state transitions are only decorated with a guard and no trigger.

This, and the fact that UML is closely related to software, brings us to filling the gap between UML and hardware. Therefore it's needed to develop a communication mechanism that can act as expected in UML (see section 3.3). Further on we need do define some rules, which coordinate the use of UML for hardware and software systems. There are three reasons to do this:

- In every Hardware Description Language (HDL) one can describe functions and situations that can't be synthesized. But if the designer follows some basic and simple rules, he can be sure that the design is synthesizable. In UML, the same situation exists. One can design a model, which can be translated neither to software nor to hardware.
- Till now, UML [9] was used to design software [10, 11] only. There is a lack of experience when it comes to creating models that can be translated to hard- and software. Defining some rules will help the designers to improve their know-how and it will bring a certain amount of quality to a model.
- Guided by these rules, the designer can be sure that a model is suitable for software/hardware codesign.

Above-mentioned rules would normally be part of a hardware/software process. Currently we are working on such a process (see section 5.2) and describing these rules now would go beyond the scope of this document. Instead, we would like to concentrate on the mapping of UML elements to VHDL code, which is done in the next section.

3.2 UML Elements

Since there are a big number of elements in UML, not all of them have been taken into account for this first approach of the UML to VHDL translation. The elements taken are classes, attributes, operations, class diagrams, objects, object diagrams, associations, ports, interfaces, events and state charts. As our real world sample shows, these elements are sufficient to model the behavior of simple systems [6, 7].

Comparing these elements to the traditional concepts used by hardware designers shows a strong parallelism [10, 12, 13]. Using state charts became a very popular concept for hardware designers to describe a design before implementing it. The top-down concept for analyzing hardware designs is also widely used. The system is seen as a black box with inputs and outputs. The black box will be broken down in smaller parts seen as black boxes again. The inputs and outputs of the black boxes will be connected to establish communication. This process continues until a certain granularity is achieved and finally the black boxes will be equipped with a behavior described e.g. with a state chart. Using object diagrams, the same analyses and design process is possible while an object corresponds to a black box. Also communication between objects is possible by using ports and interfaces. An object can be equipped with ports and interfaces, and ports are interconnected by links. Figure 5 shows a typical sample.

The next section provides more details of the translation technique we used.

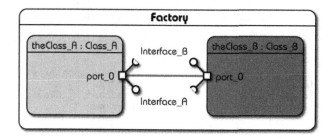

Fig. 5. UML Object Diagram

3.3 UML to VHDL Mapping

It's important to find optimal patterns to translate UML elements to VHDL. Due to the fact that an UML element can have several decorations, it is important to find a general description in VHDL that can handle all the decorations of an UML element. Not going too deep into details we will show now, which UML element looks how in VHDL. To give an idea of the translations result, figure 6 shows the VHDL code corresponding to the UML elements in figure 5. The following lines will give an overview and a brief description of the patterns used.

- The class *Factory* is translated to an **entity** construct. The entity named *Factory* consists of a list of **ports** and of an **architecture** section. By default the two inputs reset and clock are added to the entity's port list. Depending on the ports and interfaces of the class, other input and output ports may be added to the port list. In the **architecture** the main implementation (the behavior) of the class can be found.
- An object is an instance of a class. In VHDL it's possible to create an instance of an **entity**. To do this, first a **component** has do be defined inside the **architecture** containing the instance. According to figure 5 the **components** named *Class_A* and *Class_B* are defined (cf A:, B: at figure 6). The second step is to create an instance and to map the ports to other ports or to signals. The instances are called *theClass_A* and *theClass_B* (cf C:, D: at figure 6).

```
library IEEE;
use IEEE.std_logic_1164.all;

entity Factory is
port(
    reset : in STD_LOGIC;
    clock : in STD_LOGIC
    -- other ports here.
    );
end Factory;

architecture FA of Factory is
---- Declare signals to
  interconnect nested blocks.
Signal
link_0_Interface_A_methode_0:
STD_LOGIC;
Signal
link_0_Interface_B_methode_0:
STD_LOGIC;

---- A: Declare class Class_A
component Class_A
port(
    clock : in STD_LOGIC;
    reset : in STD_LOGIC;
    port_0_Interface_A_methode
_0 : in STD_LOGIC;
    port_0_Interface_B_methode
_0 : out STD_LOGIC
    );
end component;

---- B: Declare class Class_B
component Class_B
port(
    clock : in STD_LOGIC;
```

```
    reset : in STD_LOGIC;
    port_0_Interface_B_methode
_0 : in STD_LOGIC;
    port_0_Interface_A_methode
_0 : out STD_LOGIC
    );
end component;

begin
---- C: Instantiate
theClass_A
theClass_A: Class_A
port map (
    reset => reset,
    clock => clock,
    port_0_Interface_A_methode
_0 =>
link_0_Interface_A_methode_0,
    port_0_Interface_B_methode
_0 =>
link_0_Interface_B_methode_0
    );

---- D: Instantiate
theClass_B
theClass_B: Class_B
port map (
    reset => reset,
    clock => clock,
    port_0_Interface_A_methode
_0 =>
link_0_Interface_A_methode_0,
    port_0_Interface_B_methode
_0 =>
link_0_Interface_B_methode_0
    );
end Factory
```

Fig. 6. Generated Code of UML Diagram in Figure 5

- The UML elements port and interface are translated to input and output ports of an **entity**. Provided interfaces are translated as input ports and required interfaces are translated as output ports. The names of VHDL ports are the same ones as the names of the ports and interfaces in the UML model (cf A:, B: at figure 6).
- In UML, links are used to interconnect objects via ports and interfaces (see link between the two objects in figure 5). Depending on the interfaces, ports and objects used, several signals will be defined in VHDL. These signals will be used in the port map sections of components to realize a connection between components (cf C:, D: at figure 6).

The second type of UML diagrams discussed here are state charts. Figure 7 shows a simple but complete state chart that is equipped with all common elements. Comparing the state chart in figure 7 to its implementation in VHDL (figure 8), we will explain the mapping rules for state charts.

As state charts are used to describe the behavior of a class, the corresponding translation is put into the **architecture** of the VHDL **entity**. State charts are translated into a case structure where every case represents a state of the state chart. Within every case an if-construction prevents reentrant execution of the state's embedded instructions. Another if-construction is used to handle the transitions and the transition conditions.

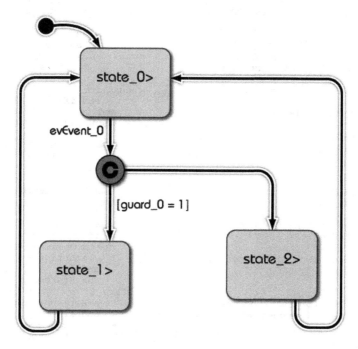

Fig. 7. UML State Chart

- The code in figure 8 shows a state chart called *Statemachine_0* within the Class *Class_A*. A state chart is realized within a VHDL **process** (cf A:, B: at figure 8). The process is triggered by the two signals reset and clock. The process consists of an a synchronous reset a part (cf C: figure 8) and of a main part synchronous to the clock (cf D: figure 8). If the reset signal goes to '1' then the circuit gets initialized and initial state is defined. The synchronous part implements the behavior of the state chart.
- Defining a new data **type** called *TFSM_States* does represent the set of states need to implement the state chart. Further on a **signal** called *FSM_Statemachine_0* is created, which type is *TFSM_States* (cf E: figure 8).
- The state chart its self is translated to a **case** structure (cf F: figure 8) that treats all possible values defined by the data type *TFSM_States*. Each state corresponds to a well-defined value of the **signal** *FSM_Statemachine_0*. A very special case or an undefined value of *FSM_Statemachine_0* is caught by the **when others** statement. This grants that the state chart does not get deadlocked and that it goes back to the initial state.

```
Library IEEE;
use IEEE.std_logic_1164.all;
use IEEE.std_logic_unsigned.all;
entity Class_A is
port(
    reset : in STD_LOGIC;
    clock : in STD_LOGIC;
    evEvent_0_reception: in STD_LOGIC
);
end Class_A;

-- A: declare the class Class_A
architecture Cl_A of Class_A is

-- E: state chart type and signal
-- definition
type TFSM_States is
(
    S_state_0,
    S_state_1,
    S_state_2
);

signal FSM_Statemachine_0:
TFSM_States;

-- multiple action exe. prevention
signal enAction: STD_LOGIC;

-- Event Reception signal def.
signal evEvent_0: STD_LOGIC;

begin
-- B: process for Statemachine_0
    Statemachine_0:process(clock,
reset)
    Begin
        -- C: asynchrony reset
        if reset = '1' then
            FSM_Statemachine_0 <=
S_state_0;
            enAction <= '1';
-- D: synchrony part
        elsif RISING_EDGE(clock) then
-- F: state chart implementation
            case FSM_Statemachine_0 is
                when S_state_0 =>
-- H: multiple execution prevention
                if enAction = '1' then
                    -- state's operartions
                    enAction <= '0';
                end if;

-- J: event handling
```

```
                if evEvent_0 = '1' then
-- K: guard handling
                    if guard_0 = '1'then
-- G: state assignment
                        FSM_Statemachine_0
<=
                            S_state_1;
-- I: enable actions
                            enAction <= '1';
                    else
                        FSM_Statemachine_0
<=
                            S_state_2;
                        enAction <= '1';
                    end if;
                end if;
                when S_state_1 =>
                    if enAction = '1' then
---- operartions of the state
                        enAction <= '0';
                    end if;

                    FSM_Statemachine_0 <=
S_state_0;
                    enAction <= '1';
                when S_state_2 =>
                    if enAction = '1' then
---- operartions of the state
                        enAction <= '0';
                    end if;
                    FSM_Statemachine_0 <=
S_state_0;
                    enAction <= '1';
                end if;
                when others =>
                    FSM_Statemachine_0 <=
S_state_0;
            end case;
        end if;
    end process;
        evEvent_0_ev_generator:
ev_generator
        port map (
            reset => reset,
            clock => clock,
            trigger =>
evEvent_0_reception,
            evOut => evEvent_0
        );
end Class_A
```

Fig. 8. Generated Code of UML Diagram in Figure 7

- Each state has one or more subsequent states. These subsequent states are assigned by statements like FSM_Statemachine_0 <= s_state_1 (cf G: figure 8).
- If in UML a state is provided with an operation, it is assumed that this operation is executed only once. To reproduce this behavior in VHDL an additional signal

called *enAction* is introduced. After a reset enAction has the value '1'. Inside the **case** structure, the value of enAction is checked for each state. If enAction's value is '1' then the state-related actions are executed. That followed, enAction is set to '0'. Doing so prohibits execution of the state's actions when reentering the same state (cf H: figure 8).

- In order to enable execution of action in case of going to another state, enAction has to be reset to '1'. This is done in the same moment as the **signal** FSM_Statemachine_0 becomes a new state (cf I: figure 8).
- As one can see in figure 7 UML defines several types of transitions. A transition can be decorated with *triggers* and *guards*. Triggers are events (generated from other parts of the model or timer events), which bring the system into another state. Guards are additional conditions that can allow or reject a state change in case of an occurring event. In this example occurring of the event evEvent_0 means that the **signal** evEvent_0 becomes '1' for exactly one clock period. If this is the case the guards are evaluated and the next state is defined as explained above (cf J: figure 8).
- Guards are realized in a simple **If** structure (cf K: figure 8). If the transition's guard is evaluated and the result is true, the system goes to the transition's target state. There can always be maximum one transition of the same source state without guard. If all transition's guards are evaluated as false, the system goes to the target state of the guardless transition.

As mentioned in section 3.1 we had to establish a communication mechanism between components. This necessity comes from the fact that within e.g. a state we can have a method call. To keep the generated VHDL code human-readable we avoid changing the anatomy of the case structure representing the state chart. To introduce a pseudo-event to translate e.g. method calls we defined a communication mechanism as shown in figure 9.

- Generating an event means changing a signals value from '0' to '1' or from '1' to '0'.
- Receiving an event is as simple as to detect a signal's value changing.
- If the event transmitting signal is initialized properly, throwing an event is as simple as inverting the signal's value. Detecting an event is slightly more complex. It's managed by a simple edge detection mechanism. As soon as the event's signal is changed, an output signal changes from '0' to '1' for exactly one period of the system clock. Figure 9 shows the different signals as mentioned above. This is not the best approach to solve the problem. E.g. sending two events to the same receiver is not possible and quickly occurring events could be missed.

For the hardware mapping we use basic elements of VHDL and well-known structures. This has a number of advantages:

- If the generated code is semantically correct, it is granted that the generated code is synthesizable.
- The generated code is platform and manufacturer independent. This is because we don't use target specific elements such as memory or multiplier blocks.

The next chapter describes a demonstrator that was created to verify the techniques exposed in this chapter.

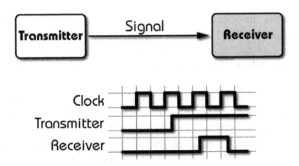

Fig. 9. Communication Mechanism to handle Events

4 Experimentation

As usual in research projects, at the end all obtained results have to be verified and proven.

A simple chronometer demonstrator was built up. As software target, we used an ARM 7 equipped board with a minimal operating system called IDF (Interrupt Driven Framework) and as hardware target a Xilinx Spartan II equipped board. The chronometer itself consists of a stepper motor, some pushbuttons and an optical sensor. An UML model of the system was created and then once synthesized for the hardware target and once compiled for the software target. Both systems were working without touching the model. All code was automatically generated, compiled, uploaded and started in the targets. Figure 10 shows the schematic of the demonstrator.

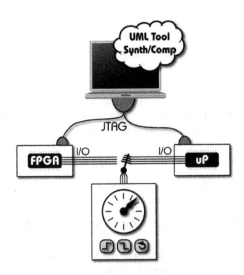

Fig. 10. Principle of the Chronometer Codesign Demonstrator

The following conclusions could be made out of the chronometer experience:

- The software code generator we used, was the built-in one of the modeling tool. For future development of the codesign project, it has to be replaced by one of the same types as the hardware code generator. This is necessary to allow correct interface integration between hardware and software.
- Moving the partition line in between of hardware and software means to involve interfaces. For this time, we implemented interfaces manually but for a real world development process it will be a must to at least semi-automate this action. This means that it should be possible to "drag & drop" ready-made interface blocks into the model and to connect them to the correct locations in the hardware and software fragment of the system's model.
- The mapping for the hardware should also be optimized. Especially it would be nice to be able to parameterize target specific matter inside the model and not to find these adaptations somewhere in the translator.
- Not all elements of UML 2.0 [9] have been used. This was partially due to the fact that the software built-in translator did not recognize them, at least not in the version of the tools we were using. This problem will automatically be corrected by introducing the "homebrew" software translator.
- More complex demonstrators must be implemented to stress- test the codesign approach we are using currently. But it must be stated that the results we obtained until now are very encouraging and that the generated systems are amazingly stable.

Having a frame, inside of which development is rolling down, would be nice. A first approach of such an all-over Development Process is briefly touched in the conclusion.

5   Conclusion

The above-mentioned experiences lead to a certain number of conclusions that have to be applied in the very near future to the described codesign approach.

5.1   Tool Chain Improvement

The most important improvements concerning the tool chain are shown in the following list:

- Improved hardware code generation patterns will be implemented in the hardware translator.
- A separate software translator will be added to the tool chain.
- Standard interfaces will be defined in UML as patterns that can be applied to a given situation.
- The whole approach will be intensively tested by the means of real world projects and demonstrators.

These are all developments that will be done around the tool chain. Another, more important development, will be to introduce a general formalism that embeds the present experimental codesign process. The reason for this is that any modeling activity requests formalism and sequencing. An outlook on this process is presented in the next section.

5.2 The 6qx Process

The definition of a simple codesign process is the logical consequence of this conclusion and because we already had defined a software centric process (6q) [14], we will extend this one into a codesign process. The 6q process has been developed in an embedded systems context and therefore provides a quite good potential to cover also hardware development aspects. The method of the 6q process is object oriented and the model is incremental. It consists of six major steps: System specification, analysis, design, translation, validation and integration.

These steps will also be contained in the new 6qx process, but will be adopted to meet codesign requirements as follows:

The first two steps, system specification and analysis, gather information about the system to be developed and map results into an UML model by the means of use-case diagrams, interaction diagrams, class diagrams, state charts and deployment diagrams. Since these steps try to specify and analyze the system, they do not care about implementation details (hardware / software). The major difference of these steps compared to the original 6q process, where hardware and software are developed in parallel, will be the removal of the hardware software partitioning decision. It is delayed into the design step, because the model covers both hardware and software of the system.

The design step will transform the flat analysis model into a well-structured model that can be partitioned into a hardware (HW) and a software (SW) partition according to various criteria (costs, speed, physical limitations and so on). The hardware partition may be split up once again into a programmable hardware (PHW) partition and an analog / digital hardware partition (DHW). Interfaces between both partitions have to be defined after partitioning or even while partitioning. The 6qx process will contain recommendations about use and implementation of interfaces in the form of interface patterns defined in UML. It will also contain hardware and software design rules (cf. section 3.1) in form of patterns defined in UML.

The translation step will regulate implementation details. Important elements that will be introduced at this moment into the system model are components that will bind the hardware and the software partition to specific targets (cf. section 3.2).

The validation step is responsible to verify correct functioning of the designed hardware and/or software. This is achieved by reusing formal descriptions of behavior from the specification and analysis step. Simulators are used to verify correct behavior.

The integration step will put it all together and finally verify correct all-over system behavior and stability. Erroneous behavior results in feedback towards the analysis pipe, insufficient stability in feedback towards the design pipe.

Figure 11 gives an idea of the 6qx process.

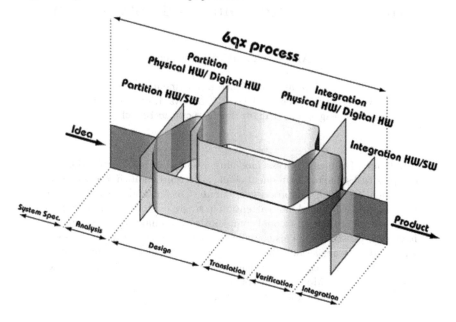

Fig. 11. Overview of the 6qx codesign process

References

[1] Keith Edwards, "Real Time Structured Methods", John Wiley & Sons, 1993.
[2] Jean J. Labrosse, "Embedded Systems Building Blocks", R&D Publications, 1995.
[3] D. L. Perry, "VHDL", second edition, McGraw-Hill, New York, 1994.
[4] IEEE, "IEE Standards VHSL Language Reference Manual", IEEE standard 1076-1987, IEEE Computer Society Press, Los Alamitos, 1987.
[5] Marylène Micheloud, Medard Rieder, "Programmation orientée objets en C++", Presses polytechniques et universitaires Romandes, 2003.
[6] McUmber & Cheng, "A general Framework for formalizing UML with Formal Languages", ICSE 2001.
[7] W. E. McUmber and B. H. Cheng, "UML-based analysis of embedded systems using a mapping to VHDL", In Proc. of IEEE High Assurance Software Engineering (HASE99), Washington, DC, November 1999.
[8] Rico Steiner, "Hardware & Software Co-Design", Diploma Thesis, HEVs, 2004.
[9] www.uml.org.
[10] Bruce Powel Douglass, "Real-Time Design Patterns: Robust Scalable Architecture for Real-Time Systems", Addison-Wesley, 2004.
[11] Bruce Powel Douglass, "Doing Hard Time: Developing Real-Time Systems with UML, Objects, Frameworks and Patterns", Addison-Wesley, 1999.
[12] S. Jones, D. Naylor, "VHDL, a logic synthesis approach", Chapman & Hall, London, 1995.
[13] Rajan "Essentials VHDL, RTL synthesis done right", USE, June1998.
[14] Medard Rieder, "A simple and complete Process for embedded Systems Development", Proceeding embedded world conference 2005, pages 876–885.

Towards Service-Based Business Process Modeling, Prototyping and Integration

Ang Chen and Didier Buchs

Computer Science Department,
University of Geneva, CH-1211 Geneva 4, Switzerland
{Ang.Chen, Didier.Buchs}@cui.unige.ch

Abstract. Business process modeling, validation and verification are complex tasks due to the frequent change of requirements in the social environment to which the process contributes. In particular, transactional business processes need more attention in stages of modeling and verification because of their additional complexities in managing the specific behavior of transactions. This contribution proposes an approach to model and validate transactional business processes by means of compositing workflow patterns constructed using Concurrent Object-Oriented algebraic Petri Nets. Moreover, a concrete framework for business process validation, prototyping and integration is proposed.

1 Introduction

Business process modeling, validation and verification are complex tasks due to the frequent change of requirements in the social environment to which the process contributes. Moreover, processes should be reusable and flexible when the underlying environment changes. The concrete execution of business processes relies on specific execution engines that interact with existing information systems, e.g. Enterprise Resource Planning (ERP) systems or Management Information Systems (MIS). The fact that business processes can be intra-organizational or inter-organizational implies that interoperability plays an important role in Business Process Management Systems (BPMS), either between different BPMS or between BPMS and other information systems.

Web Service is an emerging technology which meets the needs of interoperability between heterogeneous systems by providing a high-level general form of communication. For implementation, we will use web service as a way to interconnect modeled business processes with external information systems, but our approach is general for all service-oriented systems. Complex and error-prone configuration can exist in real systems, for instance cyclic interconnection relations, which leads to complex models as well as difficult verification. Producing prototypes and interconnecting them with real services is, in this case, an ideal manner for checking real configuration and discovering system inconsistencies.

Business process prototype simulation allows detection of process errors at design time without deploying processes into production systems, which is particularly necessary for critical systems. It must be noted that process prototypes

N. Guelfi and A. Savidis (Eds.): RISE 2005, LNCS 3943, pp. 218–233, 2006.

are cheap and risk-free. If coming with a formal foundation, process models provide facilities to test, verify business process, and validate business rules. If processes are defined using formal languages, it will be possible to automatically generate executable prototypes from process definitions.

1.1 Background

Many process modeling approaches exist, including Event-Driven Process Chains (EPCs), UML activity diagrams, business rules, service-oriented solutions and Petri nets based models. In order to define business process, most approaches propose workflow languages or notations; some languages have formal foundation and clear semantics, many others do not. Among the list, Petri nets based approaches have attracted the most attentions because of its formal semantic and graphical representation. W. van der Aalst shows three good reasons for using Petri nets as a vehicle for modeling workflow and implementing workflow management systems [1]: formal semantics despite the graphical nature; state-based instead of event-based and abundance of analysis techniques.

The workflow patterns initiative [6] aims to establish a structured approach to the issues of the specification of control flow dependencies in workflow languages. The objective is extended to data perspective and resources perspectives [3], [4]. These patterns have been used as a benchmark for comparing process definition languages and evaluating their relative expressive power. It should be mentioned that W. van der Aalst and his group have done much valuable work on business process modeling. Some of our ideas presented in this paper complete his approach, e.g. transactional workflow patterns.

Workflow Management Coalition (WfMC) [10] is trying to define standards to uniform the terminologies in the domain of business process and workflow models. Their propositions principally include XML Process Definition Language (XPDL) and reference model for workflow systems. The reference model identifies five interfaces and their specifications. Although the reference model influenced many workflow products, WfMC failed to provide a formal foundation for XPDL [5]. Nevertheless, we believe that the act of using the same vocabularies is a step towards having more precise languages and will lead to a more precise working environment.

1.2 Workflow Modeling and Prototyping

Business processes modeling rarely starts from scratch. Driven by objectives, they usually represent sequences of expected actions or events in existing information systems. They also represent relationships between the actions or events, e.g. dependency and causality. The state of a process evolves when expected events occur, e.g. user inputs, task finished, the states of running processes are monitored and controlled explicitly by BPMS.

Figure 1 depicts the proposed architecture of BPM systems and how a business process is elaborated. A common convention of process modeling is of viewing business process from several perspectives: control, data, operational, and resources, etc. Each perspective describes a specific kind of events in workflow

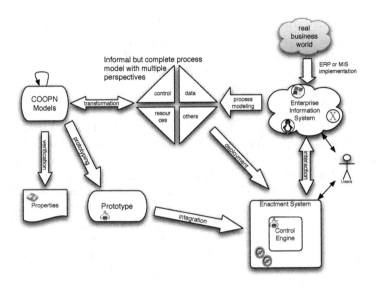

Fig. 1. BPM Architecture

systems: control flow manages the states of process instances; data flow represents information retrieval and moves between activities; operational flow represents interaction between process and other systems; resources usually represent available human or non-human resources for task distributions.

We adopt a clear separation of *Control* and *other perspectives*. In this paper we will focus on the control perspective while the used data types are merely suggested, e.g. the definition of *Case*. Figure 1 also shows the possibility of modeling business process using a precise language, performing verification of process and generating prototypes. By capturing specific information, e.g. control perspective, the informal process models can be transformed into formal models such as COOPN. Such models can be verified, and the model itself can be refined. When we have a "proven" correct model, it is possible to transform it back or generate a prototype. The reverse transformation from formal model to informal model can serve as refinement and correction of the informal model. The generation of prototype is very powerful because *the process controller prototype can be integrated directly into enactment systems, provided that the responsibilities between the prototype and the enactment system are well defined*.

Compared with process controller integration proposed in this paper, the Reference Net Workshop (Renew) [7] uses High-level Nets and net references to model and simulate workflow. Integrated with Java, it is possible to call subscribed Java code while firing a transition; moreover, the additional code does not influence the enabledness of a transition. YAWL [2] implements a web service broker to handle interaction with external systems. Service-oriented approach BPEL4WS [8] uses web services exclusively for all interaction, and it has no explicit information on the state of process instances.

In order to avoid notion confusion, some definitions about workflow management system are borrowed from WfMC [10]. The world of business process system consists of: *participants, activities, process or case instance* and *resources*. A *process definition* is a formal description of a business process or procedure. A *process or case instance* is one execution of a process definition. An *activity* is a single logical step in the process. We also agree with [8] that business processes should not reveal internal activities while interacting with external participants.

The remainder of this paper is organized as follows. After a brief overview of COOPN language in the next section, we discuss the problematic of business process modeling and show COOPN building blocks for workflow patterns in section 3; in section 4, we explain the techniques of prototype integration; section 5 concludes the paper and gives future perspectives of our research.

2   Concurrent Object-Oriented Petri Net

COOPN (Concurrent Object-Oriented Petri Nets) is an object-oriented formal specification language based on synchronized algebraic Petri nets. This language allows the definition of active concurrent objects and includes facilities for sub-typing, sub-classing, and genericity. Basically, COOPN has three types of modules: *ADT(Abstract Data Type), class, and context*: ADT represents data, class is an encapsulation of algebraic Petri nets, and context is a higher level of encapsulation which defines the contextual coordination between components. A component can be a context or an object; an object is an instance of a class.

2.1   ADT, Class and Context

COOPN ADT modules define data types by means of algebraic specifications. Each module describes one or more sorts, along with generators and operations on these sorts. The properties of the operations are given in the section *body* of the modules, by means of positive conditional equational axioms.

COOPN classes are described by modular algebraic Petri nets with particular parameterized external transitions which are defined by so-called *behavioral axioms*, similar to the axioms in an ADT. Class instance are objects; they possess methods and gates allowing specifier to model components of a system. A method call is achieved by synchronizing external transitions, according to the fusion of transitions technique. The axioms have the following structure:

Cond => event **With** synchro :: pre -> post

In which the terms have the following meaning:

- *Cond* is a set of equational conditions, similar to a guard;
- *event* is the name of a method or transition with algebraic term parameters;
- *synchro* is the synchronization expression defining the policy of transactional interaction of this event with other events, the dot notation is used to express events of specific objects. Synchronization operators are: sequence .., simultaneous //, and non-determinist exclusive choice ⊕;

– *pre* and *post* are usual Petri net flow relations determining what is consumed and what is produced in the object state places.

COOPN contexts are units of computation where included entities are coordinated following the same synchronization rules used for the class methods and gates. Contexts can be organized hierarchically and objects can move between them.

It is important to understand that the state of an object is represented by tokens in its places; tokens can be ADT terms or objects. Passing objects between two places is implemented by passing their references. Furthermore, the state of a context depends on all state of objects in the context; ADTs are immutable entities without state.

Syntactically, each module has the same overall structure, it includes an *interface* section defining all accessible elements from the outside, and a *body* section including the local aspects private to the module. Moreover, class and context modules have convenient graphical representation, which are used in this paper. The features dealing with object-orientation such as sub-classing, sub-typing and genericity are out of the scope of this paper, and can be found in [12], [13]. In the rest of the paper we will use COOPN without giving its complete description.

2.2   Representation of Services

In COOPN class and context, *methods* and *gates* describe *provided services* and *required services* of modules, respectively. Each method or gate has a signature that indicates the types of its parameters, and the value of a parameter can be an algebraic ADT term or an object. In our discussion, only algebraic ADT terms parameters are used.

Figure 2 shows two COOPN components **A** and **B**, where **A** is using a service provided by **B**. Methods are depicted by black rectangles and gates are depicted by white rectangles on the edges. The *request* and the *response* can be synchronized or not. If they are synchronized, *m2* of **A** can be considered as the "callback" method of the *request*. Depending on the state of objects, its methods can be firable or not; if a method is firable, the control is passed to external environment, e.g. context containing the objects.

Before explaining the expressive power of COOPN for service representations, we would like to refer the transmission primitives used by Web Service Description Language (WSDL [9]) to abstractly represent services. Full support of these transmission primitives makes possible the rapid integration of prototypes

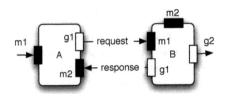

Fig. 2. Representing Services in COOPN

obtained from COOPN modeled components into a service-oriented environment. Again, our approach is generalized and applicable to all service-oriented architectures.

WSDL has four transmission primitives that an endpoint can support [9]. The *endpoints* can be considered as COOPN components:

- One-way. The endpoint receives a message.
- Request-response. The endpoint receives a message, and sends a correlated message.
- Solicit-response. The endpoint sends a message, and receives a correlated message.
- Notification. The endpoint sends a message.

As web services, COOPN services are stateless. In Figure 2, $A.m1$ and $B.m2$ represent a 'One-way' transmission, $B.g2$ is a 'Notification', the set of $A.g1$, $B.m1$, $B.g1$ and $A.m2$ is a 'Solicit-response' for A, and at the same time, it is a 'Request-response' for B.

2.3 Transactional Business Processes

Transactional business process plays an important role in the business world. It implies doing 'ALL' or doing 'NOTHING' of atomic transactions, e.g. an online shopping site should verify credit card validity and transfer money, then generate a delivery order for a client. The two actions "transfer money" and "generate delivery order" should be executed sequentially and if one fails, nothing should be executed.

In case of transaction failures, despite some business process modeling approaches that can use manual cancellation to rollback process states, most of them do not handle the transactional problems, hence rollbacks are not always possible in the process models. COOPN provides atomic sequence execution operator .. to handle the sequential transaction problems, together with two other operators: parallel // and alternative execution $\bigoplus$. We will show that it is possible to express most transactional business processes with COOPN.

3 Modeling Business Process

3.1 COOPN Building Blocks and Patterns for Business Process

The basic element of COOPN building blocks for business process is *Activity*. Activities use the set of values of type *Case* to pass control from one to another. This uniform handling of values is not ideal for methodological reasons but we will keep it for simplicity. Generic types can be defined instead and instantiated to compatible types when necessary in order to allow specificity of each building block. The ways of passing control flow between activities are summarized by some *Workflow Patterns* taken from the well-known list of W. van der Aalst [6]. A *Process Definition* consists of activities and rules used to pass control and other flows between them. In COOPN, *Case* is modeled by ADT, *Activities* are defined using *Class* and *Process* are defined using *Context*, hence the axioms of *Context* are rules for passing control flows. Note that a process can be abstracted to an activity, hence processes can be composited hierarchically.

- *Case:* In COOPN, *Case* is the super type[1] of all types used to represent a process instance in activities. We define *Case* as an ADT of pair <*ID, LocalState*>, where *ID* is the global identification of process instance and *LocalState* is the local instance value representation. For example, in an insurance company, the "client claim ID" can be a global identification of the process which handles clients' insurance claims. At each step (activity) of the process, a case may have different *states* such as "approved, not approved" and may be represented by different documents such as "claim form" and "evidence". In this example, the "client claim ID" is the global identification of case in the process; "approved claim", "rejected claim", "claim form" and "evidence" are local states used by specific activities. Note that a global identification in one process does not need to be the global identification of another process. Figure 3 shows an example of activity with 4 LocalState values. It is possible to define algebra on these ADT values to obtain "chemical reaction" on tokens (fusion, merge...) by means of specific functions; however, this subject will not be investigated in this paper.
- *Activity:* An activity accepts *cases* values and performs actions or treatments related to the cases. It can invoke external services and accept responses from external systems or users. An activity *sends out* the cases when it finishes its actions, note that an outgoing case can be any value of type *Case*, even with a different identification(workflow pattern: multiple instances). The invocation of external services can be considered as data perspective or operational perspective, which will not be discussed in this paper. The destination of outgoing case is determined by the process. *Activity* is the equivalent of *Task* in some workflow languages, however, we distinguish *Activity* from *Task* by considering *Activity* as static definition and *Task* as runtime "workitem" w.r.t. a case instance.
- *Process:* Process specifies collaboration between activities. Defined by means of COOPN context, a process instantiates activities from their definitions (classes) then specifies the causalities of events among the instances (objects) using three operators: parallel, sequence and alternative execution. Having a structure of behavior axiom similar to that of classes, contexts can use conditional expressions(on ADTs) to decide the selection of control flow.

Figure 4.a and 4.c depict the basic COOPN constructs describing an activity and a sequence of activities. The corresponding Petri Nets representation is also

---

[1] In fact, because "type" is more common in object-oriented languages, we use the term "type" instead of "sort" which is the name of a type in the theory of Algebraic Abstract Data Type.

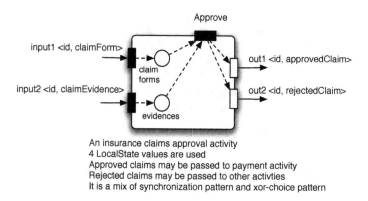

An insurance claims approval activity
4 LocalState values are used
Approved claims may be passed to payment activity
Rejected claims may be passed to other activties
It is a mix of synchronization pattern and xor-choice pattern

Fig. 3. Example of Activity and Cases as COOPN components

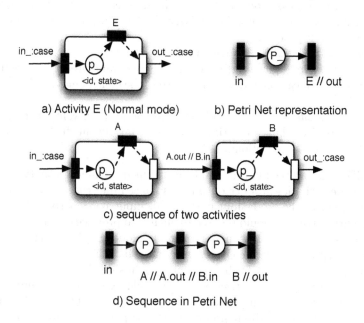

Fig. 4. Basic COOPN Building Blocks for workflow

given in Figure 4.b and 4.d respectively, with obviously less expressive power. The method $in\_:case$ accepts a token (an ADT Term) and puts it into place $p\_$. Since we don't limit the capacity of the place here, this method is always firable. The transition **E** removes tokens from the place, and according to the value of *LocalState*, it generates output to gate $out\_:case$. By simply connecting input and output of two activities, we obtain a sequence of activities. In further discussion, we will show that this basic construct of activity can be extended with little effort by adding more inputs and outputs and by specifying their corresponding

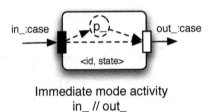

Immediate mode activity
in_ // out_

Fig. 5. Immediate Mode Activity

axioms. Figure 4.a and Figure 5 illustrate the two modes of activity, *Normal* and *Immediate*:

- Essentially, an *Activity* has one or more *inputs* receiving cases, zero or more *outputs* sending cases out and some axioms specifying the relationship between inputs and outputs. An activity without output signifies an implicit termination of process.
- *Normal Mode Activity:* A normal mode activity has *one place for each input.* A trigger (**E** in Figure 4.a) takes input cases and produces output cases according to the axioms. Like in Petri Nets, the control moves when a trigger is fired.
- *Immediate Mode Activity:* In an immediate mode activity, inputs and outputs are synchronized, hence no trigger is needed for output, furthermore, places for storing cases are optional.

The difference between normal mode and immediate mode activity is that immediate mode activities produce output as soon as input cases satisfy the output conditions (e.g. in the AND-Join pattern, all input cases arrive). In a normal mode activity, a trigger should be fired explicitly to produce outputs. Because all firable events are synchronized in an immediate mode activity, it is relatively easier to verify a process which contains only immediate mode activities. It means that if a legal input is not firable, the process has deadlocks. However, immediate mode activities have restrictions when building certain workflow patterns due to possible stabilization problems of a given system that include cycles. In consequence, our further discussion on workflow patterns will consider normal or mixed mode activities.

We distinguish three kind of methods and gates to model *control, data, operational* flows:

- Control flow: flow between activities, in general this kind of methods and gates is always firable in normal mode activities, which means an activity does not refuse incoming cases. Moreover, their parameters only contain values of the type *Cases* or its sub-types.
- Data and information flows: additional information provided by enactment system may influence control flow, they can use any ADTs as parameters.

– Operational flow: invoke external services and accept callbacks. This kind of methods and gates is not always firable, and their parameters can also be any ADTs.

In our approach, COOPN workflow models handle only control flow, the data flow and operational flow are managed by the enactment system. However, some methods and gates are used to interact with the enactment system, e.g. tell enactment system to invoke a service. Modeling of operational and data flow are out of the scope of the paper.

3.2   Workflow Patterns

Workflow patterns will be built as COOPN components with local states described by tokens, methods as input events, external events also as methods and gates as output events. Composition will be done by directly linking gates to methods. As synchronization rules will be given within pattern, only simple synchronization will be used among patterns. The workflow pattern typical list is borrowed from the pioneer work of W. van der Aalst.

Let us take an example of *synchronizing merge* to explain how to build workflow patterns with COOPN axioms. A synchronizing merge multiples paths converge into one single flow. If more than one path is taken, synchronization of the active flows needs to take place. If a token representing a case instance value is passed to the activity and presents in the place, the path is active for the case instance value. In our example Figure 6, if both *input1_* and *input2_* are active at the time we fire **E**, the two flows are merged, then *out_* is activated only once. If only one path is active at the time we fire **E**, *out_* is activated once for this path, and if afterwards another path becomes active, **E** will also be firable and *out_* will be activated another time. Note that the value of *out_* can be any value of type *Case*. For the sake of simplicity, in following figures and lists of axioms, we use **T, T1, T2** or **c, c1, c2** as values of output cases.

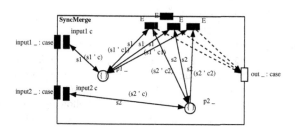

Fig. 6. Workflow Pattern: Synchronizing Merge

The following axioms describe the pattern *synchronizing merge*, an activity with two inputs and one output. T, T1, and T2 are ADT terms of type *Case*, where T=f(c1,c2), T1=f(c1), T2=f(c2). *f* is the function between inputs and outputs. Expression *c1 sameID c2* is a condition that means c1 and c2 identify the same case instance; **c**, **c1** and **c2** are variables of type *Case*; **s**, **s1** and **s2** are predefined **Sets** containing *Case* values; **s'c** is the set of adding element **c** into set **s**; **s1^s2** is the intersection set of **s1** and **s2**; # **s** is the number of elements in set **s**. *c isin s* is true if **c** is in set **s**. Initially, **s1** and **s2** are empty.

Table 1. Workflow Patterns in COOPN

Pattern name	Axioms	Comments

Parallel Split	`input c:: p s-> p s'c;`
	`E With this.out1 T1 //`
	`    this.out2 T2::`
	`    p s'c -> p s;`
		A single flow of control is split into multiple flows of control. Firing transition E will trigger gate *out1* and *out2*, sending out T1 and T2. **Synonyms:** *AND Split*

Synchronization	`input1 c1:: p s1-> p1 s1'c1;`
	`input2 c2:: p s2-> p2 s2'c2;`
	`c1 sameID c2=>`
	`    E With this.out T::`
	`    p1 s1'c1, p2 s2'c2`
	`    -> p s1, p s2;`
		Multiple flows of control converge into one. Transition E is enabled when all inputs have arrived, firing E will send out T. **Synonyms:** *AND Join*

XOR Split	`input c:: p s-> p s'c;`
	`E With this.out1 T1::`
	`    p s'c -> p s;`
	`E With this.out2 T2::`
	`    p s'c -> p s;`
		Based on a decision or value of case instance, one of several branches is chosen. Firing E will trigger one of gate out1 and out2, sending out T1 or T2. **Synonyms:** *Exclusive Choice*

XOR Join	`input1 c:: p1 s1-> p1 s1'c1;`
	`input2 c:: p2 s2-> p2 s2'c2;`
	`E With this.out T::`
	`    p1 s1'c1 -> p1 s1;`
	`E With this.out T::`
	`    p2 s2'c2 -> p2 s2;`
		E is enabled for each input. The inputs are not synchronized. **Synonyms:** *Asynchronous Join*

Multiple Merge	`input1 c:: p1 s1-> p1 s1'c;`
	`input2 c:: p2 s2-> p2 s2'c;`
	`E With this.out T1::`
	`    p1 s1'c -> p1 s1;`
	`E With this.out T2::`
	`    p2 s2'c -> p2 s2;`
		Multiple paths converge into one single flow. If more than one branch gets activated, possibly concurrently, the activity following the merge is started for every activation of every incoming branch.

Deferred Choice	`input c:: p s-> p s'c;`
	`E1 With this.out1 T1::`
	`    p s'c -> p s;`
	`E2 With this.out2 T2::`
	`    p s'c -> p s;`
		Two alternatives are offered to environment: E1 and E2 are all enabled, firing one will disable another. **Synonyms:** *Deferred XOR-split, External choice*

```
axiom1: input1 c::p1 s1 -> p1 (s1'c);
axiom2: input2 c::p2 s2 -> p2 (s2'c);
axiom3: c1 sameID c2, s3 = s1^s2, (# s3 > 0) = true,
   (c1 isin s3) = true, (c2 isin s3) = true =>
   E With this.out T:: p1 s1'c1, p2 s2'c2 -> p1 s1, p2 s2;
axiom4: s3 = s1^s2, (# s3 = 0) = true =>
   E With this.out T1:: p1 s1'c1, p2 s2 -> p1 s1;
axiom5: s3 = s1^s2, (# s3 = 0) = true =>
   E With this.out T2:: p1 s1, p2 s2'c2 -> p2 s2;
```

axiom1 and *axiom2* state that *input1_* and *input2_* will put the value c into set **s1** of *p1_* and set **s2** of *p2_*, respectively. *axiom3, axiom4, and axiom5* describe the behavior of trigger **E**: when two tokens of the same instance, **c1** is in **s1** and **c2** is in **s2**, firing **E** will remove **c1** and **c2** from the sets and send out T=f(c1,c2); if only one token exists, firing **E** will remove the token and send out a corresponding output; if there is no cases values in **s1** and **s2**, **E** will be not be firable.

Table 1 lists some other workflow patterns proposed by [6]; names and descriptions of patterns are kept for reference purpose. A complete list of workflow patterns modelled with COOPN is available in a technical report [11].

3.3   Transactional Workflow Patterns

A transaction in a workflow is one atomic event abstracting a more complex behaviour, and this is directly modeled by using synchronization mechanism on sub-models of workflows. In Figure 7 we show an example of transactional patterns, where **P** is a sub-model of workflow containing three activities **A**, **B**, and **C**: **A** is an AND-SPLIT activity, **B** is a simple activity, and **C** is an AND-JOIN activity. In particular, input *in2_* of **C** is independent of these three activities. A higher level trigger **TP** is synchronized with the triggers of these activities, specified by an axiom: **TP With TA..(TB//TC)**. When TP is fired, the model tries firing TA at first, then firing TB and TC at the same time. Since one input of AND-JOIN C might not be satisfied at the moment we try firing

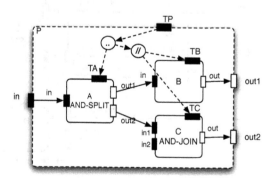

Fig. 7. Transactional workflow patterns: TP with TA..(TB//TC)

TC, TC may fail. According to the principle of synchronization, TB, TA and TP will fail, as a consequence, the case instance stays in A, neither B nor C are aware of this attempt.

In this example we observe that the synchronization propagates to an AND-JOIN activity and fails. In fact there are many reasons why a synchronization may fails, especially when dealing with immediate mode activities and operational methods e.g. invoking external synchronized services.

In general, the use of COOPN for modeling workflows is based on the principle that hierarchy of context captures the different levels of transaction while linear interconnection of components is used for describing the composition of workflow. This principle is very close to the use of COOPN for modeling Coordinated Atomic Actions [17], [18]. The hierarchical approach is not fully satisfactory, in particular for shared resources (the payment system, for instance, that can be reused in the context or other online shops). In this case the solution is to not include this resource in the surrounding context. Instead, as it must be accessible to various partners, this resource should be defined as a shared object as it was done in CAA.

4   Prototype Generation and Integration

In this section, we will explain how to validate business processes by prototyping. This will mainly be done by generating process controller prototypes from COOPN specifications and then interpreting or simulating prototypes in the CoopnBuilder environment. Finally we will compose these prototypes with the enactment systems. CoopnBuilder [16] is the latest generation of tools

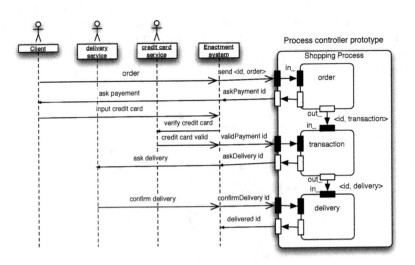

Fig. 8. Prototype Integration: an Online Shop

supporting COOPN language, this continually developing tool provides an integrated development environment to edit, verify, and visualize COOPN modules. Moreover, the included prototype generator produces executable JavaBean-like components from COOPN specifications. These components implement the underlying COOPN specifications by means of the embedded state-transition system with well-defined management of synchronization and atomicity. Methods of COOPN modules are transformed to Java methods with support for transactions. To capture outgoing events, we add *EventListener* on the *gates*.

Assuming that readers understood how to compose complex processes by means of workflow patterns, we will illustrate how the enactment system interacts with process controller prototypes and external process participants. A simple process with three activities is given in Figure 8. The *Shopping Process* is a COOPN context incorporating *order, transaction,* and *delivery* activities. Execution of activities are sequential in the process. The context delegates some methods and gates of internal activities, especially the inputs of case instance and the operational actions. All inputs and outputs of the context are handled by the enactment system. According to output messages of controller prototype, the enactment system communicates with external business process partners, who effectuate the real work of activities; when a process relevant event raises from the partners, e.g. payment by credit card is finished, the enactment system *"tells"* the controller prototype to change the state of related process instance. The controller prototype can be thought as an *"Abstract State Machine"* and the "brain" of the enactment system. An enactment system is a *"service provider"* of all embedded process controllers.

The prototype integration consists of connecting the generated process controller prototypes to an enactment system, which is like using normal JavaBeans. Further details on prototype generation and integration can be found in related work: [15] demonstrates using prototypes as controllers of embedded systems. [14] explains techniques for interfacing generated prototypes with existing Java libraries.

5   Conclusions and Future Work

This is our first attempt of using COOPN language in the domain of business process management. Through this paper, we observe some interesting results:

- Service provides an universal solution for system interaction. All interaction between the enactment system and other systems can be abstracted to services. COOPN supports the four transmission primitives proposed by WSDL [9], hence there are no surprises that COOPN can model the service-oriented components and the generated prototypes can be smoothly integrated into real systems.
- COOPN modules: *ADT, class,* and *context* can naturally represent control data, activity, and business process. Prototypes generated from COOPN models can be integrated into enactment systems as process controllers.

- By separating responsibilities of process controller and enactment system, portability and reusability of process controller are guaranteed.
- We are able to represent almost all workflow control patterns with COOPN; complex business processes are composed by these patterns. Moreover, COOPN supports transactional workflow patterns.
- Although our simple definition of value type *Case* and the separation of control from other perspectives give facilities to verify the control flow, the verification of process needs further investigations, e.g. to define useful properties.

Process controller prototype generation and integration are the most important contributions of our approach. We can have various definitions for the type *Case*, but the main modeling principle is to have an instance identification and some local representations of process instances.

As further research, we are interested in: implementing a general enactment system to automatically integrate process controllers; verification of control flow in COOPN-modeled processes; adding specific ADTs to represent data and operational flows; proposing additional patterns and analysis techniques for theses flows.

References

1. W.M.P. van der Aalst. Three Good reasons for Using a Petri-net-based Workflow Management System. In T. Wakayama, S. Kannapan, C.M. Khoong, S. Navathe, and J. Yates, editors, Information and Process Integration in Enterprises: Rethinking Documents, volume 428 of The Kluwer International Series in Engineering and Computer Science, pages 161–182. Kluwer Academic Publishers, Boston, Massachusetts, 1998.
2. W.M.P. van der Aalst and A.H.M. ter Hofstede. YAWL: Yet Another Workflow Language (Revised Version). QUT Technical report, FIT-TR-2003-04, Queensland University of Technology, Brisbane, 2003.
3. N. Russell, A.H.M. ter Hofstede, D. Edmond, and W.M.P. van der Aalst. Workflow Data Patterns. QUT Technical report, FIT-TR-2004-01, Queensland University of Technology, Brisbane, 2004.
4. N. Russell, A.H.M. ter Hofstede, D. Edmond, and W.M.P. van der Aalst. Workflow Resource Patterns. BETA Working Paper Series, WP 127, Eindhoven University of Technology, Eindhoven, 2004.
5. W.M.P. van der Aalst. Patterns and XPDL: A Critical Evaluation of the XML Process Definition Language. QUT Technical report, FIT-TR-2003-06, Queensland University of Technology, Brisbane, 2003.
6. W.M.P. van der Aalst, A.H.M. ter Hofstede, B. Kiepuszewski, and A.P. Barros. Workflow Patterns. Distributed and Parallel Databases, 14(3), pages 5–51, July 2003.
7. Moldt, Daniel; Rlke, Heiko: Pattern Based Workflow Design Using Reference Nets International Conference on Business Process Management (BPM 2003), Eindhoven, The Netherlands, Lecture Notes in Computer Science, Vol. 2678, Springer-Verlag, 2003. Pages 246–260.

8. Business Process Execution Language for Web Service version 1.1.
   http://www-128.ibm.com/developerworks/library/specification/ws-bpel/
9. Web Services Description Language (WSDL) 1.1. http://www.w3.org/TR/2001/
   NOTE-wsdl-20010315
10. Workflow Management Coalition, http://www.wfmc.org/ Workflow Reference
    Model and Standards
11. Ang Chen, Didier Buchs. COOPN Workflow Patterns. Technical Report, Computer
    Science Department, University of Geneva
12. Didier Buchs and Nicolas Guelfi, A Formal Specification Framework for Object-
    Oriented Distributed Systems, IEEE TSE, vol. 26, no. 7, July 2000, pp. 635–652.
13. Olivier Biberstein, Didier Buchs, and Nicolas Guelfi. Object-oriented nets with
    algebraic specifications: The CO-OPN/2 formalism. In G. Agha and F.De Cin-
    dioand G.Rozenberg, editors, Advances in Petri Nets on Object-Orientation,
    LNCS. Springer-Verlag, 2001.
14. Stanislav Chachkov and Didier Buchs, "Interfacing Software Libraries from Non-
    deterministic Prototypes", Rapid System Prototyping, Darmstadt, Germany, IEEE
    Computer Society Press, July 2002, pp. 92–98.
15. Stanislav Chachkov and Didier Buchs, "From an Abstract Object-Oriented Model
    to a Ready-to-Use Embedded System Controller", Rapid System Prototyping,
    Monterey, CA, IEEE Computer Society Press, June 2001, pp. 142–148.
16. Ali Al-Shabibi, Didier Buchs, Mathieu Buffo, Stanislav Chachkov, Ang Chen and
    David Hurzeler, "Prototyping Object-Oriented Specifications", Proceedings of the
    International Conference on Theory and Application of Petri Nets, Eindhoven,
    Netherlands, Wil M. P. van der Aalst and Eike Best (Eds.), LNCS(Lecture Notes
    in Computer Science), vol. 2679, Springer Verlag, June 2003, pp. 473–482.
17. Julie Vachon, Nicolas Guelfi and Alexander Romanovsky. Using COALA for the
    Development of a Distributed Object-based Application. In Proceedings of the
    2nd International Symposium on Distributed Objects & Applications(DAO'00),
    Antwerp, Belgium, 2000.
18. J. Vachon, D. Buchs, M. Buffo, G. Di Marzo Serugendo, B. Randell,
    A. Romanovsky, R.J. Stroud, and J. Xu. Coala - a formal language for coordi-
    nated atomic actions. In 3rd Year Report, ESPRIT Long Term Research Project
    20072 on Design for Validation. LAAS, France, november 1998.

Formal Development of Reactive Fault Tolerant Systems

Linas Laibinis and Elena Troubitsyna

Åbo Akademi, Department of Computer Science,
Lemminkäisenkatu 14 A, FIN-20520 Turku, Finland
(Linas.Laibinis, Elena.Troubitsyna)@abo.fi

Abstract. Usually complex systems are controlled by an operator co-operating with a computer-based controller. The controlling software runs in continuous interaction with the operator and constantly reacts on operator's interruptions by dynamically adapting system behaviour. Simultaneously it catches the exceptions signalling about errors in the system components and performs error recovery. Since interruptions are asynchronous signals they might concurrently co-exist and conflict with exceptions. To ensure dependability of a dynamically adaptable system, we propose a formal approach for resolving conflicts and designing robust interruption and exception handlers. We present a formal specification pattern for designing components of layered control systems that contain interruption and exception handlers as an intrinsic part of the specification. We demonstrate how to develop a layered control system by recursive application of this pattern.

1 Introduction

In this paper we propose a formal approach to the development of dependable control systems. Control systems are the typical examples of reactive systems. Often they run in a constant interaction not only with the controlled physical application but also the operator. The operator participates in providing the control over an application by placing requests to execute certain services and often intervening in the service provision. As a response to the operator's intervention, the controller should adapt the behaviour of the system accordingly. The task of ensuring dependability of dynamically adaptable systems is two-fold: on the one hand, we should design the controller to be flexible enough to allow the operator's intervention; on the other hand, the controller should prevent potentially dangerous interventions in its service provision.

Design of dependable control systems usually spans over several engineering domains. Traditionally abstraction, modularisation and layered architecture are recognized to be effective ways to manage system complexity [14]. Though the components at each architectural layer are susceptible to specific kinds of faults, the mechanism of exception raising and handling can be used for error detection and recovery at each architectural layer.

However, since exceptions and interruptions are asynchronous signals, several exceptions and interruptions might occur simultaneously. Incorrect resolution of such conflicting situations might seriously jeopardize system dependability. In this paper we formally analyse the relationships between interruptions and exceptions and

N. Guelfi and A. Savidis (Eds.): RISE 2005, LNCS 3943, pp. 234–249, 2006.

propose formal guidelines for designing robust interruption and exception handling. Moreover, we propose a formal approach to the development of reactive fault tolerant control systems in a layered manner.

Our approach is based on stepwise refinement of a formal system model in the B Method [1,2,15]. While developing a system by refinement, we start from an abstract specification and step by step incorporate implementation details into it until executable code is obtained. In this paper we propose a general pattern for specification and refinement of reactive layered systems in B. Our pattern contains exception and interruption handlers as an intrinsic part of the specification. We start from the specification of the system behaviour on the upper architectural layer and unfold layers by a recursive instantiation of the proposed specification pattern. Since our approach addresses the dependability aspects already in the early stages of system development, we argue that it has potential to enhance system dependability.

We proceed as follows: in Section 2 we discuss propagation of exceptions and interruptions in the layered control systems. In Section 3 we present a formal basis for designing interruption and exception handlers. In Section 4 we demonstrate our approach to formal development of fault tolerant reactive systems that contain interruption and exception handlers as an intrinsic part of their specifications. In Section 5 we summarize the proposed approach, discuss its possible extensions and overview the related work.

2 Exceptions and Interruptions in a Layered Architecture

In this paper we focus on modelling dependable control systems. In general control system consists of a plant and a controller. A plant is a physical entity monitored and controlled by a computer-based controller. Often control over the plant is provided in co-operation between a computer and an operator – a human (or sometimes another computer-based system) participating in operating the system.

Layered Architecture. Usually development of a control system spans over several engineering domains, such as mechanical engineering, software engineering, human-computer interface etc. It is widely recognized that a layered architecture is preferable in designing such complex systems since it allows the developers to map real-world domains into software layers [14]. The lowest layer confines real-time subsystems which directly communicate with sensors and actuators – the electro-mechanical devices used to monitor and control the plant. These subsystems cyclically execute the standard control loop consisting of reading the sensors, and assigning the new states to the actuators. The layer above contains the components that encapsulate the detailed behaviour of the lowest level subsystems by providing abstract interfaces to them. The component server (often called the service director) is on the highest level of hierarchy. It serves as an interface between the operator and the components.

There are several ways in which the operator can interact with the system. Normally s/he places the requests to execute certain services. A service is an encapsulation of a set of operations to be executed by the components. Upon receiving a request to execute a service, the component server at first translates (decomposes) the service into the corresponding sequence of operations. Then it initiates and monitors the

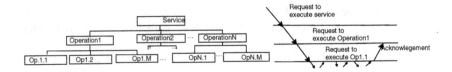

Fig. 1. Architecture of a layered system

execution of operations by placing corresponding requests on the components. In their turns, the requested components further decompose these operations into the lower level operations. These operations are to be executed by real-time subsystems at the lowest layer of hierarchy. Upon completion of each operation, the requested subsystem notifies the requesting component about success of the execution. The component continues to place the requests on the subsystems until completion of the requested operation. Then it ceases its autonomous functioning and notifies the component server about success of the execution. The behaviour of the components follows the same general pattern: the component is initially "dormant" but becomes active upon receiving a request to execute a certain operation. In the active mode the component autonomously executes a operation until completion. Then it returns the acknowledgement to the requesting component and becomes inactive again. The communication between components can be graphically represented as shown in Fig. 1.

Exceptions. While describing the communication between the layers of a control system, we assumed so far that the system is fault-free, i.e., after receiving a request to execute an operation, the component eventually successfully completes it. However, occurrence of errors might prevent a component from providing a required operation correctly. Hence, while designing a controller, we should specify means for tolerating fault of various natures. In this paper we focus on hardware faults and human errors.

The main goal of introducing fault tolerance is to design a system in such a way that that faults of components do not result in system failure [3,4,11]. A fault of a component manifests itself as an error [3]. Upon detection of an error, error recovery should be performed. Error recovery is an attempt to restore a fault-free system state or at least preclude system failure. Hence components of fault tolerant controllers should be able to detect the errors and notify the requesting component, so that error recovery can be initiated. This behaviour is achieved via the mechanism of exception raising and handling [5]. Observe that for each component (except the lowest level subsystems) we can identify two classes of exceptions:

1. *generated exceptions*: the exceptions raised by the component itself upon detection of an error,
2. *propagated exceptions*: the exceptions raised at the lower layer but propagated to the component for handling.

The generated exceptions are propagated upwards (to the requesting component) for handling. Usually the component that has raised an exception ceases its autonomous functioning. Such a behaviour models the fact that the component is unable to handle the erroneous situation. With each component we associate a class of errors from which the component attempts to recover by itself. If the component receives a propagated exception signalling about an error from this class, then it initiates error recovery by requesting certain lower layer operations. Otherwise the component propagates the exception further up in the hierarchy. Hence certain errors will be propagated to the operator, so s/he could initiate manual error recovery. This behaviour is graphically represented in Fig. 2.

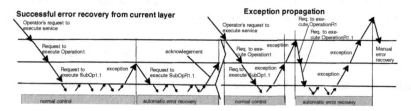

Fig. 2. Exceptions in a layered architecture

Interruptions. While discussing service provision in a layered architecture we assumed that the system accepts the operator's request to execute a certain service after it has completed execution of a previous service, i.e., in an idle state. However, often the operator needs to intervene in the service execution. For instance, s/he might change "on-the-fly" the parameters of the currently executing service or cancel it, suspend and resume service provision etc. Such interventions are usually called interruptions. Observe that a request to execute a service can also be seen as the special case of interruption.

Interruptions are dual to exceptions. They arrive from the uppermost architectural layers and are "propagated" downwards, to the currently active layer. Upon receiving

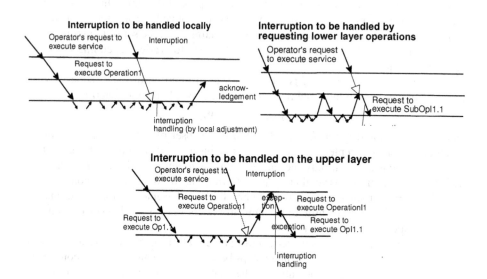

Fig. 3. Interruptions in a layered architecture

an interruption, the currently active component takes appropriate actions required to handle it. The component can either

- change the local state to adjust the execution and then resume its work, or
- generate the requests to execute certain lower-layer subservices (which might be seen as a special case of error recovery), or
- "realize" that the interruption should be handled on a higher layer of hierarchy. Then it would generate the corresponding exception, which is then propagated upwards.

The behaviour of the system while handling interruption is graphically represented in Fig. 3.

While designing dependable systems, we need to analyse the impact of interruptions and exceptions on system dependability. In the next section we will address this issue in detail.

3 Formal Analysis of Interruption and Exception Handling

Ensuring dependability of the systems that can adapt their behaviour in response to operator's interruptions is a complex task. It involves establishing a proper balance between system flexibility and dependability. For instance, if the behaviour of the autopilot deems to be faulty, the controlling software of an aircraft should allow the pilot to interrupt the autopilot and resume manual control; on the other hand, software should disallow the pilot to interrupt automatic control in a potentially dangerous way. Next we consider a formal basis for designing dependable reactive systems.

Preventing Incorrect Interventions. At first we observe that the interface of the system is the medium via which the operator requests and interrupts services. Hence design of the system interface should obey the principles of designing human-computer interfaces for error prevention (the study of those is outside of the scope of this paper). Usually the resulting system interface is dynamic, i.e., the set of the requests and interruptions which the system accepts from the operator varies depending on the internal system state.

Assume that $I = \{I_1, I_2, .. I_M\}$ is a complete set of interruptions and requests which the operator can send to the system via its interface. We define the function

$$blocking: I \rightarrow \mathbf{PI},$$

which for each interruption I_j, $j:1..M$, returns a subset of interruptions or requests which can be next accepted by the system. For instance, if the operator has sent the interruption *"Pause"* then only the interruptions *"Continue"* and *"Abort"* can be accepted next. Let us observe that some interruptions or requests are non-blocking ($blocking(I_k)=I$, for some k), i.e., they do not disable other interruptions. The function *blocking* explicitly defines how to dynamically adapt the system interface to enforce the correct operator's behaviour.

Next we study how the controller should prevent the incorrect intervention into its service provision. We define the relationships between interruptions and the controller's operations. Namely, for each operation of the controller, we identify the subset of interruptions which must be immediately handled and the subset of interruptions handling of which should be postponed until execution of the current operation is completed.

Assume that C is a component in our layered architecture. Assume also that $OpC = \{OpC_1, OpC_2, ...OpC_N\}$ is a set of operations provided by C and I is a set of interruptions and requests accepted by the overall system. For each operation in OpC, we analyse the consequences of interrupting its execution by each of the interruptions from I. As a result of such analysis, we define a function

$$atomicC : OpC \times I \to Bool$$

such that, for any $i: 1..N$ and $j: 1..M$, $atomicC(OpC_i, I_j)$ is $FALSE$ if interruption I_j received during the execution of OpC_i should be handled immediately, and $TRUE$ if handling of I_j should be postponed until completion of OpC_i. In the latter case the operation OPC_i is atomic, i.e., uninterruptible by the interruption I_j.

Since interruptions are asynchronous events and sometimes interruption handling is postponed, interruptions can be queued for handling. Let us consider the following situation: after unsuccessful attempts to recover from an error by sending certain interruption, the operator decides to cancel the execution of the current service. If the interruptions are handled in the "first-in-first-out" order, then the service will be cancelled only after all previous interruptions are handled, i.e., with a delay. This might be undesirable or even dangerous. Hence we need to distinguish between the levels of criticality of different interruptions, for instance, to ensure that, if an interruption is an attempt to preclude a dangerous system failure, it is handled with the highest priority.

We define the function

$$I\_EVAL: I \to NAT$$

which assigns priorities to interruptions and requests. The greater the value of $I\_EVAL(I_j)$, where $j: 1..M$, the higher degree of priority of handling the interruption I_j. While designing the system, we ensure that the interruptions are handled according to the priority assigned by I_EVAL.

Interruptions Versus Exceptions. Above we analysed the principles of interruption handling. However, our analysis would be incomplete if we omit consideration of the relationship between interruptions and exceptions. Indeed, since interruptions are asynchronous events, they might co-exist and "collide" with exceptions, e.g., when an interruption is caught simultaneously with the exception indicating an erroneous situation. Dealing with concurrent arrival of several signals from different sources has been recognized as a serious problem that has not received sufficient attention [4]. Incorrect handling of these signals might lead to the unexpected system behaviour and, as a consequence, can seriously jeopardize system dependability. To resolve such potentially dangerous situations, handling of simultaneous signals should be designed in a structured and rigorous way.

Let C be a component on a certain layer of our layered architecture. Let $EXC\_C = \{Exc_1, Exc_2, ...Exc_N\}$ be a set of exceptions that can be propagated to C from the lower layer components. We define the function

$$E\_EVALC : EXC\_C \to NAT$$

which assigns a certain criticality level to each exception that component receives. By defining E_EVALC for each component of our system we assign a certain priority to each exception to be handled by the system.

Let us consider now an active component C, which has currently caught the exception Exc_1 and interruptions I_1, I_2, I_3 such that $I\_EVAL(I_1) > I\_EVAL(I_2) > I\_EVAL(I_3)$. Then

- if the interruption I_1 is more critical than the exception, i.e., $I\_EVAL(I_1) \geq E\_EVALC(Exc_1)$ then the next signal to be handled is the interruption I_1,
- if the exception is more critical than the interruptions, i.e., $E\_EVALC(Exc_1) > I\_EVAL(I_1)$ then the next signal to be handled is the exception Exc_1.

Upon completion of handling the most critical signal, the caught signals are evaluated in the same way. Then the decision which signal should be handled next is made again.

Observe that the functions *blocking, E_EVALC* and *I_EVAL* can be extended to take into account its current state while making the decision about criticality of exceptions and interruptions.

Interruption and Exception Propagation. Let us now discuss the design of interruption and exception handlers. We identify three classes of interruptions:

- the interruptions, whose handling can be done locally, i.e., by changing local variables of the currently active component,
- those, whose handling requires to invoke the lower layer operations, and
- those, whose handling is possible only on some higher layer (the received interruption is converted into an exception to be propagated upwards).

The identified classes are disjoint. The proposed classification is complete in a sense that it defines all possible types of system responses on interruptions.

We define the function (for each component C)

$$I\_STATUS\_C: I \rightarrow \{Local, Down, Up\}$$

which, for any interruption, defines the type of the required handling.

In the similar way we define the types of exceptions as exceptions signalling about

- successful termination of requested service,
- recoverable error, or
- unrecoverable error.

The corresponding function (for each component C)

$$E\_STATUS\_C: EXC\_C \rightarrow \{Ok, Recov, Unrecov\}$$

defines the type of each exception and acknowledgement. If the acknowledgement notifies about successful termination then the normal control flow continues. If the exception signals about recoverable error then error recovery from the current layer is attempted. Otherwise, the exception is propagated upwards in the hierarchy.

In the latter case, we need to define the rules for converting unrecoverable propagated exceptions and interruptions into generated exceptions of the current component. After conversion, the corresponding exception of the current component is raised and propagated up. For every pair of components (C_i, C_j) such that C_i is a requesting component (client) and C_j is a requested component from the lower layer, we define the function

$$E\_CONV_{ij}: EXC\_C_i \rightarrow EXCg\_C_j$$

where EXC_C_i is the set of propagated and $EXCg\_C_j$ is the set of generated exceptions of the corresponding components. The function E_CONV_{ij} converts propagated exceptions of C_i into generated exceptions of C_j.

In a similar way, we design interruption handling converting the received interruption into an exception to be propagated upwards. For every component C, we define the function

$$I\_CONV: I \rightarrow EXC\_Cg$$

Let us observe that our exception handling has hierarchical structure: while designing exception handling we follow the principle "the more critical an error is, the higher the layer that should handle its exception". This principle should be utilized while defining the functions E_EVALC (for each component C) and I_EVAL.

In this section we formalized the principles of designing interruption and exception handling in a layered architecture. In the next section we present our approach to specification and refinement of dependable reactive systems.

4   Specification and Refinement of Reactive Fault Tolerant Systems

It is widely accepted that high degree of dependability of the system can only be achieved if dependability consideration starts from the early stages of system development [11,17]. We demonstrate how to specify layered control systems in such a way that mechanisms for interruption and exception handling become an intrinsic part of their specification. We start by a brief introduction into the B Method – our formal development framework.

The B Method. The B Method [1,15] (further referred to as B) is an approach for the industrial development of highly dependable software. The method has been successfully used in the development of several complex real-life applications [13]. The tool support available for B provides us with the assistance for the entire development process. For instance, Atelier B [16], one of the tools supporting the B Method, has facilities for automatic verification and code generation as well as documentation, project management and prototyping. The high degree of automation in verifying correctness improves scalability of B, speeds up development and, also, requires less mathematical training from the users.

The development methodology adopted by B is based on stepwise refinement [1]. While developing a system by refinement, we start from an abstract formal specification and transform it into an implementable program by a number of correctness preserving steps, called *refinements*. A formal specification is a mathematical model of the required behaviour of a (part of) system. In B a specification is represented by a set of modules, called Abstract Machines. An abstract machine encapsulates state and operations of the specification and as a concept is similar to module or package.

Each machine is uniquely identified by its name. The state variables of the machine are declared in the VARIABLES clause and initialized in the INITIALISATION clause. The variables in B are strongly typed by constraining predicates of the INVARIANT clause. All types in B are represented by non-empty sets. We can also define local types as *deferred sets*. In this case we just introduce a new name for a type, postponing actual definition until some later development stage.

The operations of the machine are defined in the OPERATIONS clause. There are two standard ways to describe an operation in B: either by the preconditioned operation PRE cond THEN body END or the guarded operation SELECT cond THEN body END. Here cond is a state predicate, and body is a B statement. If cond is satisfied, the behaviour of both the precondition operation and the guarded operation corresponds to the execution of their bodies. However, if cond is false, then the precondition operation leads to a crash (i.e., unpredictable or even non-terminating behaviour) of the system, while the behaviour of the guarded operation is immaterial since it will be not executed. The preconditioned operations are used to describe operations that will be implemented as procedures modelling requests. The guarded operations are used to specify event-based systems and will model autonomous behaviour.

B statements that we are using to describe a state change in operations have the following syntax:

$$S \ == \ x := e \ | \ \text{IF cond THEN } S1 \text{ ELSE } S2 \text{ END} \ | \ S1 \ ; \ S2 \ |$$
$$x :: T \ | \ S1 \parallel S2 \ | \ \text{ANY } z \text{ WHERE cond THEN } S \text{ END} \ | \ ...$$

The first three constructs – assignment, conditional statement and sequential composition (used only in refinements) have the standard meaning. The remaining constructs allow us to model nondeterministic or parallel behaviour in a specification. Usually they are not implementable so they have to be refined (replaced) with executable constructs at some point of program development. The detailed description of the B statements can be found elsewhere [1,15].

The B method provides us with mechanisms for structuring the system architecture by modularization. The modules (machines) can be composed by means of several mechanisms providing different forms of encapsulation. For instance, if the machine C INCLUDES the machine D then all variables and operations of D are visible in C. However, to guarantee internal consistency (and hence independent verification and reuse) of D, the machine C can change the variables of D only via the operations of D. In addition, the invariant properties of D are included into the invariant of C. To make the operations of D available through the interface of C, we should list them in the PROMOTE clause of C. If D promotes all its operations to C then C is an extension of D which can be specified by the EXTENDS mechanism.

Refinement and Layered Architecture. Refinement is a technique to incorporate implementation details into a specification. In general, the refinement process can be seen as a way to reduce nondeterminism of the abstract specification, to replace the abstract mathematical data structures by the data structures implementable on a computer, and to introduce underspecified design decisions. In the Abstract Machine Notation (AMN), the results of the intermediate development stages – the refinement machines – have essentially the same structure as the more abstract specifications. In addition, they explicitly state which specifications they refine.

Each refinement step should be formally verified by discharging (proving) certain proof obligations. Since verification of refinement is done by proofs rather than state exploration, the stepwise refinement technique is free of the state explosion problem and hence is well suited for the development of complex systems. In this paper we demonstrate how refinement facilitates development of systems structured in a layered manner.

Let us observe that the schematic representation of communication between the components of a layered system represented in Fig. 1 can also be seen as the scheme of atomicity refinement. Indeed, each layer decomposes a higher layer operation into a set of operations of smaller granularity. The decomposition continues iteratively until the lowest layer is reached. At this layer the operations are considered to be not further decomposable. From the architectural perspective, an abstract specification is a "folded" representation of the system structure. The system behaviour is specified in terms of large atomic services at the component server layer. Each refinement step adds (or "unfolds") an architectural layer in the downward direction. Large atomic services are decomposed into operations of smaller granularity. Refinement process continues until the whole architectural hierarchy is built. We argue that the refinement process conducted in such a way allows us to obtain a realistic model of fault tolerant reactive systems. Indeed, by iterative refinement of atomicity we eventually arrive at modelling exceptions and interruptions arriving practically at any instance of time, i.e., before and after execution of each operation of the finest granularity. The proposed refinement process is illustrated in Fig. 4, where we outline the development pattern instantiated to a three-layered system.

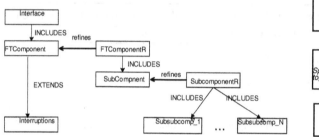

Fig. 4. Refinement process   **Fig. 5.** Abstract specification

Abstract Specification in B. The initial abstract specification consists of three machines (see Fig. 5). The machine Interface models the interface of the system. The machine Interruptions describes the data structure representing the interruptions. The machine Component contains the abstract specification of the component server, i.e., it models services which the system provides for the operator as well as interruption and exception handling on the component server layer. The interactions of the operator with the interface result in invocations of the operations of FTDAComponent. Hence Interface INCLUDES FTDAComponent.

Each refinement step leads to creating components at the lower layer by including their specifications into the refinement of the corresponding components at the previous layer. Observe that in the abstract specification the operator activates a component server by placing a request to execute a service. At the next refinement step we refine the specification of the component server to model placing requests on the lower layer component and introduce the specification of the lower layer component together with interruption and exception handling performed by it. Since the behaviour of the components on each layer follows the same pattern, the refinement process is essentially the recursive instantiation of the abstract specification pattern. Next we present the specification on the machines defining specification patterns in detail.

The specification of Interruptions contains the data structure modelling interruptions and the operations for manipulating them. The operation add_interruption inserts arriving interruptions in the sequence Inter modelling the list of interruptions to be handled. The list Inter is sorted according to the criticality assigned to interruptions by the function *I_EVAL* and the operation add_interruptions preserves this order. The handled interruptions are removed from the list via the operation remove_interruption. In addition, remove_interruption removes interruptions that have become redundant or irrelevant after handling the last interruption.

```
MACHINE  Interruptions
SETS INTERRUPTIONS
VARIABLES Inter
INVARIANT  Inter : seq(INTERRUPTIONS) &  interruptions are sorted by their criticality
INITIALISATION Inter := [ ]
OPERATIONS
   add_interruption (inter)= PRE inter is valid THEN
      add inter to Inter and ensure that interruptions remain sorted by criticality  END;

   remove_interruption (inter) =  PRE Inter is not empty THEN
      remove inter and irrelevant interruptions from Inter  END
END
```

The machine Interface given below defines how the system interacts with its environment, i.e., it models the service requests and interruptions.

```
MACHINE  Interface
INCLUDES ServiceComponent
VARIABLES current
INVARIANT  current: INTERRUPTIONS
INITIALISATION current:= No_int

OPERATIONS
   request (request_parameters) = PRE flag=stopped  THEN activate Component  END;

   interruption_1 =  PRE interruption_1 is allowed THEN
      add_interruption(interruption_name1) II current:= interruption_name1  END;

   interruption_N =  PRE interruption_nameN is allowed THEN
      add_interruption(interruption_nameN) II current:= interruption_nameN  END;

   abort = BEGIN add_interruption(Abort) II current := Abort END
END
```

The operation request models placing a request to execute a certain service. The request can be placed only when the system is in the idle state, i.e., the previous request has already been completed or cancelled. The interactions are modelled by the operations with corresponding names. Unlike requests, interruptions can arrive at any time. However, acceptance of the new interruption depends on the previously arrived interruption as defined by the function *blocking* introduced in Section 3. The preconditions of interruption_1...interruption_N check whether the previously arrived interruption, current, blocks the newly arrived interruption. If the interruption is accepted then the arriving interruption is added to the list of interruptions to be handled and the value of current is updated.

The behaviour of a fault tolerant dynamically adaptable component is abstractly specified by the machine FTDAComponent presented in Fig. 6.

MACHINE FTDAComponent
EXTENDS Interruptions
VARIABLES flag, atomic_flag, exc, exc2, state, last_int
INVARIANT
 flag : {Executing,Handling,Recovering, Pausing,Stopping,Stopped} &
 exc : EXC & exc2 : EXC2 & state : STATE & atomic_flag : BOOL &
 last_int : Interruptions & properties of exceptions, interruptions and phases
 ...
OPERATIONS
start(a_flag,cmd) =
 PRE component is idle
 THEN
  IF the requested command cmd is valid
  THEN Initiate execution
    Check a_flag and function atomic and decide whether execution of cmd can be interrupted
     by assigning the corresponding value to atomic_flag
    Start execution (flag := Executing)
  ELSE Raise exception And stop component (flag := Stopping) END
 END;

execute =
 SELECT flag = Executing THEN
  IF component generated exception because execution of cmd is unsafe or it completed cmd
   THEN stop component (flag := Stopping)
   ELSE Invoke lower layer operations and catch exc2 and start handling (flag := Handling)
   END END;

i_handle =
  SELECT flag = Handling &
   Current service is not atomic and criticality of interruption is greater than criticality of
   exception (I_EVAL(first(Inter)) > E_EVAL2(exc2)) or arrived interruption is Abort
   THEN
   IF current interruption is Abort
   THEN stop component and propagate exception
   ELSE determine the class of interruption (using I_STATUS) and handle accordingly
   END
   Remove handled interruption from the list and update last_int   END;

e_handle =
 SELECT flag = Handling &
   Current service is atomic and the arrived interruption is not Abort, or
   no interruptions has arrived, or criticality of exception is greater than that of interruption
   (I_EVAL(first(Inter)) < E_EVAL2(exc2))
   THEN Classify exceptions according to E_STATUS and handle accordingly END;

pause =
 SELECT flag = Pausing AND Newly arrived interruption is Continue or Abort
  THEN Remove handled interruption And Check system state after pausing
    Start handling (i.e., flag := Handling) END;

recover =
 SELECT flag = Recovering THEN Perform error recovery and catch lower layer exception END;

stop =
 SELECT flag = Stopping THEN Cease component's functioning (flag:= Stopped) END
END

Fig. 6. Specification of FTDAComponent

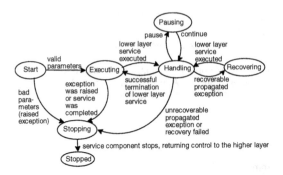

Fig. 7. Behaviour of fault tolerant reactive component

The generated and propagated exceptions are modelled by the variables exc and exc2 respectively. We abstract away from the implementation details of exceptions by choosing deferred sets EXC and EXC2 as the types for exc and exc2. The currently handled interruption is stored in the variable last_int. The local state of the component is modelled by the variable state. Each phase of execution is specified by the corresponding operation. The value of the variable flag indicates the current phase.

The operation start models placing a request to execute a service on the service component. It sets the initial state according to the input parameters of the request. The execution of the service is modelled by the operation execute. In the initial specification we model the effect of executing the lower layer command by receiving a propagated exception and updating the local state.

We assume that the interruption Abort should be handled regardless of the atomicity of the service though in certain systems it might be treated in the same way as other interruptions. Hence the operation i_handle becomes enabled either if the interruption Abort has arrived or the current service is non-atomic and the criticality of the caught interruption is higher than the criticality of the caught exception. The interruption handling proceeds according to the type of interruption to be handled – we discuss it in detail later.

The operation e_handle becomes enabled after the lower layer has completed its execution and the current interruption has a lower priority than the propagated exception or the current service is marked as atomic. The task of e_handle is to classify the propagated exception exc2 and perform handling accordingly.

The operation recover is similar to the operation execute in the sense that the lower layer is called: the state of the component is changed and a new propagated exception is received. The purpose of operation recover is to abstractly model the effect of error recovery. After recover, either e_handle or i_handle becomes enabled, which again evaluates the propagated exception and the current interruption and directs the control flow accordingly. Finally, the operation stop becomes enabled in two cases: when an unrecoverable error has occurred, or the execution of the request is completed. The behaviour of the component can be graphically represented as shown in Fig. 7.

The proposed specification can be used to abstractly specify components at each layer except the lowest one. Each component at the lowest layer has only one type of exceptions – the generated exceptions. Hence specifying exception handling is redundant at this layer. Moreover, the operations to be executed at the lowest layer are not decomposed any further and hence can be specified as the atomic preconditioned operations. Let us observe that while describing the behaviour of the component we single out handling of the interruption "Pause" because its handling is merely a suspension of autonomous component functioning.

Interruption and Exception Handlers. Now we discuss in detail the specifications of interruption and exception handlers. The interruption handler – the operation i_handle – described below analyses the interruption to be handled – first(Inter) – and chooses the corresponding interruption handling.

```
i_handle =
SELECT
  flag = Handling & (atomic_flag=FALSE & size(Inter)>0 &
  I_EVAL(first(Inter)) >= E_EVAL2(exc2,state)) or  first(Inter) = Abort
THEN
  IF first(Inter)=Abort
  THEN raise(Abort_exc) || flag := Stopping
  ELSEIF first(Inter) = Pause THEN flag := Pausing
  ELSIF I_STATUS(first(Inter))=Local THEN state :: STATE
  ELSIF I_STATUS(first(Inter))=Up THEN raise(I_CONV((first(Inter)))) || flag := Stopping
             ELSE  flag := Recovering
  END ||
  last_int := first(Inter) ||  remove_interruption
END;
```

When the interruption is Abort, the component is stopped and exception stopping the requesting component is propagated upwards in the hierarchy until all activated components are stopped. If the interruption to be handled is Pause then the component suspends its functioning and enters the Pausing phase. Some interruptions can be handled locally. This is modelled by updating the local state. Then component remains in the phase Handling and continues to analyse the caught signals. If the interruption requires handling to be performed on the higher layers of hierarchy then the component is stopped and the corresponding exception (obtained by using the function *I_CONV*) is raised. Otherwise the interruption handling is performed by requesting the operations from the lower layers, which is modelled in the operation recover.

The specification of the exception handler e_handle is done in a similar style – the function *E_STATUS* is used to define the type of exception handling required. If the exception signals about normal termination then the component continues to execute the requested service, i.e., enters the phase Executing. If the exception signals about recoverable error then the error recovery is attempted from the operation recover by executing lower layer operations. Otherwise the component is stopped, the exception is converted using the function *E_CONV2* and propagated upwards.

```
e_handle =
SELECT flag = Handling & (atomic_flag=TRUE or
   size(Inter)=0 or I_Crit(first(Inter)) < E_Crit2(exc2,state))
THEN
       IF E_STATUS(exc2) = Ok THEN flag := Executing
       ELSIF E_STATUS(exc2) = Recov THEN flag := Recovering
       ELSE raise(E_CONV2(exc2)) || flag := Stopping END
END;
```

The refinement process follows the graphical representation given in Fig. 4. We refine the abstract specification FTDAComponent by introducing the activation of the lower layer components into the operation execute. Since the refinement step introduces an abstract specification of the lower layer component, the refined specification FTDAComponentR also contains a more detailed representation of the error recovery and interruption handling procedures. The specification of the lower layer components has the form of FTDAComponent. By recursively applying the same specification and refinement pattern, we eventually arrive at the complete specification of a layered system. At the final refinement step all remaining unimplementable mathematical structures are replaced by the corresponding constructs of the targeted programming language and executable code is generated. Therefore, the result of our refinement process is implementation of a fault tolerant reactive control system.

Due to a lack of space we omit a description of the case study which has validated the proposed approach. Its detailed description can be found in [9].

5   Conclusions

In this paper we proposed a formal approach to the development of reactive fault tolerant control systems. We created a generic pattern for modelling such systems. The proposed approach is based on recursive application and instantiation of the pattern via refinement. It can be summarized as follows:

1. Specify the external interface of the system which includes requests to execute services and interruptions. Instantiate a general model to reflect interruptions, which are specific to the services under construction.
2. Define the functions for evaluating criticality of exceptions and interruptions, conversion rules and atomicity indicators of the operations. Specify functionality of the component server together with fault tolerance mechanisms modelled as exception handling. Incorporate the interruption handler. Use the defined functions to design interruption and exception handlers.
3. Instantiate the specification pattern to model components on the lower layer of hierarchy. Refine the component server by introducing invocation of operations of these components. Verify correctness of the transformation by proofs.
4. Repeat step 3 until the lowest layer of hierarchy is reached.

The use of automatic tool supporting the B Method significantly simplified the required verification process. The proofs were generated automatically and majority of then was also proved automatically by the tool.

Broy has given the formal semantics to services and layered architectures [8]. However, the proposed formalization leaves the problem of interruption and exception handling aside. Representation of exception handling in the development process has been addressed by Ferreira et al. [6]. They consider UML-supported development of component-based system with integrated reasoning about exception handling. In our approach we integrate exception handling in the formal development process and also formalize the relationships between interruptions and exceptions.

The idea of reasoning about fault tolerance in the refinement process has also been explored by Joseph and Liu [12]. They specified a fault intolerant system in a temporal logic framework and demonstrated how to transform it into a fault tolerant system by refinement. However, they analyse a "flat" system structure. The advantage of our approach is possibility to introduce hierarchy (layers) and describe different exceptions and recovery actions for different layers. Reasoning about fault tolerance in B has also been explored by Lano et al. [10]. However, they focused on structuring B specifications to model a certain mechanism for damage confinement rather than exception handling mechanisms.

Arora and Kulkarni [7] have done the extensive research on establishing correctness of adding the fault tolerance mechanisms to fault intolerant systems. Correctness proof of such an extended system is based on soundness of their algorithm working with the next-state relation. In our approach we develop a fault tolerant system by refinement, incorporating the fault tolerance mechanisms on the way. Correctness of our transformation is guaranteed by soundness of the B method. Moreover, an automatic tool support available for our approach facilitates verification of correctness.

We argue that generality of the proposed approach and availability of the automatic tool support makes our approach scalable to the complex real-life applications. In the future we are planning to overcome the current limitations of the approach such as a simplistic representation of exceptions and state-insensitive handling of exceptions and interruptions. Moreover, it would be interesting to extend the proposed approach to incorporate reasoning about parallelism.

Acknowledgements. The work reported in this paper is financially supported by IST-511599 EU Project RODIN.

References

1. J.-R. Abrial. *The B-Book*. Cambridge University Press, 1996.
2. J.-R. Abrial. *Event Driven Sequential Program Construction*. 2000, via http://www.matisse.qinetiq.com.
3. T. Anderson and P.A. Lee. *Fault Tolerance: Principles and Practice.* Dependable Computing and Fault Tolerant Systems, Vol. 3. Springer Verlag; 1990.
4. A. Avizienis. Towards Systematic Design of Fault-Tolerant Systems. *Computer* 30 (4), 1997.
5. F. Cristian. Exception Handling. In T. Anderson (ed.): *Dependability of Resilient Computers*. BSP Professional Books, 1989.
6. L. Ferreira, C. Rubira and R. de Lemos. Explicit Representation of Exception Handling in the Development of Dependable Component-Based Systems. Proc. of HASE'. USA, 2001.
7. S. Kulkarni and A. Arora. Automating the addition of fault-tolerance. *Formal Techniques in Real-time and Fault-tolerant Systems,* Pune, India, 2000.
8. M. Broy. *Service-Oriented Systems Engineering: Modeling Services and Layered Architectures*. In Proc. Of FORTE 2003, pp. 48–61, Berlin, September 2003.
9. L. Laibinis and E. Troubitsyna. Formal Service-Oriented Development of Fault Tolerant Systems. Technical Report 648, TUCS, December 2004.
10. K. Lano, D. Clark, K. Androutsopoulos, P. Kan. Invariant-Based Synthesis of Fault-tolerant Systems. In Proc. of *FTRTFT*, LNCS, Vol. 1926, pp. 46–57. India, 2000.
11. J.-C. Laprie. *Dependability: Basic Concepts and Terminology*. Springer-Verlag, 1991.
12. Z. Liu and M. Joseph. Transformations of programs for fault-tolerance, *Formal Aspects of Computing*, Vol. 4, No. 5, pp. 442–469, 1992.
13. *MATISSE Handbook for Correct Systems Construction*. 2003.
14. B. Rubel. Patterns for Generating a Layered Architecture. In J.O. Coplien, D.C. Schmidt (Eds.). *Pattern Languages of Program Design*. Addison-Wesley. 1995.
15. S. Schneider. *The B Method. An introduction*. Palgrave, 2001.
16. Steria, Aix-en-Provence, France. *Atelier B, User and Reference Manuals*, 2001.
17. Storey N. *Safety-critical computer systems*. Addison-Wesley, 1996.

Network Structure and Traffic Modeling and Simulation with CO-OPN

David Hürzeler

System Modeling and Verification Group,
University of Geneva,
24 rue du General Dufour,
1211 Geneva, Switzerland
David.Hurzeler@cui.unige.ch

Abstract. In this paper we show how network structure and traffic may be modeled and simulated using the Concurrent Object-Oriented Petri Nets formalism with system risk analysis in mind. A small example of network is given, along with its model, which is then extended and simulated. We also show the different directions we plan to take in order to make the models even more realistic and to be able to verify them.

1 Introduction

System modeling, simulation and verification represent three of the biggest challenges in computer science and software engineering and much effort has been conducted in all three of these. Risk analysis is the science studying the possibilities of failure of real systems based on conception or manipulation errors. The work presented here is part of a larger project which aims at creating a collaboration between these two domains: The long-term goal is to have software tools which help a non-expert user model a given real life system and which automatically detect and quantify risk from this model in order to prevent the above-mentioned errors. In this paper, we will present a first step in this direction by explaining how the formal logical model of a given system can be built; We will show how this model may be simulated to detect potential modeling errors, and give hints on how verification will then be tackled.

Networking raises many crucial and difficult issues in risk analysis such as bandwidth control, error (virus) propagation, router breakdown, and protocol performance. It also creates interesting problems in modeling with potentially dynamic structures, mobility and communication. We have chosen to treat this domain more specifically with the confidence that the modeling and verification results will easily translate to many other application domains. Of course, modeling networks for risk analysis implicitly leads to many abstractions; For instance, in a network, concepts of messages or router temperature are abstracted -as showed hereafter- to skeletons meeting our needs. Furthermore, other real world features such as hardware characteristics are simply omitted, as they do not directly interest us for the risks we are interested in detecting.

N. Guelfi and A. Savidis (Eds.): RISE 2005, LNCS 3943, pp. 250–265, 2006.

An other aspect is that Petri nets have been proved several times (for example [6] [5]) to be particularly well adapted to risk analysis, specially thanks to the many verification techniques for this formalism and their power of expression.

We will therefore work on a small network example, and use the Concurrent Object-Oriented Petri Nets (CO-OPN) formalism [3]. This specification language seems particularly interesting because it features several crucial network characteristics such as true concurrency, non-determinism, dynamic object creation/destruction and mobility, and proves to have several modeling advantages such as object-orientation, inheritance, subtyping [2], and coordination [1]. Also, a powerful tool has been implemented for this language and allows a user to build models, simulate them, view graphical Petri net representations of classes, and automatically generate test sets for a given specification [4]. It also has some limitations (as for instance probabilities) as described in the section on future work and which we plan to compensate by using another existing Petri net tool, GreatSPN.

The paper is divided as follows: First we will describe the small network example we plan to model and analyse. Second, we will give a first basic model of our network and show the main components of the model. We will then somewhat push this model a little further by adding queues to our routers and see how simulation helps us build better models. A small section will then be devoted to describing potential model extensions (some of which we are already studying) and showing how we plan to tackle verification itself. We will finish by giving some related works and a small conclusion.

2   The Problem

In this section, we will describe the small example we plan to work on in this paper; The network is composed of six routers, connected as described in Figure 1. Each router is connected to two to four other routers. Routers want to send each other messages, and we are interested in seeing how this happens, and how problems may occur. A message is a triple composed of a packet, the message origin, and the message destination. When a router receives a message, it must decide to which other router it should transmit it. This is described by

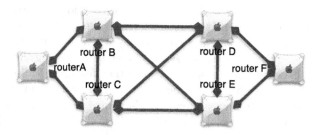

Fig. 1. Example of network

the means of a routing table defined for each router. For instance, when router B receives a message for router F, it will forward the message to either router D or router E, which in turn will give the message to router F.

Routers may break down and get repaired. In these cases, all other routers are informed of the breakdown or repair, and adapt to it. In the example above, if router E is broken down, router B always forwards the message to router D.

Routers also contain a queue of the requests they have to deal with. This queue is a bounded FIFO queue.

Finally, router activity is given by a *temperature* value, which is increased with the arrival of a new request, and which naturally decreases over time without such arrival. For a given router, temperature $T \in [0,1]$ typically evolves as described by the following equation:

$$\frac{dT(t)}{dt} = h(t) - T(t)$$

where $h(t) \in \{0,1\}$ is a heating function taking the value 1 when the router receives a request and 0 when it is idle. So, a heating (resp. idle) router sees its temperature increase (resp. decrease).

In the following section, we show how we can model such a network in CO-OPN, first without, and then with the queues (other important network features such as time or probabilities will be examined in section 5).

3   The First Model: Basic Routers

3.1   Introducing CO-OPN

In this small section, we will briefly and informally introduce the CO-OPN formalism. Concurrent Object-Oriented Petri Nets [3] is a formalism based on abstract data types (ADT), algebraic Petri nets, and IWIM (Idealized Worker Idealized Manager) coordination models [12]. It features true concurrency (in the non-interleaving semantics sense where two actions requiring a same resource may not be executed simultaneously, even if these actions do not alter the resource), non-determinism, transactional semantics, strong encapsulation and object-orientation. Another important feature which we will only mention in this paper is object mobility. CO-OPN specifications are collections of ADT, class and context (i.e. coordination) modules [15]. Syntactically, each module has the same overall structure; It includes an interface section defining all elements accessible from the outside, and a body section including the local aspects private to the module. Moreover, class and context modules have convenient graphical representations - which we will not use in this paper – showing their underlying Petri net model. Low-level mechanisms and other features dealing specifically with object-orientation are out of the scope of this work, and can be found in [14] and [3]. We will, however, show how they have been used in our example. A powerful tool has been developed for CO-OPN and is called CoopnBuilder [4]. It allows a user to build complex models, to check their syntax and types, and to simulate specifications by automatically translating them in executable Java code.

3.2 The Model

We will decompose the model description in that of data types, classes and contexts. We will not define the latter formally, but give examples with the different modules of the network model. The full formal description of the CO-OPN syntax and semantics may be found in [3]. We will start by explaining the steps that lead to the final model. So we will describe the components and the way they are interconnected, and the main concepts used to express the structure and the behaviour of the system are:

- a coordination model to describe the relations between the system components (in our example given by the Network context,
- object orientation for the structure and content of the system, and
- causality relations for the dynamic system evolution aspects that must be reflected with nondeterministic and concurrent behaviours.

We also want to insist on giving an idea of how the model is built; we think that a good approach for building systems composed of many computing entities is the use of the high-level concept of coordination programming [12]. In our mind, coordination is the management of dependencies among activities. We also think that coordination patterns can often be applied since the beginning of the design phase of the software development. This originated the notion of coordination development [5], where specific coordination models and languages were used and adapted to the specific needs encountered during the design phase. The coordination layer of CO-OPN [3][12] is a coordination language based on a IWIM (Idealized Workers, Idealized Managers) model, suited for the formal coordination of object-oriented systems. CO-OPN context modules define the coordination entities [13], while CO-OPN classes (and objects) define the basic coordinated entities of a system. So we can, in CO-OPN, cover the formal development of concurrent software from the first formal specification to the final distributed software architecture [16]. We will first quickly give an outline of the way values can be defined in CO-OPN, using algebraic data types. Then, we will describe the "components" of our formalism: The class and context modules.

Abstract Data Types. CO-OPN ADT modules algebraically specify data types. Each of these modules describes one or more sorts (which are the names of data types), with their generators and operations. The operations properties are given by the means of positive conditional equational axioms. As an example, we show below the reduced specification of the generic type Fifo(elem).

```
Generic ADT  Fifo(Elem);
Interface
    Use
        Elem; Naturals;
    Sort
        fifo;
    Generators
        [] : -> fifo;
        _ ' _ : elem, fifo -> fifo;
```

```
   Operations
      next of _ : fifo -> elem;
      insert _ to _ : elem, fifo -> fifo;
      remove from _ : fifo -> fifo;
Body
   Axioms
      (next of (elemVar1 ' [ ])) = elemVar1;
      (next of (elemVar1 ' (elemVar2 ' fifoVar1))) = (next of (elemVar2 ' fifoVar1));
      (insert elemVar1 to fifoVar1) = (elemVar1 ' fifoVar1);
      (remove from (elemVar1 ' [ ])) = [ ];
      (remove from (elemVar1 ' (elemVar2 ' fifoVar1))) = (elemVar1 '
         (remove from (elemVar2 ' fifoVar1)));
   Where
  elemVar1, elemVar2 : elem;
  fifoVar1 : fifo;
EndFifo;
```

So we see that the axioms allow us to inductively define the operations on the generators. CO-OPN allows type inheritance, which is really syntactical inheritance. In our network model, for example, we will have a Temperature type, for instance, inheriting from Naturals. Similarly, the RouterState type describing the state of routers ("on" or "off") will inherit from the Booleans type, while renaming the boolean sort name into routerState, and the generators true and false into on and off, respectively. We also define some trivial data types such as RouterId having a sort name routerId and several generators RA, RB, RC, RD, RE, and RF (one for each router in our model).

A slightly more complex data type is the type RoutingTableList. We want this to be a list of pairs of routerId values, describing, for each routerId destination of a message, to which routerId value identified router the message should be sent next. Here we can use the power of expressiveness of the CO-OPN language. Indeed, we can define two abstract generic parameterized predefined types List and Pair, and define our RoutingTableList type as a List(Pair(RouterId)); We then only need to rename the list sort name into routingTableList.

Classes. CO-OPN classes - the coordinated entities mentioned above - are described by means of modular algebraic Petri nets with particular parameterised external transitions. These are the methods (provided services) and gates (required services) of the class. Classes may also have internal transitions which firable as soon as they are enabled and all the current transactions terminate (see section 4.3). An object's state is described by the state of its places (in the Petri net sense). The call of a method (or execution of an internal transition) of a class possibly results in a change of state: The behaviour of methods and transitions are defined by behavioural axioms, similar to axioms in an ADT. The axioms have the following shape:

$$\text{Cond} \Rightarrow \text{eventname } \textbf{with} \quad \text{synchro} :: \text{test} : \text{pre} \rightarrow \text{post}$$

in which the terms have the following meaning:

- Cond is a set of equational conditions, similar to a guard;
- eventname is the name of a method with algebraic term parameters;

- synchro is the synchronization expression defining the policy of transactional interaction of this event with other events, the dot notation is classically used to express events of specific objects and the synchronization operators are sequence, simultaneity and non-determinism;
- test is a condition on the state of the object for the method to be firable, given in the form of place states which are not affected by the method firing;
- Pre and Post are the usual Petri net flow relation determining what is consumed and what is produced in the object state places.

An example follows below. In our specification we only have one class, which is the Router class. Its specification is given below, without the axioms:

Interface
 Use
  Message; RouterState; RouterId; Temperature;
  RoutingTableList; RouterIdPair;
  RouterIdStatePair; RouterStateList;
 Type
  router;
 Gates
  sendMess _ from _ to _ via _ : message routerId routerId routerId;
  stateChangeNotification _ : routerState;
 Methods
  sendReqMess _ from _ to _ : message routerId routerId;
  routerId _ : routerId;
  setRoutingTable _ : routingTableList;
  turnOff;   repairAndTurnOn;
  initRouterId _ : routerId;
  setStateOfRouters _ : routerStateList;
  changeRouterState _ _ : routerId routerState;
Body
 Place
  RoutingTable _ _ : routerId routerId;
  StateOfRouters _ _ : routerId routerState;
  RouterIdentity _ : routerId;
  TempOfRouter _ : temperature;
 Initial
  TempOfRouter 0;
 Axioms
  . . .

So the Router class has the following features (we will give the axioms for each method here):

- Four places: RoutingTable containing pairs of routerId values giving the routing tables (for each destination of message, it indicates the next router(s) to send the message to), StateOfRouters contains couples of routerId and routerState indicating the state of all the routers, and RouterIdentity and TempOfRouter respectively containing the routerId and the temperature of the current router.
- Two gates: sendMess _ from _ to _ via _ which will be connected to the right router (corresponding to the routerId specified in the via field of the gate) and stateChangeNotification _ which will communicate the new state of the current router to all the other routers.

– Several methods for initialization of routing tables, identity (initRouterId), and router states. For instance, routerId is only firable with the current router's routerId as parameter (it therefore gives a router's identity via unification methods, as we will see below with contexts):

```
routerId id::RouterIdentity id : -> ;
initRouterId id:: -> RouterIdentity id;
```

setRoutingTable and setStateOfRouters are recursive initializing methods to set a router's routing table and to initialize the knowledge of the other routers' states:

```
setRoutingTable [ ]::->;
setRoutingTable < id1 id2 > ' rtl with  this . setRoutingTable rtl:: ->
        RoutingTable id1 id2;
setStateOfRouters < id x > ' rsl with  this . setStateOfRouters rsl::
        -> StateOfRouters id x;
setStateOfRouters [ ]:: ->;
```

– Two methods turnOff and repairAndTurnOn to change the router state which are synchronized with the sending of a notification to all the other routers via the stateChangeNotification gate, and one method changeRouterState used upon reception of this state change notification from another router:

```
turnOff with  this . stateChangeNotification off::
        RouterIdentity id:  StateOfRouters id x -> StateOfRouters id off;
repairAndTurnOn with  this . stateChangeNotification on::
        RouterIdentity id:  StateOfRouters id x -> StateOfRouters id on;
changeRouterState id x:: StateOfRouters id y -> StateOfRouters id x;
```

– One method sendReqMess _ from _ to _ which computes the identity of the next router the message should be forwarded to and makes a call to the sendMess _ from _ to _ via _ gate mentioned above (which really sends the request further) with the routerId just computed as via parameter:

```
sendReqMess m from id to id1 with  this . sendMess m from id to id1 via id2::
        RouterIdentity id3, StateOfRouters id3 on, StateOfRouters id2 on,
        RoutingTable id1 id2 : TempOfRouter temp -> TempOfRouter succ (temp);
sendReqMess m from id to id1:: RouterIdentity id1: -> ;
```

Let us comment the two axioms for this method. First of all, if id1 is the routerId of the current router, there is no entry in the RoutingTable place whose first component is id1. Therefore the first axiom does not work (test condition not fulfilled) and the second axiom is used, which specifies that nothing should then be done. If id1 is not the current router identity, then a call is made to sendMess m from id to id1 via id2, where m, id, and id1 are the same parameters as for sendReqMess and where id2 is computed from the routing table. It is checked that both the local router (routerId id3) and the next one (routerId id2) are turned on, and the current router temperature is increased (succ is the successor operations in sort natural).

Of course a module specification contains variable declarations which we have omitted in the above, but which can be deduced from the interface and place definition.

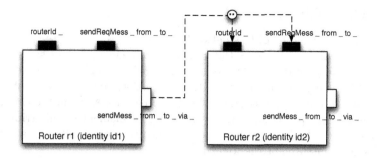

Fig. 2. Router coordination

Contexts. While the CO-OPN classes define the basic lowest-level coordinated entities, the contexts are the entities responsible for module coordination (management of dependencies among activities). Again, in this model we only have one context, which is the `Network` context. This entity contains all the router objects and gives the connection between them. A context is therefore considered as a composition of objects and other contexts. In our case, all the connections between routers are given in this context, with the following axiom (see also Figure 2):

```
r1 . sendMess m from id to idd via id2 with  r2 . routerId id2 ..
      r2 . sendReqMess m from id to idd;
```

So what this axiom does is connect the message sending by a router `r1` given by gate `sendMess _ from _ to _ via _` to the message sending given by method `sendReqMess _ from _ to _` of router `r2` identified by `iddd` (i.e. specified in the `via` field of `r1`'s gate). So in our case, if router A receives the command to send a message m from router RA to router RD, then because of the routing table of RA, it might emit a gate `sendMess m from RA to RD via RB`. This gate will be connected, in context `Network`, to `r2.sendReqMess m from RA to RD`, `r2` being the router identified by `RB` (i.e. router B). Then router B will emit the gate `sendMess m from RA to RD via RD`; this call will be connected to `r3.sendReqMess m from RA to RD`, `r3` being the router identified by `RD` (i.e. router D). This last method will do nothing, because the message is now arrived at destination. Here we can really see the power of the CO-OPN formalism, as a unique axiom specifies the connections between an arbitrary number of routers.

4   Modeling Queuing in Routers

In this section we will make the model slightly more realistic by including bounded FIFO request queues for each router. Now, when a router receives a message transfer request, he stores it in his queue (provided the latter is not already full). He then periodically proceeds to treat the first request of the queue. We will show that this extension rises some non trivial concurrency issues which we will manage with the help of the simulator.

4.1   A First Model

We will give a first model of this network "with queues". As stated, an arriving
request is immediately stored by the router in its queue. Then, the system makes
a simultaneous operation on all routers, taking each first element of their queues,
and sending the appropriate messages to the appropriate destinations. We define
a new abstract data type `Request` as a triple ⟨Message, RouterId, RouterId⟩, with
operations `mess` (resp. `snd` and `rec`) giving the first element of this triple (resp.
second and third element). In fact there are not too many differences with the
original `Router` class except the following:

- One place `SendRequestQueue` containing a FIFO list `Fifo(Request)` of requests.
  One other place `RouterSize` containing a natural indicating the number of free
  spaces in the queue.
- Method `sendReqMess` now puts the arriving requests in the queue if the latter
  is not already full:

```
sendReqMess m from id to id1:: RouterIdentity id2, StateOfRouters id2 on:
    SendRequestsQueue srq, QueueSize succ (n) ->
    SendRequestsQueue (insert < m id id1 > to srq), QueueSize n;
```

Note that putting `QueueSize succ(n)` in precondition allows us to specify that
the number of free queue spaces must be non zero.

- A method `proceedRequests` which takes the first request in the queue and treats
  it (by sending the appropriate message to the appropriate router). The axioms are:

```
(empty ? srq = false) => proceedRequests with
        this.sendMess mess (next of srq) from snd (next of srq) to
        rec (next of srq) via id1:: RouterIdentity id3,
        StateOfRouters id3 on, RoutingTable rec (next of srq) id1:
        TempOfRouter temp, SendRequestsQueue srq, StateOfRouters id1 on,
        QueueSize n -> TempOfRouter succ (temp), SendRequestsQueue remove
        from srq, StateOfRouters id1 on, QueueSize succ n;
(temp > 0) = true => proceedRequests::
        RouterIdentity id, StateOfRouters id on, SendRequestsQueue [ ]:
        TempOfRouter temp -> TempOfRouter temp - 1;
proceedRequests:: RouterIdentity id, StateOfRouters id on,
        SendRequestsQueue [ ], TempOfRouter 0:  -> ;
(empty ? srq = false), (id1 = rec next of srq) = true =>
        proceedRequests:: RouterIdentity id1: SendRequestsQueue srq,
        QueueSize n, TempOfRouter temp -> RouterIdentity id1,
        SendRequestsQueue remove from srq, QueueSize succ n,
        TempOfRouter succ (temp);
```

So if the queue is empty, nothing is done except lower the temperature
(because one logic time step has been taken nothing happens in the router)
if it is non zero. If the next request in the queue is for the router itself, then
we just remove it from the router and increase the temperature. In the other
cases, the next request is taken from the queue, examined, and sent to the
router associated to the destination of the request in the routing table of the
current router. The temperature is also increased.

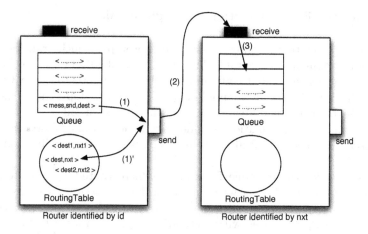

Fig. 3. One step in the journey of a message

We show in Figure 3 part of the journey of a message. Suppose a router identified by identity Id has as next request in his queue a message mess from a router identified by snd to router identified by dest (1). Then the next router to send the message to (in the picture identified by nxt) is found in the routing table (1)' and the message is sent to him (2) and placed at the top of his queue (3). The process will then continue similarly until the messages reaches the router identified by dest.

The NetworkWithQueues context is very similar to the one for routers without queues. The only difference is that it now has a proceedRouterRequests method with the following axiom:

```
proceedRouterRequests with  ((((routerA.proceedRequests // routerB.proceedRequests)
  // routerC.proceedRequests) // routerD.proceedRequests) // routerE.proceedRequests)
  // routerF.proceedRequests;
```

In other words, regularly, a method is called which treats one request in each router, all of this concurrently. The reason we have do it concurrently is the following: Suppose router A wants to send a message to router D (it has this request in its queue) and all the other routers' queues are empty. Then if the axiom was

```
proceedRouterRequests with  ((((routerA.proceedRequests .. routerB.proceedRequests)
  .. routerC.proceedRequests) .. routerD.proceedRequests) .. routerE.proceedRequests)
  .. routerF.proceedRequests;
```

we would first send the request to router B. We would then proceed the request in router B, and the above request would be sent to router D. That means that in one step, the request is proceeded to destination, which is contradictory with the model we are wanting to build. And this would not be the case if it was router D who wanted to send a message to router A (the model would then not be symmetrical).

4.2   Modeling Error Detection Through Simulation

The CoopnBuilder tool features a powerful prototyper which transforms CO-OPN specifications into executable Java code [17]. The tool executes CO-OPN transactions using generated code and translates responses back to CO-OPN notation. It also features an adapted debugger enabling step-by-step execution of queries, exhibiting the derivation tree during the execution.

When running the simulation we find out the `proceedRouterRequests` method of the `NetworkWithQueues` is never firable. We now look back at the specification to find out why.

Let us consider the example from above where router A wants to send a message to router D. Here is what happens: The `proceedRequests` of router A is called, which is synchronized with gate `sendMess`. In the `NetworkWithQueues` context, this last gate is synchronized with method `sendReqMess` or router B (for example, if that is router A's routing table specifies as next router). But this method accesses the queue resource in place `SendRequestQueue`. And concurrently to this, method `proceedRequests` of router B is called; The problem is that this method also accesses this last resource. We therefore have a resource access conflict and the transaction aborts (because it is true concurrency we have in CO-OPN), making the `proceedRouterRequests` of the network context fail. Indeed, which the transactional semantics of CO-OPN, a synchronization succeeds if and only if all of its sub-synchronizations succeed. In our case, the `proceedRouterRequests` method fails because its sub-synchronizations `proceedRequests` are in conflict and fail. So how can we solve this problem?

4.3   The Final Model

The solution is to separate these two resource accesses. And we do it by decomposing the request proceeding in two actions, one (internal transition `prepareNextRequest`) where the next request (here, $< m1, s1, d1 >$)in each router is prepared and placed in an separate place `ReadyToLeave`, and another one (method `sendRequest`) where it is actually sent out to the next router and stored in the latter's queue. What the internal transition does is put the next request in place `ReadyToLeave`. This is done immediately when a token is present in place `getNextReq` (initially filled with one token). When the message is actually sent out of the router ((see Figure 4): (1), (1)', (2), and (3)), a token is put in this last place (4) and immediately, the next request (here, $< m2, s2, d2 >$) is prepared (see Figure 5).

Now in the `NetworkWithQueuesCorrect` context we have a method `proceedRouterRequests` with the following axiom:

```
proceedRouterRequests with  (((((routerA.sendRequest // routerB.sendRequest) //
     routerC.sendRequest) //routerD.sendRequest) // routerE.sendRequest) //
     routerF.sendRequest);
```

And now simulation shows that this specification allows us to proceed requests in a correct way.

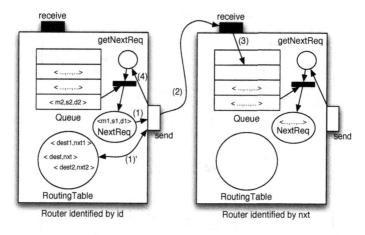

Fig. 4. One step in the journey of a message (1): Sending the request

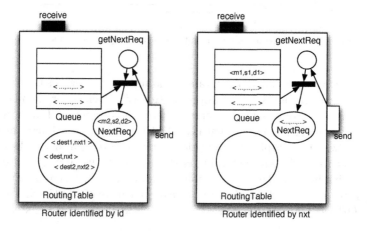

Fig. 5. One step in the journey of a message (2): preparing the next request

5   Future Work: Extensions and Verification

The work presented above is only meant to be a starting point in the modeling and analysis of networks with CO-OPN. In this section, we will show the directions we are now taking to push this work further. There are two main axis for these directions: Model extension and verification.

5.1   Model Extensions in CO-OPN

We will first present some model extensions which we find pertinent.

Scalability. This whole model has been built in a way that adding routers or sub-networks is made particularly easy. Indeed, we see that sub-networks can be

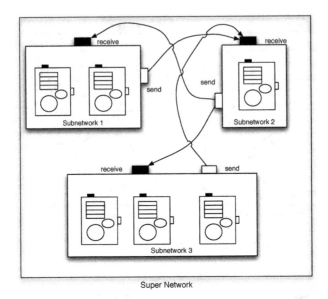

Fig. 6. Composing subnetworks into supernetworks

modeled exactly as presented above, and building super-networks is just creating new contexts which connect in an appropriate way (which is very similar to how we have connected routers in the network here) the different sub-networks contexts. This is one of the great strengths of the CO-OPN approach presented here. Figure 6 shows an example of connection between three sub-networks to make up one super-network. Another thing is that networks usually have a dynamic structure, with hosts and/or routers joining in and leaving dynamically. We can model this by using the dynamic object creation feature of CO-OPN. This shows that CO-OPN is particularly well adapted to network structure modeling.

Dynamic Routing, Message Loss and Fault Tolerance. The next extension is related to fault tolerance. In our model we have seen that the routing tables were static and depended on the other router's state. When all routers were on, the table contained non deterministic choices. We would like to have dynamic routing tables which contain only optimal paths, and which evolve with the states of the neighboring routers. This is a fairly simple addition, but which can make a big difference on larger networks in terms of performance.

Another issue is message loss. We have not treated this problem in the model presented in this paper. Obviously it is easy to add message loss per se. But modeling a decent recovery algorithm is obviously much more complex. We could add acknowledgments but as these may also be lost problems occur. There are known protocols such as the alternating bit protocol (which can be modeled in Petri nets without timeouts, with the sending of the next bit is only firable when an acknowledgment is received, and where message loss re-enables bit sending) which may help limit the number of problems, or we may abstract the protocol if the risk we are interested in is not directly connected to protocols themselves. Another way of dealing with this is to include time and timeouts.

Probabilities. Probabilities are another extension we are working on. Because CO-OPN is non-deterministic, we can implement static probabilities (i.e. with constant distributions) by adding potentially trivial axioms. For instance, if we want a method m to double the natural value of a place Place one out of three times, then we can for example have the following specification:

```
m:: Place n -> Place 2*n;
m:: Place n:   -> ;
m:: Place n:   -> ;
```

Complex Messages. Another way to extend the model is to add complex messages. What we mean is that it raises some interesting issues that routers send each other programs instead of just packets. This can fairly easily be done with either transmitting complex values (by means of more detailed ADTs) or by describing messages by CO-OPN objects. Indeed, in CO-OPN, we can send objects from and to contexts. In [2], we have given a formal extension of CO-OPN mobility which supports the sending of contexts also.

5.2 Model Extensions and Verification in GreatSPN

GreatSPN [9] is a tool on general stochastic Petri nets which allows a user to check properties on colored Petri nets with time and stochastic probabilities. It seems to us as the ideal tool to complement CoopnBuilder's modeling power. We are now working on translating CO-OPN Petri nets into nets which are usable by this tool. Of course some CO-OPN features (such as transactional semantics or some abstract data types) are not translatable. The translation is therefore composed of three phases:

- Abstraction of concepts which are not crucial to a particular property we want to check,
- "melting" or "demodularization" of all the concerned Petri nets of the CO-OPN model, and
- unfolding of part of the resulting net.

Time. As mentioned above, time is an useful extension if we want to deal with message loss and use timeouts. But time is also crucial if we are interested in performance. CO-OPN does have a full formal time extension [18] which was given, but this extension has not been implemented in the CoopnBuilder tool as of yet. Also, time and probabilities are also strongly linked together, particularly when we use stochastic Petri nets.

Probabilities. Pushing this concept further, we also want to have stochastic nets, for instance to model routers break down according to an exponential law distribution. This is currently not supported by CO-OPN. As for time though, we are now working on adding the probabilistic features on a CO-OPN algebraic Petri net on GreatSPN.

6 Related Work

In this section, we will describe some of the related work connected to risk analysis and verification for network systems. For risk analysis with Petri nets state of the art, we refer the reader to [6] which lists and compares several existing approaches focussed on calculation perspectives rather than modeling.

First of all, M. Diergardt and R. Mock [5] have used a stochastic Petri net based model to simulate the propagation of router breakdowns due to viral infection in a large network system. The authors focus on large scale simulation to analyze their system rather than logical verification and testing. The modeling approach they use is event driven. Other authors such as Yanar [10] and Fabricius [11] have also worked with continuous timed and colored Petri nets with risk analysis in mind. These approaches are really complementary to ours in the sense that they analyze their system with massive simulation on stochastic, colored and timed Petri nets, where we use simulation to validate our model and aim more at verifying system properties on the model. Also, they use a event driven modeling technique where we focus more on modularity and object properties.

Of course, much work has also been conducted with other formalisms. Parrow et al. [8], for instance, use process calculi to verify protocol algorithms (among other things). Their approach is based on proofs of process equivalences and properties. They do not, however, seem to focus on network structure modeling methodologies or probabilistic simulation as we do (or plan to do) here.

7 Conclusion

We have presented in this paper a new approach based on Concurrent Object-Oriented Petri Nets for modeling and simulating networks and their traffic. We have described, in detail, a model of a simple network example, and shown how simulation may help the modeling process. The formalism has hopefully been shown to be well adapted to the task, and we have presented the different extensions we plan to implement and how we plan to overcome some limitations of the formalism. This will be done by using the GreatSPN tool and translating CO-OPN specifications so that they are usable by this tool. GreatSPN will also be used to tackle model verification.

CoopnBuilder does not yet provide verification tools, but features a test tool which automatically generates pertinent test sets [7]. One of the directions we will also be taking is to use this tool to test potentially large network models and check for reachability-related risk (such as problematic temperature states).

Notes and Acknowledgments

This work was partly funded by the "Risk Management and Modeling for Distributed Systems" consortium hosted by the Laboratory for Safety Analysis at the Swiss Federal Institute of Technology in Zurich. The author also wishes to thank Professor Didier Buchs for useful comments on the model and paper.

References

[1] Didier Buchs, Sandro Costa, David Hurzeler; Component Based System Modelling for Easier Verification; In P. Ezhilchevan and A. Romanovski, editors, Concurrency in Dependable Computing, pp. 61–86, Kluwer, 2002.

[2] David Hurzeler; Flexible Subtyping Relations for Component-Oriented Formalisms and their Verification, PhD thesis n.3131, Swiss Federal Institute for Technology Lausanne, November 2004.

[3] Olivier Biberstein, Didier Buchs, and Nicolas Guelfi; Object-oriented nets with algebraic specifications: the CO-OPN/2 formalism. In Lecture Notes in Computer Science. Springer-Verlag, LNCS 2001, pp. 70–127.

[4] http://cui.unige.ch/smv/CoopnTools/index.html

[5] M. Diergardt and Ralf Mock, New Ways of Applying the Petri Net Formalism in Risk Analysis, Technical Report, Swiss Federal Institute of Technology, Zurich, 2004.

[6] David Vernez, Didier Buchs, Guillaume Pierrehumbert, Perspectives in the use of coloured Petri nets for risk analysis and accident modelling, Safety Science 41 (445–463), 2003.

[7] Levi Lucio, Luis Pedro, Didier Buchs: A Methodology and a Framework for Model-Based Testing. RISE 2004: 57–70.

[8] Oskar Wibling, Joachim Parrow, Arnold Neville Pears: Automatized Verification of Ad Hoc Routing Protocols. FORTE 2004: 343–358

[9] G. Chiola. A software package for the analysis of generalized stochastic Petri net models. In Proc. Int. Workshop on Timed Petri Nets, Torino, Italy, July 1985. IEEE-CS Press.

[10] Yanar, D. Modellbasierte Risikoanalyse technischer Systeme für Versicherungszwecke (PhD thesis). Laboratory for Safety Analysis, Swiss Federal Institute of Technology, Zurich, 1999.

[11] Fabricius S., Modelling and Simulation for Plant Performability Assessment with Application to Maintenance in the Process Industry (PhD thesis). Laboratory for Safety Analysis, Swiss Federal Institute of Technology, Zurich, 2003.

[12] M. Buffo. Experiences in coordination programming. In Proceedings of the workshops of DEXA'98 (International Conference on Database and Expert Systems Applications). IEEE Computer Society, Aug 1998.

[13] M. Buffo and D. Buchs. A coordination model for distributed object systems. In Proc. of the Second Int. Conf. on Coordination Models and Languages COORDINATION'97, Volume 1282 of LNCS, pages 410–413. Springer Verlag, 1997.

[14] Didier Buchs and Nicolas Guelfi, "A Formal Specification Framework for Object-Oriented Distributed Systems," IEEE TSE, Vol. 26, no. 7, July 2000, pp. 635–652.

[15] Olivier Biberstein and Didier Buchs. Structured algebraic nets with object-orientation. In Proc.of the first int. work-shop on Object-Oriented Programming and Models of Concurrency" within the 16th Int. Conf. on Application and Theory of Petri Nets, Torino, Italy, June 26–30 1995.

[16] D. Buchs and N. Guelfi, A Formal Specification Framework for Object-Oriented Distributed Systems, IEEE TSE, Vol. 26, no. 7, July 2000, pp. 635–652.

[17] S. Chachkov, Generation Of Object-Oriented Programs From CO-OPN Specifications, Phd Thesis, Software Engineering Laboratory, Swiss Federal Institute for Technology Lausanne, 2003.

[18] S. Souksavanh, Extending CO-OPN with Time, Diploma Thesis, Software Engineering Laboratory, Swiss Federal Institute for Technology Lausanne, 2002.

Balancing Agility and Discipline with XPrince

Jerzy Nawrocki[1,2,*], Lukasz Olek[1,2], Michal Jasinski[1,2], Bartosz Paliświat[1,2],
Bartosz Walter[1,2], Błażej Pietrzak[1], and Piotr Godek[2]

[1] Poznań University of Technology, Institute of Computing Science,
ul. Piotrowo 3A, 60-965 Poznań, Poland
[2] PB Polsoft, Poznań, Poland
Jerzy.Nawrocki@put.poznan.pl

Abstract. Most of the contemporary projects require balance between agility and discipline. In the paper a software development and project management methodology called XPrince (eXtreme PRogramming IN Controlled Environments) is presented. It is a combination of XP, PRINCE2 and RUP. Moreover, some experiments and tools are described that create an important basis for the methodology.

1 Introduction

The first reaction to the software crises in the late 60s was call for discipline. In the next 20 years people proposed many standards (IEEE standards, ISO standards etc.). They were followed by maturity models (CMM, ISO 15504 etc.) and discipline-oriented methodologies (e.g. PSP [13], and TSP [14]). Parallel to this process in the 70s first project management methodologies were applied to support software development. Perhaps the first one was PROMPTII created by Sympact Sytems Ltd. and adopted in 1979 by UK's Central Computer and Telecommunications Agency (CCTA). In 1989 CCTA established its own methodology called PRINCE (for PRojects IN Controlled Environments). Seven years later it was modified and since that time it is known as PRINCE2 [18]. It is quite a popular methodology also outside UK. It has got an opinion of rather restrictive but effective project management method.

However, too much discipline kills initiative and flexibility, which are necessary to successfully build complex systems with changing requirements. To help this in the mid 90s so-called agile methodologies arose. They emphasize the need for effective communication between individuals, customer orientation, software-centric thinking and fast responding to changes. Perhaps the most popular agile methodology is Extreme Programming (XP for short) [3]. As usually, there is no silver bullet and both approaches, agile and discipline-oriented, have their advantages and disadvantages. Discipline-oriented methodologies usually suffer from excessive paper work, low flexibility, slow decision processes and inability to accommodate many changes. XP's weakness is relying on on-site customer (in many projects customer representative is too busy and she/he cannot fulfill this

---

* Corresponding author.

N. Guelfi and A. Savidis (Eds.): RISE 2005, LNCS 3943, pp. 266–277, 2006.

requirement), lack of written documents (oral communication is fast but when the system is complex and there are many difficult trade-offs after some time it can be hard to remember what was the final solution and why it was chosen), and sometimes too short planning perspective.

As Barry Boehm and Richard Turner have noted, *every successful venture in a changing world requires both agility and discipline* ([5, p. 2]). In the paper an integrated and flexible software development methodology is presented along with accompanying tools which aims at balancing agility and discipline. It is called XPrince (for eXtreme Programming in controlled environments) and it is based on three other methodologies: XP [3], PRINCE2 [18], and RUP [17]. In the next section we describe a two-level approach to team organization which results in a team structure compliant with both XP and PRINCE2. In Section 3 the project lifecycle is discussed. Again our aim was to obtain a lifecycle that would be conformant with both XP and PRINCE2. Then, tools and techniques are presented that aim at providing agility and effectiveness to requirements engineering (Sec. 4) and software construction (Sec. 5). Our aim was to solve the problems associated with XP's weaknesses and preserve agility. To obtain this we have integrated a project management methodology (PRINCE2) with a software development one (XP), and we have elaborated tools that integrate various software engineering techniques. We have integrated a use-case editor with a mock-up generator and an effort estimator (the resulting tool is called UC Workbench). We have also integrated reuse with testing (test-cases are used as a query to find a function or a class).

2 Team Structure

At the thirst glance, PRINCE2 does not fit XP for a number of reasons. One of them is that roles in PRINCE2 are different from those in XP. In PRINCE2 a project is directed by its Project Board which consists of three roles (see Fig. 1a):

- *Executive* – Represents the investor and is responsible for making the project successful from the business point of view. He can cancel the project if necessary.
- *Senior User* – He coordinates end users and focuses on usability aspects.
- *Senior Supplier* – Represents the supplier organization (a senior manager).

PRINCE2 assumes that Project Board members are too busy to look after the project on the day-to-day basis. Therefore, in PRINCE2 there is another role called *Project Manager* who is responsible for tactical level of management. Among others, he prepares plans which are later on accepted by the Project Board and writes progress reports. To balance "intrinsic optimism" of the Project Manager in PRINCE2 there is an optional role of *Project Assurance* whose mission is to check if the reports send by the Project Manager meet the reality. If a project team is small the developers are immediately coordinated by the Project Manager.

XP team has no particular structure diagram. However, from the description given by Kent Beck [3] one can derive a team structure diagram presented in Fig. 1b. That diagram can be "refactored" into the diagram of Fig. 1c. This refactoring allows to see

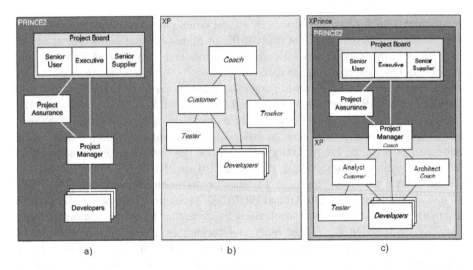

Fig. 1. Minimal project team structure in PRINCE2 (a). A team structure diagram for XP (b). XPrince team structure (c).

XP team as PRINCE-compatible. From the PRINCE2 point of view the Project Manager controls a team of developers. PRINCE2 does not impose any constraints on how the developers should be organized, so from that point of view Analyst or Architect is just a developer. On the other hand, the developers can be unaware of existence of the Project Board. From their point of view the Analyst (a role coming from RUP) is the customer and they have two coaches: Project Manager and Architect. In XP there is only one coach, but its mission is twofold: removing organizational obstacles (e.g. lack of paper) and intervene when developers encounter technical difficulties (e.g. unit tests take too long). Taking this into account we have decided to split the coach role into two roles. *Project Manager* is responsible for right organizational environment (including good contacts with the Project Board), she/he solves interpersonal problems and is rather motivating than directing [4]. A good Project Manager should build his team around character ethic proposed by Stephen Covey [10]. *Architect* is much more technically oriented. It is an additional role not present in XP nor in PRINCE2 (it also comes from RUP). From the developers point of view, Architect is a senior-designer (corresponding to Brook's Chief Surgeon [7]) who is well-experienced and can provide merit (i.e. technical) advices to the developers. The Architect is responsible for establishing and maintaining the architecture and the developers are responsible for "filling in" the architecture with the functionality. A very good description of architect's role is given by Kroll and Kruchten [17].

3   Project Lifecycle

Project lifecycle is a basis for planning. In PRINCE2 (Fig. 2a) a project begins with *Starting-up* (deciding about the management team, preparing a Project Brief and a Project Approach, planning the initiation stage). It can be very short (sometimes a few hours are enough). It is followed by *Initiating a Project* (planning a project, refining the business case and risks, setting up project controls and project files, assembling the Project Initiation Document). Then a number of *stages* appear (each stage is assigned a list of expected products and it is controlled using its own plan). A project ends with *Closing* (obtaining customer's acceptance, identifying follow-on actions, evaluating the project).

In RUP (Fig. 2b) a project consists of four phases: *Inception* (finding out what and how to build), *Elaboration* (working out the architecture, planning the project, mitigating essential risks, putting the development environment in place), *Construction* (preparing a fully functional beta version of the system), *Transition* (preparing deployment site, training users, checking that user expectations are met and deployment is complete).

XP's lifecycle is the simplest one (Fig. 2c). It consists of a sequence of releases and each release is a sequence of increments. Each release and each iteration starts with a planning session (so-called Planning Game). There is no overall project plan – planning perspective is limited to one release. Sometimes people use so-called zero-functionality increment to arrange things and prepare the development environment.

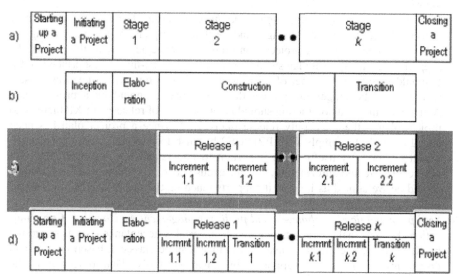

Fig. 2. Project lifecycles proposed by different methodologies: PRINCE 2 (a), RUP (b), XP (c), and XPrince (d)

In XPrince the lifecycle is a combination of all the mentioned approaches. The PRINCE2 concept of starting-closing 'brackets' is quite practical. They are completely non-technical activities, so it makes sense to separate them from the other stages (in RUP it is partially included into Inception and Transition). *Starting up a Project* is usually performed by Project Manager and it has the following objectives:

- Appoint the project management team (see the previous section).
- Produce a vision document (it is a shorter and more concrete version of PRINCE's Project Brief and Project Approach, and it contains an initial version of the business case).
- Plan the initiation stage.

The next stage is *Initiating a Project*. Its aim is to provide a plan and an organizational environment for the project. It is a combination of PRINCE's Initiation and RUP's Inception. It is mainly performed by the Project Manager and the Analyst. Some consultancy with the Architect will also be necessary. The objectives of the stage are the following:

- *Understand what to build*. If necessary, produce a lightweight version of the ConOps document [15] containing a business model based on use cases, list of problems to be solved, and key system functionality required to solve the problems. The key system functionality should be accompanied by a list of quality criteria and work products. The Analyst is responsible for the objective and for updating the risks associated with it.
- *Propose an initial architecture*. It should be a short, high-level description providing information necessary for planning the project. It should also contain a list of the tools that will be used. Nominally the Architect is responsible for the objective and its risks, but if the architecture is pretty obvious the Analyst can do the work.
- *Plan the whole project and refine the business case*. That objective is under supervision of the Project Manager and he is also responsible for maintaining the risks associated with it. A project plan presents a strategic view of the project. To support agility the project plan should be based on the first-things-first principle [10]. It should specify the number of releases and assign features (high-level use cases) to releases. The longer the project the less concrete should be a project plan. Actual planning and contracting should be at the level of releases. In XP there is no project plan – there are only release plans. In XPrince a project plan has been added not only to comply with PRINCE2 but also to provide a wider perspective which can be very useful. It is important to understand that a project plan is a source of valuable information, not an excuse to reject changes. Every change should be welcomed as long as it supports reaching the business objectives stated in the business case.
- *Set-up communication channels and project management environment*. Communication channels include reports (e.g. results of weekly acceptance tests as suggested by XP). The project management environment can be classical, based on files and documents or it can be supported by advanced tools. That objective is the responsibility of the Project Manager.
- *Plan the Elaboration stage*. The *Elaboration* stage is mainly about architecture. The Architect is to propose architectural mechanisms, identify risks associated with the proposed mechanisms, check the risks (e.g. through experiments), and create a framework that will be used by the Developers. The Analyst and the Project Manager use that stage to refine the requirements and the project plan.

Each *Release* stage consists of a number of increments which are followed by transition. At this stage the development process resembles very much XP. The Architect and the Developers produce code and test cases. The Analyst is responsible for requirements and acceptance tests. He also plays the role of on-site customer. An increment is a purely internal checkpoint. Each Release ends with a transition and then a new version of the system is deployed and passed over to end users. As in XP, each increment should have the same duration – that helps the Developers to learn what an increment is in the sense of time and, as a result, they become better at planning it.

Closing an XPrince project resembles very much its counterpart in PRINCE2. The project is decommissioned, the follow-on actions are identified, and the project is evaluated.

4 Requirements Engineering with UC Workbench

In this section we present a tool supporting requirements engineering based on use-cases. It is called UC Workbench (UC stands for Use Cases). UC Workbench was designed with XPrince's Analyst in mind.

4.1 Text or Diagram?

According to a popular saying, one picture has a value of 1000 words. Unfortunately, it seems it does not hold for requirements engineering. In March and April 2005 we have conducted an experiment at the Poznan University of Technology. The aim of the experiment was to find out which approach, text-based or diagram-based, is better from the understandability point of view. As a representative of the text-based approach we have selected use cases [8, 1]. For diagram-based approach we have chosen BPMN [27] which resembles UML but is specifically designed for business modeling. The participants of the experiment were 4th year students working on their master degrees in Software Engineering (SE) or Business Administration (BA). There were 17 SE students and 11 BA students. The process went through the following steps:

1. A *lecture* presenting an introduction to a given notation (90 minutes).
2. A *rehearsal* session during which the students were given a high level description of PRINCE2 processes expressed in a given notation with a number of seeded defects and their task was to find them. The document was 5 pages long. The session lasted for about 90 minutes.
3. An *experiment* session run in a similar way as the rehearsal. However, this time we have changed the business domain. Instead of PRINCE2 processes the participants were presented business models concerning university regulations (earning university diploma, taking the final exam etc.). They were given one hour to find the defects.

The process was performed twice (each time with different business models) to get more data. Each time there were two groups: one using use cases, and the other working with BPMN diagrams. It could happen that the two groups were not equivalent in terms of their skills. To avoid this, the second time we have switched the groups (the use-case group was given BPMN diagrams and vice versa). Students worked individually. Every detected defect was shortly described on the defect log. As the understandability measure we have assumed the number of defects detected in the document. Defect detection ratio (DDR) for a person p was defined as follows:

$$DDR(p) = \frac{\text{Number of defects detected by person } p}{\text{Number of all the defects}} \cdot 100\%$$

DDR for use cases was greater than for BPMN and that result was statistically significant (with the significance level 0.05). This justifies the following conjecture: *use cases are easier to understand than BPMN diagrams*. Thus, it is better to express business processes in the form of use cases.

We have also performed another experiment. This time one group was given a business model expressed only in use cases and the other group was given the same use cases accompanied with BPMN diagrams. The latter group detected more defects than the former and the results were statistically significant. Thus, BPMN diagrams are a valuable add-on to the use cases.

Taking into account results of those experiments we have decided that in XPrince requirements engineering will be based on use cases and diagrams will be treated as useful adornments.

4.2 UC Workbench

UC Workbench is a tool developed at the Poznan University of Technology [21] to support requirements management and business modeling based on use cases. We were surprised by the fact that there is no good tool for use-case engineering. UC Workbench provides the following functionality:

- *Editing use cases* with automatic renumbering the steps in the main scenario as well as in all the extensions.
- *Automatic reviews* with detecting 'bed smells' (e.g. undefined and unused actors, too short or too long scenarios, an extension with no steps).
- *Generating of mockups* from the collected use cases. An automatically generated mockup is based on a web browser and it consists of two windows (see Fig. 3): the *scenario window* (presents the currently animated use case), and the *screen window* (shows the screen design). In the case of business modeling the screen window would contain a BPMN diagram.
- *Composing the SRS document* based on IEEE Std. 830-1998. UC Workbench generates the SRS document from the use cases.
- *Generating effort calculators based on Use-Case Points* [16] that are to support XP's Planning Game. In XPrince planning comprises three levels: Use-Case Points (the lowest level) provide default effort estimates that can be later on changed by the experts; Wide-Band Delphi Method is used to support effort estimation by the team (experts); Planning Game (the highest level) controls a dialog between the customer (and Analyst) and the Developers led by the Architect about the scope of the next release.

We believe that appropriate tools can be very helpful in balancing agility and discipline. They can provide information available in discipline-oriented methodologies but faster and cheaper. Due to this, changing requirements are not so a big problem as it used to be.

To evaluate UC Workbench we have performed a simple experiment aiming at comparison of UC Workbench with a popular, general purpose text processor (MS Word). There were twelve participants (students of the 4th year working towards their Master degree in Software Engineering). They were split into two equal-size groups.

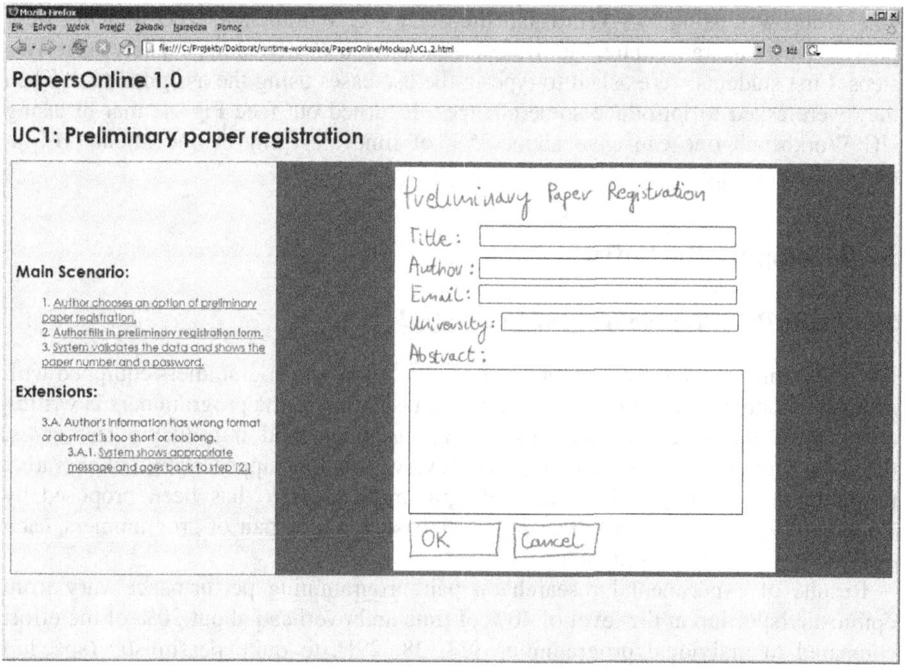

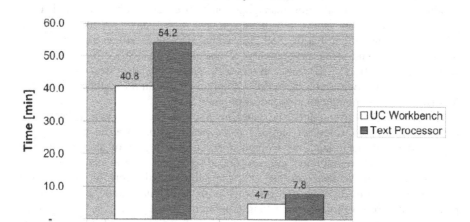

Fig. 3. A screenshot of a mockup generated by UC Workbench

Effort Comparison

Fig. 4. Effort necessary to type-in (left) and to change (right) use-cases using UC Workbench and MS Word

One group was using MS Word and the other UC Workbench. The students were provided with a draft containing 4 use cases (each 6–9 steps long). There were two steps. First students were asked to type-in the use cases using the assigned tool. Then they were asked to introduce some changes. It turned out (see Fig. 4) that by using UC Workbench one can save about 25% of time at typing-in and about 40% at introducing changes.

5 Developing the Software

5.1 To Do Pair Programming or Not To Do?

Pair Programming is one of key practice of XP. A pair of programmers equipped with a single computer is assigned a programming task. One of the programmers is writing code, while the other is watching, asking questions, and introducing test cases, therefore providing so-called continuous review. Another approach to collaborative programming – called Side-by-Side Programming (SbS) – has been proposed by Cockburn [9]. In this approach a single task is solved by a pair of programmers, each equipped with his own computer.

Results of experimental research on pair programming performance vary from optimistic (speedup at the level of 40% of time and overhead about 20% of the effort compared to individual programming [23, 28, 29]), to quite pessimistic (speedup about 20%, effort overhead about 60% [20]). Unfortunately, up-to-date there are no published experimental data concerning SbS performance.

Recent experiments performed at the Poznan University of Technology [22] indicate that classical Pair Programming is less efficient than the SbS programming. Almost 30 students were working for 6 days in a controlled environment. They were building an Internet application managing conference paper submission and review processes. They were split into three groups: SbS pairs, XP-like pairs, and individuals. It turned out that the SbS pairs were faster by 13% than the XP pairs and by 39% than the individual programmers. Consequently, the SbS effort was by 26% smaller than the effort of XP pairs and only 22% greater than the effort of individuals. This experiment shows that Side-by-Side programming is an interesting alternative to XP-like pair programming and individual programming.

Another experiment run at the Poznan University of Technology in 2005 confirms this observation. 44 volunteer subjects participated in the experiment. They were undergraduate students studying Computer Science (2nd year of study). They had completed various programming courses (including Java and C++) amounting to over 400 hours. Again we have decided that the subjects will work at the university (controlled conditions). Some students worked in XP-like pairs and the others in SbS pairs. They were given two 9-hour long programming assignments and they worked according to predefined process. The results show, that Side-by-Side programming is faster than XP-like Pair Programming by 16%–18% percent.

Interestingly, all the subjects participating in the experiment preferred collaborative programming (55%) over individual problem solving (40%). Moreover, 70% of the subjects preferred Side-by-Side approach and only 30% voted for XP-like pair programming.

In XPrince the Developers can choose between individual, SbS or XP-like pair programming. If they choose individual programming, a reviewer is assigned to check quality of the work (it is another Developer).

5.2   Code Refactoring

Refactoring is one of the core XP techniques supporting software maintenance [3]. It depends on changing source code internal structure to improve its readability and adjust it to changing requirements, while preserving its observable behaviour (that allows to reuse the 'old' regression tests) [12].

An agile project most of its life-time stays at maintenance phase because actually it constantly evolves over time. That makes refactoring (and any other software maintenance technique) very important.

Unfortunately, refactoring is also a costly and error-prone technique. Changes are likely to introduce mistakes and unexpected side-effects, which effectively alter the program behaviour. Preventing this requires additional effort, which adds even 80% to overall project cost [6]. However, the investment pays back with subsequent maintenance events: according to some authors [25], refactoring is cost effective after sixth such action. Small-scale experiment performed at the Poznan University of Technology with graduate students in Software Engineering revealed that the refactoring-related overhead in every increment decreased from 75 down to 7 percent in just three development cycles, as compared to a similar incremental process performed without code restructuring [26]. Thus, disciplined refactoring contributes to code quality, whereas its cost is justified for projects with several functional increments or maintenance actions.

As in typical XPrince project there are many increments, refactoring and programming environments supporting it (e.g. IBM Eclipse) are strongly recommended.

5.3   Integration of Code Reuse and Test-First Coding

It is a widely known fact, that code reuse can reduce software development cost and increase reliability. For instance, Toshiba reported decrease in defects by 20–30%, and Hewlett-Packard even by 76% [11]. The main problem with code reuse is finding a piece of code which can be used to accomplish some given goal. That task is definitely not a trivial one, especially when the size of repository and the number of people involved are significantly big (which is actually the situation when the systematic reuse starts paying off). Such a difficult task cannot be approached without a support of both well organized processes and well designed tools.

One of the most interesting approaches to improving the search process is so-called behavioural retrieval [2, 24]. A behaviour of a class or a method is specified by a small program showing the input and expected output. That idea was first proposed by Podgurski [24]. Unfortunately, it was not widely used in practice because of a common belief that specifying a class or a method is not trivial and it will be faster to write a piece of code than to find it in a repository (the technique of behavioural retrieval is oriented towards relatively small pieces of code like functions or classes).

But in XP (and in XPrince as well) coding is preceded by preparing test cases (it is so-called test-first coding). To support code reuse and test-first coding we have developed a tool that takes test cases written in jUnit and using the technique of behavioural retrieval searches through a code repository looking for a class or a method which potentially satisfies this rough specification. If it succeeds, the Developer can check more precisely if the found piece of code satisfies his requirements and if so, the work is done. If not, he can start programming as he did if he was just doing classical test-first coding.

The proposed technique is not to replace existing methods of searching through repositories. It is rather a complementary solution designed to operate well for small pieces of code, for which commonly used techniques as text-based retrieval or faceted classification may not be sufficient.

To evaluate the proposed tool we have performed a simple test. Nine programmers (5th year students) were given description of 10 relatively simple program units (the descriptions were given in a natural language). They were asked to provide a set of test cases that would allow finding the units in the code repository. In 9 of 10 cases the programmers correctly specified the units. The only problem was with a class representing strings that can be matched with regular expressions (4 of 9 programmers made a wrong assumption).

6 Conclusions

By integrating different methodologies and supporting them with appropriate tools one can obtain a balance between agility and discipline. The solutions presented in the paper follow from our 7-years long experience in running the Software Development Studio at the Poznan University of Technology. The described methodology (XPrince) and the first version of UC Workbench went also through in-field testing – they have been used in a commercial project for a government agency.

Acknowledgements

We are thankful to PB Polsoft, a software company with headquarters in Poznan who provided us with a feedback from a real industrial project run according to XPrince, and personally to Grzegorz Leopold who created that opportunity.

This work has been financially supported by the State Committee for Scientific Research as a research grant 4 T11F 001 23 (years 2002-2005).

References

[1] Adolph, S., Bramble, P., Cockburn, A., Pols, A., *Patterns for Effective Use Cases*, Addison-Wesley, 2002.
[2] Atkinson S., *Examining behavioural retrieval*, WISR8, Ohio State University, 1997.
[3] Beck, K., *Extreme Programming Explained. Embrace Change*, Addison-Wesley, Boston, 2000.
[4] Blanchard, K., Zigarmi D., Zigarmi P., *Leadership and the One Minute Manager*, 1985.
[5] Boehm, B., Turner, R., *Balancing Agility and Discipline. A Guide for Perplexed*, Addison-Wesley, Boston, 2004.
[6] Bossi P., Repo *Margining System*.
http://www.communications.xplabs.com/lab2001-1.html, visited in 2004.

[7] Brooks, F., *A Mythical Man-Month*, Addison-Wesley, Boston 1995.

[8] Cockburn, A., *Writing Effective Use Cases*, Addison-Wesley, Boston, 2000.

[9] Cockburn, A., *Crystal Clear. A Human-Powered Methodology for Small Teams.* Addison-Wesley, Boston, 2005.

[10] Covey, S., *The Seven Habits of Highly Effective People*, Simon and Schuster, London, 1992.

[11] Ezran M., Morisio M., Tully C., Practical Software Reuse, Springer, 2002.

[12] Fowler M., *Refactoring. Improving the Design of Existing Code.* Addison-Wesley, Boston, 1997.

[13] Humphrey, W., *A Discipline for Software Engineering*, Addison-Wesley, Reading MA, 1995.

[14] Humphrey, W., *Introduction to the Team Software Process*, Addison-Wesley, Reading MA, 2000.

[15] *IEEE Guide for Information Technology – System Definition – Concept of Operations (ConOps) Document*, IEEE Std. 1362–1998.

[16] Karner, G., Use Case Points – Resource Estimation for Objectory Projects, Objective Systems SF AB, 1993.

[17] Kroll, P., Kruchten, Ph., *The Rational Unified Process Made Easy*, Addison-Wesley, Boston, 2003.

[18] *Managing Successful Projects with PRINCE2*, TSO, London, 2004.

[19] Nawrocki, J., Jasiński, M., Walter, B., Wojciechowski, A., Extreme Programming Modified: Embrace Requirements Engineering Practices, 10th IEEE Joint International Requirements Engineering Conference, RE'02, Essen (Germany), IEEE Press, Los Alamitos (2002) 303–310.

[20] Nawrocki, J., Wojciechowski, A.: Experimental Evaluation of Pair Programming. In: Maxwell, K., Oligny, S., Kusters, R., van Veenendaal, E. (eds.): Project Control. Satisfying the Customer. Proceedings of the 12th European Software Control and Metrics Conference ESCOM 2001. Shaker Publishing, London (2001) 269–276.

[21] Nawrocki, J., Olek, L., UC Workbench – A Tool for Writing Use Cases and Generating Mockups. **In**: Baumeister, H., Marchesi, M., Holcombe, M., (Eds.) Extreme Programming and Agile Processes in Software Engineering, *Lecture Notes in Computer Science* 3556, (2005), 230–234.

[22] Nawrocki, J., Jasinski, M., Olek, L., Lange, B.: Pair Programming vs. Side-by-Side Programming. Proceedings of the European Software Process Improvement and Innovation Conference, *Lecture Notes in Computer Science* 3792 (2005), 28–38.

[23] Nosek, J. T., The Case for Collaborative Programming. *Communications of the ACM*, Volume 41, No. 3 (1998) 105–108.

[24] Podgurski, A., Pierce, L., *Retrieving reusable software by sampling behavior,* ACM TOSEM, Volume 2 , No. 3 (1993) 286–303.

[25] Stroulia E., Leitch R., K., *Understanding the Economics of Refactoring.* In: Proc. of the Fifth ICSE Workshop on Economics-Driven Software Engineering Research. Portland, 2003.

[26] Walter B., *Analysis of Software Refactorings.* PhD dissertation, Poznań University of Technology, Poznań (Poland), 2004 (in Polish).

[27] White, S., Introduction to BPMN, http://www.bpmn.org/Documents/_Introduction%20to%20BPMN.pdf, visited in 2005.

[28] Williams, L.: *The Collaborative Software Process.* PhD Dissertation at the Department of Computer Science, University of Utah, Salt Lake City (2000).

[29] Williams, L. et al.: Strengthening the Case for Pair Programming. *IEEE Software*, Volume 17, No. 4 (2000) 19–25.

Extreme89: An XP War Game[*]

Jerzy Nawrocki and Adam Wojciechowski

Poznan University of Technology, Institute of Computing Science,
ul. Piotrowo 3a, 60-965 Poznan, Poland
{Jerzy.Nawrocki, Adam.Wojciechowski}@put.poznan.pl

Abstract. *Extreme89* is a simulation game designed to introduce software teams – programmers and customers – to Extreme Programming practices. The game is run by a moderator and lasts 89 minutes – this is the reason why we named it *Extreme89*. Several teams build-up of customer representative and programmers compete to earn maximum number of points. Teams earn points for delivering properly produced artifacts. Artifacts in the game correspond to software modules delivered to customer in real software projects. Every artifact in the game is assigned a Fibonacci-like function. Manual computing values of the functions performed by the programmers substitutes real programming. Rules of *Extreme89* closely correspond to XP practices. The game has two releases while each release is build-up of two increments. *Extreme89* with its atmosphere of the competition and time-compressed active lesson of XP was successfully introduced to Computer Science students at Poznan University of Technology.

1 Introduction

Extreme Programming (XP) is a paradigm shift in software development. What makes it different from classical approaches is, among others, adaptation to changing requirements, intensive oral communication, many short releases providing rapid feedback from end users, and strong business orientation (a customer makes all the business decisions concerning the project) [1]. Such a radically new methodology requires a new approach to teaching. It is well known that behavioral aspects cannot be effectively learned solely by attending lectures and reading textbooks. Active learning can be very useful.

One of pedagogical patterns for active learning is *war game* [5, 6]. It is a simulation game based on a metaphor of real situations, where several individuals or teams earn credits while they solve the same problem in parallel or play one against another. We know of two simulation games oriented towards XP. The first war game for XP is *Extreme Hour* proposed by Peter Merel [3]. In *Extreme Hour* programming is replaced by designing a fun device e.g. an improved mousetrap. Participation in the game encourages extensive oral communication and resembles brain storming. Unfortunately, there is no distinction between customer's and programmers' knowledge - in

---

[*] This work was financially supported by State Committee for Scientific Research as a research grant 4 T11F 001 23 (years 2002–2005).

N. Guelfi and A. Savidis (Eds.): RISE 2005, LNCS 3943, pp. 278–287, 2006.

XP customer is an expert in business domain but he can be a layman in Information Technology and the programmer is opposite. Another weakness of *Extreme Hour* is lack of changes in requirements or conditions on the market which may force the customer to change his original preferences during the process.

Another XP 'process miniature' [2] was proposed by Alistair Cockburn [4, p. 140]. He changed *Extreme Hour* by introducing real programming to the game and stretching time to 90 minutes. One must notice that Cockburn's experience was oriented rather to demonstrate the two iteration XP process than to make it a war game (a war game is a process miniature with a kind of competition). Working in those strict time-limits the most spectacular part of the experience was the Planning Game, when the customer had to make decisions about the scope and functionality of the project. To emphasize our game is not Cockburn's one, we planned it for 89 minutes and named it Extreme89.

Extreme89 is a war game that aims at introducing programmers and customers to XP practices. The game is run by a moderator. Several teams compete in one session (in parallel) to earn maximum number of points. Each team consists of one customer and at least two programmers (all of the teams should have the same number of programmers). Teams earn points for delivering properly produced artifacts. Artifacts in *Extreme89* correspond to software modules delivered to customer in real software projects. A list of the artifacts to be 'produced' and their worth is given to the customer in the beginning of the game. The programmers get information on how to 'produce' the artifacts. Every artifact in the game is assigned a recursive Fibonacci-like function. To produce an artifact means to compute manually value of the recursive function assigned to the artifact. The winner in the game is the team which collects the maximum total worth of produced artifacts.

Rules of *Extreme89* closely correspond to XP practices. To simulate an XP project each session is split into two releases, worth of the artifacts is changing during the game and arguments of the recursive functions are also subject to change reflecting changes in implementation. The customer knows current worth of the artifacts but he does not know how to 'produce' them while the programmers get definitions of recursive functions but they do not know how much they earn for delivering artifacts. This way knowledge of the customer and the programmers is clearly separated.

In the following sections of the paper we present roles of *Extreme89* participants, rules and complete scenario of the simulation game. In section 4 we show how Extreme Programming practices are mapped onto game activities. Finally we present evaluation of the game conducted at the Poznan University of Technology to try and understand XP practices.

2 Roles in *Extreme89*

The main aim of *Extreme89* is to introduce participants to XP practices and to show the importance of communication and collaboration in a software team. The result of the collaboration between the customer and the programmers is the final product, which scope and quality depends on both – programmers competence and effectiveness of communication in the team. To force communication between team members, knowledge, given to customer and programmers, is separated. To learn 'what the other side knows' programmers must talk to the customer and vice versa.

2.1 Programmers

The role of programmers in *Extreme89* is 'producing' artifacts. They calculate manually values of recursive functions associated with the artifacts. Examples of the functions are given below:

$F(a, b, 1)= a$
$F(a, b, 2)= b$
$F(a, b, n)= F(a, b, n-2) + F(a, b, n-1) \text{ div } 2 \quad$ if $n>2$

$G(a, b, 1)= a$
$G(a, b, 2)= b$
$G(a, b, n)= G(a, b, n-2) + G(a, b, n-1) \text{ div } 10 \quad$ if $n>2$

One should notice that function F can be defined as follows:

$F(1)= a$
$F(2)= b$
$F(n)= F(n-2) + F(n-1) \text{ div } 2 \quad$ if $n>2$

Function G may be defined in analogical way. This form is easier for manual calculations and clearly shows the role of parameters *a* and *b* – the initial values in the sequence. However, the advantage of the first form (functions F and G defined with 3 input parameters) is the ease to demonstrate which value of the sequence (beginning with *a* and *b*) is the result. For example: $F(x_1, x_2, 5)$, where $x_1=1$ and $x_2=7$ we have:

$F(1)= x_1 = 1$
$F(2)= x_2 = 7$
$F(3)= F(1) + F(2) \text{ div } 2 = 1 + 7 \text{ div } 2 = 1 + 3 = 4$
$F(4)= F(2) + F(3) \text{ div } 2 = 7 + 4 \text{ div } 2 = 7 + 2 = 9$
$F(5)= F(3) + F(4) \text{ div } 2 = 4 + 9 \text{ div } 2 = 4 + 4 = 8$

Associations of artifacts and functions are given to programmers. They know how to 'produce' the artifact. An example list of artifact-function associations is given below:

Counter	$= F(x_1, x_2, 18)$	**Data**	$= F(x_3, x_4, 18)$
Stylesheet	$= F(x_5, x_6, 18)$	**Web-page**	$= \text{Data} + F(x_5, x_6, 35)$
Catalogue	$= F(x_7, x_8, 18)$	**Search**	$= F(x_9, x_{10}, 18)$
Orders	$= \textbf{Search} + F(x_7, x_8, 35)$	**Invoice**	$= F(x_{11}, x_{12}, 18)$
Credit-card	$= F(x_{13}, x_{14}, 18)$	**Payment**	$= \textbf{Invoice} + F(x_{13}, x_{14}, 35)$
E-shop	$= G(\text{Orders div } 100, \text{Payment div } 100, 70)$		

It is possible to start calculations only if programmers know actual values of functions' parameters. An example set of parameters x_i is given below:

$x_1 = 2$	$x_2 = 3$	$x_3 = 2$	$x_4 = 4$	$x_5 = 2$	$x_6 = 5$	$x_7 = 2$
$x_8 = 6$	$x_9 = 2$	$x_{10} = 7$	$x_{11} = 2$	$x_{12} = 8$	$x_{13} = 2$	$x_{14} = 9$

2.2 Customer

The customer represents business aspects of the project. He knows the market value of each artifact (see table 1.), which is the current worth that team earns for delivering particular artifact. The customer expects that programmers are able to 'produce' all the artifacts, however he does not know how difficult it is. The customer is aware that within limited time of the game (89 minutes) the team has no chance to 'produce' all the artifacts. Thus he must communicate with his programmers to learn how much time they need to calculate functions associated with particular artifacts and what is the risk of an error in calculations. It is customer's job to make strategic decision what artifacts will be 'produced' in particular release.

Table 1. Current worth (market value) of the artifacts

Artifact	Worth
Counter	3
Data	3
Stylesheet	4
Web-page	24
Catalogue	4
Search	4

Artifact	Worth
Orders	20
Invoice	5
Credit-card	3
Payment	20
E-shop	100

The artifacts correspond to modules of a system and some of them are logically dependent, e.g. in order to 'produce' artifact *web-page* the programmers need to calculate functions associated with *stylesheet* and *data* (however, *web-page* is not a sum of *stylesheet* and *data*). Those logical dependencies between artifacts are given to the customer on a graph (see fig. 1.).

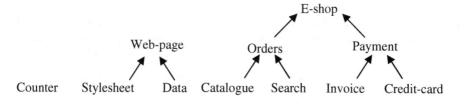

Fig. 1. Dependencies between artifacts

Except the current worth of the artifacts, customer knows ranges (upper and lower bound, see table 2.) associated with all the artifacts. Proper value of an artifact calculated by programmers is always located within the corresponding range. It corresponds to acceptance tests. If value of an artifact calculated by the programmers is located within the corresponding range the customer cannot reject this result. One may say – 'the artifact passes acceptance test based on customer's knowledge'.

However, one cannot exclude a situation where implementation defect is not detected during acceptance tests. Thus the customer knows only the ranges and any value of an artifact beyond its bounds must be rejected.

Range bounds (given in Table 2) help the customer to eliminate results that are definitely faraway from the correct solution. Customer and programmers may freely exchange their knowledge but they must communicate orally. Customer cannot read programmers' sheet of knowledge and vice versa.

Table 2. Ranges for artifacts

Artifact	Range	Artifact	Range
Counter	100..400	Orders	14100..15900
Data	150..450	Invoice	250..800
Stylesheet	170..190	Credit-card	300..330
Web-page	12500..12800	Payment	21200..22900
Catalogue	210..230	E-shop	5400.5700
Search	200..700		

2.3 Moderator

The game is run by the moderator. He is responsible for:

- Preparing materials with knowledge for customer and programmers.
- Animating the game by giving new portions of knowledge to the participants according to game scenario.
- Acceptance test and final assessment of collected results.

3 Game Scenario

3.1 Accessories

Extreme89 war game can be organized almost everywhere. Although it simulates work in a software team there is no need to use computers, because programming is replaced by computing values of recursive functions. The list of required accessories include:

- Printed materials with domain knowledge for customer and programmers.
- Sheets of paper and ball-pens for programmers.
- Table, chairs and a partition used as a holder for sheets with domain knowledge presented separately to programmers and customer.
- A clock for precise time management during the game.

All the team members sit around one table (customer face to face with his programmers). It corresponds to work in the open space, one of key XP practices [1]. Entire team may easily communicate during the game. Partition placed on the table should guarantee that knowledge presented to programmers cannot be red by customer and vice versa (see Fig. 2.).

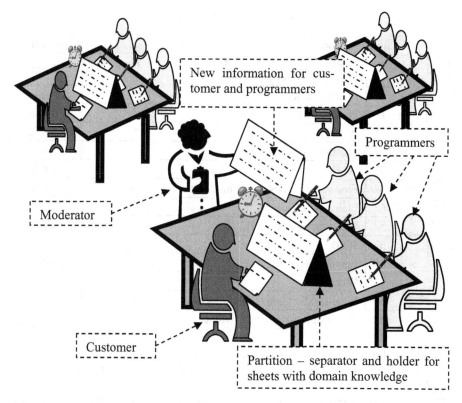

Fig. 2. *Extreme89* war game. Teams compete to earn maximum worth for produced artifacts

3.2 Timetable

The game is run according to strict time-limits described in form of scenario (see table 3.). The process is split into two releases while each release consists of two increments. Product – set of artifacts delivered at the end of each release – goes to moderator for assessment. Only the moderator has the list of proper values of the functions associated with the artifacts.

Knowledge of programmers, customer's experience and conditions on the market are subject to change during the process of producing software system. In *Extreme89* programmers' competence and customer experience grow systematically. In the beginning of the game programmers have blanks in function definitions – they do not know how to produce an artifact. At particular stages of the game (according to the timetable) participants get new, more precise, data from moderator. On programmers' side some blanks in function definitions are filled and some parameters are corrected. Customer get better acceptance tests (ranges are getting narrow and narrow), but there are possible surprises on the market – worth of the artifacts may change.

Table 3. *Extreme89* timetable

Time	Action	Period
0	Customer and programmers read and learn their domain knowledge	5 min.
5	Planning release I	5 min.
10	Planning increment I.1	5 min.
15	Work	12 min.
27	Planning increment I.2	5 min.
32	Work	12 min.
44	First release goes to the moderator for assessment	3 min.
47	Planning release II	5 min.
52	Planning increment II.1	5 min.
57	Work	12 min.
69	Planning increment II.2	5 min.
74	Work	12 min.
86	Final product goes to the moderator for assessment	3 min.
89	Congratulations for the winners	

Meaning of the icons on the left side of the table:

New (more precise) domain knowledge delivered to team members.

New (corrected) set of initial function parameters delivered to the programmers.

Product (artifacts produced by the programmers and accepted by the customer) is assessed by the moderator. The team gets the information about earned credits.

4 *Extreme89* vs. Extreme Programming

Extreme89 was proposed to give participants a chance to experience the atmosphere of team work according to XP practices. Here we present mapping of main XP practices that have very evident parallel in rules of the game.

- **On-site Customer.** Live contact of the customer who knows the business aspects of the project with programmers who have competences and technical skill to produce artifacts.
- **Planning Game.** Strictly limited time of the game requires proper planning. Scope of the project must be adjusted to programmers possibilities and to conditions on the market to earn maximum worth for delivered product.
- **Coding Standard.** In many cases calculations used to 'produce' an artifact may be reused by the same or another programmer to calculate another artifact. It easier to

find an error in somebody's calculations if they are in compliance with agreed standard.

- **Small Increments.** Very short time for increments forces planning small task that add value to product 'produced' by the team.
- **No Overtime.** Artifacts delivered late do not add value to final score of the team.
- **Pair Programming.** Programmers are not forced to work in pairs, however they may try it and observe differences in quality of work produced by pairs and individuals.
- **Simplicity.** There is no place for adding 'functionality' to artifacts produced in *Extreme89*.

5 Initial Experience with *Extreme89*

Extreme89 was played for the first time in March 2003 at Poznan University of Technology. Participants of the war game were 3rd, 4th and 5th year students of Computer Science. All together is was 120 students divided into teams of 3 to 6 persons. For about 80 3rd year students it was the first experience with XP practices while older students already had some practical experience from managing projects being developed according to XP. To enforce emotional engagement in the game the winners in each group were rewarded with computer accessories and sweets.

Right after the game all the participants filled a questionnaire where they expressed their impression of the *Extreme89*. The game was welcomed very warmly and more than 80% of participants assessed the tutorial to XP with the highest mark. Among the strongest advantages of the game students indicated:

- Intensive course of Extreme Programming.
- Possibility to observe and experience how much depends of fluent communication in a project team (especially when knowledge of a customer and programmers is separated).
- Good fun.

Ten months later we played *Extreme89* again with a group of 20 students. At that time all of them had some experience with team work on a software project and much better theoretical background in XP in general. After the game they were asked to assess their impression of the game once again. Here are some of the results:

Question	Yes	No	No clue
Does *Extreme89* help to understand XP?	95%	-	5%
Would you recommend *Extreme89* for younger students as intro to XP?	95%	-	5%
Did the game convince you to XP?	65%	20%	15%
Would you like to play from time to time to remind XP practices?	45%	45%	10%

Since the first time *Extreme89* was played we did several experiments playing the game with various groups of participants. We tried to play the game prior to and after the lecture on eXtreme Programming. Playing *Extreme89* before giving the lecture introducing to XP practices is an opportunity for a team to practice and discover the most effective way of team work by themselves. A significant outcome from that experiment was that majority (above 70%) of winning teams developed their own practice of pair work. It seemed to appear very naturally when the Customers observed many mistakes in artifacts delivered by singles. During the lecture following the game participants could compare XP practices to their natural behavior. Students tried to relate their way of playing the game to XP practices. After the lecture, during a discussion, some of students (Programmers in the game) confirmed that they underestimated importance of Planning Game and instant communication with the Customer. Strong pressure to produce quickly, closed some programmers' eyes to wider understanding of system being build. Calculations performed to deliver particular component might be re-used during calculating values of other artifacts but some Programmers did not noticed that fact.

Extreme89 was also played during a commercial workshop dedicated to software engineering. Participants of the event were mainly software project managers and programmers. In this case Extreme89 followed a lecture introducing to XP practices. A significant observation reported by participants was underestimating the importance of communication within the team. It happened that two or more persons worked on the same artifact without knowing that they do the same task. Although in the context of the game it might make some sense to confirm results produced independently by two programmers, participants reported this case as lack the control over the project. The workshop participants assessed the game very good.

6   Further Development of *Extreme89*

Currently we work on a web-based version of *Extreme89*. Electronic system makes it possible to observe which team delivered an acceptable solution and instantly lower the number of points that other teams may get for the same solution delivered later. It is to simulate market behavior where the first deliverer of a product wins the biggest profit. Another important feature of the new Internet version of *Extreme89* will be the possibility of introducing various task – including also programming. The game will be played in computer laboratories and there will be no restrictions for using computers to obtain the results. What must remain not changed from first version of the game is separation of Programmers' and Customers' knowledge. In the web-based edition the Programmers and Customers will have separate logins and different pieces of information on their screens. Equipped with the new tool we will try to assess how far e-mails, telephones and messengers can substitute personal contact between Programmers and Customer.

Moving the game to computer network environment will provide the basis for running the game simultaneously in several locations. This way we will prepare a platform to play national contest in XP team work.

7   Summary

In the paper we presented *Extreme89* – a war game designed to introduce software teams to XP practices. Emotional engagement in the game of the participants is stimulated by competition between teams. First assessment of *Extreme89* was quite positive, however it revealed also some weaknesses. For instance students suggested to simplify calculations in order to produce more artifacts during the game. Evaluation showed that participants consider the game a very attractive form of learning XP.

An Internet-based version of Extreme89 (currently under development, soon to appear) will provide us with a tool for estimation the influence of personal contact of the customer and programmers on project progress.

References

[1] Beck K., Extreme Programming Explained. Embrace Change, Addison-Wesley, 2000.
[2] Cockburn A., Process Miniature, http://c2.com/cgi/wiki?ProcessMiniature.
[3] Cockburn A., Process Miniature, http://c2.com/cgi/wiki?ExtremeHour.
[4] Cockburn A., *Agile Software Development*, Addison-Wesley, 2002.
[5] O'Callaghan A., Simulation Game Workshop Pattern,
    http://sol.info.unlp.edu.ar/ppp/pp22.htm, Model and Implement,
    http://sol.info.unlp.edu.ar/ppp/pp23.htm.
[6] Eckstein J., Bergin J., Sharp H., Patterns for Active Learning, Pedagogical Patterns Project, http:// www.jeckstein.com/pedagogicalPatterns/activelearning.pdf.

Author Index

Lecture Notes in Computer Science

For information about Vols. 1–3882

please contact your bookseller or Springer

Vol. 3929: W. MacCaull, M. Winter, I. Düntsch (Eds.), Relational Methods in Computer Science. VIII, 263 pages. 2006.

Vol. 3928: J. Domingo-Ferrer, J. Posegga, D. Schreckling (Eds.), Smart Card Research and Advanced Applications. XI, 359 pages. 2006.

Vol. 3927: J. Hespanha, A. Tiwari (Eds.), Hybrid Systems: Computation and Control. XII, 584 pages. 2006.

Vol. 3925: A. Valmari (Ed.), Model Checking Software. X, 307 pages. 2006.

Vol. 3924: P. Sestoft (Ed.), Programming Languages and Systems. XII, 343 pages. 2006.

Vol. 3923: A. Mycroft, A. Zeller (Eds.), Compiler Construction. XIII, 277 pages. 2006.

Vol. 3922: L. Baresi, R. Heckel (Eds.), Fundamental Approaches to Software Engineering. XIII, 427 pages. 2006.

Vol. 3921: L. Aceto, A. Ingólfsdóttir (Eds.), Foundations of Software Science and Computation Structures. XV, 447 pages. 2006.

Vol. 3920: H. Hermanns, J. Palsberg (Eds.), Tools and Algorithms for the Construction and Analysis of Systems. XIV, 506 pages. 2006.

Vol. 3918: W.K. Ng, M. Kitsuregawa, J. Li, K. Chang (Eds.), Advances in Knowledge Discovery and Data Mining. XXIV, 879 pages. 2006. (Sublibrary LNAI).

Vol. 3917: H. Chen, F.Y. Wang, C.C. Yang, D. Zeng, M. Chau, K. Chang (Eds.), Intelligence and Security Informatics. XII, 186 pages. 2006.

Vol. 3916: J. Li, Q. Yang, A.-H. Tan (Eds.), Data Mining for Biomedical Applications. VIII, 155 pages. 2006. (Sublibrary LNBI).

Vol. 3915: R. Nayak, M.J. Zaki (Eds.), Knowledge Discovery from XML Documents. VIII, 105 pages. 2006.

Vol. 3914: A. Garcia, R. Choren, C. Lucena, P. Giorgini, T. Holvoet, A. Romanovsky (Eds.), Software Engineering for Multi-Agent Systems IV. XIV, 255 pages. 2006.

Vol. 3910: S.A. Brueckner, G.D.M. Serugendo, D. Hales, F. Zambonelli (Eds.), Engineering Self-Organising Systems. XII, 245 pages. 2006. (Sublibrary LNAI).

Vol. 3909: A. Apostolico, C. Guerra, S. Istrail, P. Pevzner, M. Waterman (Eds.), Research in Computational Molecular Biology. XVII, 612 pages. 2006. (Sublibrary LNBI).

Vol. 3908: A. Bui, M. Bui, T. Böhme, H. Unger (Eds.), Innovative Internet Community Systems. VIII, 207 pages. 2006.

Vol. 3907: F. Rothlauf, J. Branke, S. Cagnoni, E. Costa, C. Cotta, R. Drechsler, E. Lutton, P. Machado, J.H. Moore, J. Romero, G.D. Smith, G. Squillero, H. Takagi (Eds.), Applications of Evolutionary Computing. XXIV, 813 pages. 2006.

Vol. 3906: J. Gottlieb, G.R. Raidl (Eds.), Evolutionary Computation in Combinatorial Optimization. XI, 293 pages. 2006.

Vol. 3905: P. Collet, M. Tomassini, M. Ebner, S. Gustafson, A. Ekárt (Eds.), Genetic Programming. XI, 361 pages. 2006.

Vol. 3904: M. Baldoni, U. Endriss, A. Omicini, P. Torroni (Eds.), Declarative Agent Languages and Technologies III. XII, 245 pages. 2006. (Sublibrary LNAI).

Vol. 3903: K. Chen, R. Deng, X. Lai, J. Zhou (Eds.), Information Security Practice and Experience. XIV, 392 pages. 2006.

Vol. 3902: R. Kronland-Martinet, T. Voinier, S. Ystad (Eds.), Computer Music Modeling and Retrieval. XI, 275 pages. 2006.

Vol. 3901: P.M. Hill (Ed.), Logic Based Program Synthesis and Transformation. X, 179 pages. 2006.

Vol. 3900: F. Toni, P. Torroni (Eds.), Computational Logic in Multi-Agent Systems. XVII, 427 pages. 2006. (Sublibrary LNAI).

Vol. 3899: S. Frintrop, VOCUS: A Visual Attention System for Object Detection and Goal-Directed Search. XIV, 216 pages. 2006. (Sublibrary LNAI).

Vol. 3898: K. Tuyls, P.J. 't Hoen, K. Verbeeck, S. Sen (Eds.), Learning and Adaption in Multi-Agent Systems. X, 217 pages. 2006. (Sublibrary LNAI).

Vol. 3897: B. Preneel, S. Tavares (Eds.), Selected Areas in Cryptography. XI, 371 pages. 2006.

Vol. 3896: Y. Ioannidis, M.H. Scholl, J.W. Schmidt, F. Matthes, M. Hatzopoulos, K. Boehm, A. Kemper, T. Grust, C. Boehm (Eds.), Advances in Database Technology - EDBT 2006. XIV, 1208 pages. 2006.

Vol. 3895: O. Goldreich, A.L. Rosenberg, A.L. Selman (Eds.), Theoretical Computer Science. XII, 399 pages. 2006.

Vol. 3894: W. Grass, B. Sick, K. Waldschmidt (Eds.), Architecture of Computing Systems - ARCS 2006. XII, 496 pages. 2006.

Vol. 3893: L. Atzori, D.D. Giusto, R. Leonardi, F. Pereira (Eds.), Visual Content Processing and Representation. IX, 224 pages. 2006.

Vol. 3892: A. Carbone, N.A. Pierce (Eds.), DNA Computing. XI, 440 pages. 2006.

Vol. 3891: J.S. Sichman, L. Antunes (Eds.), Multi-Agent-Based Simulation VI. X, 191 pages. 2006. (Sublibrary LNAI).

Vol. 3890: S.G. Thompson, R. Ghanea-Hercock (Eds.), Defence Applications of Multi-Agent Systems. XII, 141 pages. 2006. (Sublibrary LNAI).

Vol. 3889: J. Rosca, D. Erdogmus, J.C. Príncipe, S. Haykin (Eds.), Independent Component Analysis and Blind Signal Separation. XXI, 980 pages. 2006.

Vol. 3888: D. Draheim, G. Weber (Eds.), Trends in Enterprise Application Architecture. IX, 145 pages. 2006.

Vol. 3887: J.R. Correa, A. Hevia, M. Kiwi (Eds.), LATIN 2006: Theoretical Informatics. XVI, 814 pages. 2006.

Vol. 3886: E.G. Bremer, J. Hakenberg, E.-H.(S.) Han, D. Berrar, W. Dubitzky (Eds.), Knowledge Discovery in Life Science Literature. XIV, 147 pages. 2006. (Sublibrary LNBI).

Vol. 3885: V. Torra, Y. Narukawa, A. Valls, J. Domingo-Ferrer (Eds.), Modeling Decisions for Artificial Intelligence. XII, 374 pages. 2006. (Sublibrary LNAI).

Vol. 3884: B. Durand, W. Thomas (Eds.), STACS 2006. XIV, 714 pages. 2006.

Vol. 3883: M. Cesana, L. Fratta (Eds.), Wireless Systems and Network Architectures in Next Generation Internet. IX, 281 pages. 2006.